Decision Support Systems:
An Applied Managerial Approach

Decision Support Systems: An Applied Managerial Approach

◆ ◆ ◆

Vicki L. Sauter
University of Missouri—St. Louis

JOHN WILEY & SONS, INC.

New York   Chichester   Brisbane   Toronto   Singapore   Weinheim

ACQUISITIONS EDITOR   Beth Lang Golub
MARKETING MANAGER   Leslie Hines
PRODUCTION SERVICE   University Graphics, Inc.
MANUFACTURING MANAGER   Mark Cirillo
PHOTO EDITOR   Lisa Passmore
ILLUSTRATION COORDINATOR   Anna Melhorn
This book was set in 10/12 ITC Garamond Light by University Graphics, Inc. and printed and bound
by R.R. Donnelley, Crawfordsville. The cover was printed by Lehigh Press.

ISBN 0-471-31134-0

Printed in the United States of America

10 9 8 7 6 5 4 3

This book is dedicated, with love, to
My Late Father, Leo F. Sauter, Jr.,
My Husband, Joseph S. Martinich,
and
My Son, Michael C. Martinich-Sauter,
with thanks for their steadfast inspiration and encouragement.

Preface

◆ ◆ ◆

Information is a crucial component of today's society. Due to our shrinking world, accelerating communications, and growing interests, information relevant to a person's life, work, and recreation has exploded. However, many believe this is not all good. In a book entitled *Information Anxiety,* Wurman notes that the information explosion has backfired, leaving us stranded between *mere* facts and *real* understanding. Similarly, Peter Drucker notes in a *Wall Street Journal* editorial entitled, "Be Data Literate—Know What to Know," that although executives have become computer literate, few of them have mastered the questions of what information they need, when they need information, and in what form do they need information. Further, Drucker notes, executives will need better information in the future if their companies are to be competitive; more information is not profitable unless it is relevant information.

This is both good news and bad news for designers of Decision Support Systems (DSS). The good news is that if, as Drucker claims, the future success of companies is through the astute use of appropriate information, then the future of MIS will be the design of DSS that facilitate intelligent uses of appropriate information. The bad news is that where DSS are available, they may not be providing enough *support* to the users. Too often the DSS are designed as a substitute for the human choice process or an elaborate report generator.

Decision support systems, by definition, should aid in and strengthen some kind of choice process. In order for DSS designers to know what information to retain and how to model the relationships among the data so as to best complement the human choice process, we must understand the human choice process. To that end, this book illustrates what is known about decision making and the different styles that decision makers demonstrate under various conditions. This "needs assessment" is developed on a variety of levels: (a) what is known about decision making (with or without a computer) in general; (b) how has that knowledge about decision making been translated into specific DSS needs; and (c) how does one actually program those needs into a system. Hence, all topics are addressed on three levels: (a) general theory; (b) specific DSS theory; and (c) hands-on applications. These are not separate chapters, but rather an integrated analysis of what the designer of a DSS needs to know.

The second impetus that drives the content and organization of this book is an overriding focus totally upon decision support systems. Many books spend a significant amount of time and space explaining concepts that are important, but ancillary to the development of a DSS. For example, many books discuss the methods for solution of mathematical models. While accurate solution methods for mathematical models are important for a successful DSS, there is much more about the models that needs discussion in order to implement a good DSS. Hence, I have left model solutions and countless other topics out of the book in order to accommodate topics of direct relevance to DSS.

Writing this book was clearly a labor of love. I believe in decision support systems and their contribution. Those who know me well know that when I believe in something, I share it with enthusiasm and zeal. I think those attributes show in this book and make it better.

◆ MAJOR FEATURES OF THE BOOK

Integration of Theory and Practice: It is the integration of theory with practice, and abstract with concrete, that makes this book unique. This characteristic reflects a personal bias that it is impossible to understand design concepts until you actually try to implement them. It also reflects a personal bias that unless we can relate the DSS concepts to the "real world" and the kinds of problems (opportunities) the students can expect to find there, the students can not understand the concepts fully.

Although the book contains numerous examples of many aspects of DSS, there is one example that is carried throughout the book: a DSS to facilitate car purchases. I have selected this example because most students can relate to it, and readers do not get bogged down with discussion of company politics and nuances. Furthermore, it allows a variety of issues to be compared in a meaningful fashion.

Focus on the "Big Picture": The representation throughout the book focuses on "generic" DSS, which allows discussion of design issues without concern for whether it is a group system, an organizational system, or an individual system. Furthermore, it allows illustration of how seemingly specialized forms of DSS, such as Geographic Information Systems or Purchasing Support Systems, actually follow the same principles as a "basic" DSS.

Although I show implementation of the concepts, I do not over-focus on the tools. There are example screens of many tools appearing in the book. Where I show development, I create my examples using Level 5 Object, a generator from Information Builders. However, if you elect to use another tool, these examples can be understood generally by students and adapted easily to other tools.

Strong Common Sense Component: We MIS folks can get carried away with the newest and greatest toy, regardless of its applicability to a decision-maker. It is important to remember the practicalities of the situation when designing DSS. For example, if we know that a company has a commitment to maintaining particular hardware, it would not make sense to develop a system relying upon other hardware. These kinds of considerations and the associated implications for DSS design are highlighted in the book. However, this is not to say that some of these very interesting, but currently infeasible options are not discussed. Clearly, they are important for the future of MIS. Someday, these options will be feasible and will be practical, so they are discussed to some extent.

Integration of Expert Systems: Unlike many texts, this book does not address expert systems as a topic separate from decision support systems. The decision to integrate expert systems into the DSS coverage was a conscious one that reflects my perception of how expert systems are used today, and how they will be used into the future. Ten years ago, expert systems were primarily seen as stand alone systems; most of them were available as demonstration or nonessential systems. Over the years, however, expert systems have evolved into an integrated component of many decision support systems provided to *support* decisions makers, not replace them. To accomplish such a goal, the expert systems could not be stand alone, but rather needed to be integrated with the data and models used by these decision makers. In other words, expert systems (or intelligence) technology became a modeling support function, albeit an important one, for decision support systems. Hence, the coverage of the topic is integrated into the modeling component in this book. However, I do acknowledge there are some special topics needing attention to those who want to build the intelligence. These topics are covered in a supplement to Chapter 4, thereby allowing instructors to use discretion in how they integrate the topic into their classes.

International Issues Coverage: As more companies become truly multinational, there is a trend toward greater "local" (overseas) decision-making that needs to be coordinated. These companies can afford to have some independent transaction processing systems, but will need to share common decision support systems. If the DSS are truly to facilitate decision making across cultures, then they must be sensitive to differences across cultures. This sensitivity includes more than just changes in the language used or concern about the meaning of icons. Rather, it includes an understanding of the differences in preferences for models and model management systems, and for tradeoffs and mechanisms by which information is communicated and acted upon. Since future designers of DSS will need to understand the implications of these differences, they are highlighted in the book. Of course, as with any other topic, the international issues will be addressed both in "philosophical" terms and in specific technical terms.

Object-Oriented Concepts and Tools: Another feature of the book that differentiates it from others is the use of object-oriented technology. Many books either present material without discussion of implementation, or use traditional programming tools. I have found that students have difficulty making the jump from these traditional programming tools to object-oriented tools. However, we know that a reliance upon object-oriented technology can lead to easier maintenance and transfer of systems. Since decision support systems must be updated to reflect new company concerns and trends, designers must be concerned about ease of maintenance. So, while the focus of the book is not on object-oriented programming, the nuances of its programming will be discussed wherever it is practical. In addition, there is a chapter that focuses upon this topic that can be included in the curriculum.

Web Support and Other Instructional Support Tools: There is a complete set of Web links that provide instructional support for this book. Example syllabi, projects, and other ideas can be viewed and downloaded from the Web. All figures and tables appear on the Web so you can use them directly in the class or download them to your favorite demonstration package to use in class. In addition, there are lots of Web links to sites you can use to supplement the information in the book. Some of these links provide access to demo versions of decision support packages for download and use of some sample screens. These provide up-to-date examples of a variety of systems that students can use or instructors can demonstrate to bring the practice into the classroom. Other links provide access to applications descriptions, war stories, and advice from practitioners. Still others provide a link to a variety of instructors (both academic and nonacademic) on the topic. I strived to provide *support* for the class from a variety of different perspectives. You can see the information at *http://www.Wiley.com/college/Sauter.* Further, there is information at the end of every chapter about the kinds of materials found in support of that chapter on the Web; directions for direct access to the chapter information is given in those chapters. More important, in the true spirit of the Web, I will update these links as more information becomes available. So, if you happen to see something that should be included, please email me at *Vicki_Sauter@umsl.edu.*

In addition to the DSS support, I have accumulated links regarding automobiles and their purchase and lease. This Web page would provide support for people who want to explore the car example in the book in more depth, or for students who want to use different information in the development of their own automobile DSS. You can link to this from the main page or go to it directly at *http://www.umsl.edu/~sauter/DSS/automobile_information.html.*

For those who do not have access to the Web, or who prefer more traditional forms of instructional support, there are similar materials included in an instructor's manual that is available with the book.

◆ ACKNOWLEDGMENTS

If a book is a labor of love, then there must be a "coach" to help one through the process. In my case, I am lucky enough to have a variety of coaches who have been with me every step of the way. First, in a very real sense, my students over the years have provided a foundation for this book. Even before I knew I was going to produce this work, my students provided an environment in which I could experiment and learn about decisions, decision making, and decision support systems. It is their interest, their inquisitiveness, and their challenge that have led me to think through these topics in a manner that facilitated the writing of this book. I have particular gratitude to Mary Kay Carragher, Mimi Duncan, Joseph Hofer, Timothy McCaffrey, Richard Ritthamel, and Phillip Wells for their efforts and support.

Second, there are numerous people at John Wiley and Sons who helped me achieve my vision for this book. I am grateful to each one for his or her efforts and contribution. In particular, I would like to thank my editor, Beth Lang Golub, who believed in this project long before I did, continued to have faith in it when mine wore thin, and was willing to stand by decisions because she believed they were right. I could not have produced this book without her. In addition, I want to thank Elisa Adams, my style editor, who helped to make my ideas accessible through direct and constructive changes in the prose.

Third, I would like to thank the following faculty reviewers who reviewed drafts of the chapters and provided superb comments to improve its style and content: Thomas E. Sandman, California State University-Sacramento; Brother Matthew Michelini, Manhattan College; Jane Fedorowicz, Bentley College; George Federman, Santa Barbara City College; Charles Butler, Colorado State University; Bruce White, Dakota State University; Robert J. Berger, University of Maryland; Jim Courtney, Texas A & M University; Richard Irving, York University; T.M. Rajkumar, Miami University; Robert T. Sumichrast, Virginia Polytechnic Institute and State University; Linda Volonino, Canisius College; Lawrence A. West, Jr., Florida State University; Madjid Tavana, La Salle University; Theresa M. Vitolo, Penn State University.

Finally, I want to thank my friends and family for their support, encouragement, and patience. My husband, Joseph Martinich, has been with me every step of the way—not only with this book, but in my entire career. I sincerely doubt that I could have done any of it without him. My son, Michael Martinich-Sauter, has demonstrated infinite patience with his mother throughout this project. More important, he has inspired me to look at every topic differently and more creatively. I have learned much about decisions, decision making, and decision support from him, and I am most grateful he has shared his wisdom with me. Finally, I want to acknowledge Lady Alexandra (a.k.a. Alex–the dog) who has made me laugh when I really needed it.

Contents

◆ ◆ ◆

◆ ◆ ◆

Introduction to Decision Support Systems

Introduction

◆ ◆ ◆

Virtually everyone makes hundreds of decisions each day. These decisions range from the inconsequential, such as what to eat for breakfast, to the significant, such as how best to use a scarce resource in a production process. All other things being equal, good outcomes from those decisions are better than bad outcomes. While some individuals are "lucky" in their decision-making processes, for most of us, good outcomes in decision making are a result of making good decisions.

"Good decision making" means that we are informed and that we have relevant and appropriate information on which to base our choices. In some cases, we support decisions using existing, historical data, while other times we collect the information especially for a particular choice process. The information comes in the form of facts, numbers, impressions, graphics, pictures, and sounds. It needs to be collected from various sources, joined together, and organized. The process of organizing and examining the information about the various options is the process of modeling. Models are created to help decision makers understand the ramifications of selecting an option. The models can range from quite informal representations to complex mathematical relationships.

For example, when deciding on what to eat for a meal, we might rely on historical data, such as those available from tasting and eating the various meal options over time, and our degree of enjoyment of those options. We might also use specially collected data, such as cost or availability of breakfast options. Our model in this case might be simple: select the first available option that tastes good. Other decisions may require more extensive and managed information collection and modeling support. For example, when deciding on a production process, we might collect information regarding the needs for various raw materials, their relative cost and scarcity, and the relative demand for finished products and their profit margins. To make the choice of how to produce those finished products, we might develop a mathematical model of the optimal production plan.

The quality of the decision depends on the adequacy of the available information, the quality of the information, the number of options, and the appropriateness of the modeling effort available at the time of the decision. While it is *not* true that more information is better, it is true that more of the appropriate type is better. In fact, one might say that to improve the choice process, we need to improve the information collection and analysis processes.

One way to accomplish that goal is to use decision support systems (DSS). Decision support systems are computer-based systems that bring together information from a variety of sources, assist in the organization and analysis of information, and facilitate the evaluation of assumptions underlying the use of specific models. In other words, these systems allow decision makers to access relevant data across the organization as they need it to make choices. The DSS allow decision makers to analyze data generated from transaction processing systems and other internal information sources *easily*. In addition, DSS allow access to information from outside the organization. Finally, DSS allow decision makers the ability to analyze the information in a manner that will be helpful to that particular decision and will provide that support interactively.

So, the availability of decision support systems provides the opportunity to improve the data collection and analysis processes associated with decision making. Taking the logic one step further, the availability of decision support systems provides the opportunity to improve the quality and responsiveness of decision making and hence the opportunity to improve the management of corporations.

◆ DSS AND THE DECISION PROCESS

To see how decision support systems can change the way in which decisions are made, consider the following example[1] of a Manhattan court. New York spends in excess of $3 billion each year on criminal justice, and the number of jail beds has increased by over 110% since 1977. In Manhattan, developers have spent billions of dollars refurbishing neighborhoods and providing good-quality living, business, and entertainment areas. Yet people continue not to feel safe in them, and minor crimes depreciate the quality of life for residents. Furthermore, the likelihood of repeat offenses is high; more than 40% of the defendants seen in a year already have three or more convictions.

While there is clearly a problem, the facts that crime exists, that enormous amounts of money are spent, and that people do not feel safe are examples of bad *outcomes*, not necessarily bad decisions. However, three facts do suggest that the quality of decisions could be improved:

- Criminal justice workers know very little about the hundreds of thousands of people who go through the New York court systems;
- There has been little creative thinking about the sanctions judges can use over time; and
- Most defendants get the same punishment in the same fashion.

---

[1]Assael, S., "Moving justice from expert witnesses to expert systems," *Wired*, Vol. 2.03, March 1994.

Specifically, these suggest that with more information, more modeling capabilities, and better alternative-generation tools, better decisions, which could result in superior outcomes, might be achieved.

In the Manhattan case, citizens, court officials, and criminal justice researchers noted the problem of information availability and have developed a process to address it for "quality of life" crimes, such as shoplifting and street hustling. Specifically, the city, landlords, and federal funding representatives jointly created a new court and located the judge in the same building as city health workers, drug counselors, teachers, and nontraditional community service outlets to increase the likelihood of the court working with these providers to address the crime problem innovatively. The centerpiece of this effort is a decision support system that provides judges with more and better information *as well as* a better way for processing that information in order to make an impact on the crime in Manhattan.

This example illustrates some of the important characteristics of a DSS. A DSS must access data from a variety of sources. In this court example, the system accesses the arresting officer's report, including the complaint against the offender and the court date. In addition, the DSS provides access to the defendant's criminal record through connections with the New York Division of Criminal Justice. These police records are supplemented with information gained by an independent interviewer, either at the police precinct or at the courthouse. These interviewers query defendants regarding their lifestyles (e.g., access to housing, employment status, health conditions, drug dependencies). Finally, an intermediary between the court and the services available—called a court resource coordinator—scans the person's history, makes suggestions for treatment, and enters the information into the system.

A second characteristic of a DSS is that it facilitates the development and evaluation of a model of the choice process. That is, the DSS must allow users to transform the enormous amount of "data" into "information" that helps them make a good decision. The models may be simple summarization or sophisticated mathematical models. In this case, the modeling takes a variety of forms. The simple ability to summarize arrest records allows judges to estimate recidivism if no intervention occurs. Further, the summarization of lifestyle information encourages the development of a treatment model. In addition, with the DSS, the judge can track community service programs and sites to determine which is likely to be most effective for what kinds of offenses. Hence, the judge can model the expected impact of the sanctions on a defendant with particular characteristics. In other words, the DSS can facilitate the evaluation of programs to determine if there is a way to have greater impact on particular defendants or on a greater number of defendants.

The design team is in the process of adding additional modeling capabilities. Soon, they hope to integrate mapping technology that will plot a defendant's prior arrest record. The judge can evaluate this map to determine (a) if there is a pattern in offenses that can be addressed or (b) where to assign the community service sentence to optimize the payback to society.

The third characteristic that is demonstrated by this DSS is that it must provide a good user interface through which users can easily navigate and interact. There are enormous amounts of raw data in this system—equivalent to a 3-inch file folder on most individuals. Providing access to the raw data and the summarized information in a meaningful fashion is challenging. In this case, the designers used a Windows environment[2] and summarized all information into a four-window, single-screen format. As shown in Figure 1.1, the current incident is shown on the main (left-to-right) diagonal. The system locates the complaint in the top-left quad-

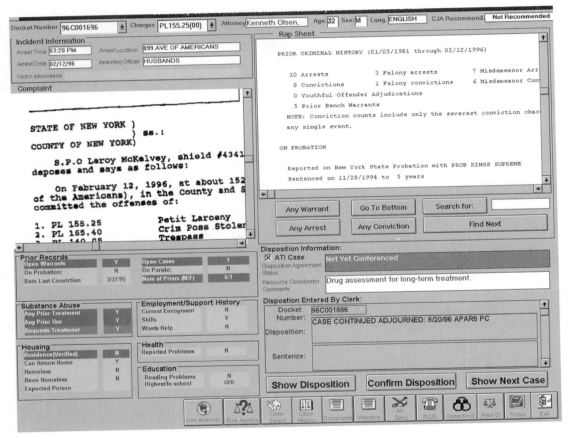

Figure 1.1   Manhattan Court DSS—defendant overview screen.

---

[2]In April 1995, Microsoft Corporation Chairman Bill Gates awarded the Midtown Community Court the fourth annual Windows World Open Competition Award for exemplary use of technology in the public sector. This prestigious competition recognizes innovative technology that transforms the way organizations do business.

rant and leaves the bottom-right quadrant for the judge's decision. At the top right, the DSS provides a summary of the historical offenses for the defendant. The bottom-left quadrant summarizes the lifestyle questions and the interviewer's recommendations for changes.

While the summary information provides an overview of the information about the defendant, the judge can drill down any of the quadrants to obtain more detailed information. For example, the lifestyle summary screen displays the education level, housing status, and drug dependency problems. However, the judge can drill down in this screen to find precisely what drugs the person uses and for how long or with whom the defendant lives and where. In addition, the system highlights problematic answers in red so the judge can locate them immediately. This further allows the judge to establish how many problems the defendant has by the amount of red displayed on the screen: the more red on the screen, the greater the number of problematic lifestyle choices the person has made. This drill-down-screen evidence is shown in Figure 1.2. Demonstration of the flexibility in analyzing the data is shown in Figure 1.3.

In this case, it is too early to determine if better decisions will result in better outcomes. However, early evidence is promising. For example, to date, only 40 percent of defendants in the standard Manhattan courts complete their community service sentence, while 80 percent of the defendants going through the courts using this DSS complete their sentences. Further, almost 20 percent of the defendants sentenced to community-based sanctions[3] *voluntarily* take advantage of the social services. Finally, the system was awarded the National Association of Court Management's Justice Achievement Award for 1994.

In this example, the decision makers are attempting a strategic change in how they do business—by using a DSS among other changes—in order to tackle their problem. Not all DSS are associated with strategic changes or with public sector applications. In fact, many readers of *Datamation* believe that DSS are critical to the success of their organizations. In *Datamation*'s annual "Industry Outlook," readers were asked about their priority projects for the upcoming year. In 1993, 1994, *and* 1995, 12 percent of the readers ranked decision support system applications as "critical." Further, about one-third of those surveyed in those three years ranked DSS applications as "very important" to their organizations. The only projects rated as more critical were systems maintenance, such as network management, electronic mail and database administration, or customer service systems and financial applications. Since some projects labeled "customer service systems" or "financial systems" might actually be decision support systems, their importance in businesses today is probably greater than the published statistic. Similarly, in the "Information Revolution 1994" special issue of *Business Week*, the third-highest "in-

---

[3]Community-based sanctions include projects such as sweeping streets, removing graffiti, cleaning bus lots, maintaining street trees, painting affordable housing units, and cleaning and painting subway stations. All work is done under the supervision of the appropriate metropolitan agency.

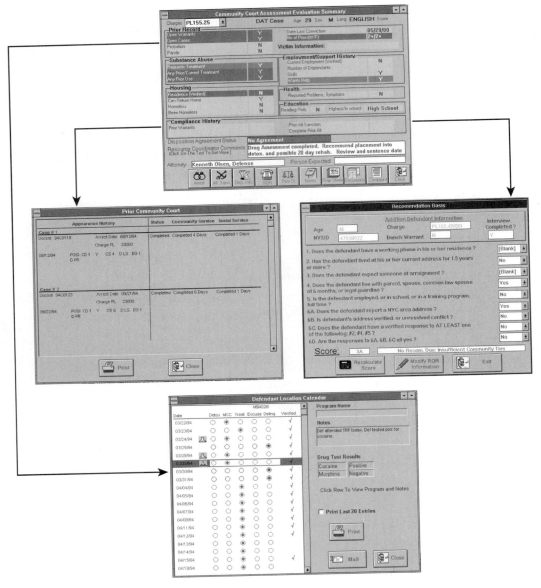

Figure 1.2 Manhattan Court DSS—drill-down screens.

formation priority" was the organization and utilization of data. That is, the senior information executives polled see DSS as being critically important. The only factors of more significance were reengineering processes through information technology and aligning information services and corporate goals.

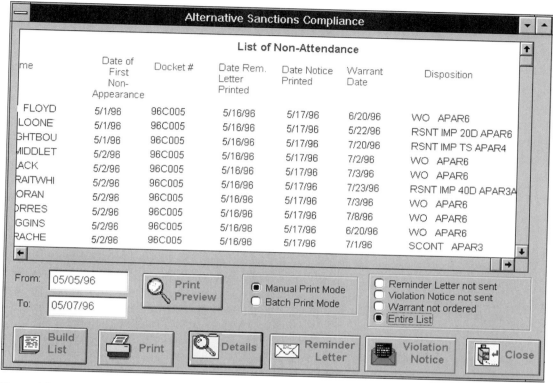

Figure 1.3 Manhattan Court DSS—flexibility in data analysis.

◆ THE ACCEPTANCE OF DSS

The obvious question is Why? People have been making decisions for thousands of years without DSS. In fact, business managers have been making good decisions, with good outcomes, for hundreds of years. Why should DSS technology *now* be important to the choice process? As shown in Figure 1.4, four major factors contribute to the importance of DSS in today's market.

One factor contributing to the acceptance of DSS technology is that desktop computing has made technology easier to use and portable. Historically, computing meant interaction with a mainframe in a batch mode from a fixed terminal, generally in one's office or in a lab. This meant that one submitted a job and waited up to a week for a response. Even if the job was supposed to be run immediately, response time was often slow and not conducive to helping the decision maker think. Often the mainframes were "down" or unresponsive at exactly the time they were needed. And often the decision maker was not in his or her office, or was not accessible via a modem, at the time that the data needed to be analyzed. By

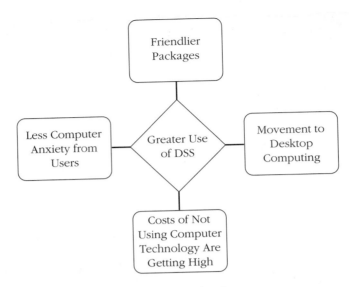

Figure 1.4   Factors contributing to acceptance of DSS.

contrast, today's desktop computers can download the data and analyze it at any time the decision maker is ready. One does not need to be concerned with connectivity to a mainframe. Similarly, with laptop technology, one can process data anywhere at anytime. Hence, the computer is ready when the decision maker is ready, not the other way around.

The second factor contributing to the acceptance of computer-based systems is the development of friendlier packages, even to novice users. No longer must one know the special "Job Control Language" and write in a specialized language just to be able to access data on a computer. Rather, one can import the data into a spreadsheet package and begin looking at trends, graphs, and interrelationships just by using a menu. This friendliness is a feature users have come to expect. Hence, software written for special purpose also tends to be easier to use, with greater reliance on online help options and context-sensitive help.

This change in how software is written has been instrumental in the third factor contributing to the acceptance of DSS. Fewer upper-level managers experience computer anxiety. In fact, a study a few years ago estimated that among Fortune 500 companies, about 10 percent of CEOs and about 33 percent of high-level managers use computers regularly in their decision-making processes. This number increases each year. Many CEOs and high-level managers already have been exposed to computers, either at home or in the office, and therefore they are less likely to fear their use in the decision-making process.

These three factors clearly contribute to the acceptance of technology, but the fourth factor is the one pushing the use of DSS technology: decision makers are using DSS because the cost of not using the technology is getting very high. To

◆ DSS Designs Insights ◆

Nobel laureate economist Herbert Simon points out: "What information consumes is rather obvious: it consumes the attention of its recipients. Hence a wealth of information creates a poverty of attention, and a need to allocate that attention efficiently among the overabundance of information sources that might consume it." (*Scientific American*, Sep 95, p. 201) Hence, as the amount of information increases, so does the need for filtering processes that help decision makers find that which is most important and meaningful.

understand this completely, one needs to compare the businesses of today to those of earlier times. Historically, most businesses were relatively small, were relatively focused, and served a small target area. Good managers were ones who remembered well and who could analyze problems well. They were knowledgable about their businesses because they typically worked their way up, learning about the organization and the business in the process.

Many companies are finding economies of scale in being larger organizations. In addition, these companies are diversifying to make themselves less vulnerable to changing economies. No longer do companies pull their workforces from a small geographic area. Now, some parts of the process are likely to be conducted in another country where costs are lower or where plants are closer to a necessary resource. In fact, in some corporations, parts are produced in multiple countries and assembled in yet another country. Companies no longer compete with just the companies in that city, state, or region. Now, competition for sales, for workforce, and for inputs is on a worldwide basis. Other smaller companies are using the technology to maintain their competitive advantage over the larger, more diversified corporations.

This change in the way business is conducted means that the corporation is more complex than ever before. It is difficult for managers to see all aspects of the process, much less to master them. The amount of information that needs to be processed is much greater than it ever has been. Simultaneously, the amount of time managers have to respond to data has shrunk. With rapid communication, fax machines, electronic mail, and worldwide telephone use, information is available quickly and needs to be responded to quickly.

It is obvious that both the amount of information and the number of ways of getting that information have increased substantially in the last several years. Further, if one notes that the types of sources that have been added in recent years are all "instant access" sources, one can see how the demands for faster analyses of more data could put pressure on decision makers. When one combines the existence of so much information, the speed at which information can be transmitted, and the significant competition for labor and markets, it becomes obvious that the costs of making errors can be quite consequential. The availability of a DSS gives the decision maker access to the data and the tools to respond to his/her environment in more reasoned ways. As an example, consider the following case from Motorola's Government and Systems Technology Group (GSTG)[4], which provides communications systems for customers such as NASA, the U.S. Space Station project, the U.S. Department of Defense, and aerospace corporations.

Consider the problem. Marketing managers, who often visit client sites or Washington, D.C., carry their records about business pursuits with them. While immediate access to their records gives marketing managers the ability to negotiate successfully with current clients, it used to mean that GSTG's business acquisition teams, back at the plant, did not have details that could help them effectively leverage other new deals; certainly they did not have access to the most up-to-date information because it was being recorded away from the plant. This posed a problem because current clients and potential opportunities are highly interdependent. Since each opportunity can relate in some fashion to a number of customers, a large number of active and prospective opportunities need to be managed simultaneously. The stakes are high also: a lost opportunity could mean millions of dollars of lost revenue. To maximize effectiveness, all relevant team members need to have accurate and up-to-date information on any given opportunity at any time, so that all members can exploit it properly. Business teams need absolute clarity about who will follow up on opportunities.

The solution was an innovative implementation of a DSS running on office machines *and* laptop computers that would facilitate a process of collecting, sorting, and sharing data. Managers can record relevant intelligence and progress in the system—the data are organized into folders that can be accessed easily by others. In addition, other data are sent from the mainframe to team members via e-mail messages. When necessary, the user can click on an icon that pulls the data out of the e-mail message, converts the file into appropriate format, and updates the database. All information is summarized on the new business opportunity screen. From there, users easily can access planning and scheduling details. Further, the various team members can generate a variety of reports, using information from a variety of sources to view the necessary perspective.

The DSS is also helpful with regular review meetings. Prior to the availability of the DSS, managers were required to use large quantities of *printed* reports during review meetings. These reports provided summaries and forecasts, but not the significant supporting documents. The DSS, on the other hand, allows decision makers access to both: decision makers can test assumptions and change viewpoints to check the sensitivity of a solution.

Decisions made during these meetings become effective immediately, so everyone understands the range of the impact. The DSS can be shared during such a meeting by attaching it to an overhead projector, allowing managers and new business team members to review each opportunity simultaneously. Changes to assignments, budgets, or schedules that relate to new business can be entered dur-

---

[4]"Motorola launches intelligent business opportunity support using Level 5 Object," *Information Builder News*, Spring/Summer 1994, pp. 42–45.

ing the meeting by an NBIS administrator, and the revisions are immediately entered into the NBIS database. At any time, managers can extract any portion of the database, including all active opportunities.

The result, in Motorola's opinion, is a success because it helps managers to be more responsive to customer inquiries and content in proposals. The bottom line is that Motorola is better able to meet its corporate objective of total customer satisfaction.

◆ WHAT IS A DSS?

As stated previously, a DSS is a computer-based system that supports choice by assisting the decision maker in organizing information and modeling outcomes. Consider Figure 1.5, which illustrates a continuum of information systems products available. In this diagram, the conventional management information system (MIS) or transaction processing system (TPS) is shown at the far left. The MIS is intended for routine, structural, and anticipated decisions. In those cases, the system might retrieve or extract data, integrate it, and produce a report. These systems are not analysis oriented, and they tend to be slow, batch-processing systems. Therefore, they are not good for supporting decisions.

The far right of Figure 1.5 illustrates the expert system (ES). ES are intended to reproduce the logic of a human who is considered an expert for the purposes of a particular decision. The systems generally process a series of heuristics that are believed to mimic that logic. They are good at supporting decisions, but only those decisions that they have been programmed to process.

In between those two is the area of the decision support system and the executive information system (EIS). These two types of systems are intended to help decision makers identify and access information they believe will be useful in processing poorly structured, underspecified problems. They provide *flexible* mechanisms for retrieving data, *flexible* mechanisms for analyzing data, and tools that help understand the problems, opportunities, and possible solutions. They enable the decision makers to select what they want in both *substance* and *format.*

For example, an MIS might provide a report of profit by item on a monthly basis, typically in written form. A DSS, on the other hand, would store the profit by

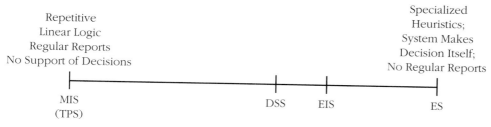

Figure 1.5 Continuum of information systems products.

item for later analysis. The system would allow decision makers to decide whether the analyses were for individual products, groups of related products, products in a particular region, and so on. In addition, it might flash a notice to the manager (at the first availability of the data) when a product has a profit that is outside its typical range—either high or low. Decision makers can then decide whether the shift represents a need for corrective action for a problem or the possibility of an opportunity. In this way, it makes it easier to collect information, easier to put it in a form that allows analysis, and easier to have it available when it is needed.

Similarly, the MIS provides no help in generating alternatives. If it does provide some sort of model, it provides only the results. Typically, there is no provision for what-if analyses to determine how sensitive the answer is to the assumptions made. The DSS would typically provide access to these sensitivity analyses. In addition, a DSS might prompt users to consider sensitivity analyses or provide suggestions on how to improve the analyses.

Four components comprise a decision support system, as shown in Table 1.1. We will discuss these components briefly here, and each of these components will be discussed in depth later in this book. The database management system (DBMS) provides access to data as well as all of the control programs necessary to get those data in the form appropriate for the analysis under consideration, without the user programming the effort. It should be sophisticated enough to give users access to the data even when they do not know where the data are physically located. In addition, the DBMS facilitates the merger of data from different sources. Again, the DBMS should be sufficiently sophisticated to merge the data without explicit instructions from the user regarding how one accomplishes that task.

◆ **DSS in Action** ◆

The Geographic Environmental Modeling System (GEMS) at Carnegie-Melon University is a decision support system that facilitates the evaluation of air quality in a region. GEMS provides a consistent graphical user interface (GUI) that accesses all system capabilities. Through this user interface, a GEMS user can select from multiple scientific models and multiple forms of output. For example, in the screen shown below, the user has access to four distinct windows: the overview window (top left), the toolbox, the graph, and the map (right window). Further, GEMS provides capabilities for analysis of the data generated by the underlying air quality models. Data from several different control strategy scenarios can be compared to find the best strategy. This is shown in the screen below, which shows maps of the air quality with no intervention (top-left map) and a particular intervention (top-right map) as well as the difference between the two (third map). Further, the DSS provides advanced capabilities for viewing the data generated by the air quality models. The picture in the second screen shows an area where the concentration of ozone exceeds standard levels. The map merges together information obtained from satellite imagery and from political boundaries derived from the Census Department's TIGER database. Data management tools provide the appropriate data conversions from different formats and merge together information from different databases.

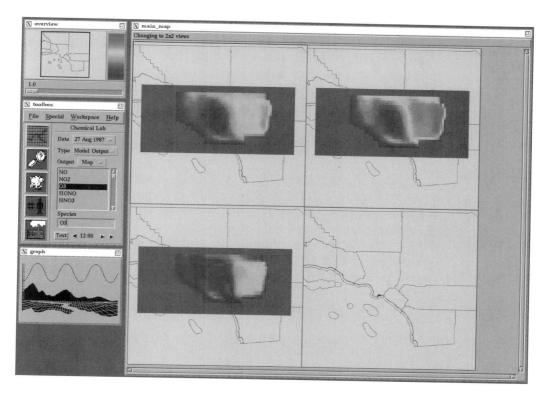

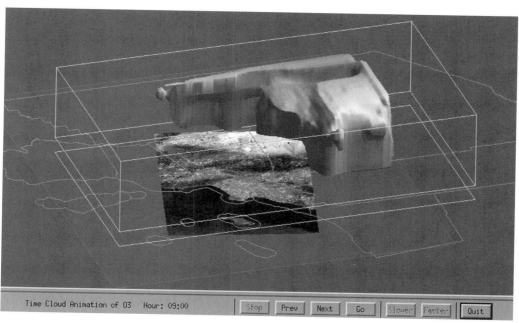

The model-base management system (MBMS) performs a similar task for the models in the DSS. It keeps track of all the possible models that might be run during the analysis, as well as controls for running the models. This might include the syntax necessary to run the jobs, the format in which the data need to be put prior to running the model (and to put the data in such a format), and the format the data will be in after the job is run. The MBMS also links between models so that the output of one model can be the input into another model. Further, the MBMS provides mechanisms for sensitivity analyses of the model after it is run. Finally, the MBMS provides context-sensitive and model-sensitive assistance to help the user question the assumptions of the models to determine if they are appropriate for the decision under consideration.

As the name suggests, the user interface represents all the mechanisms whereby information is input to the system and is output from the system. It includes all the input screens by which users request data and models. In addition, it includes all the output screens through which users obtain the results. Many users think of the user interface as the *real* DSS, because that is the part of the system they see.

Whereas there is general agreement of the existence of the first three components of a DSS, there is a fourth, relatively new component of a DSS, referred to as the mail or message management system (MMS). This component allows for the use of electronic mail as another source of data, modeling, or general help in the decision-making process. Since electronic discussion groups, electronic mail among workers, and other resources are quickly becoming an important resource to decision makers, they need to be managed and integrated as do other components of a DSS if they are to be a resource for decision making.

Decision support system use is *not* programming and is *not* data entry. That is, decision makers do not write computer code to analyze data when using a DSS. Rather, the DSS provides a framework through which decision makers can obtain necessary assistance for decision making through an easy-to-use menu or command system. Generally, a DSS will provide help in formulating alternatives, accessing data, developing models and interpreting their results, selecting options, or analyzing the impacts of a selection. In other words, the DSS provides a vehicle for accessing resources external to the decision-making process for use in that choice process, as shown in Figure 1.6.

Similarly, decision makers generally do not enter data when they use a DSS, but rather avail themselves of corporate and public databases already available. From time to time, decision makers will want to enter some of their own data in a private database, but it is kept to a minimum. Neither is a DSS simply the use of a

Table 1.1.   Four Components of a DSS

- Database Management System
- Modelbase Management System
- User Interface
- Mail Management System

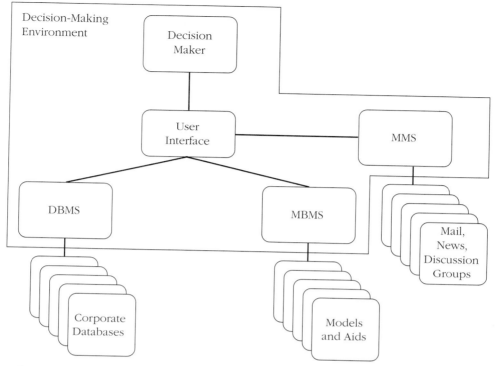

Figure 1.6 Components of a DSS.

◆ DSS in Action ◆

Jewish Hospital Healthcare Services uses various DSS applications in the areas of productivity, cost accounting, case mix, and nurse staff scheduling. The systems include modeling, forecasting, planning, communications, database management systems, and graphics. Furthermore, all the data are drawn from key clinical and financial systems so that there is not inconsistency in the data used by different decision makers. This allows decision makers to consider problems *and opportunities* from more dimensions, with better support than ever before. For example, the DSS includes a "nursing acuity system" for classifying patients by the severity and nursing needs associated with their illnesses. These calculations can be used by the nurse staff scheduling system to estimate the demand for nurses on a daily basis. Not only does this system help nurse managers to plan schedules, the DSS helps them to evaluate heuristics they might employ in developing the schedule. For example, they can compare the estimated nurse staffing needs to the actual levels to determine if there are better ways of managing their staffs. In this era of managed care, such analyses help the hospitals use scarce resources more effectively.

Butters, S., "Jewish Hospital Healthcare Services uses DSS," *Journal of Systems Management*, 43, June 1992, p. 30.

Equifax provides too many of America's Fortune 1000 companies DSS and supporting databases that allow these businesses to make more effective and profitable
business decisions. The system allows users access to more than 60 national databases, mapping software, and analysis tools so that users can define and analyze
their opportunities in a geographic area.

The tool enables retailers, banks, and other businesses to display trade areas and
then to analyze demographic attributes. In particular, this DSS integrates customer
information with current demographic and locational data. For example, *Consumer-
Facts* offers information about spending patterns of more than 400 products and
services in more than 15 major categories, with regional spending patterns incorporated. Further, it provides five-year projections that reflect the impact of dynamic
economic and demographic conditions, such as income, employment, population,
and household changes, on consumer spending that can be integrated with a corporation's own customer information.

This coupling of data and analysis of reports, maps, and graphs allows decision
makers to consider questions of customer segmentation and targeting; market and
site evaluation; business-to-business marketing; product distribution strategies; and
mergers, acquisitions, and competitive analyses. For example, the DSS facilitates
consideration of crucial yet difficult questions such as:

- Who are my best customers and where are they located?
- Which segments respond positively to my marketing campaign?
- How will the addition of a new site affect my existing locations?
- How can I analyze and define my market potential?
- How can I estimate demand for my products and services accurately?
- What impact will an acquisition have on my locations?
- How is the competition affecting my business?

spreadsheet package or modeling package. Spreadsheets and modeling packages
simply provide the tools to do analysis. They do not provide a mechanism for accessing data unless one already knows where it is and how it should be accessed.
Further, these tools do not provide assistance in the wide range of decision support generally associated with a DSS.

◆ USES OF A DECISION SUPPORT SYSTEM

Throughout this chapter, there are examples of decision support systems in operation today. The applications range from strategic planning to operations management, and they exist in the public sector as well as the private sector, including
both the for-profit and not-for-profit branches. So, if there is not a particular application area, how does one know when it would be appropriate to use a system?

Decision support systems are most useful when it is *not* obvious what information needs to be provided, what models need to be used, or even what criteria are most appropriate. Said differently, they are useful when it is not obvious *a priori* how the choice should be made. Furthermore, since DSS proceed with requests from decision makers in the order and manner selected by the user (and not necessarily linearly in their application), they tend to be associated with situations in which users proceed differently with each problem. However, that does not mean a DSS cannot be useful for a more structured problem.

LaPlante (1993) notes that DSS are most useful when (a) managers and their staffs spend significant time locating and analyzing data that are already stored electronically; (b) management meetings stall because people challenge the validity of the data; (c) management is frequently surprised by the data when end-of-month–type reports are generated; and (d) decisions are too frequently made based on anecdotal evidence instead of on appropriate data, even when data might be collected regularly. In short, she notes that if the data are collected electronically, but are not used to their full potential, a DSS is warranted.

Hogue and Watson (1983) note that DSS might be developed for other reasons. Although their study notes that the number-one reason for using a DSS is to obtain accurate information, it states that many users develop such systems to obtain *timely* information or because *new* information is needed. Other corporations develop DSS because they are viewed as "organizational winners," or because management has mandated the use of a system. In these cases, managers believe that their image of using the DSS affects their clients' views of their product. In very few cases (only about 6 percent of those that Hogue and Watson studied) the DSS is used because it reduces cost.

The industrial revolution provided machinery to make jobs easier. The information revolution is supposed to provide the same level of help to the knowledge worker. Just as the automobile did not replace the human, the DSS does not replace the human. Similarly, the availability of automobiles did not solve all the transportation and transshipment problems—just the problem of how to get one or more people with one or more items somewhere else faster, more comfortably, and using less energy. Likewise, a DSS will not solve all the problems of any given organization. However, it does solve some problems well. Generally, it is accepted that DSS technology is warranted if the goal is to help decision makers:

- Look at more facets of a decision;
- Generate better alternatives;
- Respond to situations quickly;
- Solve complex problems;
- Consider more options for solving a problem;
- Brainstorm solutions;
- Utilize multiple analyses in solving a problem;
- Have new insights into problems and eliminate "tunnel vision" associated with premature evaluation of options;

- Implement a variety of decision styles and strategies;
- Use more appropriate data;
- Better utilize models; and
- Consider what-if analyses.

The software facilitates one's own processes. One should remember, however, that a badly designed DSS can make one's life difficult—just as a lemon of an automobile can make one's transportation difficult.

DISCUSSION

This book uses a liberal definition of the term DSS to allow a wide variety of technologies to be included. This allows exploration of the greatest range of opportunities available for DSS. The possibilities will be pursued in terms of the four components defined in Table 1.1. Once the concepts of the "generic" DSS have been cultivated, we will add the special issues and opportunities associated with more "advanced" DSS concepts, such as group decision support systems (GDSS), executive information systems (EIS), geographic information systems (GIS), and Groupware.

◆ O N   T H E   W E B ◆

On the Web for this chapter provides additional information to introduce you to the area of Decision Support Systems. Links can provide access to demonstration packages, general overview information, applications, software providers, tutorials, and more. Further, you can see some DSS available on the Web and use them to help increase confidence in your general understanding of this kind of computer system. Additional discussion questions and new applications will also be added as they become available.

- *Links provide overview information.* For example, one link provides a brief history of DSS and its relationship with other related disciplines. Similarly, another link provides a glossary of DSS terms. Finally, there are links to bibliographies about DSS available on the Web.

- *Links provide access to DSS examples in business, government and research.* Some links provide access to papers on the Web describing DSS applications and their uses. Others describe the process used to develop the application.
- *Links provide access to information about DSS providers and software tools.* Many software companies have Web pages that describe their tools and the application of those tools.
- *Links provide summaries of applications in particular industries.* For example, summaries of how the use of DSS can help solve business problems related to manufacturing and marketing are available on the Web.

You can access material for this chapter from the general WWW Page for the book, or directly from the following URL.
http://www.umsl.edu/~sauter/DSS/intro.html

QUESTIONS

1. What factors inhibit the growth of DSS in today's businesses?

2. Define DSS. How is it different from transactional processing systems?

3. List the major benefits of DSS.

4. What conditions suggest the need for a DSS?

5. Consider popular descriptions of computerized systems you have encountered over the last several months. Are any of these systems DSS? Why or why not?

6. Find an application of a DSS in an area of interest to you. What are the good aspects of the DSS? In a real DSS, some of the technical niceties are generally sacrificed for the realities of the situation. What technical niceties were sacrificed in your system? Were they reasonable sacrifices?

7. The literature often separates "expert systems" applications from "decision support systems" applications. Discuss why they should be considered separately.

8. Discuss examples of when one would want "expertise" integrated into a DSS.

9. Why must a corporation have good transactional processing systems before implementing a DSS?

10. Consider the system developed for the Manhattan court system at the beginning of this chapter. What attributes of the system make it a decision support system? How do you know it is not a transaction processing system or an expert system?

SUGGESTED READINGS

Alter, S., *Decision Support Systems: Current Practice and Continuing Challenge*, Reading, MA: Addison–Wesley, 1980.

Assael, Shaun. "ROBOCOURT," *Wired*, Vol. 2.03, March 1994, p. 106–111.

Burrows, P., "Giant killers on the loose," *Business Week: The Information Revolution*, Special 1994 Bonus Issue, Spring 1994, pp. 108–110.

Butters, S., "Jewish Hospital Healthcare Services uses DSS." *Journal of Systems Management*, 43, June 1992, p. 30.

Evans, J.R., "A microcomputer-based decision support system for scheduling umpires in the American Baseball League," *Interfaces*, 18(6), November/December 1988, pp. 42–51.

Evans-Correia, K., "Putting decisions through the software wringer: Intel uses decision support software for supplier selection," *Purchasing*, 110, March 21, 1991, pp. 62–64.

Fuerst, W.L. and P.H. Cheney, "Factors affecting the perceived utilization of computer-based decision support systems in the oil industry," *Decision Sciences*, 13(4), October, 1982, pp. 554–569.

Gorry, G.M. and M.S. Scott-Morton, *Decision Support Systems: An Organizational Perspective*, Reading, MA: Addison–Wesley, 1978.

Hogue, J.T. and H.J. Watson, "Management's role in the approval and administration of decision support systems," *MIS Quarterly*, 7(2), June 1983, pp. 15–26.

"IS meets business challenges head on," *Datamation*, 39(1), January 1, 1993, pp. 27–35.

LaPlante, A., "Liberate your data," *Forbes*, October 1993, pp. 58–68.

Martin, E.W., D.W. DeHayes, J.A. Hoffer, and W.C. Perkins, *Managing Information Technology: What Managers Need to Know*, New York: Macmillan Publishing Company, 1991.

"Motorola launches intelligent business opportunity support using Level 5 Object," *Information Builder News*, Spring/Summer 1994, pp. 42-45.

Paul, S. "European IS managers get down to business," *Datamation*, 40(5), March 1, 1994, pp. 78-84.

"Removing the roadblocks," *Datamation*, 40(1), January 7, 1994, pp. 22-24.

Rathnam, S., M.R. Arun, A. Chaudhury, and P.R. Shukla, "MUDRAPLAN—A DSS for media planning: From design to utilization," *Interfaces*, 22(2), March/April, 1992, pp. 65-75.

Rizakou, E., J. Rosenhead, and K. Reddington, "AIDSPLAN: A decision support model for planning the provision of HIV/AIDS-related services," *Interfaces*, 21(3), 1991, pp. 117-129.

Sage, A.P. *Decision Support Systems Engineering*, New York: John Wiley and Sons, 1991.

Sager, I., "The great equalizer," *Business Week: The Information Revolution*, Special 1994 Bonus Issue, Spring 1994, pp. 100-107.

Sauter, V.L., "The effect of 'experience' upon information preferences," *Omega*, 13(4), June 1985, pp. 277-284.

Sauter, V.L. and J.L. Schofer, "Evolutionary development of decision support systems: What issues are really important for early phases of design," *Journal of Management Information Systems*, 4(4), 1988, pp. 77-92.

Sauter, V.L. and M.B. Mandell, "Using decision support concepts to increase the utilization of social science information in policy-making," *Evaluation and Program Planning*, 13, 1990, pp. 349-358.

Scott-Morton, M.S., *Management Decision Systems: Computer-Based Support for Decision Making*, Cambridge, MA: Harvard University Press, 1971.

Shannon, P.W. and R.P. Minch, "A decision support system for motor vehicle taxation evaluation," *Interfaces*, 22(2), March/April 1992, pp. 52-64.

Sprague, R.H. and E.D. Carlson, *Building Effective Decision Support Systems*, Englewood Cliffs, NJ: Prentice-Hall, 1982.

Sprague, R.H. and H.J. Watson (eds.), *Decision Support Systems: Putting Theory into Practice, Third Edition*, Englewood Cliffs, NJ: Prentice-Hall, 1993.

C h a p t e r   2

Decision Making

◆ ◆ ◆

As we saw in the previous chapter, a decision support system is a computer-based system intended to help decision makers identify and access information they believe will facilitate their choice processes. As such, it is a system with *flexible* mechanisms for retrieving and analyzing data that allows decision makers to consider what they want and how they want it, so they can better understand the problems, opportunities, and potential solutions associated with a choice process.

Before we can discuss how to *support* the choice process, it is necessary to review what we know about the choice process. The considerable amount of known information could not be chronicled here. Instead, this chapter gives an overview of the general ideas about decision making as they apply to the *design* of a decision support system. The guiding principle of this literature is that different decision makers will need quite different information to support their choice processes. Similarly, a particular decision maker will need different support when facing different choices in different choice environments. Designers of good decision support systems will be cognizant of those needs and respond to them in order to provide decision makers with the flexibility to change the emphasis they place on various criteria.

◆ RATIONAL DECISIONS
Definitions of Rationality

The place to begin is with a definition of *rationality*. Everyone knows that rational decisions are better than those that are not rational. But what does *rational* mean? The dictionary defines it as "based on, or derived from reasoning...implies the ability to reason logically."[1] Clearly, rational decisions require information about the alternatives, which must be identified and evaluated with regard to some set of criteria and some forecast of future conditions. In addition, we must judge these

---

[1]Guralnik, D.B., *Webster's New World Dictionary, Second College Edition*, New York: Simon and Schuster, 1980, p. 1179.

alternatives in terms of their relative use of resources, their impact on our constraints, and their benefits in terms of our objective.

While this provides some guidance, it leaves a significant amount of room for interpretation about what should be included in a decision support system. Rational decisions certainly are based *partly* on economic factors, and therefore optimize the economic condition of the firm, such as minimizing costs, maximizing profits, or maximizing return for investors. So decision support systems need to be able to reflect how much each alternative will cost or how much profit will result from each alternative. Consider, for example, a situation in which a decision maker selects a vehicle from a range of automobiles. Economic rationality would dictate listing the costs of the various automobiles. In addition, it might include more extensive information such as the fuel mileage (to estimate the fuel costs during ownership), the maintenance record (to be able to estimate maintenance costs), special insurance issues (such as high theft rates or other attributes that raise the cost of insurance), and life expectancy of the automobile (to know when the automobile is likely to need replacement). Few of us can imagine purchasing or leasing an automobile without considering the price in some way.

The clear importance of economic considerations means that DSS need to include some economic data and models for evaluating those data. Unfortunately, since many individuals over-emphasize this criterion, many DSS are built to include *only* the economic characteristics of the problem. However, just as few of us would consider buying a car without some fiscal evaluation, few of us would consider *only* economic issues in the choice process. In fact, as Figure 2.1 summarizes, there are six forms of rationality associated with a reasonable decision process.

Upon reflection, almost everyone would agree that technical rationality is assumed in a reasonable decision making process. Technical rationality asserts that if the options will not work, they should not be considered in the choice process. That is, choices should be consistent with the attainment of our goals or objectives. For example, will a particular mix of materials provide the needed strength, or will a particular software package allow the user to perform necessary computations? Even before we look at the economic benefit of the alternative, we should ensure that the solution will actually solve the problem and meet the needs of decision makers. Therefore, a decision support system must include appropriate data and models with which to evaluate the technical aspects of the choices. These might be the engineering specifications of an alternative or information regarding

Figure 2.1   Forms of rationality.

Economic
Technical
Legal
Social
Procedural
Political

the strength of materials relative to needs. In addition, the system might incorporate a model for testing a design. Finally, it might include a plan of action to meet some specific need, with references and information about the success of such a plan in meeting needs in other locations.

To return to our automobile example: what technical characteristics allow the decision maker to decide whether or not the automobile would meet the needs of the owner? For example, if the goal of the owner is high performance, technical criteria should include the engine size, the horsepower, and the availability of possible options for improvement of the performance, such as better-grade wheels and tires. If instead the goal of the owner is to be able to carry certain cargo or a certain number of passengers, then technical criteria include the type of trunk, the capacity of the trunk, the number of seats, or the size of the automobile. *Consumer Reports* data, highway testing data, insurance data, and other performance information might be relevant. The question of technical rationality is whether the particular automobile will meet the specific needs of the user.

In most corporations, legal rationality, the third form of rationality in Figure 2.1, is assumed in a reasonable decision process. Legal rationality prescribes that before a choice is accepted, the decision maker(s) should ensure that the action is within the bounds of legality in the jurisdiction in which the activity will take place. That is, if the manufacturing process is to be completed in Indonesia, then the decision makers understand that the process complies with the legal statutes of Indonesia, as well as with those statutes of the corporate headquarters and/or the country to which parts will be shipped. At the very least, rationality would suggest that the decision makers be aware of the risk and implications of violating statutes.

While most corporations evaluate the legal ramifications of a decision, few look at the legal issues as an active component of the choice process. While decision makers might share decisions with lawyers and ask their opinions, it is generally *after* most of the generation of alternatives, tradeoffs, and evaluation has occurred. Rarely is the legal counsel enough a part of the decision making team to participate actively in what-if kinds of analyses. A DSS that will truly *support* the decision makers will provide access to data and models through which to check the legality of the choices under consideration.

Consider again the choice of an automobile. The owner needs to guarantee that the automobile of choice would meet the legal requirements of the state. This might not be as straightforward as it appears at first glance. For example, suppose the owner wants to purchase a pre-owned automobile, and suppose the system's database includes many automobiles manufactured before 1970, when seat belts were not required on U.S. automobiles, including many "classic" and antique cars. The law does not prescribe that these cars be retrofitted with seat belts, so there is no legal issue associated with the purchase of the car. However, there may be a legal issue associated with the use of the car if, for example, the owners have small children who will ride in it. Car seats, which are required in many states, cannot be secured properly without seat belts. Hence, if the owner purchased a classic car or an antique car that had not been retrofitted with seat belts, the children could not ride in the car legally, because their car seats could not be secured, especially in the back seat. If the owner was not familiar with the seat belt law, they might not consider this issue until after they had already purchased the car. However, if the DSS truly provided *support*, it would provide users such information about legal issues as they were narrowing down alternatives. Most decisions have some legal issues that should be considered during the decision process.

Social rationality is a consideration of the ethical nature of the choice from the perspective of both society as a whole and the decision unit as a group. It suggests that decision makers will not make choices that are "good for the company" if they are bad for themselves or their departments. Similarly, decision makers will not select an option if it is in conflict with the prevailing ethics of society.

While we *hope* most business decisions are reviewed for their ethical nature, the real concern is whether such issues are considered in the context of the DSS. That is, are the ethical or other societal issues considered during alternative generation and evaluation, as are the financial or technical issues? Such inclusion in the *process* generally is believed to result in potentially better choices at the end. Consider again the automobile example. Societal rationality in that context might help the users to evaluate the amount of air or noise pollution created by an automobile. Or it might help the user to understand the environmental impacts of replacing automobiles too often. Information about such ethical issues should be included as an easily accessible component of the DSS so that this dimension can become a part of the tradeoff analysis associated with a choice.

Another aspect of rational decisions is procedural rationality. While it might be economically desirable, technically feasible, and legal to adopt a choice, if the procedures cannot be put into place to implement a particular alternative, it is not rational to do so. In other words, a fifth aspect of choice is whether the appropriate people are in place, the logistics can be handled, and the facilities can be arranged. The DSS must support procedural or substantive rationality, as well.

Consider again the automobile example. Suppose a particular type of automobile satisfies the potential owner in terms of economic, technical, ethical, and legal issues, but the only place to have the automobile serviced is a two-hour ride from home. Or suppose the automobile uses a unique type of fuel that might not readily be available. For an active, busy individual, buying this car might not be a rational decision. Similarly, purchasing a car that will require substantial cuts that one is not likely to make in one's budget, would not be considered rational. Or, on the other hand, suppose the decision maker is considering leasing a car and one of the criteria is that the car be maintained in spotless condition. If the decision maker has several young children, this might not be a procedurally rational decision.

It is not difficult to see that most reasonable individuals would believe logically reasoned decisions should include an investigation of the technical, procedural, legal, ethical, and economic aspects of the alternatives. The last type of rationality—political rationality—is somewhat harder to imagine in a decision support system. The strongest argument for its inclusion is that the political aspects of decisions are considered in the "real world." If we believe that the DSS helps decision makers consider choices better, then we should want to help the decision maker use the political aspects of the decision to their fullest.

Political rationality requires the decision maker to be aware of the relationships between individuals, between departments, and perhaps even between organizations when evaluating a choice process. It implies that decision makers will evaluate the alternatives in light of what is favorable to them and their personal or unit goals. This might include information regarding the probabilities of others adopting a particular strategy and the possible outcomes associated with those strategies. Further, it might include information regarding the mandates and budget of a particular person or unit and how that affects the decision makers and their own units. Political rationality reflects the values of the individual and those of other key players, as well as their relative roles. It suggests a shrewd and practical evaluation of the impact of a particular action on those relationships and the decision maker's perception of the desirability of that impact. Hence, information for the DSS might include data regarding other individuals (or other units) who might be involved in, affected by, or competing with the choice process under consideration. Further, it might include the political agenda or strategies of these groups, the manner by which these groups could be influenced, and strategies for working with these other groups.

Political issues might affect the purchaser of an automobile. For example, consider the message that the car purchased for an elected official conveys to his or her constituency. In particular, consider such an acquisition for an official of a city that is in financial difficulty because many corporations are abandoning the city, and therefore many individuals are out of work. While there may be money available in the budget to acquire and operate a luxury automobile for such an official, and while it may be perfectly legal to acquire the car, it would not be politically rational to obtain such an automobile. The message that the purchase would convey to the constituency undergoing hardship would be negative. There are other examples of political rationality being involved in a decision. In some corporations, image is crucial and can be influenced by the kind of automobile one drives. Appearing too flashy or too conservative, or too similar or dissimilar to the automobiles of others, could affect the desirability of the automobile. If these are, in fact, issues, DSS could include photographs of the car and the associated colors.

Not all systems will contain information regarding all forms of rationality equally. However, since we know that decision makers consider—or should consider— these various facets of rationality, designers should try to provide support for them.

Bounded Rationality and Muddling Through

Just as we need to be aware of the full implications of the meaning of the term rationality, we need to understand how decision makers will use the information provided. Many designers assume that decision makers are only interested in the *best possible* action. In turn, this implies that decision support systems must provide techniques and data that help identify that choice. In many cases this would mean enormous amounts of data and complicated models. Needless to say, the assumption can be quite constraining and limiting for a decision support system.

Simon, in his Nobel Prize–winning research on decision making (see, for example, Simon, 1955; Simon, 1956), suggests that decision makers *do not* optimize their decisions. Rather, these decision makers generally *satisfice*; that is, they find not the best possible action, but rather one that is *good enough*. Simon recognized the limitations of data, processing capability, and methods as well as limitations on the intelligence level of decision makers. He argued that decision makers make rational decisions that are bounded by these limitations (hence, the term *bounded rationality*). In addition, he argued that the advantage in terms of improved decision making does not merit the costs associated with overcoming those limitations. Others have added that even rational choice requires certain predictions about consequences of particular actions as well as projections of future preferences. Therefore, there will always be uncertainty in the system anyway.

Still others add that managers tend to have relatively little time to collect or analyze data or even to consider possible actions. In this light, the concept of bounded rationality, which argues for a *good*, but not necessarily the *best*, decision seems necessary. If, in fact, the system cannot provide something that is easy to follow in a reasonable time frame, the decision maker might not consider it at all.

One way of illustrating the bounded rationality approach to decision making is the theory of "muddling through" (see, for example, Lindblom, 1959; Braybrooke and Lindblom, 1970). "Muddling through" describes decision makers' unwillingness to make bold changes through their choices. Rather, they prefer minor decisions that cause only incremental changes in their environment. So, while they select in concert with their goals (for example, profit maximization, customer satisfaction), decision makers do so by taking small steps in the appropriate direction. In particular, they steer away from long-range or strategic planning, because that often requires large, significant changes in policies or actions. Hence, decision makers will consider only information that is absolutely necessary to make these incremental changes, generally limited information regarding a selected few dimensions. Further, decision makers tend to prefer only the *marginal* effect of a change of policy from the status quo.

What does this mean to DSS design? First, it suggests that designers of systems should not endeavor to make available *all* information or all models that could possibly be used by those making choices. Decision makers are likely to consider only a limited amount of information available in their choice process. In fact, they may not even consider available information if it would require a large shift of focus. This is particularly true if the decision maker has a concern about the quality of the model or of the information available in a DSS.

Not using all possible information is not necessarily bad. However, often the choice to use limited information is associated with biased or uninformed decision making. Clearly, the bias (especially if it is unintentional) and the absence of crucial dimensions of an alternative are problems. Since we know that these dimen-

In her book, Cynthia Crossen* sites a variety of studies on the relationship between the consumption of walnuts and cholesterol levels. For example, she sites a study from the *Archives of Internal Medicine*:

> The story began with a study of 31,209 Seventh-Day Adventists. Researchers questioned them about their consumption of 65 different foods. To the researchers' surprise, those who ate nuts at least five times a week had only half the risk of fatal heart attacks as those who had nuts less than once a week.

Her analysis of the bias in the study included the following:

> *Unfortunately, we do not know from this account how many of the sixty-four other foods were associated with a lower risk of heart attacks. We do not know if the nut eaters shared other characteristics besides eating nuts that may have explained their lower rate of fatalities. Seventh-Day Adventists do not smoke or drink, which makes them an abnormal population to study. And according to this account, the study was based on their memories, not observation.*

In other words, the study was biased. Decision makers who might attempt to make choices based on this study might not select the important characteristics to modify. Crossen continues with another walnut-cholesterol study.

> This time, the researchers put 18 healthy volunteers on two carefully controlled diets for two months. One was a nut-free version of a standard low-cholesterol diet. The other was nutritionally similar, except 20 percent of the calories came from about 3 ounces of walnuts per day . . . On the no-nuts diet, the volunteers' cholesterol levels fell 6 percent. When they switched to the walnut diet, their cholesterol declined an additional 12 percent. Everyone's cholesterol dropped while eating nuts, and the average decrease was 22 points, from 182 to 160.

Her analysis:

> *While not a fatal flaw, eighteen subjects is a very small study. The subjects were put on a low-cholesterol diet, which means their cholesterol was going to drop no matter what. Think about eating three ounces of walnuts every day. It comes to more than fifty pounds a year. . . . They lost me. Did all the subjects first eat no nuts, then the nuts regime? Or were there two groups, one starting with no nuts and one starting with nuts? Did the 22-point cholesterol drop include the decrease attributable to the low-cholesterol diet alone? How long did the study go on—that is, would the cholesterol level have continued to drop from the low-cholesterol diet with or without the nuts? Those walnuts displaced other food—was the drop a substitution effect alone?*

In other words, because of the bias in which the data were collected and summarized, we actually know nothing from either study. However, upon first reading, it appears as though information is unbiased. It is this subtle bias that is unintentional to the decision maker which can reduce the value of the DSS significantly.

*Crossen, C., *Tainted Truth: The Manipulation of Fact in America*, New York: Simon and Schuster, 1994, pp. 224–225.

sions may exist, even with our best intentions, we must design decision aids that protect against biases. Hence, decision support systems should include assistance that not only helps the decision makers use the mechanics of the system correctly but also helps them use the data and models correctly. These ideas will be addressed more completely in later chapters.

Finally, designers of DSS should not feel compelled to include models that are not cost-effective. However, they should help decision makers learn the most they can from the information available through easy integration of information, effective use of models, and encourage analysis of the sensitivity of the costs and benefits of alternatives to the underlying assumptions.

The Nature of Managers

In addition to being aware of the various types of rationality and the ways in which rationality is and can be implemented in the choice process, designers of decision support systems should know how decision makers work. Otherwise, it is unlikely that the systems will actually *support* the decision makers in their choice process.

Mintzberg has studied decision makers over a number of years (see, for example, Mintzberg, 1990). In his work he has found several characteristics of decision makers that can influence the design of decision support systems. First and foremost, different decision makers operate and decide in very different ways. However, most of them *want* to operate *their way* because it has been successful for them. As a result, decision support systems must also be designed to allow their users to *do things their way*. In other words, they must include substantial flexibility in their operations. Otherwise, they are unlikely to be used.

Mintzberg did find some similarities among decision makers. Most high-level decision makers dislike reflective activities, do not want substantial aggregated data, and consider most choices in a short time period (often less than 15 minutes). Furthermore, managers prefer verbal media for dissemination of information (meetings and/or telephone calls) over written media (such as reports). Although we might at first think that this is bad news for decision support systems, it could be viewed as guidance for their design. In particular, it calls for (a) flexibility in analyses; (b) access to a wide range of databases; (c) access to historically innovative types of databases; and (d) tight integration of electronic mail and electronic discussion group technology with the decision support systems. These will be discussed briefly in the following paragraphs as well as in later chapters.

What do Mintzberg's conclusions tell us about information? First, managers prefer informality and efficiency in the manner in which they obtain information. Meetings and telephone calls typically have less formality than does a report. Likewise, if designed appropriately, a DSS can provide an informal and nonthreatening environment in which to be considering alternatives. This is particularly true if it integrates access to many databases and a useful electronic mail feature. The former allows the decision maker quick access to facts or information that might other-

In his book *The Pursuit of WOW!*, Tom Peters discussed principles of management. In Principle 49*, he notes how people respond to uncertainty:

The Greeks knew little of the way their world worked by the standards of Copernicus or Newton, let alone Einstein. Yet they developed a system of meaning as finely articulated as any you'll find in a modern quantum mechanics text.

The translation to everyday life is clear. When confronted with anything unusual, from a new ache or pain to a new boss, we try to build a theory of how things are going to work out. And, says experience and psychological research, the less we know for sure, the more complex the webs of meaning (mythology) we spin.

While Peters goes on to explain the lesson of keeping customers informed, this principle can have other lessons to DSS needs. That is, without current and appropriate information and decision aids, decision makers will still develop a model of the choice context and make decisions based on that model. With reasonable support and information, decision makers are likely to develop a prudent model. Without reasonable support and information, decision makers are likely to develop defective views of reality, which can lead to imprudent choices being made. Hence, decision support—even fairly limited support—can increase the likelihood of discerning choices being made.

*Peters T., *The Pursuit of WOW! Every Person's Guide to Topsy-Turvy Times*, New York: Vintage Books, 1994, p. 74.

---

wise be obtained by asking a subordinate to find them. In this way, the decision maker can access information without concern of others' opinions of acquiring the information. In addition, if the sought information provokes other questions, the decision maker has more freedom to pursue information in support of those questions.

The latter allows decision makers the option of integrating the informally obtained information with that found in the DSS. Many individuals find electronic mail considerably less formal than written communication. Matters of style and structure are generally abandoned in favor of the quick, to-the-point question–answer format more frequently found in verbal communication. In fact, e-mail is often written "off the cuff," and a form of nonverbal cue, referred to as "Smileys," has even developed to fill the nonverbal vacuum and minimize misunderstandings. Smileys are combinations of computer keyboard characters typed to fit on a single line that generally follow the punctuation and represent the writer's emotions.

Second, Mintzberg's work suggests that managers do not always think in a linear manner. In a meeting or telephone call, decision makers can digress from the main discussion for a while to handle issues that surface. Such behavior is much

◆ DSS Designs Insights ◆

Symbols such as :-) and :-(can convey simple happy (or silly) and unhappy (or disappointed) sentiment.

Variations on the theme can include (look at them sideways)

:-) 8   for a dapper look,

% + {   to indicate you lost a fight, or

; -)   to indicate that you are just kidding.

Some have even been defined to represent particular famous people or events, such as = = | :-)> to represent Abraham Lincoln.

more difficult to accommodate in a report. We must start at the beginning and read until we get the necessary details. Then, if we have questions, we must request another report and repeat the process. In other words, in designing a DSS, it is important to allow managers the ability to move around in their analyses as new questions arise. A "hypertext" design process is necessary.

Third, managers want to know the source of their facts. Many managers do not make a decision on the basis of the information presented to them, but rather on the basis of *who* presents the information. If managers have faith in the people presenting the option, they will have faith in the option. This has three implications for the design of a decision support system. It means that there must be some way to assign sources to the information available in the system. In addition, it means there must be a manner by which users can obtain, store, access, and aggregate others' opinions and analyses of options under consideration. This might include the integration of an electronic mail system. E-mail would allow the decision maker the ability to pose questions or insights and obtain reflections on them from relevant others. Further, the system must include electronic access to magazines, newspapers, wire services, and other media, and it must be storable because it might be usable in the future. Once it is stored, you must give the decision maker the ability to access it easily and summarize it.

Fourth, it means managers want to have some predigestion of information. Decision makers are busy. Therefore, they need help in understanding all the information they receive in a day. Again, the electronic communications capability will facilitate this goal. In addition, the DSS must provide easy access to a database of position papers or other statements that can be searched in a flexible manner. Or, in some circumstances, it is necessary to have prepared analyses (in a hypertext format) available for the manager to access.

Fifth, it means managers value involvement. One reason for meetings is to allow all parties to become involved in the planning and "buy into" it. Electronic discussion groups, electronic mail, and general sharing of documents can provide the same effect, if managed properly.

◆ APPROPRIATE DATA SUPPORT

Decision support systems need to provide a range of information without overwhelming the decision maker. In fact, there is a rule of thumb, called the "Seven Plus or Minus Two Rule," that says decision makers can, on average, assimilate only five to nine ideas before they are overwhelmed.

This section discusses theories of information processing, including pattern recognition and learning in the choice process. After this section, we will have a better basis for answering questions about how to identify specific data and specific models for a given decision support system.

Information Processing Models

Information processing requires the decision maker to perceive and process information, recognize patterns in the information, and remember past events to understand information currently available. For example, consider the process of reading. We must be able to see the letters on the page and to recognize differences between the individual characters. In addition, we must remember patterns of letters and their associated meaning so as to understand what a particular combination of characters appearing on the page means. Similarly, we need to perceive what combinations of words mean, particularly to recall the specific nuances of certain combinations.

Although reading is not difficult for most adults, it can be quite challenging for the child just beginning because that child understands neither what aspects of the differences in characters are important nor what differences in combinations of words are important. Similarly, students in an introductory statistics course have difficulty processing information in a discussion problem. They do not have skill in understanding how the information can be structured into a mathematical format. Often, they do not have sufficient experience to understand what information is crucial and what is superfluous.

Most decision makers have similar problems. The goal of the decision support system is to help them separate the crucial from the irrelevant and to understand it better. To achieve that goal, decision makers must acquire information from the system in a meaningful fashion. The acquisition process has three unique phases: (1) sensation, (2) attention, and (3) perception. In the sensation process the decision maker has some awareness of the existence of the information. In the second stage, attention, the information has gained the concentration of the decision maker. Finally, in the third stage, perception, the decision maker begins to interpret the meaning of the information and to process it into memory. This third phase is the moment when information and its meaning are apparent to the decision maker in a manner that allows its use.

Prior to the third stage, the decision maker might filter out information without explicit notice. Such filtering is a crucial component of concentration because of the huge number of stimuli, such as the sound of fire engines and the coffee pot, coming from one's environment. This filtering is done to remove information believed to be irrelevant to the task under consideration.

We will discuss in a moment how these factors affect the actual perception process. However, at this point it is important to know that information might be filtered on the basis of something beyond the control of the designer of the decision support system. That means that it is not sufficient simply to have information available, or even to display information. Decision makers may not take the time to look for information passively provided by the DSS. Even if it is displayed, the decision maker may not notice it or absorb its meaning. If the decision maker really needs to see the information, there must be some mechanism of ensuring that he or she does so. Some designers use unambiguous pop-up screens that require the user to take action before they disappear. Other designers use flashing lights, beeps, or other sensorial stimuli. The manner of action depends on the system itself.

The way decision makers screen with regard to task is well known. For example, when selecting stocks for investment, decision makers will most likely consider the financial aspects of performance of the stocks as well as financial measures of performance and liquidity of the companies. (This material is well documented in finance books.) They are unlikely to consider issues such as the color of the paper of the stock certificate or the phase of the moon. How decision makers screen with regard to experience is less well documented. What we do know is that experience affects what information decision makers will seek and how they expect to have that information conveyed.

Consider, for example, the models of information processing proposed by Piaget. He indicates that people develop in their information processing needs as a function of their maturation, experience, education, and self-regulation. Specifically, he suggests that inexperienced decision makers will seek more concrete informa-

---

◆   **DSS Designs Insights**   ◆

If our mind allowed all the signals from our environment to reach our consciousness, we would be unable to process information. To obtain a physical representation of how difficult it would be to perceive the meaning of stimuli, listen to the *Holiday Symphony* by Charles Ives. In that symphony, Ives' goal was to bring together all the stimuli perceived by a young boy at a celebration in a small town. In one movement, "Decoration Day," Ives begins with the music that might have been heard in a New England town celebrating Memorial Day in the early twentieth century. Of course, there is music from the bands. However, Ives intersperses sounds remembered by a small boy, such as the church bell ringing, errors made by musicians, and the sounds of soldiers mourning the loss of their comrades. Once listeners have taken the time to identify the individual components, they can appreciate the music and its meaning. If listeners do not take that time, the music appears to be nothing more than the random clashing of sounds. That is, without direction, it is difficult to identify patterns in the activities that lead to the music.

tion than do their more experienced counterparts. Inexperienced decision makers are more comfortable with methods drawn from their personal experiences. Furthermore, they use elementary classification schemes and generalize only with regard to tangible and familiar objects. They use direct cause–effect relationships of the form, "If A happens, then I look at ratio B." Finally, these decision makers tend to be "closed" in the sense that they will not voluntarily explore possibilities outside those specified in their elementary classification schemes. In short, they tend to follow the rules specified in their formal training.

Most individuals in an elementary statistics course make decisions about their exam questions in this way. Specifically, these students look at a problem and attempt to find another "just like it." Then they decide on a solution technique because "I used this solution technique on the sample problem and it was correct. Therefore, it should be correct to use it on the exam question." These students follow very elementary rules to put problems into categories, and they expect to find exam questions that fit their classification schemes. Once they have found a pattern in the questions, they will not look for other factors that might help them decide on a solution technique more efficiently or more effectively. Invariably the instructor does not understand their classification scheme and puts a question on the exam for which the scheme will not specify the appropriate solution technique.

Novice users are less willing to seek a wide range of information about potential automobiles. In the earlier car-purchasing example, the system might ask the novice user questions such as "What car do you drive now? What things do you like about it? What things do you not like about it?" and make a recommendation based on this very limited information.

As decision makers become more experienced, they reflect more on information provided to them and seek possibilities they have not considered previously. They can imagine other options and other information to support their hypotheses about options. In fact, their decision making tends to be more open-ended, involving more speculation about unstated possibilities. In other words, they become more analytical about their evaluation.

In the car-purchasing example, these decision makers can handle more abstract questions, such as the desirability of new options on a car. They will also be more appreciative of and accepting of a deductive reasoning system that allows them to select automobiles by specifying features.

Rasmussen similarly identifies experience as an important predictor of the information needs of decision makers (Rasmussen, 1983). In particular, he notes that decision makers are guided by past experience and the success of that past experience. For example, if a decision maker has faced a problem and experienced a good outcome resulting from the choice, then he or she is likely to use similar approaches and techniques the next time a similar problem arises—whether or not those approaches and techniques had anything to do with the outcome. If, on the other hand, the decision maker experienced a bad outcome resulting from the choice, he or she is likely to move away from those approaches and techniques—even if they were appropriate.

If the decision makers are novices or have never approached a decision similar to the one under consideration, they are likely to employ more tactical rules in evaluating their alternatives. These rules are defined and employed rigidly, and decision makers are unlikely to stray from them. Like Piaget, Rasmussen believes these decision makers follow a data-driven approach to choices. They look at the characteristics of an alternative and compare those to something they know and understand. For example, when a novice examines a car for potential purchase, he or she tends to compare that car to known cars such as those owned by friends and family. So such a decision maker may look at the size of a new car compared to that of the currently owned car, the features with regard to the features of a currently owned car, and so on.

At the intermediate level, information is viewed as evidence of the similarity of this choice situation to related past situations. The degree of similarity will guide decision makers in the selection of rules, as outlined earlier. They are not goal oriented; rather, they are mimicking the process they have experienced earlier. However, they are willing to generalize somewhat further.

Experienced decision makers are goal oriented. They actively select goals to achieve and seek information relevant to their achievement. They tend to move into a "hypothesis and test search strategy." For example, these decision makers might begin the search process with a belief that they might like driving a larger automobile. Rather than compare how easy or difficult it might be to drive, park, and maneuver the differently sized car, these decision makers are likely to test drive a variety of cars to determine whether they like the feel and operation. In the process, they may refine other, related characteristics, such as head room or comfort, that should also govern their choice of automobile. In this way, they constantly modify their own functional model as they gain additional information. Hence, these decision makers are more likely to investigate information deeply without prompting. Of course, they also run the risk of inappropriately generalizing. Finally, at its highest level, Rasmussen indicates that decision making becomes virtually instinctual.

Knowledge of these different decision making styles tells the designer of a decision support system how to incorporate models. Rasmussen suggests that *sole* reliance on quantitative models does not adequately reflect the needs of many decision makers. Rather, qualitative systems would offer support for the user at any of the more advanced behavior levels. Such systems would be especially useful at the knowledge-based level, where information must be used in unfamiliar ways and where there are not pre-established, quantitative rules for processing data. Qualitative measures should guide the overall analysis, while quantitative models can be used for more detailed analyses of the system.

Klein also developed a model of decision making based on the experience of the decision maker (Klein, 1980). While many of the ideas are parallel to those expressed by Piaget and Rasmussen, Klein adds a description of experts and their decision making process. Specifically, he indicates that experts tend to reason by analogy. They do not follow explicit, conscious rules. Neither do they disaggregate situations into components, but rather analyze the entire situation *in toto*. In fact, he asserts that attempts to force experts to specify their rules explicitly, or to examine only selected components of a problem, might reduce performance quality. Such an artificial process could stifle or mask the process that comes naturally.

These expert decision makers, then, need decision aids that will let them recognize analogous situations. One approach is to include a background artificial intelligence system that could analyze particular choices and "learn" the rules that experts employ. If such rules were ascertained, they could be parlayed into further assistance, which would illustrate why a particular approach was or was not appropriate in the current context.

A somewhat more practical use of Klein's model is in helping decision makers see how a current choice context is similar to one they faced previously. A DSS might also include helping decision makers understand how the current context is *different*, and hence why different strategies might work. Specifically, this means a DSS should have decision aids that support users' ability to recognize trends. This might include the development of a database with which to track options, the relevant factors, and the outcome of choices. It might also include an alternative generation option that assists decision makers in introducing new choices that address problems perceived in the past. Finally, the DSS could help decision makers perform the necessary computations to assess the impact of various choices.

Another model, proposed by Dreyfus and Dreyfus (see, for example, Dreyfus and Dreyfus, 1986), describes six levels of expertise in decision making through which decision makers progress as they become more expert in their decision making. Along the way, they change the kind of information they seek and the manner in which they expect to have the information represented. The first level is *novice*. These decision makers decompose their environment into context-free, non-situational components. They rely on standardized rules for determining action. Since they do not have experience, they have no basis for judging the quality of their decision making efforts. This behavior is similar to that which most students employ in an introductory statistics course. Since they are not entirely sure why certain computations are carried out, they simply replicate them exactly like the example in the book or the example from class. This is a very regimented, "cookbook" approach to decision making.

The second level is *advanced beginner*. These decision makers follow much the same procedure as do the novices, except that they can understand some rudimentary differences between situations. Like novices, they require explicit instruction regarding the procedures for decision making. This might include recommendations about the data that should be acquired, the models that should be employed, and the order in which analyses should be done. In addition, they would need decision aids aimed at helping them understand unique features of a given situation.

Competent decision makers, those in the third category, begin to develop a perspective of a problem and can single out important and irrelevant factors in the choice context. Similarly, they can identify unique characteristics of the choice context, analyze them, and develop some guidelines for addressing those characteristics independently.

The last level of *analytical approaches* to decision making (and the fourth level overall) is *proficiency*. Proficient decision makers have increased practice in applying the rules of data analysis and modeling. They can recognize important characteristics of problems and can generally determine whether or not they have approached a problem correctly. They are still considered analytical, because they still follow a specified set of principles that guide their action. Unlike less skilled decision makers, however, they have memorized the principles and follow them naturally. An example of this level of decision making is the student who has specialized in statistics and has just received a bachelor's degree. Such students understand the differences between regression and autoregressive models and know how to apply each one correctly in a regulated environment. However, they still decide which to employ and how to employ them by using well-defined rules of action.

The last two types of decision making, *expertise* and *mastery*, are more intuitive approaches to decision making. For these decision makers, an occurrence triggers an action intuitively. Unlike the analytical decision makers who know that "*A* happened and therefore we must apply technique *A1*," these decision makers simply "know" they should apply technique *A1*. In fact, if one queried a decision maker of mastery level, he or she might not be able to tell you offhand why technique *A1* was selected or why technique *A2* was not. The major difference between these two high levels of decision making is the monitoring function. Those at the expertise level still monitor their own performance of decision making, but they can do it internally. Master-level decision makers do not monitor their choices.

So, what does this mean to the design of a DSS? Well, we can see that as decision makers develop, they will follow less regimented processes. A novice decision maker will need a great deal of structure in his or her system, while a master decision maker will need a great deal of flexibility. Not only does this structure/flexibility criterion apply to the user's movement through the system and to the user interface, but it also refers to the modeling procedures and their requirements. While warning messages and suggestion boxes would be well received by novices, they will actually weaken the decision-making behavior of those at the expertise and mastery levels.

Consider the example of the automobile purchase. A novice may have no idea what information to consider about an automobile. While concerned about purchase price, he or she may not be aware of the extras associated with options. In addition, the novice might not realize how much sales tax or interest adds to the total amount of money needed to purchase the car. Systems in support of these individuals must provide such information explicitly and help the user apply it appropriately.

Similarly, novice and advanced beginner decision makers will need help in monitoring the quality of their decision processes. This means they need guidance and supervision of their selection of data and models during the choice process. In addition, they will improve their performance if, over time, the outcomes of their choices are monitored and relayed back to them. In this way, they can determine what has worked well and what has worked poorly. Consider, again, the automobile example. Novice and advanced beginner decision makers need assistance in understanding the implications of their choices. For example, suppose the decision maker is interested in high performance but is also financially constrained. If a sports car is chosen, the system must help the user to understand the amount of additional money that will be spent on insurance and on fuel. That is, the system must help the user to comprehend the total package of costs.

Not only do the type and amount of structure and of decision aids change with experience, but the actual information preferred by decision makers changes. For example, Sauter (Sauter, 1985; Sauter and Schofer, 1988) found that novice decision makers prefer very explicit, quantitative data regarding the resources available. As they gain more experience, they move from seeking feasibility information to seeking information about the performance of alternatives under consideration. These decision makers tend to prefer more qualitative information and even speculations regarding the past performance of an alternative under scrutiny. With additional experience comes a move toward evaluation of the efficiency of alternatives. These decision makers seek quantitative, factual information regarding the process or internal operations of an alternative.

This result suggests that the kind of database and model support required by decision makers will shift over time. The middle-level decision makers will provide the greatest challenge to designers of decision support systems. They will need not only conventional database support, but also access to databases in which they can store as well as search and summarize opinions, some of which could

---

◆ DSS in Action ◆

Decision makers change the criteria and the weighting of criteria as a function of their environments. In an article in *ORMS Today**, Totten and Tohamy describe logistics support systems that facilitate efficient routing of trucks and their cargoes for large firms. In it they describe systems that can learn how to weight the various corporate objectives as they change throughout the year. For example, around the holidays, the driver "get-home request" has the top priority. In contrast, during the remainder of the year, customer requirements have top priority. Hence, the system needs to be able to change the models used to facilitate decision making easily. With this change in priority comes the creation of new alternatives, such as load swapping, for the decision maker to consider.

*Totten, L. and N. Tohamy, "Home for the Holidays," *ORMS Today*, 22(6), December 1995, p. 24–29.

exist in public databases. Other stored opinions will need some level of security to support them, so they would appear only in private databases for the exclusive use of the decision maker. For example, in the automobile example, users might want access to comments in publications such as *Consumer Reports* regarding the desirability of automobiles. In addition, they might want a personal database in which to store comments about cars they have seen or test driven, or the comments of friends and relatives. Once the data are stored, users need access to scan and retrieve them and to summarize them in a useful fashion.

Of course, other factors, such as the amount of stability in the relevant environment and the focus of the decision, can affect what kinds of information users seek as well. While we will discuss this in more depth in later chapters regarding the design process, it is important to note here that the needs of the decision maker will change over time. Hence, the system must have the flexibility to change with the decision maker and accommodate changes in both the information sought and the models employed.

◆ GROUP DECISION MAKING

Understanding decision making processes is difficult because there is so much variability across individuals in terms of the phases they adopt, the methods they employ, and the data that are important to them. However, variability in these issues increases tremendously when groups make decisions, thereby making support of a group decision making activity that much more difficult.

When we identify group decision making, we refer to several individuals working together to complete some task as a unit. These individuals might be people who always work together, and hence have some shared history of performance. Or they may have been brought together for just this one decision and hence have no appreciation for the skills and knowledge that each brings to the task. Similarly, the group could be in one location meeting together, or in multiple locations meeting via teleconferencing, or working in one location but at different times.

In theory, groups are developed to address a task because they can provide better solutions than can one person. For example, through discussion, groups can develop a better understanding of the complexity of a problem. Furthermore, since groups have more skills and understanding than any one individual, they can generate more and richer alternatives for problem solving. Similarly, since there are many individuals involved, there is a greater chance that errors may be found at early and thus easily reparable stages. Finally, if a group participates in a decision, the members are more likely to accept the decision and hence not resist the outcome of the process.

However, group decision making does not always occur in the fashion we anticipate. Since the process generally requires meetings, it can be slow and time-consuming, especially if the tasks are not well managed. In particular, there is a tendency to waste valuable time in waiting, in socializing, in having people repeat concepts, or in listening to people speak just for the sake of speaking. As in many group projects, group members may rely on others to "pick up the slack" and not contribute properly.

There are, in addition, two major problems associated with group work. First, there is the tendency to conform to a given solution too early. Social pressure may convince some individuals to accept a solution before they are ready to do so. Similarly, social pressure, especially among busy individuals, may lead to an incomplete analysis of the task and incomplete use of information. People tend to want to not "buck the trend," and conform to the group too readily, especially if they have not carried their fair share of the workload. Related to this is the second major difficulty associated with group work: the problem of group dynamics. Too often, the person with the highest authority, the person who has been there longest, the person with the best credentials, or the person with the loudest voice or the most dominant personality dominates the discussion and therefore the generation of alternatives and resolution of the task. Shy, relatively inexperienced or new individuals have difficulty being heard. This can be a particular problem if they have drastically different views of a problem or skills. Whereas group members *should* be relying on the *substance* of the information and the *appropriateness* of the alternatives to guide them in deciding how pivotal they are to the discussion, they too often view the personality or the group dynamics when deciding the merit of an argument.

If we are building a decision support system to advance a *group* decision making effort, we must consider not only all the issues discussed previously, but also features that can enhance the positive attributes of groups and minimize the negative. For example, tools that can encourage all individuals to brainstorm alternatives and question assumptions will take advantage of the positive aspects of group decision making. Tools that can mask who is presenting information and limit the amount of time each individual has to communicate can counteract the negative.

DISCUSSION

The purpose of this chapter is to introduce some of the thoughts on decision making available in the literature. These theories and views will be expounded on later, as we discuss exactly *how* they are implemented in a decision support system. Individual aspects of the user interface, databases, model management issues, and connectivity with external resources will be developed in the following four chapters. A later chapter will address the design of group decision support systems.

◆ O N   T H E   W E B ◆

On the Web for this chapter provides information about the theory of decision making as it pertains to the design and use of Decision Support Systems. Links can provide access to demonstration packages, general overview information, applications, software providers, tutorials, and more. Additional discussion questions and new applications will also be added as they become available.

- *Links provide access to general overview information.* For example, one link provides a brief history of the literature on decision making, others discuss particular aspects of the choice process, and some provide access to bibliographies on the discipline of decision making.
- *Links provide access to tools.* Some links are provided to DSS functioning on the Web that will help you consider how you make decisions and seek information.

- *Links provide access to exercises about decision making.* Some links give examples and exercises that will help to analyze your decision making style, the criteria that support it and conditions under which it changes.
- *Links provide access to information about purchasing and leasing an automobile.* Decision making is the foundation for the four components of a DSS. The next four chapters, give examples for purchasing or leasing an automobile. Begin now to think about how people make these decisions; some links on the Web can help you learn about the kinds of systems, and the information and models that could support that choice among options that are available.

You can access material for this chapter from the general WWW Page for the book, or directly from the following URL.
http://www.umsl.edu/~sauter/DSS/dm.html

QUESTIONS

1. Discuss how the model proposed by Dreyfus and Dreyfus provides guidance for the evolutionary design of decision support and expert systems.

2. Describe how DSS can illustrate the tenets of decision making. That is, identify how systems can provide support in a manner that is prescribed by the decision making literature covered in this chapter.

3. What changes would you make to an electronic book catalog system (such as you find in your library) to transform it into a good decision support system.

4. Describe the decision support system you might provide to Sherlock Holmes. Be sure to describe all components of a DSS.

5. Consider a company that has had major financial difficulties in the recent past. Discuss how the use of a decision support system might have helped management to discover and repair problems earlier. Be specific in your treatment of a company.

6. Suppose you were attempting to justify the development of a DSS for a corporation. Discuss how you would justify the expenditures.

SUGGESTED READINGS

Braybrooke, D. and C.E. Lindblom, *A Strategy of Decision*, New York: Macmillan Publishing Co., 1970.

Churchman, C.W., *Design of Inquiring Systems*, New York: Basic Books, 1971.

Crossen, C., *Tainted Truth: The Manipulation of Fact in America*, New York: Simon & Schuster, 1994.

Cyert, R.M. and J.G. March, *A Behavioral Theory of the Firm*, Englewood Cliffs, NJ: Prentice Hall, 1963.

DeSanctis, G. and R.B. Gallupe, "A foundation for the study of group decision support systems," *Management Science*, 33(5), May 1987, pp. 589–609.

Dreyfus, H.L. and S.E. Dreyfus, *Mind Over Machine: The Power of Human Intuition and Expertise in the Era of the Computer*, New York: The Free Press, 1986.

Gray, P. and L. Olfman, "The user interface in group decision support systems," *Decision Support Systems*, 5(2), 1989.

Huber, G.P., "The nature of organizational decision making and the design of decision support systems," *MIS Quarterly*, 5(2), June 1981, pp. 1–10.

Huber, G.P., "Cognitive styles as a basis for MIS and DSS designs: Much ado about nothing," *Management Science*, 29(5), May 1983, pp. 567–579.

Langley, A., "In search of rationality: The purposes behind the use of formal analysis in organizations," *Administrative Systems Quarterly*, December 1989 pp. 598–631.

Lindblom, C.E., "The science of *muddling through*." *Public Administration Review*, 19, Spring 1959, pp. 155–169.

Lindstone, H. and M. Turroff, *The Delphi Method: Technology and Applications*, Reading, MA: Addison-Wesley, 1975.

Keen, P.G.W., "The evolving concept of optimality." *TIMS Studies in the Management Sciences*, 6, 1977, pp. 31–57.

Klein, G.A., "Automated aids for the proficient decision maker," *Proceedings of the 1980 IEEE Systems, Man, and Cybernetics Conference*, October 1980, pp. 301–304.

March, James G., "Bounded rationality, ambiguity and the engineering of choice," *Bell Journal of Economics*, March 1978, pp. 587–608.

Miller, G.A., "The magic number seven, plus or minus two: Some limits on our capacity for processing information," *Psychological Review*, 63, 1956, pp. 81–97.

Mintzberg, H., *The Nature of Managerial Work*, New York: Harper and Row, 1973.

Mintzberg, H., "The manager's job: Folklore and fact," *Harvard Business Review*, March/April, 1990, p. 163–176.

Mintzberg, H., D. Raisinghani, and A. Theoret, "The structure of the 'unstructured' decision processes," *Administrative Science Quarterly*, 21, June 1976, pp. 246–275.

Mockler, R.J., *Computer Software to Support Strategic Management Decision Making*, New York: Macmillan Co., 1992.

Nunamaker, J.F., A.R. Dennis, J.S. Valacich, D.R. Vogel, and J.F. George, "Electronic meeting systems to support group work," *Communications of the ACM*, 34(7), July 1991, pp. 40–61.

Rasmussen, J., "Skills, rules and knowledge: Signals, signs and symbols, and other distinctions in human performance models," *IEEE Transactions on Systems, Man, and Cybernetics*, 13(3), May/June, 1983, pp. 257–266.

Rasmussen, J., *On Information Processing and Human-Machine Interaction: An Approach to Cognitive Engineering*, New York: North Holland, 1986.

Robey, D. and W. Taggart, "Human information processing in information and decision support systems," *MIS Quarterly*, 6(2), June 1982, pp. 61–73.

Sage, A.P., *Decision Support Systems Engineering*, New York: John Wiley and Sons, 1991.

Sanderson, D.W. and D. Dougherty, *Smileys*, New York: O'Reilly and Associates, 1993.

Sauter, V.L., "The effect of *experience* on information preferences," *Omega: The International Journal of Management Science*, 13(4), 1985, pp. 277-284.

Sauter, V.L. and J.L. Schofer, "Evolutionary development of decision support systems: Important issues for early phases of design," *Journal of Management Information Systems*, 4(4), Spring 1988, pp. 77-92.

Simon, H.A., "A behavioral model of rational choice." *Quarterly Journal of Economics*, 69, 1955, pp. 99-118.

Simon, H.A., "Rational choice and the structure of the environment, *Psychological Review*, 63, 1956, pp. 129-138.

Simon, H.A., *Models of Man*, New York: Wiley, 1957.

Simon, H.A., "From substantive to procedural rationality," in S.J. Latsis (ed.), *Method and Appraisal in Economics*, London: Cambridge University Press, 1976, pp. 129-148.

Simon, H.A., "Rational decision making in business organizations," *American Economic Review*, 68, May 1978, pp. 1-16.

Simon, H.A., *Models of Thought*, New Haven, CT: Yale University Press, 1979.

Sprague, R.H. Jr., "A framework for the development of decision support systems," *MIS Quarterly*, 4(4), pp. 1-26.

Taylor, R.N., "Concepts, theory and techniques: Psychological determinants of bounded rationality: Implications for decision-making strategies," *Decision Sciences*, 6(2), 1975, pp. 409-427.

Thompson, J., *Organizations in Action*, New York: McGraw-Hill, 1967.

Van de Ven, A.H. and A.L. Delbecq, "The effectiveness of nominal, delphi and interacting group decision making processes," *Academy of Management Journal*, 14, 1971, pp. 203-213.

PART II

◆ ◆ ◆

Components of a DSS

Chapter 3

Data Components

◆ ◆ ◆

Data are things known or assumed. The term generally refers to facts and/or figures from which conclusions can be drawn. For example, the raw counts of walnut consumption and cholesterol levels discussed in Chapter 2 represent data. Similarly, the cost of commercial time and the distribution of viewing audiences of a set of television programs represent data relevant to marketing plan choices. Details about shipping procedures, cost, and reliability of various haulers represent data that are relevant to a logistics plan.

However, these are not the only kinds of details that might be considered data for the purposes of DSS. When making choices, some decision makers value the opinions of trusted colleagues. For example, when purchasing managers consider new, unknown vendors, they often seek opinions regarding service and reliability from colleagues at other corporations who have purchased from those vendors. They would not use these opinions solely, but would use them to enrich a cost model developed from more objective data. Similarly, when developing a long-range plan, a CEO enlists knowledgable subordinates to gauge the expected changes in regulations, governments, vendors, competitors, and clients over a 20-year period. These opinions are melded with quantitative models, which alone do not provide reliable long-range forecasts, as the basis of a long-range estimate of the company's needs. In each of these cases, opinions and judgments are used as inputs to a choice process. They supplement standard "objective" data to represent aspects of the choice that would otherwise be lacking. Since the DSS is intended to *support* the choice process, it must accommodate such subjective data and opinions and provide efficient ways of searching for and using these data.

For other decisions, decision makers might need data that are not stored in conventional ways. For example, decision makers considering the choice of textiles for the manufacture of furniture believe the support provided by pictures is superior to that provided by verbal descriptions of the colors, patterns, and textures. Images supplement data such as price, vendor, or shrinkage that would be accessed in a standard fashion. Decision makers considering a large-scale disaster relief plan might need a video report of the affected area to assess the problems and needs of an area fully. Such a video might be supplemented with a hypertext stack to allow a decision maker immediate access to land use plans, damage estimates, or population statistics for each affected area. Or, a symphony music director might find it beneficial have CDs (audio data) of possible selections so that balanced and appealing programs can be chosen. With audio data and a database describing programs, audience size, reviews, and comments, the director could develop models that maximize the number of new compositions played by an orchestra while still being sensitive to the expected size of the audience, thus pairing new selections and established favorites in a pleasing fashion.

With the advent of virtual reality technology, decision makers might also need access to "experiences" before they can select alternatives. For example, if the DSS supported a company in the telecommunications industry, virtual reality might be created to allow users to see and navigate nodes and links, analyze node data, and re-route traffic quickly and efficiently. Or, if the DSS incorporated geographical information systems tools, virtual reality might be used to allow the user to travel through new cities, add buildings to see how they fit, and check for power lines and other support services.

◆ WHAT ARE DATA?

Thus we might think of the data in a decision support system as anything fed into models[1] and used by decision makers to evaluate alternative actions, whether numbers, words, pictures, videos, or experiences. The important aspect of the data is that they are *valuable* to the decision maker. Of course, the difficulty for the designer is in determining what will be valuable and/or useful to the decision maker.

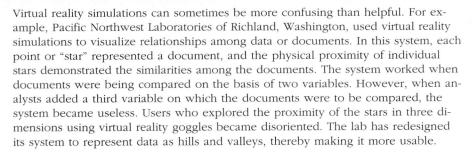

◆ DSS in Action ◆

Virtual reality simulations can sometimes be more confusing than helpful. For example, Pacific Northwest Laboratories of Richland, Washington, used virtual reality simulations to visualize relationships among data or documents. In this system, each point or "star" represented a document, and the physical proximity of individual stars demonstrated the similarities among the documents. The system worked when documents were being compared on the basis of two variables. However, when analysts added a third variable on which the documents were to be compared, the system became useless. Users who explored the proximity of the stars in three dimensions using virtual reality goggles became disoriented. The lab has redesigned its system to represent data as hills and valleys, thereby making it more usable.

Coy, P. and R.D. Hof, "3-D computing: From medicine to war games, it's a whole new dimension," *Business Week*, September 4, 1995, pp. 70–77.

---

[1]This includes the modeling technique identified as complete enumeration. Specifically, sometimes the decision maker "models" by scanning all the data available in order to identify unanticipated patterns.

Figure 3.1 illustrates the evolution of needs and capability over time. Specifically, it shows the relative magnitude of data needed by decision makers (the left circle in each pair) and the data available in machine-readable form (the right circle in each pair) from the early days of DSS to now. Notice that the amount of information needed by the decision makers has increased (as indicated by the relative size of the left circle of each couple). During the last three decades, business decisions have become more complex. The number and range of competitors and consumers have increased. No longer do companies rely primarily on local or regional sources for inputs, work force to complete production, or consumers to purchase their products. This means decision makers must be aware of trends, activities, customs, and regulations around the world and therefore must have easy access to considerably more information. In addition, events happen today at much faster rates than ever before, and hence the relevant statistics to which the decision makers must respond also change rapidly. This, too, contributes to increased information needs. Fortunately, at the same time, improvements in storage capabilities, the speed of processors, and the quality of programs have led to increases in the amount of data available in machine-readable and processable form over this period of time.

During the early days of DSS, the challenge was to provide decision makers access to enough information to allow them to make choices. Now, the challenge is not to provide *enough* information for decision makers; rather, it is to access *useful* data without overwhelming or misleading the decision maker. The shaded regions in Figure 3.1 indicate the amount of data available in machine-readable (and processable) form that decision makers actually *need*. In the early days of DSS, very few of the relevant materials were available in machine-readable form. Even if the materials were available, the programs to process the data were not sufficiently sophisticated, or the computers on which the DSS was run were not powerful enough to process the data. Hence, there was very little support possible, as

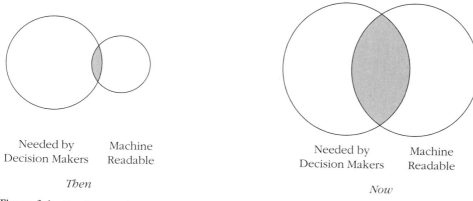

Needed by   Machine
Decision Makers   Readable

Then

Needed by   Machine
Decision Makers   Readable

Now

Figure 3.1   Evolution of user's needs and DSS capabilities.

indicated by the small shaded area. The challenge at that point was to find better ways of collecting and storing data so they could be used in a DSS.[2]

That challenge has been met. Today, we are much better at computerizing more and different kinds of information. This presents advantages, disadvantages, and, of course, new challenges. From a positive perspective, it means that more of the data necessary to support decisions are, in fact, machine readable and processable and thus can be incorporated into the DSS. However, since it is now possible and relatively inexpensive to computerize large and varied amounts of data, there is the temptation to computerize everything that can be computerized and let the decision makers sort out what they need. While this philosophy probably ensures that useful, machine-readable data are incorporated, it also allows for incorporation of more data that are *unnecessary* to the decision. This can lead to decision makers becoming overwhelmed with the amount of information they need to process. With a large amount of data, they could easily miss data that are relevant to their decision. In addition, they might inappropriately use irrelevant information or use relevant data in an inappropriate way. Of most concern, though, is the fact that they may become discouraged with the system and just not use it. Hence, the challenge of DSS today is to include all (or the greatest percentage possible) of the necessary machine-readable/processable information (as indicated by the shaded region) in the DSS and to ensure that the remaining machine-readable data are not included. This means that it is important to include only data that are *useful* to the decision.

◆ INFORMATION

The first step in determining the usefulness of information is to contrast it with data. We've said that the term *data* represents things known or assumed. In contrast, the term *information* means acquired knowledge, or an "informing." While that seems to be a subtle difference, it is an important one because it represents the difference between a computer application and decision support. Generally, raw facts and figures represent data, and processed facts and figures represent information. Processing can be a summarization (either numerical or graphical) or the output from one or more models. For example, a list of scores on an exam in a particular class represent data; each score represents performance by the corresponding individual. However, they do not represent information. This list does not help you, as an individual student, decide how to respond to your performance on the exam. Once the data are processed, however, they do support your decision. With a computation of class mean and standard deviation, or the identification of cutoffs associated with each letter grade, students can decide whether they performed at a personally acceptable level, whether they should study harder, and whether they should drop the class.

---

[2]Regrettably, many developers met this challenge by attempting to convince decision makers that what they should think is valuable is that which could be provided.

In the simplest terms, if the data are not in and of themselves information, or if the data cannot be transformed into information, then they should not be included in the database. While this requirement is theoretically appealing, it is difficult to operationalize. There are three approaches to operationalization. The first is to take a normative approach to the information needs: what information *should* the decision maker want in order to make this type of decision? This approach assumes that information that meets the standard guidelines for making a particular decision will be useful in a given decision making situation. It is the material taught in business administration courses, advocated in text books, or specified in company or profession guidelines or standards. For example, when making a decision regarding inventory policy, standard operations management texts advocate knowing the distribution of demand for some time period, the expected demand for that time period, the costs of ordering the product, and the costs of holding the product in inventory. Hence, the normative approach says that those are the kinds of information that should be included in an inventory support system.

Few decision makers approach choices as straightforwardly as is taught in business courses, and so the normative approach is not sufficient to guide the database development alone. Most decision makers believe that the theoretical approach to solving their problems is not sufficient to respond to the variety of issues encountered in real decision contexts. Specifically, these approaches do not address the question of how to make a decision if the data are not available or are not sufficient, nor how to include necessary political factors in the process.

So the designer of a DSS must also use a subjective approach to judging the usefulness of information. *Subjective* here refers to the perspective of the decision makers—what do they *think* will be useful? This allows decision makers to specify the full range of information they might consider in the process, whether or not it is specified by the normative approach. For example, decision makers might indicate that when deciding how much of a product to order for inventory, they must address a wide range of issues in addition to cost. For example, the decision of how much of an item to acquire might mean making tradeoffs between this order and the availability of other products (because of competition for space or capital) or opportunity costs. Further, the question of how many items to have on hand might be linked to image considerations. This would tell the designer of a DSS to include these additional factors in the database for the DSS.

A third viewpoint is the realistic approach, which asks whether decision makers will use particular information if it is included in the database. Some decision makers might not have confidence in sophisticated models, either because they do not understand or appreciate them, or because they have had bad experiences with them in the past, or because it might be politically difficult to use them in certain contexts. Designers of DSS should be realistic about whether such information will, therefore, ever be used. If it is not likely that decision makers will use it, designers need to evaluate how much including the information will cost, and whether that money, time, or opportunity might be put to better uses.

DSS designers realize that choices regarding inclusion of data in a DSS involves compromise between the normative view of decision making, the subjective view of what is useful, and the realistic view of whether and how information can really be used in the choice process. Sometimes this means that data are dropped from the system, while other times it means that parallel data (more palatable to the decision makers) are included in the system. Still other times, compromise means adding help screens and warning messages to make it easier for decision makers to use the information.

Characteristics of Information

In addition to its content, other aspects of the data can determine whether they might be valuable. We must ask whether the data can be used effectively by the decision makers to improve the expected outcome of the decision in their current form. To do this, we evaluate 12 characteristics of the information, as listed in Table 3.1. Appropriateness for each of these 12 categories is defined in terms of the choice context, the decision maker, and the decision environment under consideration. It is important to realize that there is no universally correct or universally incorrect value that each of these takes on. Before discussing how to determine what is or is not valuable, let us define the terms.

Timeliness

Timeliness addresses whether the information is available to the decision maker soon enough for it to be meaningful. Consider the following time line.

Event Occurs	Data Updated	Data Available to Decision Makers

Typically decision makers do not know immediately that an event has occurred; there is some delay between the occurrence and the time the data in the system have been updated. Further, there is a delay between when the data have been updated and when they are available to decision makers. For example, suppose the decision involves inventory of Star Wars toys. When a new shipment of Star Wars toys arrives in the warehouse, the computerized database is not instantaneously updated. Instead, there is a lag during which the inventory is checked. Then the data enter a queue for being keyed or scanned into the system. Typically even after the data have been entered, there is a delay until the database can be updated. Such a delay might be due to a technical decision involving when enough resources are available to process the database effectively. Or, it might be due to a managerial decision that dictates that no changes to a database can occur when one or more individuals are using the database. Once the database has been updated, the data are generally available to the decision makers. Of course, if the decision maker receives only daily reports or has not rerun a necessary model, there might be further delay in getting the information to the user.

Table 3.1. Characteristics of
Useful Information

1.   Timeliness
2.   Sufficiency
3.   Level of detail and aggregation
4.   Understandability
5.   Freedom from bias
6.   Decision relevance
7.   Comparability
8.   Reliability
9.   Redundancy
10. Cost Efficiency
11. Quantifiability
12. Appropriateness of format

Timeliness of information refers to the reporting delay, or the length of time between the event's occurrence and the decision maker's knowing of the event. The rule of thumb is that the DSS should provide information quickly enough to meet the needs of the users without unnecessary cost or sacrifice of another attribute of information. If users are developing a long-range plan for the development of warehousing space, they do not need immediate knowledge of the number of widgets received. Similarly, if the users are developing a marketing plan, they do not need up-to-date information about the number of children born in a particular county that day.

On the other hand, if the users are planning production runs and they are using just-in-time methods, it is desirable to have the information available as soon as possible. Similarly, if the data represent stock transactions as input to a system for recommending stock trades, it is crucial that the information be available in a timely fashion. Likewise, if the data describe lost or stolen credit cards, the sooner the information is in the approval database, the more likely decision makers are to reject inappropriate purchase approval.

There is a temptation to attempt to provide everyone with information instantaneously. While there is nothing inherently wrong with such a goal, it does incur a cost, in terms of both data entry and model use. If the data change quickly, someone will need to enter those data quickly. If decision makers are tempted to rerun models to ensure that they have the best information, it may adversely affect some other aspect of the data, such as its reliability or comparability. DSS designers need to weigh the benefits of speed against cost from the perspective of the decision maker.

Sufficiency

The second issue needing evaluation is whether the data are adequate to support the decision under consideration. Sufficiency might refer to whether the sample size is large enough to support the kind of differentiation the decision maker wishes to make. For example, suppose a decision maker wants to estimate the nationwide advertising revenue associated with particular headings in yellow pages directories. Three directories would not provide sufficient insights into the revenue generated nationwide because there are vast regional differences in the data due to publisher, size of metropolitan area, and type of competitors. If, however, the goal were to estimate the number of ads in a particular metropolitan area, information about three directories might be adequate.

Similarly, sufficiency includes whether the time horizon is long enough to observe the true effect of a change in policy. For example, suppose the goal were to evaluate a program designed to reduce juvenile delinquency, and so a database is created including measures of the level of delinquency before the program was initiated and at sometime after the program begins. If the database only includes measurements two months after initiating the program, the decision makers do not have sufficient information on which to decide the impact of the programs and whether those effects can or will be sustained. On the other hand, if the purpose of the decision is to determine which budgets are on target, the two-month time horizon might be sufficient.

Since sufficiency can affect the decision makers' ability to draw inferences from the data, it is crucial that designers of decision support systems be sensitive to both the expressed and the implied needs of decision makers. However, since over the life of the DSS the system is likely to be used for support that had not been envisioned at the time of design, it is important to build warning devices into the system to help decision makers know when the data are not sufficient for the task at hand. The most direct approach is to generate a caution screen that specifies the population from which the sample has been drawn and suggests that decision makers evaluate the similarity of that population to the one about which they would like to make an inference.

When the data needs and applications can be projected into the future, designers can build intelligent caution windows that help decision makers grasp the extent to which generalizations can be made. For example, if the DSS is designed to help with market research studies, the majority of analyses will involve consideration of the preferences of a sample. Although it is not possible to determine *a priori* all the possible samples, it is possible to embed intelligence into the system that automatically scans the data available for an analysis and generates a caution screen that states the extent to which the sample is generalizable.

Level of Detail

The aggregation level of the data is also an important factor for determining the usefulness of information in a DSS. The goal in DSS design is to provide data at meaningful aggregation levels for the choices under consideration. Unless the scope of support can be estimated fairly well, this generally means storing data at low levels of aggregation and allowing the decision maker to aggregate the data as needed. For example, suppose a DSS is being used to determine ways of improving productivity. The supporting database could include production details from each of several plants nationwide. If the database includes only annual production data for each of these plants, users would be unable to glean seasonal differences among the plants that might highlight opportunities for change. Alternatively, if the database includes daily production data, with no tools for aggregating the data into larger time blocks, the users might not be able to ascertain monthly trends. Or, if the data are available in appropriate time chunks but are not detailed with regard to different plants, then it might be impossible to see relative differences in productivity.

Similarly, if the DSS is intended to support marketing decisions, users must be able to aggregate data in ways that are meaningful to launch marketing campaigns. That is, they should be able to aggregate data by age group, region of a country, or socioeconomic status in order to determine the group most favorable to their strategies.

Modeling with different levels of aggregation can help managers discover problems or opportunities. By varying an analysis from a "big picture" perspective to a focused perspective, decision makers can glean trends they might not otherwise notice. However, aggregation can also be used to defend a decision once it is derived from other modeling efforts. For example, suppose a DSS were implemented in Congress to help senators and representatives evaluate spending bills more effectively. These elected officials *might* use the system to consider more aspects of the problem, model better, and use more information to make better decisions. However, these same individuals are responsible to their own voting constituencies. The advantage of being able to consider the impacts at a national level *and* at the level they represent helps them to defend their decision to those constituencies. In this case, the user could have enough information to address the facts and not need to talk around the issues.[3]

In general, the best approach is to provide a database with totally disaggregated data. Not only does this allow the decision maker the flexibility to select the level at which the data should be aggregated, it allows different decision makers the ability to view the problem on distinct levels. Of course, total disaggregation requires that the system provide an easy mechanism by which the decision maker can view the various fields on which data can be aggregated, and an easy method for specifying the aggregation appropriate for the application. This is, in fact, the approach many systems employ with data warehousing techniques, and it will be discussed later in this chapter.

Understandability

If decision makers cannot understand what is in the database, or if the database lends itself to perceptual errors, decision makers cannot use it effectively. The key is to simplify the representation in the database without losing the meaning of the

---

[3]Of course, the availability of better information is a necessary, but not a sufficient, condition to cause this scenario to occur.

data. One aspect of understandability is the encoding scheme. If data are encoded and the legend for those codes is not available or obvious, decision makers may not be able to use the data. For example, if one enters "M" and "F" for a field labeled "sex," most English-speaking individuals can determine the coding scheme. However, entering "1" and "2" in that same field causes ambiguity with regard to the code's meaning. This code must be explained in the system. Similarly, obscure names for fields, such as SPLQ002-15, especially if they are not identified, make it difficult for the user to comprehend.

Designers need to be concerned about representation of quantitative data as well. For example, it is common to drop a decimal point when recording data and have it logically re-inserted by a modeling package. If the data will always be used within a model that can handle the transformation, it is an acceptable practice. However, if the data might be scanned by users for some reason, the absence of the decimal point might be confusing.

One approach to ensuring that decision makers can understand the fields is to include an electronic data dictionary. Such a document would provide explanations for the fields as well as for the representations of those fields. Depending on the application, it might also be desirable for the dictionary to include aliases by which fields are known in different departments, as well as information about the source of the information and how it might be used. Access to this document could be provided through a general search of the dictionary upon request, or through user-activated context-sensitive help screens. The latter is preferred from the perspective of providing better support, although the former is an easier programming task.

Freedom from Bias

It is not appropriate for the designer to bias the analyses if it can be avoided. Bias can be caused by a wide variety of problems in the data, such as nonrepresentativeness with regard to time horizon, variables, comparability, or sampling procedures. For example, consider a decision about how to assign technicians to emergency care. The goal of the system might be to ensure that the percentage of emergency care technicians is highest when the likelihood of accidents is highest. In support of this decision, a database could be created that counted the number of accidents per hour. Decision makers might find that the number of lives lost in automobile accidents was small between 3 and 5 A.M. but large between 3 and 5 P.M. Although *apparently* unbiased, this statistic actually provides a quite biased perspective of the likelihood that a life will be lost in an accident. It does not reflect the relative number of cars on the streets during those periods of time. The statistic from the early-morning hours, while low as an absolute number, might be high as a percentage of cars on the road. In this way, it actually could indicate a much higher likelihood of death than the raw number would suggest, and therefore would suggest that more technicians be placed in emergency care during that time period.

The variables included in the system can also bias the meaning of an analysis.

For example, only having data regarding "the number of lives lost" under different scenarios without having the dual data, "the number of lives saved" under those same scenarios tends to bias analyses toward more conservative actions.

Designers can also bias a database by including only material from a nonrepresentative subset of the set of interest. For example, if a DSS is to support marketing designs, the designer can bias the outcomes by including information only from one region of a country, or one country from a group of several. Similarly, selecting a nonrepresentative time horizon can bias results of some analyses. For example, if decision makers need to make choices regarding alternative delivery methods, and data are included only for mid- to late-December, results are likely to be affected. This is particularly true if the time horizons reflect different company data.

Three aspects of information—relevance, comparability, and reliability—can cause problems of bias in the data. As with sufficiency, it is crucial that designers of decision support systems be sensitive to both the expressed and the implied needs of decision makers. When the data needs and applications can be projected into the future, designers can build intelligent caution windows that help decision makers grasp the extent to which bias exists in the sample. Otherwise, designers should provide caution screens that remind decision makers that bias might be present and affect the meaningfulness of the analyses.

Decision Relevance

Perhaps the most obvious issue to consider when building a database is the relevance of the information to the choices under consideration. DSS designers sometimes are tempted to computerize anything available, because it might, someday, be useful. Clearly, the policy can lead to inefficiencies in storage and use of data. However, the dangerous aspect of that concept is that if data are available, the users might use them—whether they are relevant or not. For example, many regression users put every variable they can conceive into a model in hopes that something will show relevance. It is crucial to protect users from such an approach and give them data that can be built into a model that will truly provide decision relevance and significance of results.

We define decision relevance, as a function of the choices and alternatives available to the decision makers. It is crucial that these boundaries of the decision be carved carefully. Consider a DSS intended to help a major automotive dealer address inventory control. One part of such a system might be information regarding the available inventory of parts at other dealers in a nearby area. The type of data seem relevant. However, if the term, "nearby area" is not defined properly, these data might not be at all relevant to the decision maker. For example, suppose a database is designed to include all dealerships in a particular state. A dealership located at one edge of a state might be able to determine whether a part is available 300 miles away, but not whether it is available at a location 30 miles away because that location is in another state. Hence, the information provided is not *relevant* to the decision since the dealership is unlikely to tap the resource 300 miles away.

Comparability

When deciding whether data are valuable, we need to assess whether they can be compared to other relevant data. *Comparable* means that, in important ways, measurement conditions have been held constant. Of course, "important ways" depends on the situation under consideration. It might be relevant for the data to have similar time horizons. Or it may be necessary for the data to represent the same unit of measure. The bottom line is that the meaning of any differences between two statistics can be attributed to one and only one difference because all other conditions are the same.

For example, suppose a particular DSS is being used to support the manager of a LAN. The question under consideration is whether to purchase additional copies of some software and decrease access to other software. One of the attributes the manager wants to consider is whether demand for particular software packages has increased or decreased over time. Comparisons between past and present use are possible only if the data represent usage over a similar time horizon and are represented in a similar fashion in the database. If, for example, the current usage statistics (the number of requests for package X) are measured over 20 days, and the previous statistics are measured over 52 days, they are not comparable. Or if the previous statistics are measured for all CASE tools, and the current statistics are measured for a specific tool (the one for which decisions are being made), the data are not comparable. Obviously, some transformations are possible to make the two points in time comparable, but only if the DSS allows this to occur. If not, the analyses are not worthwhile.

The problems with comparability might be subtle, though. Suppose decision makers compare mortality rates of cities. As a baseline, they compare those individual city mortality rates to that of the Navy during the same period of time. Suppose further that the period of time corresponds to one at which the Navy is actively participating in war. The decision makers could find that the mortality rate in a particular city is far higher than that of the Navy during a specific war. Does this mean the city is "unhealthy"? In a sense, the data are comparable because both statistics represent the same time period and both are represented as a rate (say, per 1000 individuals). Yet, these are not actually comparable because they represent two entirely different populations, from which one would expect to obtain different levels of mortality. Individuals serving in the Navy tend to be young, healthy women and men who maintain good physical fitness. While the civilian population includes some similar individuals, it also has representation of infants, elderly, and infirm, all of whom have a higher mortality rate. So, even though the individuals in the Navy have an increased risk due to war-related mortality, they have a much lower likelihood of mortality due to other causes. Hence, the comparison is meaningless.

As with the level of detail, the safest way to design is to provide a database with totally disaggregated data. This allows the decision makers the ability to shape the way their analyses are done so they can be compared with other, known comparisons. Of course, total disaggregation requires that the system provide an easy method for specifying the selection appropriate for the application. If possible, the system should include the types of intelligent help and/or caution screens discussed earlier.

Reliability

Decision makers will assume that the data are correct if they are included in the database; designers therefore need to ensure that they are accurate. They should verify the input of data and the integrity of the database. For example, suppose the DSS supports police detectives. For the detectives to have confidence in such a system, they must be certain that the suspects appear in the database associated with the correct personal data. That is, if the system is used to identify a suspect from a set of fingerprints, it must reliably provide the name and address of that suspect, not those of a sibling or someone with a similar name. Similarly, if the database includes erroneous data regarding the availability of inventory or other resources, it cannot help the user to plan production strategies effectively.

◆ DSS in Action ◆

The Motor Carrier Taxation DSS (MCTDSS)* was developed for use in evaluating motor vehicle taxation legislation in the state of Idaho; for any proposed tax structure, the MCTDSS shows the impact on revenue as well as the anticipated tax shifts (that is, what groups will benefit and what groups will pay higher taxes). The MCTDSS illustrates some of the tradeoffs of conceptual elegance necessary to achieve timely and cost-effective decision support. As is often the case with DSS, the necessary data were often nonexistent or in an inappropriate format. For instance, differences in the computer systems used to process motor vehicle registrations and actual revenue collections make it difficult or impossible to match records across systems. To address the problem, MCTDSS comprises more than 200 distinct programs and several dozen data sets. Each program creates a transformation of some transaction data set to create another, more usable data set. The programs and data sets must be managed to ensure that programs are executed in the proper order and that when data or programs change, programs are selected and ordered properly to maintain the validity of the ultimate outputs.

*Shannon, P.W. and R.P. Minch, "A decision support system for motor vehicle taxation evaluation," *Interfaces*, 22(2), 1992, pp. 52–64.

Redundancy

In a perfect world, we would repeat the least possible information in order to use the least storage. This goal is laudable because it should not limit the user's ability to link data from multiple sources. In many real-world situations, however, some redundancy is useful. First, if information appears in two databases and one of them becomes corrupted, we can rebuild the information easily. In this way, the redundancy acts as a mechanism for ensuring validity of the data in a particular field.

Second, the "perfect situation" assumes that all data are stored in relations or tables that can be joined flexibly and quickly. This assumes that *a priori* the designer has anticipated possible links and defined indices between the tables so that those links can be made. Further, it assumes that the computing power to associate data from multiple databases is available to ensure that users get their information fast. This might not always be the case. As organizational environments change and decision makers change, the kinds of inquiry change. If these changes have not been anticipated, the existing normalized databases cannot meet their needs. However, some redundancy allows these unanticipated queries to be processed efficiently. Hence, one needs to think ahead in evaluating the benefit of redundancy for a given application.

Cost-Efficiency

The benefit of improved decision making capability must outweigh the cost of providing it, or there is no advantage in the improvement. Said differently, data are only cost-efficient in a database if there is positive value in the changed decision behavior associated with acting on the data in question after the cost of obtaining those data is subtracted.

All information has some cost associated with it. There are costs of obtaining the data either through primary collection such as a survey or secondary collection such as the access to an existing database. There are also costs of making those data available in machine-readable form, as represented in the cost of data entry and verification of those data. In addition, there are storage costs, including the storage medium and the infrastructure for maintaining that medium. Finally, there are processing costs, which increase as the amount of data increases.

It is obvious that the direct costs of obtaining information need to be included. However, it is also necessary to consider the opportunity costs of including some information. If a survey staff is busy implementing a survey regarding Product X, it obviously cannot be implementing a survey regarding Product Y. So the cost associated with obtaining the information with regard to Product X must include some indication that information is being lost with regard to Product Y. If the information regarding Product Y is crucial, then this can be a substantial cost.

On the benefits side, we must decide how much the decision would be improved with the additional information. If the additional data do not change the kind of choice the decision maker would select, there is no benefit of including that information in the database. In all other circumstances, one needs to evaluate the *improvement in* or *incremental benefit* to the decision making capability associated with the addition of the data.

We could, of course, employ statistical techniques such as decision theory to determine the anticipated costs and benefits associated with each additional field. In most applications, however, such an approach is not practical. Most real decisions are not defined strictly and the associated probabilities are not identified, and most uses of information are difficult to assess. Hence, typically we use a substitute approach, subjectively assessing the bottom line. In an extreme case, for example, it does not make sense to spend $10,000 to collect additional data that could improve the decision (and thus the benefit to the company) only by $1,000.

Quantifiability

Quantifiability does *not* assume that all valuable measures are quantified. Rather, it means the data are quantified at the appropriate level and that only appropriate operations can be performed on them. The level of quantification, referred to as the *scale*, dictates the types of meaningful mathematical operations that can be performed with the data. If data are valuable, the user assumes that *if* measures are quantified, it is appropriate that they be so; if it is not appropriate, the system prevents further manipulation of the data.

Consider first the various scales: numbering scales can be nominal, ordinal, interval, or ratio. If they are nominal, the number is simply a label (for example, assigning the color yellow to the number 1, blue to the number 2, orange to the number 3). The label does not mean anything; it simplifies coding or data entry. Ordinal scales, on the other hand, imply that the increase or decrease in the label is associated with the corresponding change in some attribute. For example, assigning the number 1 to small, 2 to medium, and 3 to large is an ordinal scale because the size of an object is getting larger as the label increases.

Interval scales imply that the distance between two labels has meaning and that it is ordinal, but that no absolute value for zero has been defined. For example, temperature[4] is an interval scale because the distance between 50 and 51 degrees is the same as the distance between 70 and 71 degrees and because 70 degrees is hotter than 50 degrees. However, it does *not* imply that 100 degrees is twice as hot as 50 degrees.

---

[4] Of course, whether temperature is measured on an interval or ratio scale depends on how you measure temperature. Environmental temperature measured on conventional scales, such as the Fahrenheit or Centigrade scales, does not have a point at which "no heat" exists. Rather, these scales are standardized to a point where materials undergo a phase change, such as water boiling or freezing. As such, there is no real zero point, so ratios of temperatures have no meaning. If temperature is measured on an absolute scale, such as Kelvin or Rankine, then a meaningful zero point is defined and hence the scale is ratio.

Ratio scales are the highest level because they afford the greatest flexibility in the meaningful manipulation of data. Not only do relative differences have the same meaning and the labels represent an order, but the ratio of two labels is also meaningful. For example, length is a ratio scale. The difference between 8 feet and 7 feet is the same as the difference between 4 feet and 3 feet. In addition, one can say that the ratio of 8 feet to 4 feet is the same as the ratio of 4 feet to 2 feet.

Quantifiability says that if the system allows unrestricted manipulation of data, the data must be ratio-level data. If the manipulations assume only an interval or ordinal scale, then lower levels of scale can be allowed. Finally, if data are represented on a nominal scale, no manipulations can be performed.

Such a restriction can be handled in two ways: either disallow representation of nominal, ordinal, or interval levels, or let the system intelligently prohibit certain models to be implemented regarding certain data. The latter option means the system needs embedded rules that check the data type before executing a requested model, and that it will provide users with an error indicator when they request inappropriate manipulations of the data. Otherwise, users will assume that if they can implement a model, it is appropriate to implement a model and might make decisions based on evaluations that are meaningless.

Appropriateness of Format

The final determinant of the value of information is whether it is displayed in an appropriate fashion. This refers to the medium for the presentation, the ordering in which data are presented to the decision maker, and the amount and kind of graphics that are used.

Most data in a DSS will naturally be a visual display. The question is, when is this appropriate? Documents that are very long or very wide are quite difficult to read and grasp if displayed only onscreen. Typically, decision makers can cope with them better if they are available on paper copy. If this is not an option, the question is whether or not the data can be summarized differently so they are easier to read.

The order of the presentation can also affect the manner in which decision makers evaluate data. If meaningful data are presented at the end of some module, if they are optional, or if they are crowded on the display, the decision maker may never notice them. In addition, what they see first and last will affect how decision makers evaluate new information. If "really bad" statistics are presented first, the decision makers might evaluate moderately good statistics more negatively. If the most recent case evaluated had quite good statistics, a moderately good option might be discarded prematurely. Often the order is chosen by the decision maker and so is out of the control of the system. It is therefore especially important for the developers of the model management system to take care in the way supplemental characteristics are provided (see Chapter 4) and for the developers of the user interface to be aware of the decision making style of the users (see Chapter 5).

Finally, the way data are displayed can affect the conclusions drawn from them.

If the decision makers are attempting to draw conclusions regarding trends in the data, they can see such trends far better from a graph than they can from a list of numbers. On the other hand, if the decision maker needs to understand the value of a particular data point, then it is difficult to obtain it from a graph; a tabular presentation is better. Inappropriate use of graphing techniques (including bar charts, pie charts, or iconic representations) can also affect the decision. For example, trends can be magnified by reducing the scale or truncating the axes of the graph; they can be diminished by increasing the scale. Similarly, differences of scale between the two axes or the omission of portions of the graph can obscure the true trend. These and other problems of graphing will be discussed in Chapter 5.

◆ DATABASES

Historically, data were kept in files associated with an individual application. This meant that each time something changed with regard to the data, the appropriate files associated with each application that used the data also needed to be changed. For example, suppose the decision support system were developed to facilitate planning in factories. One of the inputs would be demand for each of the products manufactured. Using the historical file-processing approach, each plant manager would need to forward information about production of each of the products to the DSS data manager, who would update the appropriate files. Then each sales manager would need to forward information to the DSS data manager regarding the sales of those items, as well as information regarding unfulfilled demand. Hence, data are entered by some mechanism once into some format appropriate for its original purpose. One or more files are forwarded to the DSS data manager, who transforms the data into a format that is appropriate for use in the DSS and updates these files. The frequency of these updates depends on the timeliness needs of the DSS, the data maintenance for the original purpose, and the volume of activity. It is clear, however, that this file transfer process, particularly if the files are kept in different formats (as is generally the case) is, at best, inefficient. Errors of data entry are hard to fix across all applications, and it is difficult to ensure that all users are accessing the same values. As needs in the various applications change and fields are inserted or deleted, the problem gets even worse. Of course, since the same data are kept in many places, it means storage media also need to be duplicated.

As corporations have recognized the importance of data as a corporate resource, they have improved the collection and maintenance processes. One of the most significant advances was the creation of corporate databases. These databases are collections of interrelated data. The goal of the database concept is to store related data together, in a format independent of the DSS. Since data storage and data use are independent, decisions regarding storage are made independently of decisions regarding usage. Those who maintain the data can focus on minimizing redundancy in storage; if the data are maintained only once in a corporation, storage is reduced.

Furthermore, a variety of decision support systems can use the same databases in very different ways. These data are linked together so that information from different physical locations on the storage medium can be joined together for transmission to the users' screens with a minimum amount of trouble. As applications needs change, the addition or removal of a field can be performed efficiently. Furthermore, decisions can be coordinated more easily because everyone is using the same updated version of the data. So the system on the factory floor can use disaggregated inventory data to ensure that specific necessary raw materials are available when needed, while the system in the corporate planning office can use aggregate inventory data to determine whether the orders might be placed more efficiently if combined and hence processed less frequently.

Consider, for example, a student database at a university. All the data about the students, including their names, addresses, telephone numbers, high school records, college grades, majors, and financial needs are kept in a database. The financial aid office probably has no reason to access high school information or specific college grades, but it needs significant information regarding the financial status of the student. Hence, its DSS can be developed to access only the basic performance data such as GPA and the financial information. However, the advisor has no need for information about financial needs, but rather needs access to specific course grades to determine whether the student is prepared to take an advanced class or has successfully completed graduation requirements. While it does not appear so to the users, they are actually accessing the same database. The designers give them access only to information that is relevant to their decision processes.

In most corporations today, there is very little debate regarding the choice between traditional file processing and database use. While the move from file processing to database technology is difficult and expensive, once the transition is complete, the technology provides flexibility and consistency, and uses minimum storage space. These benefits promote the use of DSS. From the perspective of the user, it does have some disadvantages, however. If a file is developed for one application, it allows that person to have greater control over the data and faster access to the data. Since the storage can be adapted to a particular application, it can be stored efficiently for that application, thereby making processing somewhat easier, cheaper, and faster. All these benefits sound good until the application is changed and the needs change. Then, users must start all over again, and rebuild the databases. This costs money and effort. These costs, coupled with the ease of merging data, the increased number of fields available, the longer time horizon that is generally available, and the reduced cost of maintenance, help to sway the preference toward database technology.

Kinds of Databases to Support Decision Making

The corporate database provides the foundation of a decision support system. These systems generally provide data about a vast array of transactions conducted in the normal business operation of a corporation. Internal databases record information regarding sales, purchases, costs, personnel, schedules, forecasts, and other aspects of the organization. The data, then, can serve as the foundation of models in the decision support system. While important, these official records of the corporations are not sufficient to support most of today's decision making.

External Data

Today through the next century, decision makers will not be able to make decisions in the absence of information about one or more factors outside the corporation, referred to as *external data.* Such external data might be as obvious as customer preference information, demand for competitors' products in particular sales regions, census data, or industry reports. Or, it might be information about the reputation and performance history of potential vendors, or the legal and ethical standards in various areas of the world and projections of how they might change in the long run.

Public Data

Some data will be collected and maintained by the corporation. For example, a marketing department might collect market share information and/or demographic data regarding its own customers. These data might be accumulated over a number of years and used in a number of marketing applications. Other data will be available from public sources. For example, Figure 3.2 illustrates the availability of census data accessible by any Web browser over the Internet. These data can be downloaded and analyzed with other corporate or public data.

Some databases are available only for dial-up or direct-access searches through their own networks. Examples of these are Nexis-Lexis from Mead Data Central and databases from CompuServe, Inc., I.P. Sharp Associates, Inc., and Dow Jones News Retrieval. Others are available for greater access through the internet, sometimes for a fee. Each day brings greater availability to databases around the world that might be of use in supporting decisions. Government documents, transcripts of speeches, trade agreements, newspapers, and news sources such as that shown in Figure 3.3 can be secured, searched, or downloaded to a personal computer. Census data, geological data, the Federal Register, results from the World Health Organization, laws, regulations, and even a current listing of plants and gymnosperms in specific countries are available. Even books, reference materials, and journals are available in electronic form to supplement decision making.

There are many ways of helping decision makers use such public databases. First, if the databases are resident in-house, designers need to ensure that access can be provided through the DSS just as with the corporate data. Similarly, if the database is provided on the internet, designers need to provide not only the interface to access the database but also a link to the internet through a network or modem connection.

Fortunately, once the connection to the internet has been made, there are tools

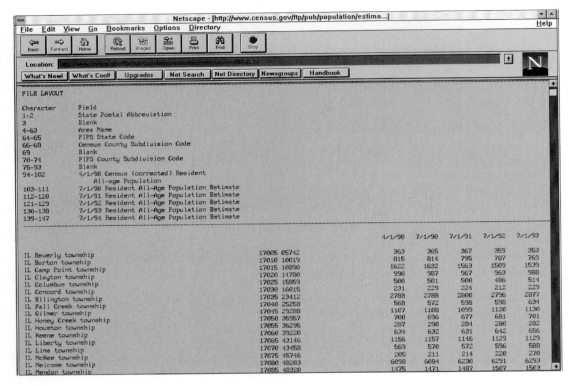

Figure 3.2   Census data availability.

available to facilitate the mining of the data. For example, developers using LOTUS Notes can avail themselves of flexible tools for searching, querying, and incorporating information available on the Web. In addition, standards for Version 3.0 of Hypertext Markup Language (HTML 3.0) and above allow developers to embed some functional programs into Web pages.

Consider, for example, the third-party tool Formula One/NET, which facilitates incorporation of interactive worksheets in a Web page. Figure 3.4 illustrates a

◆   DSS in Action   ◆

A new World Wide Web server for financial information is available for browsing free of charge, thanks to DTN Wall Street, an electronic quotes and news service. Using a graphical browser, users can view current stock and securities prices (with a 15-minute delay), plus historical graphs of the Dow Jones Industrial Average and the S&P 500—including performance over the last 25 years.

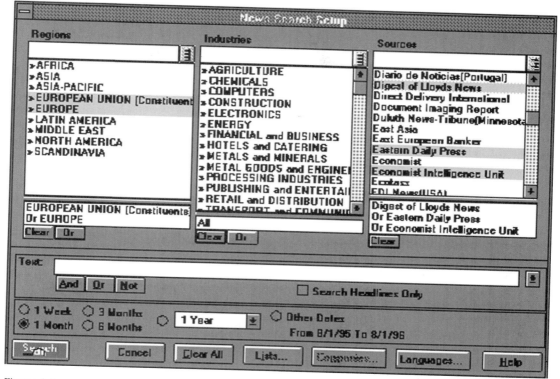

Figure 3.3 Internet-based news services.

spreadsheet with which clients can interact via the Web. Once data are entered in the "Amount to Invest" field, the spreadsheet finds recent data for the performance of the listed mutual funds and forecasts expected return on this investment. Further, the spreadsheet embeds buttons with hypertext links. So, for example, if a client activated the link associated with one of the funds, he or she would be transferred to a page describing that fund.

Or an organization could use not only the data but also the analytical tools available at the Web site for analysis. Consider Figure 3.5. This example shows how a client might access the current rates of a financial institution and, by using the available analytical tools, determine the payment associated with different loan amounts and terms.

Finally, charts can be embedded into a Web page that are automatically updated as the underlying data change, thereby creating a live chart, as shown in Figure 3.6. Decision makers can then access this page as part of their analysis if appropriate.

In addition to linking to particular pages or particular data, DSS developers can also equip decision makers by providing indices of related databases that might

| Click a Fund for More Info | Cur YTD | 1 Year | Annualized | | | Bull 10/90-9/95 | Bear 5/90-10/90 |
			3 Years	5 Years	10 Years		
Enter Your Amount to Invest: $150,000							
Fidelity Blue Chip	$187,500	$180,150	$182,550	$187,950	N/A	$475,500	$129,600
Fidelity Contrafund	$197,400	$190,200	$178,950	$188,400	$180,000	$477,450	$132,300
Fidelity Dividend Growth	$193,350	$188,100	N/A	N/A	N/A	N/A	N/A
Fidelity Low-Priced Stock	$180,000	$176,400	$177,750	$187,950	N/A	$478,200	$129,900
Fidelity Magellan	$202,950	$194,400	$180,000	$183,900	$178,200	$426,750	$124,200
Fidelity OTC Portfolio	$204,750	$199,200	$175,200	$183,450	$175,350	$413,550	$125,400

Figure 3.4   The *Formula One/NET* interactive web spreadsheet.

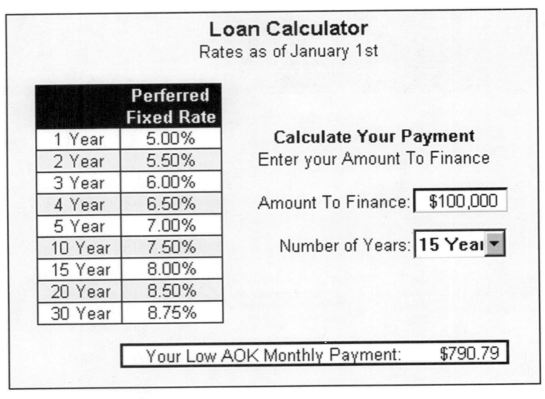

Figure 3.5   The *Formula One/NET* updated screen.

be of interest. This provides a form of passive support whereby decision makers, if they choose, can scan the relevant pages for what in Chapter 2 we called "intelligence." Such indices would need to be updated regularly, preferably by automated means. In addition, the system should allow the decision maker the ability to scan other related databases on demand.

Private Data

Not all data are stored in shared databases. Most decision makers use rules of thumb to help make choices when data cannot be weighed algorithmically. In addition, they have data about past decisions, including the process and the result. They may have data they have collected privately that they can use to obtain a strategic advantage in their corporation. Sometimes, they simply keep notes of political processes in the organization and how they might influence or be influenced by a particular decision.

Real decision makers formulating real alternatives use these supplementary data to facilitate their choice process. For example, some hotels provide general man-

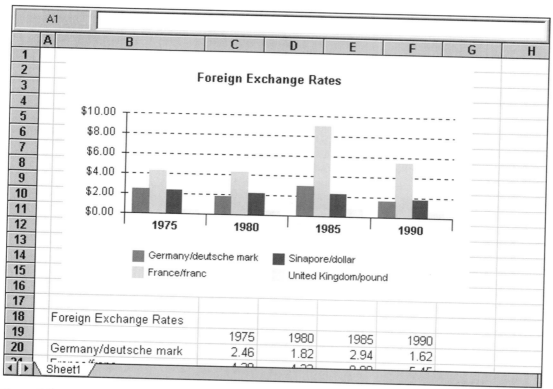

Figure 3.6 *Formula One/NET* interactive Web graphics.

agers with DSS capability. While these systems include information about profits, transactions, and physical facilities, they also provide the managers with the ability to maintain information collected during their decision making process. This information might include a database of major upcoming events, such as changes in tourist attractions, changes in office availability, or conventions, that could be accessed as input to decisions about special promotions. Alternatively, these decision makers might keep records about special abilities of employees that would influence scheduling decisions.

If a DSS is really going to provide the kind of support for decisions advocated by industry, it must facilitate the development and maintenance of these private databases. That is, the systems will need to help the decision maker generate and populate these databases, as well as provide easy access to the data and a wide range of retrieval and summary of their results. If the system resides on a PC, it is easy to provide access to other databases. Even if the system resides on a mainframe or a distributed environment, it is possible to maintain private databases on one's PC. However it is done, of course, it is crucial to provide sufficient security to ensure that only the decision maker can access the information.

Data Uses

While Shakespeare might have believed that naming conventions do not influence the usefulness of data[5], designers of decision support systems know better. The same data stored in different ways can go from being useful to useless. Nongraphical files can be maintained as text files or as image files.[6] If they are stored as text files, they can be searched for words, phrases, or character combinations. These text files require less storage and are easily transferred from one machine to another. However, they do not lend themselves to a realistic rendering of some visual image. If stored as images, however, these files require much more space and they cannot be searched with today's technology. When searches are needed for the image files, a separate text file of keywords is stored with them for this purpose. The keyword file can then be searched, but it does not allow the full range of examination that searching a full text file can. Hence, the format in which the data are stored can affect their usability. The designer needs to know not only *what* the user wants, but also *how* the information will be used in order to provide adequate decision support.

Knowing how the decision makers use information could also affect whether the data are stored as compressed or uncompressed files for the decision support system. The tradeoff between these two methods of storage is between storage space and speed of access. Compressed files have the advantage of using less disk storage resources. However, because they must be uncompressed before use, they have the disadvantage of slower response time. In addition, because they are stored

---

[5]Shakespeare said "a rose by any other name would smell as sweet" in *Romeo and Juliet*.
[6]Graphical or pictorial information is always stored as images today. In the past, some individuals attempted to store graphical images as text. However, the poor resolution and the difficulty of creating the images has caused this approach to be discontinued.

differently, they are more difficult to merge with other data sources. Uncompressed files have the opposite features. Clearly then, we must look to issues of file size and frequency of use before deciding what format to select.

◆ DATABASE MANAGEMENT SYSTEMS

Historically, computer systems were created using a file-processing approach. In this way, the applications and their data files were independent of one another. So standards and guidelines for applications developed in the accounting department were not in any way affected by standards and guidelines for applications on the factory floor. In addition, the data-supporting applications in accounting were entered, maintained, and updated separately from those for the factory floor operations. For example, when new raw material inventory came to the corporation, someone in the accounting department entered the information and processed the charges for payment. Similarly, someone supporting the factory application entered the existence of the new raw material for inventory control. The data were entered twice, and stored twice, thereby introducing inefficiencies into the system. Further, when reports from the two departments were generated, the reports might not agree if one department had more recent information than the other.

This file-processing system provided individual departments with complete control over their own data. Departments could tailor applications to their own specifications. In addition, they had easy and efficient access to and manipulation of the data. Further, because storage could be tailored to an individual application, the data could be stored efficiently.

On the other hand, the file-processing system provided significant disadvantages for departments. It introduced additional costs associated with data entry and storage. Individual departments had to build and maintain separate databases, especially as new applications were developed. More importantly, the various departments could find themselves with inconsistent data sets.

As organizations moved to greater computerization of their data and processes and better techniques were developed in the field, companies began to move from the file-processing philosophy to a consolidated database philosophy. This means that the collection of interrelated corporate data was consolidated and organized in some flexible fashion and made available to a variety of users.

Clearly, the dictate that most data would be held centrally would not, of itself, cause departments to abandon the file-processing philosophy. The carrot that encouraged individual departments to support this change was the introduction of database management systems (DBMS) to facilitate the use of databases. The DBMS serves as a buffer between the needs of the applications and the physical storage of the data. It captures and extracts data from the appropriate physical location and feeds it to the application's program in the manner requested.

The primary advantage the DBMS provides is an independence between the *actual* arrangement of data (as they are physically represented) and the *apparent* arrangement of data to the application. Users in the accounting department can have access to the same data, displayed on the same type of screen and manipulated in the same fashion, as they had in the file-processing application. Similarly, users on the production floor can have access to the same data, displayed on the same type of screen and manipulated in the same fashion, as they had in the file-processing application. The DBMS provides the translation to the application so that the application's programmers can take that data organization as a given. As applications are improved or new applications are added, they simply need to be hooked to the DBMS, saving considerable time in development. Even the process of adding new fields to the database is considerably easier than adding them to traditional files. Hence, since more applications could get greater access to more data and do more with the data than before, departments were willing to support the concept.

The database approach is particularly important when data access across functional and departmental boundaries is desirable and when future needs are uncertain with regard to the type of data that are important and/or associations between data fields that are necessary. In addition, database technology is important when users frequently need rapid access to data to answer ad hoc questions. All these reasons, of course, provide another way of saying that the database technology is crucial if designers are to provide the kind of flexibility necessary to maintain decision support systems.

When considering database technology from the perspective of decision support systems, it is important to note that not all database structures are equal with regard to flexibility and/or usability. There are three fundamental database structures—hierarchical structure, network structure, and relational structure—each of which has advantages and disadvantages (to be explained shortly). In light of all these advantages and disadvantages, the relational structure is the most promising from the perspective of decision support systems.

Hierarchical Structure

The hierarchical structure describes data in terms of tree structures, which results in a set of nested one-to-many and one-to-one relationships. For example, suppose the database included information about employees within an organization. Consider Figure 3.7.

Using this database, it is easy to find information about a specific employee. However, it is not easy to discover any lateral relationships. For example, suppose a decision maker were attempting to build a planning team and wanted to include everyone who had either an undergraduate or a graduate degree in civil engineering and everyone who had attended specific training programs. Using this structure, it would be impossible to obtain this information unless one examined the records of each employee in the program. Any query that is not defined at the outset as a subset of another group cannot be conducted efficiently.

Similarly, if employees report to different supervisors for different projects, we could not represent the relationships efficiently using this structure. The hierarchical structure allows each record to be the target of only one relationship. It could

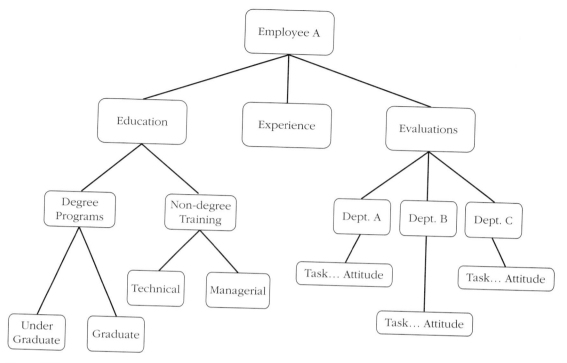

Figure 3.7 Hierarchical database structure.

show Employee A reporting to Supervisor 1, but could not show Employee A reporting to Supervisor 2 on a different project, unless all the information regarding Employee A were replicated under Supervisor 2.

Network Structure

A somewhat more flexible structure is represented by the network structure, which is shown in Figure 3.8. The motivation for this structure was to eliminate some of the redundancy caused by situations such as that described for the hierarchical structure and to allow greater flexibility of queries.

As you can see, the network model allows multiple superior and subordinate relationships. For example, you can see that there are two departments, with Department A housing Jones, Ganga, and Summers and Department B housing Milo, Smith, and Chen. In addition, there are three projects under construction. Project 1 includes Jones and Milo, Project 2 includes Ganga and Smith, and Project 3 includes Summers and Chen. Unfortunately, this model permits relationships that involve two record types, as in the department and project example. Similarly, it would allow product and vendor relationships, but not product, vendor, and ware-

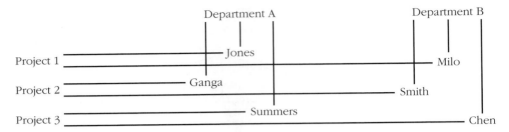

Figure 3.8   Network database structure.

house relationships. To obtain more complex relationships, the system creates a "master" record type that includes all the relationships of primary interest and a pointer file that allows the system to find and examine transaction information that describes a record of events for that primary item.

A second problem in the network data model is that only relationships that are explicitly included at the time the database is designed can be used in processing. Therefore, the system provides limited help for ad hoc queries or for queries and reports that change over time.

The final problem is maintenance. It is quite easy to create loops as users attempt to form new structures. Similarly, each time new information is added to the database, the pointer system needs to be updated. This does not facilitate flexibility.

Relational Structure

The ultimate in flexibility in database design today, and the structure that ideally should be included in decision support systems, is the relational structure. This structure is constructed by using tables to collect and store data. With the use of indices, these tables can be logically connected to represent any relationships among data. Since the tables can be connected, there is no reason to replicate information among them, with the exception of the index that connects data. This process of reduction of duplication, known as *normalization*, helps to ease the maintenance burden associated with large databases.

For example, consider the information represented in Figure 3.9. Information regarding the employees' skills is located in the first table, while information about their departments appears in the second table. The only element that is shared by the two is the last name of the employee. However, if we wanted to summarize the skills available in each of the two departments, we could logically join these two tables and easily obtain the information.

◆ DATA WAREHOUSES

In a typical organization, the available operational databases have been designed to meet the needs of the regular procedures. These might include the insertion of an order, an update of a reservation, or a summary of transactions for a particu-

EMPLOYEE SKILLS RELATION

Employee Name	Skill–Coding	Skill–Analysis	Skill–Documentation	Skill–Presentation
Jones	High	Low	High	Low
Milo	High	Moderate	Low	High
Smith	Moderate	Moderate	Moderate	Moderate
Ganga	Moderate	Low	Low	High
Chen	High	High	Moderate	High
Summers	Low	Moderate	Low	Low

DEPARTMENT RELATION

Employee Name	Department
Jones	A
Milo	B
Smith	B
Ganga	A
Chen	B
Summers	A

Figure 3.9   Relational structure of databases.

lar user. While regular procedures occasionally include queries, they typically are quite simple. Generally, therefore, the transaction databases just provide current information about the organization.

Unfortunately, no matter how efficiently the databases of an organization are designed, they typically cannot meet the informational needs of a DSS because they lack historical data and data stability that are crucial to the analyses required by decision makers. For example, decision makers might query the system with questions such as How did the promotion affect sales last quarter in comparison to the same promotion last year? or Did the new crime prevention program affect the number of quality-of-life crimes? Was its performance different in different regions? In addition, data tend to reside on different operational systems, which have very different data organizations. In fact, combining data from DB2, Oracle, and COBOL with data in databases from Sybase or Informix can be tricky and can make data analyses more difficult. Operational databases generally are of a size and structure that are quite inefficient for general analyses. As a result, since the needs of the operational databases are quite different from those of a DSS, they are not optimized for DSS. This results in poor performance for DSS queries, which can cause poor performance for the operations originally supported by the system.

Historically, this has meant the DSS was not as useful as it might be because crucial data were not accessible in a timely manner. To compensate, some adopted frozen extracts of the system for analyses. These extracts provided information about *selected* entities at *one point in time*. While using these extracts was more efficient than using the transaction database directly, the extracts lacked the breadth of information necessary for complete analyses or flexible ad hoc queries. In other words, even with the benefits of this solution, it did not provide an environment conducive to the use of a DSS.

The alternative gaining popularity is to create a data warehouse to support the DSS needs. A *data warehouse* is a database management system that exists separate from the operations systems. It is subject and time variant and integrated, as are the operational data. However, data warehouses are nonvolatile and hence capable of supporting a variety of analyses consistently. Generally, these databases are archives for operational data that have been chosen to support decision making and optimized to interact with the DSS of an organization. Generally, they are relational databases that can support a wide variety of queries in a wide variety of formats; they may be composed of hundreds of tables optimized for typical queries.

Data warehouses include information of interest to middle- and high-level decision making. They typically hold significant amounts of data. Consider, for example, an organization such as H.E.B. of San Antonio, Texas. This organization maintains approximately 257,000 items per store and two years of data by week, by item, and by store. This is about 400 million detail records. Summary files are maintained by time and total company. Summary files at the category level, for example, would have to be recalculated each time an item is moved from one category to another, which apparently is done often. The goal of the system is to have all queries answered in 4 seconds, but some trend reports with large groups of items over long periods of time may take 30–40 seconds. Hence, with the data warehouse, H.E.B. managers can now make fact-based decisions to determine which products to put in which stores, how much product to send to a store, and the proper product mix. In other words, the kind of knowledge that used to come only from years of working with a particular product in a particular environment can now be replicated with analysis.

Similarly, consider another example of successful data warehousing in the Gloucestershire Constabulary, one of the 43 police forces serving England and Wales. It covers a diverse rural and urban area with a population of more than half a million people. In a typical year, the Gloucestershire Constabulary addresses more than 60,000 crimes and 170,000 incidents, with varying levels of severity. To meet their reporting and analysis needs, officers must analyze 25 different performance indicators on those crimes and incidents. The data warehouse allows officers to draw together information from a variety of sources easily and quickly, thereby making better use of their scarce resources.

Data warehouses are created by a process such as that shown in Figure 3.10. Data are taken from a variety of sources of operations data. Once transferred, the data are scrubbed to ensure that they are meaningful, consistent, and accurate. They are then loaded in relational tables that can support a variety of analyses and

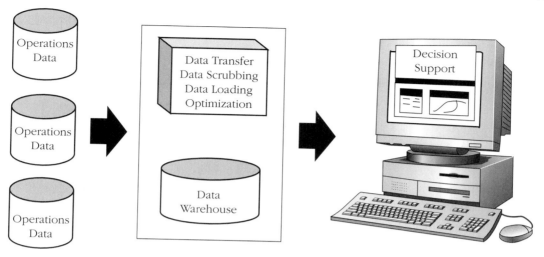

Figure 3.10   Data warehouse.

queries and optimized for those that are expected to occur most frequently. Finally, they are stored for later use with decision support systems.

The development of a data warehouse is a difficult and time-consuming process that costs most organizations considerably. While the processes of moving and optimizing data are not terribly difficult, the processes of identifying relevant data, blending them, and ensuring that they are scrubbed appropriately are difficult. In addition, in order for the warehouse to be most effective, designers must identify key fields on which to index the data and a format for indexing that makes data use most efficient.

For example, H.E.B. of San Antonio began the creation of a data warehouse with seven months of extensive interviews to gather information about the needs of all users. This is a standard practice in application development. If there is already some knowledge of what decision makers need, designers build a working model first and ask for user feedback based on the model. Furthermore, as we will see in Chapter 8, generally it is recommended that designers begin with the creation of small data warehouses for use by selected users over some period of time to ensure that their needs are understood well.

Once the data warehouses have been created and optimized, it is a straightforward process to load them efficiently, loading new data when decision support activities are not being performed. However, as data are multiplied over time, designers need to define new syntax and query formats that are faster and easier, as well as new approaches for joining relational tables and for mining these very large databases using "intelligent agents."

Data Mining and Intelligent Agents

Although data warehouses provide access to information that will help decision makers understand their operations and environment better, users can become lost in the enormous possibilities for analysis and miss the forest for the trees. Less experienced users particularly need a tool to help them mine the value of the information available in these warehouses. Such a tool could help users to find the kinds of data that seem to discriminate among alternatives the best, identify cases that meet some criterion, and then summarize the result or find patterns in the data to highlight important trends or actionable situations.

Intelligent agents are pieces of software that complete specific, repetitive tasks on behalf of the user. They are not new to computers; they are commonly in use on systems to monitor CPU and peripheral use and capacity. Other intelligent agents are associated with e-mail systems, where they help sort and prioritize e-mail by sender or topic on behalf of the user. Their new use is as a means to search through relational databases to find relevant data for decision makers. Even more exciting is the combination of search protocols with analysis capabilities that will cause the intelligent agent not only to find data but also to analyze it to find examples of trends or patterns the decision maker might miss on his or her own. In addition, the intelligent agent can get at the information faster to detect unusual occurrences so the decision maker can act on them more quickly.

For example, consider the product DSS**Agent** from MicroStrategy, as shown in Figure 3.11. This product surfs a data warehouse for information and summarizes it for decision makers. Users can schedule intelligent agents to execute on a one-time basis, periodically, or based on events. For example, decision makers can perform regular scanning of absenteeism or missing reports to highlight indicators that problems might need attention. Or decision makers can schedule intelligent agents to find information after planned promotions or after a particular indicator reaches some prespecified value. Using workflow triggers, users can specify both pre- and postagent macros that can integrate with other modeling components of the DSS. For example, the agent could find information that would automatically be imported to a forecasting application to compute projected demand. If desired, another agent could be triggered to mail results of the application automatically to people on the management team.

Many intelligent agents today provide a set of options through which the user can scan the data warehouse. For example, users can define filters based on specific qualifying criteria. Or users can define percentile and rank filtering; using this option, decision makers could identify the source of the top 10% of their raw materials, for example. Similarly, intelligent agents can be launched using conditional metrics. Thus, users can specify information to be found regarding a particular business unit and compared to that of multiple business units or to the company as a whole.

To fully exploit the data mining capability, however, the intelligent agents need to be combined with artificial intelligence so the software can find not only the data, but also the patterns in the data. In fact, if it works well, data mining should

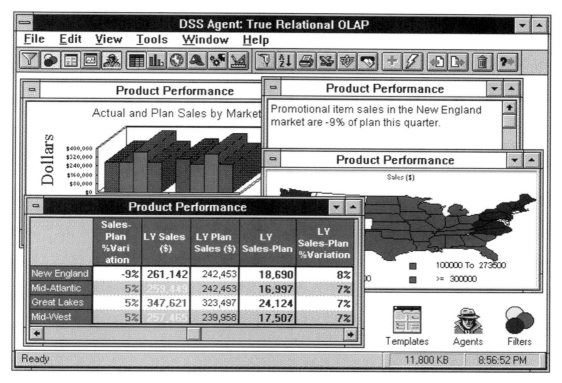

Figure 3.11   The DSS**Agent** opening screen.

find answers in the data that the decision maker has yet to consider asking. Data mining tools find patterns in the data, infer rules from them, and then refine those rules based on the examination of additional data. The patterns and rules might provide guidelines for decision making, or they might identify the issues on which the decision maker should focus during the choice process.

Data mining can yield five kinds of results: associations, sequences, classifications, clusters, and forecasting. To distinguish these, consider a data warehouse of information about students. *Associations* are events linked with regard to a single criterion, such as two or more courses that students tend to take together, such as Decision Support Systems and Database Systems. The fact that students take the courses together might not be apparent without the analysis. However, after the analysis, we know that the two courses should not be scheduled at the same time. *Sequences* are events linked over some period of time, such as patterns the students employ for taking courses over multiple semesters. For example, a student who takes a statistics course this semester is unlikely to take the forecasting course for two subsequent semesters. This will help the department plan course offerings.

Classification identifies patterns that are unique for members of a particular group. It examines existing items that have already been classified and infers a set of rules from them. For example, the system might classify attributes of those students who complete their degree in a specified number of years from those who do not. By finding the similarities among students who do not successfully complete their degrees, the system might find "early warning signals" on which the administration can act. A similar process is *clustering*. It also infers rules about groups that differentiate them from other groups. It differs from classification, however, in that there are no items classified *a priori*, and hence the agent needs to determine the groupings as well. In this case, the system might be used to separate students who are likely to respond to an innovative program from those who would better be served by traditional methods. Finally, *forecasting* is the process of estimating the future value of some variable.

As we will see in the next chapter, four analytical tools—neural networks, decision trees, rule induction, and data visualization—as well as conventional analyses are used to complete these five kinds of analyses. To be successful, the approach and the product must meet the needs of the user and a particular data warehouse. Other criteria for the evaluation of data mining products are illustrated in Table 3.2.

◆ THE CAR EXAMPLE

In this section, and in parallel sections in the next three chapters, we will consider the topics of interest with regard to a DSS intended to facilitate acquiring an automobile. This system should allow consideration of purchase and lease decisions;

Table 3.2. Criteria for Evaluating Data Mining Products[1]

What approaches does the tool use to model the data?
What kinds of problems does it solve?
What hardware and operating systems does it use?
Does the tool require a database extract, or can it read the data directly?
What type of user interface does it use for data entry and data interpretation? Is it easy to use and understand?
What is the maximum number of variables and rows it can handle?
How does it support categorical data and continuous data?
How sensitive to "noise" data is it? To what amount and kind of aberrant data is it particularly sensitive?
How long does it take to get useful answers from the data?
How clear are the results?

[1]Table is adapted from Edelstein, H., "Mining data warehouses," *Information Week*, 561, January 8, 1996, pp. 48–51, and used with permission.

for purchase decisions, the system should allow consideration of both new and used automobiles. Further, since different users will have different concerns, the DSS needs to accommodate a wide range of analyses.

Possible Criteria

The goal of the DSS is to provide support for users from a broad range of experiences and expertise. Consider the range of criteria people use for selecting an automobile. Some individuals select a particular manufacturer because they have always purchased from that manufacturer; they simply look for the model within their price range from a particular manufacturer. Others are more willing to look across manufacturers but are tied to selecting an automobile within a particular price range. Still others want to look at the long-term costs associated with a particular automobile, taking into account not only the monthly payments, but also gasoline costs, upkeep, insurance, and maintenance.

For another segment of the population, safety is the most important characteristic. Within this group, some potential purchasers select the largest automobile they can find because that one will, by their definition, be the safest. Others look for safety tests and judge cars on the basis of those tests. Still others want to include the likelihood of a malfunction that might be associated with a safety risk or the likelihood of the automobile being stolen.

Another group of individuals evaluates automobiles on the basis of performance characteristics. To some, performance is associated with the fuel efficiency of the vehicle. To others, performance is determined as a function of power, such as the number of cylinders, the size of the engine, the speed at which the automobile can accelerate, or the type of transmission in the vehicle.

For other groups, comfort is the main criterion for car selection. These people might be interested in obtaining the largest car possible, the one with the largest trunk capacity, or the one with the most legroom or headroom. Still others might be interested in the types of options associated with the vehicle. Finally, they might be interested in knowing who would be responsible when something does not work.

Other groups might be interested in the image suggested by a particular car. For example, does the car suggest a socially active single person, a fast-track career person, a serious parent, or something different? For others, it might be the specific activities it can support: will it haul 2x4s or the soccer team?

In essence, then, there is a wide range of data that could be requested in support of the automobile purchasing decision. Different people will approach the problem quite differently. Furthermore, given individuals approach the problem differently after some experience. Finally, given individuals with a given level of experience may approach the problem differently if the system can provide guidance as to how to use the information.

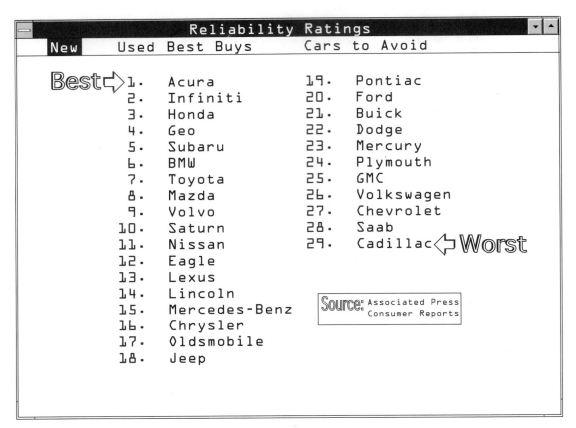

Figure 3.12   Historic background information: previously owned automobiles.

The Data Warehouse

To provide the user with a valuable tool, the DSS must contain comprehensive information, not only about current models, but also about the history associated with the manufacturer and model. The user may have a need to look at trends with regard to a particular model and its maintenance record. While this may not be possible, the system should be able to identify the ten most reliable cars and the ten least reliable cars in a format that will facilitate analyses. Similarly information about safety should be provided. (See Figures 3.12, 3.13, and 3.14.)

The challenge in this kind of DSS is not in finding information that someone might use, but rather in helping the user *limit* his or her data focus. Consider, for example, the kinds of information available from popular periodicals about new automobiles. *Kiplinger's Buyer's Guide* provides many tables of information about automobiles.

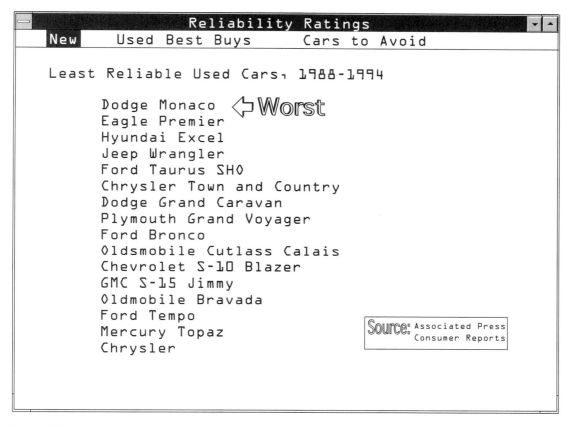

Figure 3.13 Historic background information: new automobiles.

Some of the attributes it includes are shown in Table 3.3. In addition, *Kiplinger's* provides summary tables of other useful information about the automobiles. For example, Table 3.4 summarizes *Kiplinger's* analysis using the National Highway Traffic Safety Administration's (NHTSA) ratings and insurance ratings of automobiles.

Data are even available via the Internet today. Figure 3.15 illustrates the kinds of information that Edmund's maintains online.

In addition to keeping the decision maker from being overwhelmed by the data, the system must store the data efficiently so that users need not have excessive delays in their analyses. Finally, there is the question of how to use the data in the DSS.

Information Uses

In Chapter 2 we discussed 6 types of rationality that need to be considered in a DSS: economic, technical, ethical, legal, procedural, and political. If these are valid, there needs to be information from which the decision maker can evaluate po-

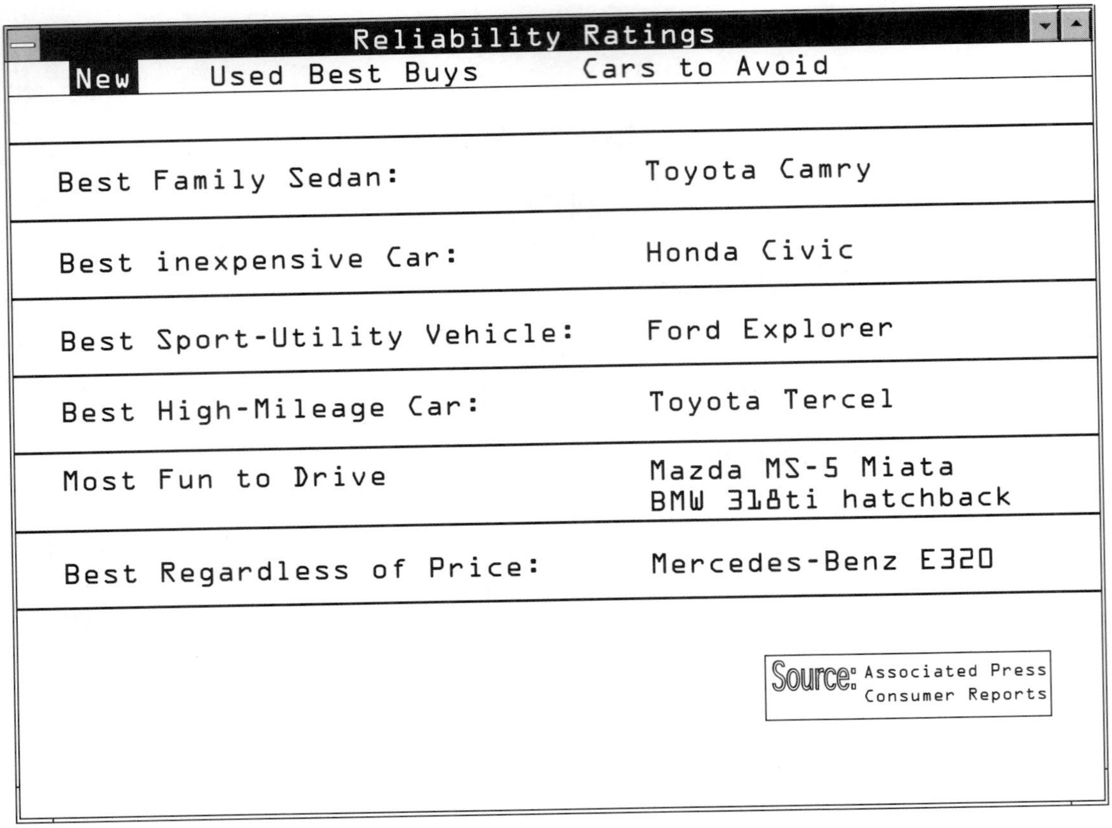

```
┌─────────────────────────────────────────────────────────────┐
│ ─               Reliability Ratings                ▼│▲ │
│ ┌─────┐                                                       │
│ │ New │    Used Best Buys          Cars to Avoid             │
│ └─────┘                                                       │
├─────────────────────────────────────────────────────────────┤
│                                                               │
│   Best Family Sedan:            Toyota Camry                 │
├─────────────────────────────────────────────────────────────┤
│   Best inexpensive Car:         Honda Civic                 │
├─────────────────────────────────────────────────────────────┤
│   Best Sport-Utility Vehicle:   Ford Explorer               │
├─────────────────────────────────────────────────────────────┤
│   Best High-Mileage Car:        Toyota Tercel               │
├─────────────────────────────────────────────────────────────┤
│   Most Fun to Drive             Mazda MS-5 Miata            │
│                                 BMW 318ti hatchback         │
├─────────────────────────────────────────────────────────────┤
│   Best Regardless of Price:     Mercedes-Benz E320          │
├─────────────────────────────────────────────────────────────┤
│                                                               │
│                              ┌──────────────────────────┐    │
│                              │ Source: Associated Press │    │
│                              │         Consumer Reports │    │
│                              └──────────────────────────┘    │
│                                                               │
└─────────────────────────────────────────────────────────────┘
```

Figure 3.14   Historic background information: targeted by category of automobile.

Table 3.3.   Automobile Attributes Included in *Kiplinger's 1996 Buyer's Guide: The New Cars*

Manufacturer	Curb weight
Model	Wheelbase
Body style	Length and width
Suggested retail price	Turning circle (feet)
Dealer cost	Legroom in the front and rear
Resale value in 2 and 4 years	Headroom in the front and rear
Insurance cost index	Cargo space
Engine size	Antilock brakes status/cost
Number of cylinders	Automatic transmission status/cost
Miles per gallon in the city and on the highway	Air conditioner cost

Table 3.4.   Ratings by Kipplinger's[1]

| | | | | | SAFETY FEATURES | |
MAKE AND MODEL	OVERALL SCORE	DRIVER HIC	PASSENGER HIC	INSURANCE SCORES	RESTRAINT SYSTEMS	ABS@
Acura Integra 4dr sedan	10	585	637	108	belts	opt.
Acura Legend 4dr sedan*	10	897	660	56	bags	std.
BMW 325i 4dr sedan*	9	705	698	102#	bag	std.
Buick Century Custom 4dr sedan*	9	542	931	67	bag	—
Buick Century Special 4dr sedan	11	815	1,144	67	(bag)	—
Buick Regal 2dr	9	880	535	91	belts	opt.
Chevrolet Astro van*	17	2,065	1,815	76	belts	std.
Chevrolet Beretta 2dr	5	343	739	108	bag	std.
Chevrolet Caprice 4dr sedan	11	533	1,101	62	bag	std.
Chevrolet Cavalier 4dr sedan	9	770	485	120	belts	std.
Chevrolet Corsica 4dr sedan	9	493	956	100	bag	std.
Chevrolet Geo Metro 2dr hatch*	13	860	870	173	belts	—
Chevrolet Geo Storm 2dr hatch	9	417	981	147	bag	—
Chrysler Concorde 4dr sedan	10	770	622	95	bags	std.†
Chrysler New Yorker 4dr sedan	10	674	929	73	bag	opt.†
Dodge Caravan van*	6	407	427	59	bag	opt.
Dodge/Plymouth Colt 4dr sedan	10	919	561	105	belts	opt.
Dodge Daytona 2dr hatch	4	399	297	144	bag	opt.
Dodge Dynasty 4dr sedan*	10	674	929	87	bag	opt.
Dodge Intrepid 4dr sedan*	10	770	622	95	bags	opt.
Dodge Shadow 4dr hatch	6	503	457	136	bag	opt.
Eagle Vision 4dr sedan	10	770	622	95	bag	opt.†
Ford Aerostar van*	9	485	723	80	bag	std.**
Ford Crown Victoria 4dr sedan*	8	907	331	63	bag(s)	opt.†
Ford Mustang 2dr convertible	8	651	438	97	bag	—
Ford Probe 2dr hatch*	13	784	995	117	bag	opt.
Ford Taurus 4dr sedan*	8	647	431	80	bag(s)	opt.
Ford Taurus 4dr wagon	5	480	258	61	bag(s)	opt.
Ford Tempo 4dr sedan*	10	655	772	113	(bag)	—
Ford Tunderbird 2dr	7	541	496	83	belts	opt.†
Honda Accord 4dr sedan*	7	501	558	91	bag	opt.
Honda Accord SF. 4dr sedan*	9	555	799	91	bags	std.
Honda Civic 4dr sedan*	12	744	903	127	bag	opt.
Honda Prelude 2dr*	6	510	555	102	bags	opt.
Hyundai Excel 2dr hatch	9	696	419	173	belts	—
Hyundai Excel 4dr sedan*	9	520	544	179	belts	—
Hyundai Scoupe 2dr	12	870	618	212	belts	—
Lincoln Continental 4dr sedan	9	863	492	60	bags	std.
Mazda 626 4dr sedan*	9	589	694	102	bag	opt.
Mazda Miata 2dr convertible*	11	920	531	85	bag	opt.

(*Continued*)

Table 3.4.   Continued

| | | | | | SAFETY FEATURES | |
MAKE AND MODEL	OVERALL SCORE	DRIVER HIC	PASSENGER HIC	INSURANCE SCORES	RESTRAINT SYSTEMS	ABS@
Mazda Protege 4dr sedan	11	779	612	126	belts	—
Mitsubishi Eclipse 2dr hatch	9	772	612	138	belts	opt.
Mitsubishi Galant 4dr sedan	14	1,024	711	105	belts	—
Mitsubishi Mirage 4dr sedan*	10	919	561	148	belts	opt.
Nissan 240SX 2dr hatch	6	407	525	120	belts	opt.
Nissan Altima 4dr sedan*	7	610	499	95	bag	opt.
Nissan Maxima 4dr sedan*	11	818	864	89	bag	opt.
Nissan Sentra 4dr sedan	9	660	613	137	(bag)	opt.
Oldsmobile Eighty-Eight 4dr sedan*	9	473	829	66	bag	std.†
Plymouth Acclaim 4dr sedan	9	762	446	100	bag	opt.
Plymouth Bonneville 4dr sedan*	8	359	768	68	bag(s)	std.†
Pontiac Trans Sport van	7	761	595	71	belts	std.
Saturn SL 4dr sedan*	13	705	1,063	112	bag	opt.
Toyota Camry 4dr sedan*	6	390	650	96	bag	opt.
Toyota Celica 2dr	11	834	685	125	bag	opt.
Toyota Corolla 4dr sedan*	11	522	771	129	bag	opt.
Toyota Previa van*	11	711	983	71	bag	opt.
Volkswagen Passat 4dr sedan	14	1,182	604	91	belts	opt.
Volvo 240 4dr sedan*	6	282	835	93	bag	std.

@ Anti lock brakes. * Insurance scores are for earlier models than those tested by NHTSA. # Injury statistic for two-door car. — Not applicable. † Traction control optional. ** Rear-wheel ABS. ( ) Available as an option.
[1] Ratings were created by combining federal crash-test scores with insurance injury claims data. The overall score is composed of 30% from the HIC; 25% from the passenger HIC; Driver chest-injury scores are 10% of the score; Leg injury scores make up 5% and insurance claims represent 10%. The lower the score, the better.
The NHSTA conducts crash tests of automobiles. HIC scores of 500 or less indicate almost no chance of head injury in a frontal crash at 35 mpg. A score of 1,000 means that one in six occupants may have a life-threatening skull injury in such a crash. The Insurance Institute for Highway Safety compiles data based upon personal injury protection claims for each type of car. Scores are relative, with 100 representing an average loss. A score of 120, for example, means that claims for that car are 20% higher than average.
Table is adapted from "Safety by the Numbers," *Kipplingers*, August, 1993, p.62.

tential automobiles in each dimension of interest. This presents some fairly significant data requirements on the system. If we consider just economics for a moment, then we still need to provide a significant amount of information in the database. Look, for example, at Figure 3.16. According to this worksheet, even if we *only* wanted to consider financial aspects of the automobile, we would need to estimate or retrieve 10 fields for each automobile.

When purchasing automobiles, image can play a key role in the decision process. Providing actual pictures of the automobiles could help some users identify possible alternatives or help the user to cull out nonalternatives. Pictures could display several angles of a vehicle's exterior, console, and interior

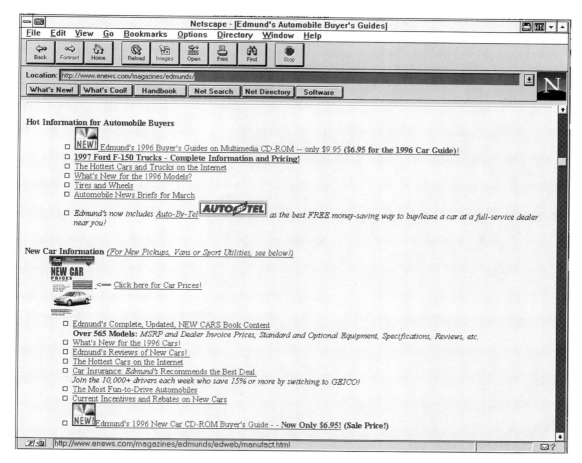

Figure 3.15 The Edmund's web-based information service.

Annual Ownership Costs		Cost of Car Per Year	
Depreciation	$_____	Annual Ownership Costs	$_____
Finance Charge	$_____	Annual Operating Costs	$_____
Insurance	$_____		
Taxes	$_____	Total	$_____
License and Registration	$_____		
Miscellaneous Costs	$_____	Annual Operating Costs	
		Maintenance, Repairs	$_____
Total	$_____	(Including Tires)	
		Gas and Oil	$_____
		Total	$_____

***Worksheet has been adopted from *Kiplinger's 1996 Buyer's Guide: The New Cars*.

Figure 3.16 Annual automobile cost worksheet.

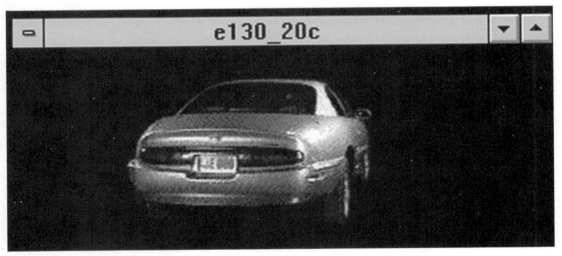

Figure 3.17   Virtual reality simulation of the exterior view of an automobile.

or possibly a view under the hood. In fact, General Motors provides such images in *QuickTime* format on the Web. Users can simulate walking around the automobile and seeing the exterior from all sides, as shown in Figure 3.17. Similarly, users can simulate sitting in the driver's seat and viewing the interior and mirrors, as shown in Figure 3.18. Once such clips are available to the designer of the DSS, it is simple to run an external viewer such as *QuickTime* to use the clips.

Figure 3.18 Virtual reality simulation of automobile as seen from driver's seat.

Even more information could be provided if the designer wanted to include additional video clips. Users could simulate the responsiveness of the automobile to curves and bumps, inclines, and declines by watching a movie of the front and rear views as seen in the driver's seat. Enhancing this with audio clips would make it more realistic. Audio clips can easily be run with external "viewers" that provide seamless integration into the DSS.

Images can also be displayed in other forms. Suppose the user wants the automobile he or she acquires to reflect a particular image. The user might query what automobiles people who display that image might drive. The system should be able to address this. For example, if the user wanted to have the same image as employees of Apple Computer Corporation, he or she might ask what kinds of cars these employees generally drive. The DSS might bring up information such as that shown in Table 3.5 about the automobiles driven by said employees. It may be sufficient to list these automobiles. Or it may be necessary to select only these cars for further consideration.

Obviously, the data in this system must be current. New car buyers will want information about the newest features and problems. Information from the latest car reports should be incorporated into the system as soon as possible. Recall notices and identified problems may also provide critical information to a user. Similarly, upcoming models need to be included in the database as soon as possible since a buyer may need to make a choice between getting the current year's or the next year's model.

The user must have the ability to specify the level of detail. The system should present the user with basic, standard information, and allow him or her to drill as

Table 3.5.   Most Popular Cars Among Apple Employees

	MAKE	MODEL	PERCENT (COUNT)
1.	Honda	Accord	9.5% (58)
2.	Honda	Civic	9.0% (55)
3.	Acura	Integra	4.9% (30)
4.	Toyota	Corolla	4.1% (25)
5.	Toyota	Camry	3.9% (24)
6.	Ford	Explorer	3.0% (18)
7.	Acura	Legend	2.8% (17)
8.	Toyota	Celica	2.6% (16)
9.	Ford	Mustang	2.5% (15)
10.	Ford	Taurus	2.1% (13)

These data were found in *Wired* magazine, July 1994. The magazine cites their source as *Wired* operative Todd Goldenbaum. Survey of 610 cars taken at the Infinite Loop parking lots and several other garages and lots at Apple in Cupertino, California.

deeply as desired and to compare automobiles with regard to factors that are important to that user.

An electronic field definition dictionary could be useful, particularly for first-time users. This dictionary could be used to define technical terms such as EFI, MPGH, and MPGC or the scale for collision and insurance ratings. Further, the dictionary could explain concepts such as purchasing a car through a broker or standard lease terms. Other users may want explanations to more technical questions such as why they would care how many valves are available in the car or the difference between a single and dual overhead cam.

"How To"

Once the databases have been created and identified, the actual use of the databases in the DSS is not difficult because much of the operation is, in fact, addressed by the database management system. For example, within the tool Level 5 Object, we find a system-defined object for a database, as shown in Figure 3.19.

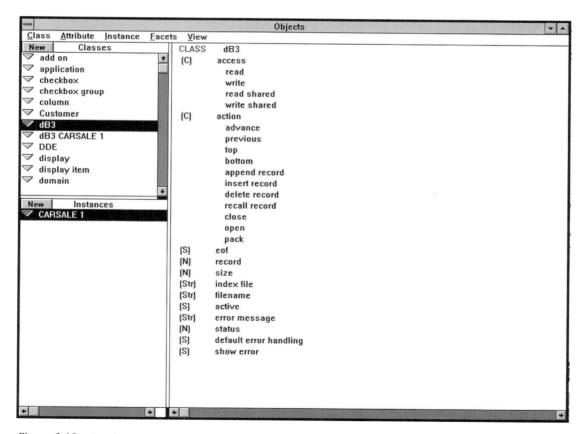

Figure 3.19 Database system object definition in Level 5 Object.

The attributes of this object provide basic database operations, such as opening or closing the database, movement around the database records, adding and deleting records, or even the index that might be used with regard to a particular database. The specific code required to actually insert a record in an existing database, or to find the end of file, for example, are already provided within the DSS generator.

When we create a specific database and identify it within Level 5 Object, the database actually inherits all the system-defined attributes, as shown in Figure 3.20. These inherited attributes supplement the user-defined attributes, which include the field names, types, and sizes.

When we need information from this database, then, we can use it similarly to other query systems. Suppose, for example, we needed some information about a

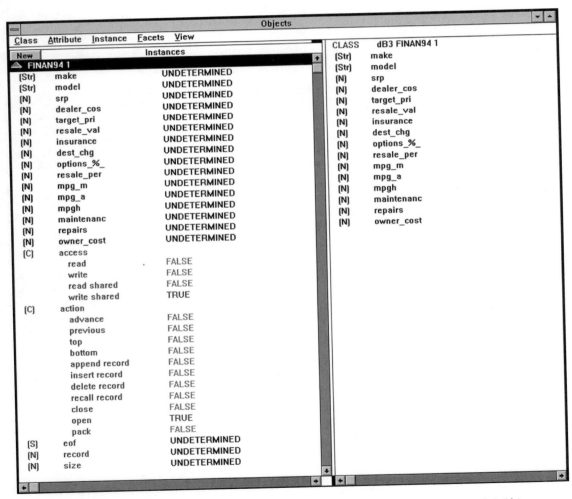

Figure 3.20   Example of inheritance of attributes: a specific database definition in Level 5 Object.

particular car that has been selected for a customer. This might be as a result of a customer specifying a particular automobile, or as a result of an analysis through which the DSS identified a desirable automobile. Figure 3.21 illustrates how one might complete such a search. The FIND sequence tells Level 5 Object to search the database named FINAN94, which contains financial information. Specifically, the code asks the system to find an entry in this database that matches the car identified as appropriate for the customer (Cmake OF Customer).

If the system identifies a match between the customer's preferred car and an entry in the database, it will create a temporary database, called Possible Car, with two entries: the model and the price of the automobile. The system will continue to cycle through the database until it reaches the end of file. Each time the system identifies a match, it will create an entry in this temporary database. Of course, if we were interested in more information about that automobile, we could create more fields in the temporary database.

We could, of course, write these entries to a permanent database that could be stored for later use by the decision maker. The code would look quite similar, except that we would now need to use the database function of appending a record, as shown in Figure 3.22.

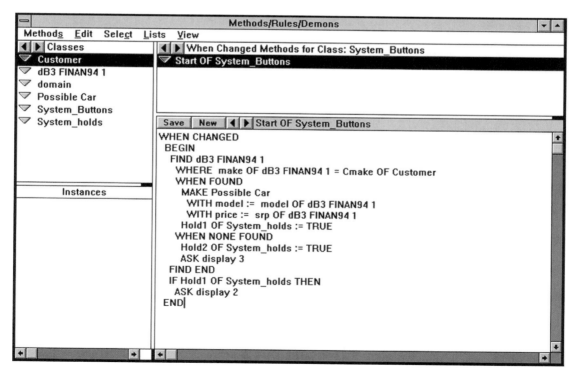

Figure 3.21   Level 5 Object code to search database and display results to screen.

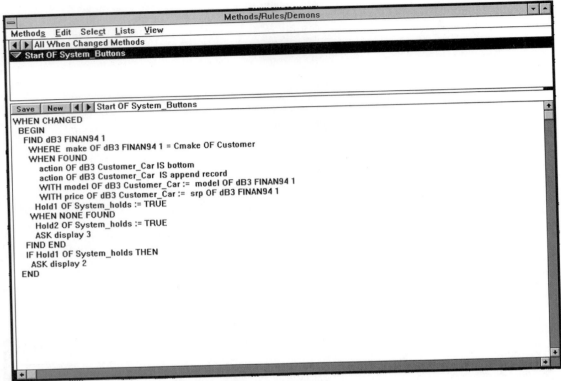

Figure 3.22   Level 5 Object code to search database and to save results of the search to another database.

Finally, we set a flag, Hold2 OF System_holds, if at least one match was found. This flag can be checked later to determine whether a display figure should appear (as it does in this program) or additional analyses and searches should be launched, as illustrated in Figure 3.23.

Of course, it is possible that no match will be found in the database. The code we write must anticipate this outcome and direct the system for its next action. In this simple example, we request that the system display a message that tells the user no match was found.

Another function designers would need to understand is how to create or supplement a particular database. In the previous examples, the system created a temporary database of the options available for the user. Often, however, the user will need to save the information for later operations. These might include the creation of a personal database, as defined earlier in the chapter, or the storage of intermediate steps so the user can try other analyses at a later time. Such an operation begins much the same way the previous searches were conducted; the designer still needs to create a temporary database with the results of a search. However, by using a code such as that shown in Figure 3.24, the user can update a permanent database.

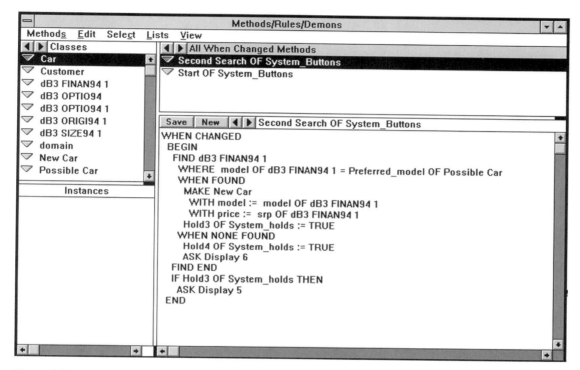

Figure 3.23 Level 5 Object code to search database and set a flag to indicate further analyses.

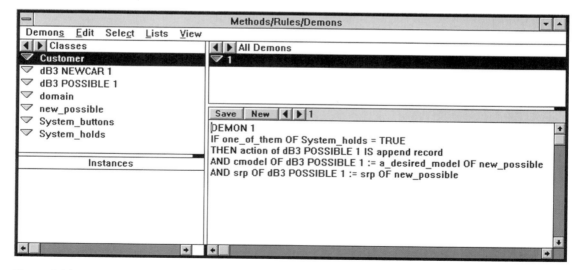

Figure 3.24 Level 5 Object code to respond to the flag set in Figure 3.23.

DISCUSSION

The fundamental database concerns for a DSS revolve around ensuring that the appropriate data are available and that they can be manipulated in the desired fashion efficiently. While this seems straightforward, it often is considerably more difficult than it sounds. First, various decision makers use different information at different points in time. Hence, the designers need to complete analysis and knowledge engineering to determine what data might be relevant. Second, data need to be collected from the various transaction processing systems and other sources, scrubbed, checked, and verified before they can be stored in a warehouse. Of course, once in the warehouse the data need to be organized into tables to optimize the searches from the DSS. Finally, the data management system needs to provide assistance to the users to help them understand what implications the data have for the choice process and how they can be used more effectively.

QUESTIONS

1. Consider the decision to register for courses in a given semester. What kinds of data would you use in that choice process? Why would you use those data?

2. Consider the data discussed in Question 1. How would you process those data to transform them into information?

3. Comment on the following statement:

    A good DSS should provide the manager as much information as possible and that information should be provided no more than five seconds after requested.

4. How would a DSS designer determine what information is most important to users?

5. Under what circumstances might designers be more concerned about the "appropriateness of format" of the information than the "timeliness" of the information?

6. Is material found on the World Wide Web "information" or "data"? What factors did you use to make that determination?

7. What kinds of private data might retail sales buyers maintain in a DSS?

8. Discuss the limitations for providing decision support that are imposed if data is stored in an hierarchical database or a network database.

9. Discuss how data warehousing has improved usability of DSS in corporate settings.

10. What kinds of validity threats do you have if data was obtained through data mining activities?

◆ O N   T H E   W E B ◆

On the Web for this chapter provides additional information about data, information, database management systems, data warehousing, and data mining. Links can provide access to demonstration packages, general overview information, applications, software providers, tutorials, and more. Additional discussion questions and new applications will also be added as they become available.

- *Links provide access to information about database and data warehouse products.* Links provide access to software information, software comparisons and reviews, and general information about both database management systems and data warehousing products.
- *Links provide access to descriptions of applications and development tricks.* In addition to information about the software, the Web provides links to worldwide applications of the software. You can access chronicles of users' successes and failures as well as innovative applications.

- *Links provide access to the changing technology of data mining.* This area is changing rapidly. The Web can provide access to information about tools and procedures for data mining, as well as press information about its impact.
- *Links provide access to information about automobiles.* An enormous amount of data about automobiles is available on the Web. You can scan the links to determine what kinds of information is most useful under what circumstances. Further, you can determine what kinds of impediments are introduced by various storage and retrieval mechanisms. Finally, the links can provide evaluations for information and storage capabilities.

You can access material for this chapter from the general WWW Page for the book, or directly from the following URL.
http://www.umsl.edu/~sauter/DSS/dbms.html

SUGGESTED READINGS

Agarwal, R., M.R. Tanniru, and M. Dacruz, "Knowledge-based support for combining qualitative and quantitative judgments in resource allocation decisions," *Journal of Management Information Systems*, 9(1), Summer 1992, pp. 165–184.

DePompa, B., "There's gold in databases," *Information Week*, 561, January 8, 1996, pp. 52–54.

Edelstein, H., "Mining data warehouses," *Information Week*, 561, January 8, 1996, pp. 48–51.

Fedorowicz, J., "Evolving technology for document-based DSS," in Sprague, R.H., Jr. and H.J. Watson (eds.), *Decision Support Systems: Putting Theory into Practice, Second Edition*, Englewood Cliffs, N.J.: Prentice–Hall, 1989, pp. 125–136.

Garnto, C. and H.J. Watson, "Investigation of database requirements for institutional and ad hoc DSS," in Sprague, R.H., Jr. and H.J. Watson (eds.), *Decision Support Systems: Putting The-*

ory into Practice, Third Edition, Englewood Cliffs, N.J.: Prentice-Hall, 1989, pp. 111–124.

Kimball, R. and K. Strehlo, "Why decision support fails and how to fix it," *Datamation*, 40(11), June 1994, pp. 40–43.

Kraemer, K.L., J.N. Danzinger, D.E. Dunkle, and J.L. King, "The usefulness of computer based information to public managers," *MIS Quarterly*, 17(2), June 1993, pp. 129–148.

McFadden, F.R. and J.A. Hoffer, *Database Management*, Menlo Park, CA: Benjamin Cummings, 1985.

Orr, K., "Data warehouse technology," *An Information Builders' White Paper*, 1995, pp. 1–21.

Radding, A., "Support decision makers with a data warehouse," *Datamation*, 41(5), March 1995, pp. 53–56.

Sauter, V.L. "Some insights into the requirements of information systems for public sector decision-makers," *Policy and Information*, 8(1), 1984, pp. 9–23.

Sauter, V.L. "The effect of 'experience' on information preferences," *Omega: International Journal of Management Science*, 13(4), 1985, pp. 277–284.

Sauter, V.L. and M.B. Mandell, "Transferring decision support concepts to evaluation," *Evaluation and Program Planning*, 13, 1990, pp. 349–358.

Subramanian, A., et al, "Strategic planning for data warehousing in the public sector," *Proceedings of the HIICS International Meeting*, Hawaii, January 1996.

Wallace, P., "Multimedia boosts Holiday Inn's training system," *InfoWorld*, 15(24), June 14, 1993, p. 62.

West, L.A., Jr. and J.F. Courtney, "The information problems in organizations: A research model for the value of information and information systems," *Decision Sciences*, 24(2), Spring 1993, pp. 229–251.

White, C., "The key to a data warehouse," *Database Programming and Design*, February 1995, pp. 23–25.

Chapter 4

Model Components

❖ ❖ ❖

Modeling is the simplification of some phenomenon for the purpose of understanding its behavior. Most people have their first experience with models as children, such as in model airplane building. Everyone knows that a model airplane is not a real airplane and hence will not perform all the functions of a real airplane. However, certain attributes of the plane are created realistically, such as the number of wings, the number of propellers, the relative size or colors of the plane, and its markings. A child might be able to ascertain the development of planes by noting the evolution of number and placement of wings, the use of propellers, and even how the shape of the plane has changed over time. Another child, with different interests, might use these models to learn the colors and markings of planes associated with different countries. Hence, the amount of detail and the kind of detail necessary for the model airplanes is dependent on the interests of the child at that moment. In other words, whether or not the model is sufficient is dependent on the needs of the decision maker (in this case, the child).

Business modeling fulfills the same objective. The purpose of a model is to simplify the choice context so that decision makers can clearly understand options and their ramifications. When statisticians develop regression models, their goal is to determine the factors essential to understanding the variability in the phenomenon of interest. Market research specialists, for instance, use regression to predict demand for a particular product. They understand that many factors affect a person's decision whether or not to purchase a product. However, in developing their marketing campaigns, it is useful to know whether their product appeals to young, unmarried professionals or to retired blue collar workers and whether the desirability of the product is different in different regions of the country.

Models represent an important part of decision support systems. Most business decisions have a large number of influential factors. Hence, most decision makers need to filter the essential components of the situation from the irrelevant ones. While it seems obvious that models fill this need, not everyone feels comfortable with models. Often it is not clear what model is most appropriate. Other times it is clear what kind of model is needed, but the data are not there to support it. Finally, sometimes it is not the result of the model that is so important, but rather the model's sensitivity to particular market conditions.

Although models can be applied without decision support systems, their power is magnified with decision support systems because of the inherent flexibility, friendly interfaces, and query capability of DSS. Historically, decision makers needed to rely on others to develop and interpret models for them because of the difficulty of running the computer programs associated with models. With DSS, decision makers are given personal access to appropriate models and appropriate data, and immediate access to results.

It is this *easy* and *friendly* access that makes DSS-based models so attractive. Decision makers can understand the implications of their judgment and modify those judgments when they appear to be inconsistent with what is known. In addition, because of the speed and efficiency of analysis, decision makers can examine more alternatives in order to find a good strategy. Furthermore, the model encourages decision makers to investigate the variables that are most sensitive to assumptions. Improvement in these aspects of problem analysis, in turn, aids decision makers in advocacy and implementation of the chosen solution because they understand more facets of the problem better. For example, the New Zealand yacht-

---

◆   DSS in Action   ◆

Intel chose Apian Software's *Decision Pad* to help it make choices among suppliers fairly and accurately. This DSS allows users to set multiple criteria for any decision, weight the criteria in importance, and do "what if" manipulations—using both quantitative data and qualitative information. In other words, the DSS goes beyond spreadsheet comparisons and number crunching to give real value to criteria that cannot be compared easily. The DSS allows users to record, annotate, manipulate, and compare the multiple components of supplier evaluations in an orderly fashion: alternatives, preferences, and criteria, and their relative importance. In addition, the user gives an assigned weight of importance he or she feels each criterion should have in determining the final outcome. Hence, the purchasing manager can compare each individual alternative against each criterion, attaching documentation notes to each conveniently. The system uses up to 250 items, although Intel focuses on five main criteria: price, service, capabilities, competitiveness, and stability; under those criteria are subcriteria such as on-time delivery, operation management, and labor relations. Further, the system allows the models to compute information with incomplete variables. However, the DSS will warn the user if the incomplete information is sufficient to fairly determine an outcome. For instance, if two suppliers are very close in score, additional information could sway the outcome. Then the user can decide whether to go back and complete the matrix. Finally, since the DSS allows the use of both quantitative and qualitative information, it helps the decision makers see how they are accounting for information.

Evans-Correia, K., "Putting decisions through the software wringer: Intel uses decision support software for supplier selection," *Purchasing*, 110, March 21, 1991, pp. 62-64.

racing team exploited the benefits of alternative generation and evaluation in its designs of *Black Magic 1* and *2*, which competed in the America's Cup in 1995. More than 10,000 options were considered during the four-month competition, which allowed the team to make constant improvements in the design of the yachts at the waterfront facility. Many believe this systematic evaluation of alternatives led to the remarkable performance in which the New Zealand team swept the field 5 to 0.

◆ MODELS

A model is a generalized description of a decision environment. The goal of creating it is to simplify a phenomenon in order to understand its behavior. While that is a nice definition, it does not help decision makers to understand how to model or even how to identify a model.

Decision support systems can include several types of models, some of which you have studied in your other classes. For example, statistical models include regression analysis, analysis of variance, and exponential smoothing. Accounting models include depreciation methods, budgets, tax plans, and cost analysis. Personnel models might include "in basket" simulations or role playing. Marketing models include advertising strategy analyses, consumer choice models, and product switch models. The characteristics of these models differ substantially, as do their uses; each represents simplification of a decision phenomenon that is useful for understanding some component of behavior. The skills needed to build and use these models and the kinds of support needed to help less skillful users utilize the models effectively also differ considerably. Part of the challenge of creating a DSS is knowing what models need to be included and how they can be supplemented to make them meaningful and useful for the decision maker. The remaining sections of this chapter address the challenge of how to make the models more meaningful and useful for decision makers.

We will use three different dimensions to describe models: (a) the representation; (b) the time dimension; and (c) the process, as shown in Figure 4.1.

Representation

The first dimension, the representation, describes the kind of data needed in a model, which, in turn, dictates the necessary approaches used to collect and process the data. In particular, we are distinguishing between models that rely on experiential data and those that rely on objective data. The difference between the two is the process by which the model is generated, not the answer that is derived.

Experiential models rely on the preparation and information processing of people, either individually or as a group. These models might include judgments, expert opinions, and subjective estimates. For example, diagnostic software used by physicians to help in prescribing treatment for tumors or blood diseases models

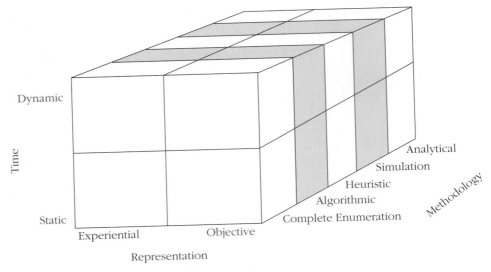

Figure 4.1   Dimensions of models.

the experience of expert practitioners. Similarly, in-basket personnel simulations or virtual reality simulations can represent experiential modeling. In such modeling, the information used and the manner in which it is used to make a choice is up to the decision maker.

For example, a forensic animation simulation was created to convict a Florida man of vehicular homicide. The simulation showed how his truck drove into a group of children (one of whom was killed) and then left the scene of the accident. One of the problems associated with the use of such models is their subjectivity in use. If two individuals attempt to use the same behavioral model, they may come to different conclusions because they are drawing on different experiences and are likely to weight those experiences differently. In this case, the verdict was appealed on the basis of the use of the simulation, which, according to the defense, misrepresented the scene of the accident (which happened at night) and the automobile.

Objective models, on the other hand, rely on specified, detached data and its analysis by known techniques. They are considered "objective" because the data considered and the way they are used are specified, constant, and independent of the specific decision maker's experiences. Consider the Reuters Money Network system shown in Figure 4.2. This system allows decision makers to access almost real-time stock quotes, historical data, and models for analyzing the data. The return on investment computed by one user for a particular option will be the same as the return on investment computed by another user for that same option. Hence, there is no subjectivity associated with the analysis.

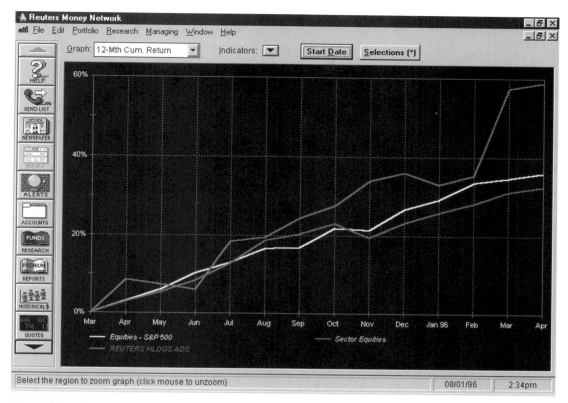

Figure 4.2 Objective data analysis with Reuters Money Network.

However, that in no way means that they are unbiased or lead everyone to the same conclusion. We can bias results by the selection of the variable, time period, or sample group. For example, conclusions about the yield of investments can vary substantially by the time horizon considered; stock market investments tend to provide poor yields when examined over short time horizons, but excellent yields, on average, when examined over multiple decades. Both provide an "objective" view of the performance of a portfolio, yet they provide very different conclusions; not providing both views presents a biased view of the problem. The ability to recognize such biases and thereby study multiple aspects of a problem is one of the advantages of using a DSS.

Neither the experiential nor the objective model is appropriate all the time, and each has its own strengths and weaknesses. Objective models have the advantage of being straightforward to apply and easily replicated with new data. In addition, they can save time in that they do not require the establishment of extensive experience such as that needed for some forms of behavioral modeling. These models have limitations as well. The basic assumption underlying objective modeling is that the simplification of reality necessary to create a mathematical model does not eliminate the essential issues controlling the decision environment. That is, it assumes that the most important factors, such as competition, regulation, prices, and technology are represented in the simplified model in a manner similar to that in the actual decision environment. If these factors change in a significant way, the mathematical models would not be appropriate because the essence of the decision environment and its probable reactions would not be represented. Under these circumstances, it is important to rely on experiential models.

Some DSS allow for the integration of both the objective and experiential models. For example, the DSS facilitating the U.S. Army plans for future needs of materiel incorporates both kinds of modeling. Objective models are built based on quantitative analysis of historical data. In this case, the historical data represent past demands for and uses of the materiel over time. The projections combine models that first assume a continuation of past patterns of materiel use, and then take into account planned activities such as major exercises. These forecasts are supplemented with heuristics about possible changes in the needs during the upcoming time horizon; expert opinions and human judgment are included to alter the projections. The DSS helps the user evaluate the combined model performance by continually measuring trends and alerting the decision maker to changes in the trends.[1]

Time Dimension

The time dimension identifies how much of the activity of the decision environment is being considered. The two ends of the continuum are static models and dynamic models. At the static end, models represent a snapshot in time of all factors affecting the decision environment. Such models assume that everything will remain the same. Similarly, such models assume that there is no dependence of later decisions or actions on the choice under consideration. Dynamic models, on the other hand, consider the decision environment over some specified time period. They may consider the same phenomenon during different periods of time, or they may consider interrelated decisions that will be considered during different time periods.

Methodology Dimension

The third dimension, methodology, addresses how the data (whether objective or experiential) will be collected and processed. There are five general methodologies: (a) complete enumeration; (b) algorithmic; (c) heuristic; (d) simulations; and (e) analytical. In complete enumeration, by far the hardest and most expensive op-

---

[1]Stovall A.A., Jr., *Army Command, Leadership and Management: Theory and Practice*, Carlisle Barracks, PA: U.S. Army War College, 1995–1996, pp. 17-18–17-19.

tion, information about *all* feasible options is collected and evaluated. Under many circumstances, complete enumeration is impractical. However, there are some contexts for which it is necessary or desirable. For example, the U.S. Census is an example of complete enumeration in which all individuals in the United States are identified and *counted*.[2] The purpose of counting all individuals is to understand the population shifts in the United States so representation in the Congress can reflect actual population density. Rather than sampling various areas in each state, the government identifies every person individually.

Complete enumeration also has been useful in the application of neural networks of transaction files for pattern recognition. For example, a neural network system was constructed for Mellon Bank of Chicago to identify suspicious credit card activity that might be indicative of stolen credit cards. Historically, both human auditors and electronic expert systems identified dubious transactions through abrupt increases in either the number or the size of transactions. By examining all the transactions, the neural network identified a change in *small* purchases as an indicator of stolen credit cards. In fact, at that time, card thieves were using small purchases, often as little as $1, in pay-at-the-pump gas stations, to determine whether the cards were still being accepted. It was this complete enumeration of transactions, supplemented by pattern-recognition capabilities, that allowed the system to respond quickly to the presence of criminal behavior.

The second approach, the algorithmic model, is the development of a set of procedures that can be repeated and will, eventually, define the desired characteristics of the decision environment. Such models are best represented by the field of operations research/management science. Algorithms have a set of repetitive calculations that can be implemented to find the best answer. The set of calculations itself is based on the characteristics of a particular problem. Unlike total enumeration, an algorithm identifies promising information that can be used to identify the best outcome without first evaluating all possible options. An example of such a modeling technique is the Simplex Algorithm. To use this model, we need to represent a problem as a linear program, determining an objective function that can be optimized (either maximized or minimized) and a set of constraints. Typically the objective function uses the minimization of costs, the maximization of utility, or some related concept. The constraints define the availability of scarce resources such as time, money, and inputs. If we can represent the problem as a linear program, we can use repetitive operations based on matrix row reduction calculations and find the best solution to the problem.[3] These repetitive operations are simple arithmetic operations; the process of applying them is the algorithm. (See the following box.)

---

[2] It has been noted in the 1990 U.S. Census that the process used does not count homeless individuals and underestimates their numbers. Strictly speaking, then, the census is not a complete enumeration.

[3] There are some special problem structures that cannot be solved using this algorithm. In addition, some problems cannot be solved *practically* with this technique because the number of variables and/or constraints is so large it would take a prohibitively long amount of time to solve the problem.

◆ **Technical Information** ◆

To understand algorithms and their use, let us consider a specific problem.

As MIS club plans to sell two special fruit baskets for the upcoming holiday season. Fruit Basket A contains 3 apples, 4 oranges, and 1 honeydew melon and sells for $8. Fruit Basket B contains 4 apples, 3 oranges, and 2 honeydew melons and sells for $12. The amount of each fruit available and their costs to the MIS club are shown in the table below. If it is assumed that the MIS club can sell all the baskets it makes, how many of each one should it make?

Fruit	Quantity Available	Cost per Piece
Apple	160	$0.30
Orange	180	$0.20
Melon	60	$1.20

The first step is to represent the problem mathematically. In this case, we will have two variables, x and y, where x represents the number of Fruit Basket A to make and y represents the number of Fruit Basket B to make. We know that each Fruit Basket A sells for $8 and each Fruit Basket B sells for $12, but in order to know how much profit we will make, we must compute the cost of each basket. Basket A contains 3 apples @ $.30, 4 oranges @ $.20, and 1 melon @ $1.20, so it costs $2.90 to make up the basket (if we assume that the actual basket is free). Hence, the net profit from Basket A is $5.10. Using a similar method, we can find that the net profit from Basket B is $7.80. Hence, our objective is to

$$\text{maximize } 5.10x + 7.80y$$

However, there are constraints dictating the availability of fruits that must be met. Using the quantities above, they are

Apples:	$3x + 4y \leq 160$
Oranges:	$4x + 3y \leq 180$
Melons:	$1x + 2y \leq 60$

Algorithms are used widely today in business, organizations, and government. They can help decision makers know how to place investments, where to advertise products, or how to assign staff to projects. One area where algorithms are used heavily is in personnel planning and scheduling. For example, many hospital systems use algorithms to assign nurses and other staff to shifts. In some cases, the systems include measures of "intensity" of patient illnesses so that they can determine whether the optimal general staffing levels will meet the specific needs on a daily basis.[4] Similarly, the U.S. Army uses an algorithm-based DSS called *ELIM-*

---

[4]Butters, S., "Jewish Hospital Healthcare Services uses DSS," *Journal of Systems Management*, 43, June 1992, p. 30.

Conceptually, the algorithm for solving this problem looks at possible values for x and y and selects the one that maximizes our objective. Consider the following graph:

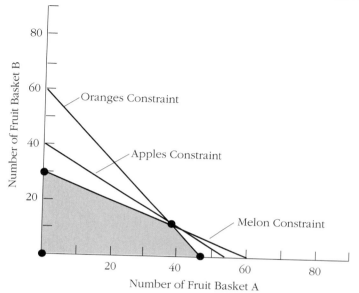

The algorithm "knows" to look for the feasible combinations of the two types of fruit baskets, as shaded in the graph. Further, it knows that the best combination is going to be one of the four "extreme," or corner, points highlighted above. The algorithm evaluates an extreme point with regard to the objective (5.10x + 7.80y). It then looks at the adjacent corners to determine if one of them gives a better solution. If so, the algorithm moves to that new point and begins again. In essence, the algorithm moves from corner to corner, always improving the value of the objective. With large problems, the process is important because one can have many variables and many constraints resulting in millions of corner points. Since the algorithm follows a systematic approach to improvement, it ends up checking only a small percentage of the possible points. In this case, it is the combination of 36 Fruit Baskets of Type A and 12 Fruit Baskets of Type B, giving a profit of $277.20 to the MIS Club.

COMPLIP with input from other modeling forecasting systems to plan for deployment of personnel to various tasks so as to meet their strength needs as specified in the Force Structure Allowance.[5]

The third possible model process is heuristic. Generally, heuristics are applied to large or ill-structured problems that cannot be solved algorithmically. The goal

---

[5]Stoval, A.A., Jr., *Army Command, Leadership and Management: Theory and Practice*, Carlisle Barracks, PA: U.S. Army War College, 1995–1996, pp. 18-2–18-3.

is to find a satisfactory solution that is reasonably close to optimal. All heuristics involve searching, evaluating, learning, and more searching to find a good solution. They are usually developed for a particular problem in order to take advantage of the structure of a problem. Some heuristics are designed to construct solutions; others are designed to improve existing solutions. Since heuristics are so dependent on a particular representation of a problem, they are not often generalizable to other problems.

Heuristics can be quantitative solutions to a problem or behavioral solutions to a problem. In the former case, the model is a numeric representation of a choice and we focus on numeric processing. Typically, a quantitative heuristic is developed as an alternative to using a quantitative algorithmic approach, if, for example, a reliable algorithm is not available, if the computation time is excessive, if the data are limited, or if the problem is so big it cannot be reasonably simplified otherwise. For example, if the decision variables in a problem are restricted to dichotomous (0 or 1) values or integer values, known algorithms may fail to find an optimal solution. This might include a firm's assignment of production processes to particular production facilities or a financial institution's assignment of deposits to lockboxes. Similarly, if the objective to a problem is nonlinear, or if there are many variables or constraints, known algorithms may fail to find an optimal solution. Some heuristics can be identified that take advantage of the mathematical structure of a problem to find good answers to these problems.

If the heuristic is behavioral, then we consider the relationships between concepts and use symbolic processing of the data. In fact, this kind of behavioral heuristic is generally referred to as *expert systems* (a branch of artificial intelligence). Expert systems use rules, frames, objects, and meta-rules (often referred to as demons or daemons[6]) to replicate the solution technique that an expert would use to solve an ill-structured, nonquantifiable problem. These models can give meaning and context to the symbol and incorporate subjective information about the validity of an answer or the way in which the answer should be used to obtain a solution.

The fourth approach to modeling is simulation. Unlike algorithmic and heuristic modeling, which provide a normative answer, simulation provides descriptive results. The goal of simulation is to imitate reality either quantitatively or behaviorally. Typically, this involves the repetition of an experiment and the description of the characteristics of certain variables over time. For example, a simulation of a factory would include a variable that measures the amount of time an average part spends waiting in lines and the amount of time it takes to process the in-

---

[6]The term *demon* or "daemon" in a programming environment refers to a portion of code that lies dormant until a particular event, such as the change in the value of a variable, causes the code to process. These daemons might cause particular actions to occur, such as the searching of a database, or they might prohibit actions to occur and take the user along a different path of code.

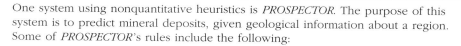

◆ Technical Information ◆

One system using nonquantitative heuristics is *PROSPECTOR*. The purpose of this system is to predict mineral deposits, given geological information about a region. Some of *PROSPECTOR*'s rules include the following:

RULE 1.
    IF the igneous rocks in the region have a fine to medium grain size,
    THEN they have a porphyritic texture (0.5).

RULE 2.
    IF the igneous rocks in the region have a fine to medium grain size,
    THEN they have a texture suggestive of a hypabyssal regional environment (2, 0.000001).

RULE 3.
    IF the igneous rocks in the region have a fine to medium grain size and they have a porphyritic texture,
    THEN they have a texture suggestive of a hypabyssal region environment (100, 0.0000001).

RULE 4.
    IF the igneous rocks in the region have a texture suggestive of a hypabyssal regional environment,
    THEN the region is a hypabyssal regional environment (65, 0.01).

RULE 5.
    IF the igneous rocks in the region have a morphology suggestive of a hypabyssal regional environment,
    THEN the region is a hypabyssal regional environment (300, 0.0001).

RULE 6.
    IF the region is a hypabyssal regional environment,
    THEN the region has a favorable level of erosion (200, 0.0002).

RULE 7.
    IF Coeval volcanic rocks are present in the region,
    THEN the region has a favorable level of erosion (800, 1).

The system processes these and other rules much the way an expert geologist would to examine the geological, geophysical, and geochemical data to predict where ore-grade minerals could be found. The numbers in parentheses indicate measures of certainty with the conclusions that are built into the reasoning process.

PROSPECTOR rules were taken from Waterman, D.A., *A Guide to Expert Systems*, Reading, MA: Addison–Wesley Publishing Company, 1986, p. 58.

ventory. Using the mathematics underlying the simulation, we could vary the demand for products, the raw materials arrivals, and the number and types of production lines and study the impact of these variations on the amount of time one part spends waiting in line and making a transaction. With today's simulation software, decision makers can vary decision variables and see the impact with animation, such as that shown in Figure 4.3.

Simulations help decision makers understand how external influences can affect the outcomes of their decisions. For example, Compaq relied heavily on simulation in deciding when to introduce its microcomputers with Pentium processors. The simulation was designed to model customer demand, pricing, and dealer inventories to help managers decide when to introduce their newest products. It is a complicated model that can simulate a variety of relevant conditions, such as component price changes or even the impact of a rival model. In this way, the managers can evaluate the risk *before* taking the risk. While it is too early to evaluate the full impact of this strategy change, early results were good. When Hewlett-Packard dropped prices by 22%, the simulation had predicted the change within a few dollars. Hence, Compaq's decision had already taken this strategic move into consideration.[7]

Similarly, personnel departments use in-basket simulation exercises to help individual managers determine the best approaches to addressing the problems that arise in managing people. In this case, the manager measures not a mathematical variable, but rather the reaction of another individual in order to experiment with positive and negative reactions and determine which will provide the desired effect. Finally, today's technology can make it possible to simulate how it feels to drive a given automobile over a variety of surfaces and in a variety of conditions to determine which car provides the most desirable ride given its cost.

The essence of constructing simulation models is to simplify the elementary relationships and interdependencies of the situation being considered. While it does simplify the conditions, simulation also allows us to build in real-life complexities that might affect the variables being measured. It is descriptive in its answer, thereby encouraging "what if" kinds of experimentation in which many alternatives can be considered independently, and time is compressed so that long-term effects can be measured quickly.

Simulations are not without their disadvantages, however. They do not provide an optimal solution; instead, they provide information about conditions from which we can glean a good, or possibly an optimal, solution. Like heuristics, inferences are not transferable beyond the specific type of problem being considered. Finally, and most important, the construction of simulations can be slow and costly.

The last type of methodology is the analytical model. Analytical modeling refers to the process of breaking up a whole into its parts, and the associated process of examining the parts to determine their nature, proportion, function, and inter-

---

[7]McWilliams, G., "At Compaq, a desktop crystal ball," *Business Week*, March 20, 1995, pp. 96–97.

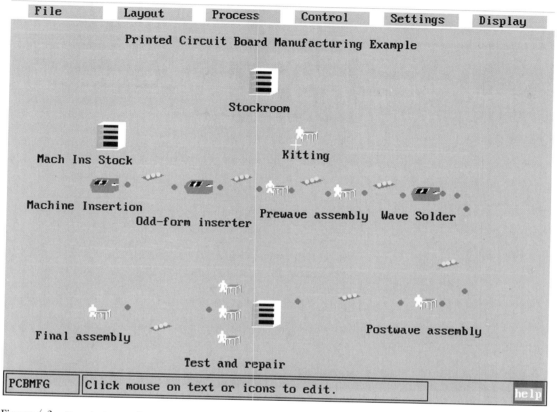

Figure 4.3 Simulation software support.

relationships. Where phenomena are well defined, analytical approaches solve for related variables that have specified properties within limits. For example, the phenomenon of gravity is well defined so that we can use specified equations to describe how an object will fall. Where phenomena are not well defined, which includes virtually all business-related phenomena, the analytical approach determines how to separate a given problem into its constituent parts and determine what subcomponents are most important in affecting the interactions with other subcomponents. Statistical analyses, especially regression and other predictive models, provide good examples of analytical modeling.

Consider, for example, the process of creating strategies for football games. The interdependence of the players and the complexity of the plays make it difficult for any individual to make choices without help. National Football League teams use decision support systems with sophisticated analyses to make these decisions. The DSS helps the coach understand the tendencies of the opposition and hence

◆ **DSS in Action** ◆

The U.S. Military is one of the most significant users of simulations in the world to-day. The *Generalized Air Mobility Model*, or GAMM,* simulates the entire theater airlift system's movement of cargo from source to destination. Hence, the DSS pro-vides simulation of flights, airdrops, overland cargo transshipment, and the surviv-ability of cargo in the various modes of transportation. (The DSS does *not* simulate the outcome of the campaign, just the ability of the airlift system to meet the oper-ational demands of a given scenario.)

The quality of the insight from this simulation, as in any simulation, comes from the quality of the measures that were built into the system for evaluation. Histori-cally, the military used measures such as rate-of-cargo movement, average aircraft flying time per day, utilization rate, and departure reliability. While these measures provide some indication of the basic throughput of the operation, they do not mea-sure the effectiveness of the mission, nor how it supports combat forces. Hence, GAMM has factors of evaluation such as

- timeliness of deliveries;
- effectiveness in making multi-flight deliveries within narrow time and location constraints such as those necessary for combat missions; and
- ability to move large, oversized items.

In addition to providing operational logistics for a particular campaign, GAMM also can predict where long-term airlift characteristics need to be changed and hence of-fer insights into future designs.

*Auclair, P.F., S.J. Wourms, and J.J. Koger, "Ideas take flight," *ORMS Today*, 20(4), August 1993, pp. 24–29.

◆ **DSS Design Insights** ◆

Computer simulations are not replicas of reality. For example, Boeing Co. engineers used simulation to design a fuse pin that held the engines to the wing for its 747 cargo plane. After El Al Airlines had a crash in 1992, in which the plane killed more than 40 people in the Netherlands, engineers reviewed their simulation. They found that the simulation had missed several weak points in the design of the fuse pin. The fuse pin had, in fact, broken, causing the crash.

Coy, P. and R.D. Hof, "3-D computing: From medicine to war games, it's a whole new dimension," *Business Week*, September 4, 1995, pp. 70–77.

to plan strategies that will respond to them. In fact, when the Giants won the Super Bowl in 1991, Coach Bill Parcells, who used such a DSS, gave some of the credit for the win to the system.[8]

◆ MODEL-BASE MANAGEMENT SYSTEMS

The DSS provides the decision maker with more than the models themselves. Through the model-base management system (MBMS), the DSS provides easy access to models and help in using those models. Clearly, the library of models is an important aspect of this component. Such a library should provide decision makers access to a wide variety of statistical, financial, and management science models as well as any other models that could be of importance to the particular problems to be encountered.

Easy Access to Models

The library of models is provided to allow decision makers *easy* access to the models. Easy access to the models means that users need not know the specifics of how the model runs or the specific format rules for commanding the model. For example, consider the DSS built using *Which & Why*, shown in Figures 4.4 and 4.5. In Figure 4.4, we can see that users can easily select a model simply by clicking on one of the tabs shown at the top. In Figure 4.5, we see how the user can manipulate the tools once they are chosen with simple keystrokes or mouse movements.

The model-base management system should facilitate easy entry of information to the model. Unlike conventional modeling software, which often requires that information be entered in a specific order and a specific format, DSS should allow flexible input of the data. The role of the model-base management system is to translate the user-friendly form of the data into the appropriate format for a particular model. For example, if a model requires that the data be input in a rigid line-and-column framework, such as

1.22	15	3
2.31	21	6
3.11	11	9

the user can input the data (if they are not already in a database) flexibly in a format that might be more comfortable, such as 1.22, 2.31, 3.11, 15, 21, 11, 3, 6, 9. The MBMS will put the data in the format appropriate for the particular model(s) being used.

Similarly, users of the system need not be aware of the specific syntax required to execute a particular model. The MBMS should generate the necessary commands

---

[8]Goldstein, M., "Laptops in sports," *PC LapTop Computers Magazine*, 4(4), April 1992, pp. 28–33, 85.

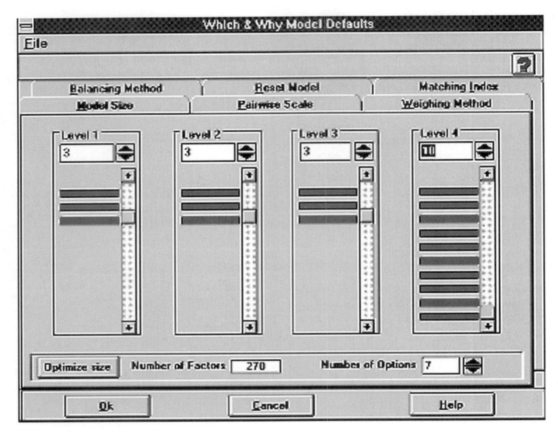

Figure 4.4   Simple model selection.

to tell the machine where the model is located and what commands are necessary to cause the model to execute. For example, the user should not need to remember (or even know) the requirements for naming or formatting the data to utilize them in a model. Rather than the user needing to remember the code, such as that shown in Code Box 4.1, the user would simply click on the icon for accounts data. Clearly, someone would need to program the system to associate a particular icon with a given place in the database. More important from the perspective of the MBMS, though, is the fact that the data have been identified in the appropriate format as input to a particular package (in this case, SAS).

Further, it is important that the program be notified that there is something "unusual" about the data, such as the record length. Not only might users be unaware of the appropriate syntax through which to share this information, they might not even know that the information needs to be provided. Similarly, users should not

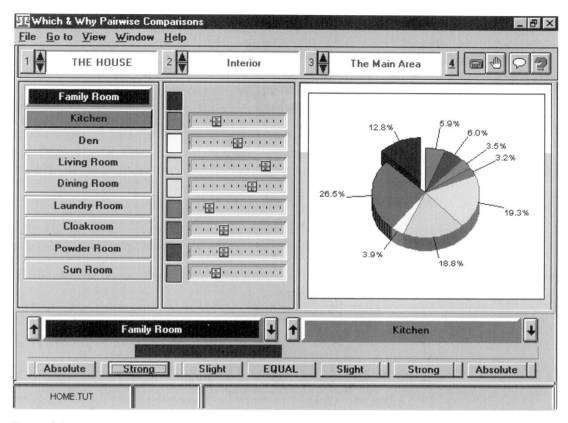

Figure 4.5 Simple manipulation of model.

need to remember the control sequences for testing hypotheses (Code Box 4.2); they could simply type *is there a difference in absenteeism in the different groups?*

Of course, in order to provide this easy access to models, the designer must make certain assumptions about how the decision makers want their analyses conducted. In this case, the designer made assumptions about the specific test of the differences of means among the groups by specifying the model, the test, the procedure, and the format of output. On one hand, this makes analysis easier for the decision makers because they can access the model immediately without needing to specify assumptions, look up syntax, or write code. On the other hand, it constrains those decision makers who need different assumptions for their particular tests. This presents somewhat of a dilemma for the designer of the system in knowing how to make the tradeoff between flexibility and control.

Regrettably, there is not a standard answer to this question, and only knowledge of the decision makers, their preferences, their agreement on their preferences, and the likelihood of their changing preferences will define how much flexibility is

---

◆ CODE BOX 4.1: Sample SAS Code to Input Data ◆

```
CMS FILEDEF ACCOUNTS DISK ACCOUNT DATA A1 (LRECL 135);
      DATA SAMPLE;
      INFILE ACCOUNTS;
      INPUT DEPARTMENT $ 1-7 EMPLOYEE $ 9-25 NUMBER 27-32
      ABSENT_FULL 34-36 ABSENT_HALF 38-42 REASON 80-133;
          TOT_ABSENT = ABSENT_FULL + ABSENT_HALF;
       :
       :
```

---

needed in the model features. However, a designer can compromise. If, for example, most decision makers want the features set in a particular way, but not all accept this option, the features could be set with a default setting and easy access to change the settings. Upon the selection of the test, a window such as that shown in Figure 4.6 could appear. As the users click a mouse (or press Enter) on any one of those, they would see another window that allows them to change the options.

There are variations of this approach. If, for example, the differences in features are person specific, the designer could build intelligence into the system with a rule that specifies that if the user is PERSON X, use the Gabriel test rather than the Duncan test. In this way, PERSON X always has the preferred test as the default and all others have their preferred test as the default. Or, the designer could provide a check box that would allow users to change defaults before running the test if they desire. While it is tempting to force the user to acknowledge and accept each option individually, it is not recommended. Such a sequence will increase the average amount of time it takes for a user to run a model. Unless many users often change the options, this is an unnecessary waste of time. In addition, many users will quickly tire of these repeated entries, learn to ignore them (by pressing Accept for each option), and become frustrated with the system. Furthermore, they will not be any more likely to actually read the entries.

◆ CODE BOX 4.2: Sample SAS Code to Process Data ◆

```
PROC ANOVA;
      CLASS A B C;
      MEANS A B C A*B/ DUNCAN LINES;
      MODEL Y = A |B(A)| C / INT INTERCEPT;
      TEST H = A A*C E = B(A);
          TITLE 'ABSENTEEISM BY DEPARTMENT, SENIORITY, JOB';
```

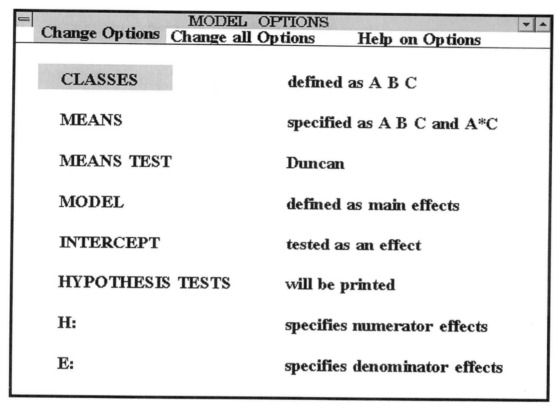

Figure 4.6   Model option selections.

Understandability of Results

In addition, the DSS should provide the results to the user in an understandable form. Most models provide information to the user employing at least some cryptic form that is not comprehensible for people who do not use the package frequently. For example, the results from a regression could be presented using a standard SAS output format, such as that shown in Figure 4.7. Regular users of SAS can find most of the information that they need to evaluate the model and begin forecasting with it. However, even a person who is familiar with statistics but unfamiliar with the output of SAS or other statistical packages might not be able to interpret the meaningfulness of the results. Certainly a decision maker not familiar with either statistics *or* SAS would be unlikely to be able to answer even the simple question of how many items one would expect to sell if the price were $1.24 and the advertising expenditures were $15/month. Consider instead a screen such as that shown in Figure 4.8.

In Figure 4.8, the results are labeled clearly and all the relevant information is provided to the user in a conclusion format. The user does not need to remember too much about the technique "regression" because the screen explains the types of issues that should be of interest. Furthermore, it encourages the user to experiment with the model (by entering data) to become more comfortable with it and the results. Since one of the fundamental assumptions in DSS design is that the supported decisions are "fuzzy" and infrequently encountered, it is important not to assume that the user can remember the nuances of the output of each model that might be accessed.

Note that we are not simply talking about the *appearance* of the results. In Figure 4.8, we are literally helping the user to understand the *meaning* of the output by removing some of the jargon implicit in the computer printout and rephrasing in terms the decision maker can understand. For example, consider the boxed information in the lower left. The purpose of the box is to highlight the meaning of the slope coefficient associated with each of the variables as well as their associated interval estimates. In contrast, Figure 4.7 lists the slope in the column "parameter estimate" next to the respective variable name. The appropriate standard error appears in the following column. To use the information from the SAS output,

MODEL: EQ1		SSE	109.03877		F RATIO	47.92
		DFE	48		PROB>F	0.0013
DEP VAR: SALES		MSE	2.271641		R-SQUARE	0.9319

VARIABLE	DF	PARAMETER ESTIMATE	STANDARD ERROR	T-RATIO	PROB>|T|
INTERCEPT	1	16.406365	4.342519	3.7781	.0069
PRICE	1	- 8.247580	2.196057	-3.7556	.0071
ADVERTISING	1	.585101	0.133672	4.3771	.0032

	A	B				
1						
2						
3						
4						
5	MONTH	WEEK				
6						
7	January	1				
8		2				
9		3				
10		4				
11	February	1	10	55	52	10	58
12		2	10	54	37	7	30
13		3	69	66	42	6	4
14		4	61	89	44	10	31
15	March	1	76	86	53	10	48
16		2	89	47	46	13	28
17		3	73	86	36	8	1
18		4	52	147	55	12	35
19	April	1	64	83	71	7	51
20		2	68	68	61	7	35
21		3	109	112	57	12	8
22		4	62	171	62	7	33
23	May	1	60	109	87	7	55
24		2	65	25	56	11	31
25		3	77	112	33	10	0
26		4	61	170	71	13	26

Figure 4.7   Traditional results format.

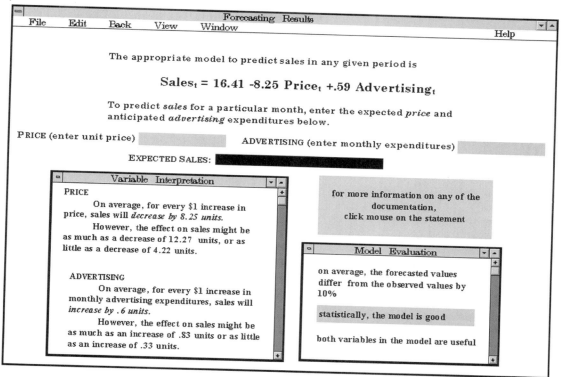

Figure 4.8 Results with decision support.

the decision maker needs to know what each of these terms means and that a slope can have a physical interpretation. Furthermore, the decision maker needs to know that all point estimates have intervals associated with them and that we determine the interval by multiplying the standard error by the critical value of t associated with 48 degrees of freedom, found in a standard t-table, not found on Figure 4.7! This is a lot to expect from the decision maker, especially given that each model has its own unique notation and set of issues. The box in Figure 4.8 does not require the decision maker to know all the intermediate steps or to compute anything. In short, Figure 4.7 provides results from the model; Figure 4.8 provides *support* for a decision.

Clearly, different individuals will require different levels of support. Figure 4.8 provides only the minimal quantitative information. However, it can be tied to other output screens that could provide additional support if the decision maker selects it. For example, in Figure 4.8, the instructions note that the user can obtain additional information about a specific topic by clicking the mouse on that statement. In this screen, the statement "both variables are useful" is highlighted. If the decision maker clicked on that space, the system would display Figure 4.9, which provides additional information, including the mathematics and assumptions behind the statement.

The previous example provides information to the decision makers only if they select it. However, sometimes you want to make sure that the decision maker sees additional help screens because it is crucial. In this case, the system can "force" a particular area of the screen to be highlighted, create a pop-up notice about a problem, or emit a sound to catch the decision maker's attention. Suppose, for example, that the variable price in the model described in Figure 4.8 were *not* statistically significant. It is possible to provide the information in a box, as shown in Figure 4.10.

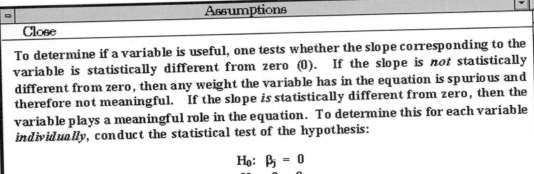

Figure 4.9   Detailed model support.

This box provides information about the validity of the model. However, it is passive and does not highlight the problem or tell the decision maker the implications of the problem. Instead, consider Figure 4.11. In this screen, we are highlighting some of the information on the printout so that it is not missed by the decision maker. Not only does this additional screen call attention to the easily missed note about the variable being not statistically significant, but the CAUTION message box tells the decision maker the implications of not taking action on this problem. In this way, the DSS is helping the clients clarify their assumptions about the implications of the results. So, in fact, the DSS is helping the decision maker to use the information correctly.

The way we provide support for interpreting results depends on what kind of DSS generator and modeling package we are using. In an abstract sense, there must be a code that causes the computer to scan the results of the model and creates the base screen with the results. In this case, the modeling package must return the results of the F-statistic, the t-statistics, the probabilities associated with those t-statistics, and the mean squared error. Further, there must be some intelligent link that fires to interpret the results and to place those results in the appro-

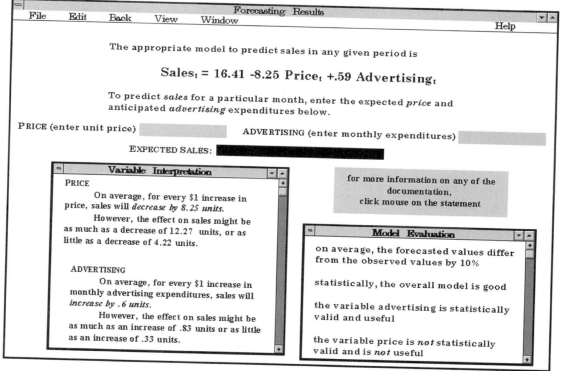

Figure 4.10   Passive warning of model problems.

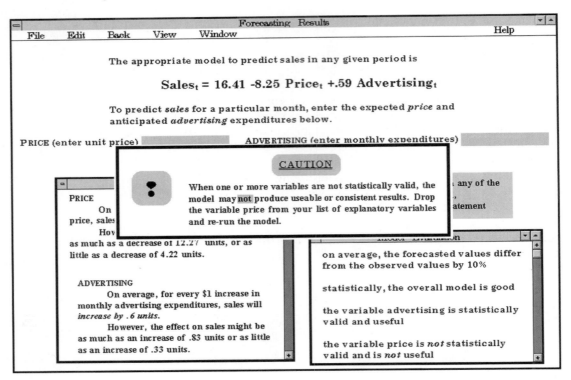

Figure 4.11   Active warning of model problems.

priate window. Finally, there must be another intelligent link that fires when one of the variables is not significant, to cause the CAUTION message box to appear.

Clearly, to create this kind of help in a traditional language is difficult. The fourth-generation languages and object-oriented languages available today allow the designer much flexibility. First, such languages allow the user to create pop-up windows that are linked to particular results or variables. In this case, each of the four items noted in the results window might actually be a different window that is linked to code checking the appropriate result. The border might actually be a hyper region that serves no purpose but an aesthetic one. Furthermore, the CAUTION message box might be linked to an indicator of nonsignificance of a variable. An alternative CAUTION message box might be linked to a condition in which two or more of the variables are not significant.

Integrating Models

Another task of the MBMS is to help integrate one model with another. For example, suppose the user needs to make choices about inventory policy and selects an Economic Order Quantity (EOQ) model, as shown in Computations Box

4.1. To use this formula to determine the optimal order quantity, we need information about expected product demand, the costs associated with an order, and the typical holding costs (with consistent monetary and time units). If the decision makers can input the data or read the data directly, there is no problem. Typically, however, this is not the case. Generally, the order costs need to be computed by combining the costs of personnel, supplies (such as forms), and services (such as phone resources) needed to execute an order. In addition, since holding costs can vary over time, we need to average holding costs to obtain a current estimate. Finally, unless demand is well specified, it needs to be forecasted based on historical data. Hence, upon selection of the EOQ model, the MBMS needs to complete several tasks:

1. Search database for a single value for the order costs.
2. If no specific order cost information is available, invoke model to compute order costs by summing personnel costs, supply costs, services costs, and the order costs charged by the vendor.
3. Feed the computed order costs to the EOQ model.
4. Obtain data about holding costs.
5. If historical data are available, estimate holding costs.
6. If no historical data are available, invoke model to determine holding costs.
7. Feed computed holding costs value to the EOQ model.
8. Invoke model to forecast demand for the time period(s) served by the order.
9. Feed forecasted demand to the EOQ model.
10. Compute economic order quantity.

Not only should the user not need to intervene in this process, but the user need not even know the process is occurring. However, since the meaningfulness of the EOQ is dependent on the quality of the forecasts and estimates, the user should be provided the forecasts and information about the quality of those forecasts. This might be accomplished by a screen such as the one in Figure 4.12.

Sensitivity of a Decision

One of the tasks of the model-base management system in a decision support system is to help the decision maker understand the implications of using a model. This is not always easy because decision makers may not be inclined to ask ques-

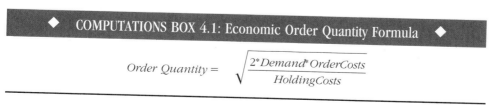

◆ COMPUTATIONS BOX 4.1: Economic Order Quantity Formula ◆

$$Order\ Quantity = \sqrt{\frac{2 * Demand * OrderCosts}{HoldingCosts}}$$

tions particularly if they do not know what questions need to be asked. Consider the examples in the following paragraphs.

Example 1

Peara's Personalized Computers uses an assembly line to build desired configurations. One of the employees on the line has suggested a change in procedure that Andrew Peara thinks might improve the efficiency of the operations. Andrew Peara wants to determine if his intuition is correct, and if the change would be worth implementing. To investigate this, using historical data he determines that the mean length of time to perform a certain task or a group of tasks on an assembly line is 15.5 minutes, with a standard deviation of 3 minutes. Because he understands the importance of collecting data, he selects 16 employees and teaches them the new procedure. After a training period, he finds that these employees, on average, take 13.5 minutes to perform the task with the new procedure. The question Andrew needs to answer is whether these results provide sufficient evidence to indicate that the new procedure is really faster and thus should be implemented. This statistical analysis for this problem is shown in Computations Box 4.2.

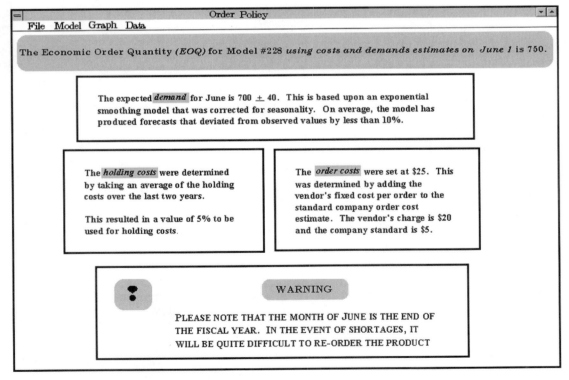

Figure 4.12 Seamless integration of models.

◆ DSS in Action ◆

AIDSPLAN is a DSS resource that allows health care workers in Great Britain to plan resources for HIV/AIDS-related services better. The system explicitly encourages decision makers to focus on "what if" questions so they can creatively experiment with strategies that might prove useful in meeting the needs of this increasing care-needing group. The DSS can be used to explore the consequences of alternative strategies or investments in resources, as well as the sensitivity of those consequences to particular assumptions about uncontrollable and unpredictable factors. This, in turn, allows decision makers to examine the impacts of the decisions in terms of likely overload, need for further resources, and flexibility to meet future uncertainties.

Forecasts of demand within particular localities are derived from the COX National Forecasts by patient categories. Decision makers can elect whether to examine these forecasts at their low, medium, or high range. This projection of patient demand, in turn, forms the basis for experimentation with care options. Costs of care options by patient category are used to estimate the costs and resources required to treat the projected patient demand.

The model's analysis is based on a division of patients into categories that, for planning purposes, can be considered relatively homogeneous in their demand for services. Criteria that can be used to classify patients include clinical state, possible drug abuse, age, dependency, housing situation, and the presence or absence of informal support at home.

For each category, the health authority needs to identify alternative care options. A care option is a costed combination of service inputs that constitutes a clinically acceptable method of treating or supporting a member of the client group. It is defined in terms of the basic resources needed to supply appropriate care and treatment. Model users can adopt the list of resources provided with AIDSPLAN or change it to suit their special concerns or circumstances. Up to 32 different resources can be accommodated in the model. Once users have established such lists of resources, they can express any given care option as a particular combination of recourses from the list in specified amounts.

For any particular assumptions made about future demand, AIDSPLAN computes the resources and cost consequences of the identified care strategy. Using a menu, the user can display summaries of the results at different levels to see the effect of the input assumptions and to identify where further analyses may be needed. In fact, medical personnel currently are using AIDSPLAN to facilitate discussion of the consequences for services of using AZT prophylactically and the impact of day care facilities on the provision of inpatient beds.

Rizakou, J. Rosenhead and K. Reddington, "AIDSPLAN: A decision support model for planning the provision of HIV/AIDS-related services," *Interfaces*, 21(3), 1991, pp. 117–129.

Based on the analysis, Andrew Peara knows that there is reason to believe the new procedure will reduce the amount of time it takes to perform the task. However, it is unlikely that this is the only information the decision maker will want to know in order to make the decision. It is obviously necessary to determine whether the value of the additional computers that could be produced (because it takes less time to perform each one) offsets the cost associated with the training. We could then estimate that instead of producing 3.87 computers per hour (one every 15.5 minutes), the average person will be able to produce 4.44 computers per hour. Said differently, this is an increase of 4.59 computers per shift or 22.98 computers per week for an average worker. With this information, and some information about the revenue per computer and the cost of training, the decision maker can easily decide whether the additional 23 computers per week per worker will increase revenue sufficiently to justify the costs of training.

However, this analysis is built on some assumptions that may not be clear to the decision maker. One of the characteristics of good decision support is that it helps the decision maker understand these assumptions and evaluate whether or not they are reasonable. Before discussing how to display the information, we need to know the assumptions.

1. *A major assumption underlying this analysis is that these 16 individuals really represent the employees who will perform this task.* While the description of the problem indicated that the 16 were "randomly selected," it is important to be sure that they are representative. In real-world cases, "randomly selected" might mean

---

◆   COMPUTATIONS BOX 4.2: Sample t-test   ◆

In introductory statistics, you learned that this type of problem is a one-tailed test of the mean. From a statistical point of view, the question is

$$H_0: \mu = 15.5$$
$$H_A: \mu < 15.5$$

where μ is the true mean task time. To test this, given the sample size of 9 and the estimated standard deviation, one uses a t-test:

Reject H_0 if |computed t| is greater than the critical t-value, $t_{1,8} = 1.8331$, or

$$t = \left| \frac{\overline{X} - \mu}{\frac{s}{\sqrt{n}}} \right| > 1.8331$$

In this problem,

$$t = \frac{\overline{X} - \mu}{\frac{s}{\sqrt{n}}} = \frac{13.5 - 15.5}{\frac{3}{\sqrt{16}}} = -2$$

Since the calculated value for t is less than the critical value of t (found in standard t-tables, -1.8331), one can reject the null hypothesis.

the 16 people who volunteered, the 16 best workers, the 16 biggest problems for the supervisor, or the 16 people who happened to make it to work on a very snowy day. Since you are not provided with information regarding how the sample was selected, it is important to test whether these employees really were representative by comparing their task times prior to the introduction of the new procedures to their times afterward (such as through a paired t-test).

Consider the three possibilities and how they could affect the decision. If the 16 employees' average pretraining assembly time was not statistically different from that of the entire group, then the original conclusion appears valid. If instead their average pretraining task times were statistically larger than that of the group, the results are potentially more impressive. This fact should be brought to the attention of the decision maker as even more evidence that the training is good. However, if their average pretraining assembly time already was statistically lower than 15.5 (especially if it was statistically lower than 13.5), Andrew Peara would need to know that the training might not be as effective as the test first indicated.

2. *A second assumption is that the variance associated with task completion will not be increased.* The original description of the case indicated that the standard deviation is 3 minutes. Since one of the major causes of bottlenecks on assembly lines is increases in variation of assembly time, it is necessary to determine whether the posttraining standard deviation is still 3 minutes. Problems in balancing the line and/or quality control will almost certainly occur with an increase in the variance.

3. *One of the basic assumptions is that there is demand for the extra capacity.* The benefits of achieving this new efficiency can only be realized if either there is demand for additional items or the workers can be used profitably in some other task. If not, regardless of the results of the test, incurring the cost of the new training is not worthwhile.

As with most aspects of decision support, there is no universally correct way to provide this information to the decision maker. The basic options are (a) check the assumptions automatically and note the results on the screen in a pop-up box; (b) check the assumptions automatically and only note the violations of the assumptions on screen; (c) note the assumptions on screen and allow users to decide whether they need to be checked (either individually or as a group); and (d) ignore the assumptions and assume that the users know enough to check them without system help. Clearly, each option has advantages and disadvantages. If we provide total information (the results of the tests on the screen), the user is informed about the reasonableness of the use of the statistic. However, users may find that this information clutters the screen, especially if many assumptions are evaluated for a given test. In addition, users may not take the time to scan the information box and hence may not notice the violations. Similarly, if we simply give the users the option of checking assumptions, they may not take the time because they do not know the value of the additional information. However, if the users are quite knowledgable about their data, this option saves processing time and hence provides a faster response to the user. By not warning the users of the potential problems, we fail to provide decision *support.*

$$\overline{X} = 15.5 - 1.8331 * \frac{3}{\sqrt{16}} = 13.67$$

The remaining option, check the assumptions and list only those that are not validated by the check, provides the support necessary to help users apply the techniques better. In addition, since only problems are noted on the screen, the results do not become tedious and users know they should pay attention to them. Of course, testing the assumptions can take more processing time, and hence slow response time. If this is perceived to be a problem, we can always allow the user to set options to ignore the testing of one or more assumptions prior to running the test. Furthermore, we can build these preferences into a profile for each user so they do not need to be set each time a model is invoked.

In addition to testing assumptions to verify that a model is being appropriately used, the decision maker might simply want to develop a better intuition for the problem. The MBMS should help users investigate more facets of a problem easily. Typically, such additional analyses are menu options, not automatic procedures.

Consider the types of additional analyses that might be undertaken in the problem of the mean task times just considered. Additional analyses are more crucial if the results of the analysis suggest that there is no difference in the two means. Such intuition can be facilitated by the system giving information about the sensitivity of the results to the various conditions of the problem. For example, it might be quite reasonable to provide some information about what mean time would be necessary to produce a statistically significant result. This can be determined by using the same equation, but solving for the sample mean necessary to achieve the critical value of t (from a statistical table), as shown in Computations Box 4.3. So as long as the new procedure takes, on average, less than 13.67 minutes, it will produce a statistically significant improvement. Alternatively, we might want to know how large a sample would have been necessary to obtain significance with the result of an average time of 13.5. Again, it is simply an issue of considering the base formula in a slightly different manner, as shown in Computations Box 4.4.

$$n \geq \left[\frac{\dfrac{(13.5 - 15.5)}{4}}{-1.8331} \right]^2 \geq 3$$

In this case, the results suggest that it was only necessary to have three subjects with the data that are available. If the test had not been significant, and Andrew Peara would want to rerun the test with a different number of subjects, this equation would tell him how many subjects to select.

Example 2

Consider another example, in which a decision maker selects regression to help solve a problem. In this case, a manufacturer wants to know the relationship between the age of machinery and the annual maintenance costs. A sample of 50 machines is taken and the following costs are obtained.

Age	Costs	Age	Costs	Age	Costs
1	81	21	59	41	543
2	35	22	52	42	457
3	114	23	59	43	491
4	36	24	57	44	588
5	91	25	67	45	596
6	134	26	73	46	602
7	45	27	66	47	580
8	130	28	77	48	654
9	170	29	68	49	559
10	141	30	73	50	678
11	188	31	81		
12	145	32	76		
13	220	33	84		
14	119	34	79		
15	134	35	82		
16	196	36	477		
17	154	37	456		
18	207	38	431		
19	188	39	447		
20	226	40	505		

If we constructed a screen for the results of this regression that paralleled that in Figure 4.8, it would look like the one shown in Figure 4.13. It appears from the information provided in Figure 4.13 that the model is good and should be used. However, this is not true. Although the relevant statistical measures of the model have been checked and are significant, they do not convey the complete story about the implications of using this model. Consider the graph of the maintenance data shown in Figure 4.14. With a quick examination of the data, it becomes obvious that there is some phenomenon occurring in the middle of the data. This change in process is undoubtedly affecting the equation. More important from a prediction point of view, of course, is the fact that the equation is not particularly good at predicting costs for those machines. This suggests that the age of the machinery is not sufficient to determine maintenance costs and that some other phenomena need to be considered. From the user's perspective, the graph suggests that while age might be a good indicator in general, it is necessary to understand the maintenance issues better.

It is difficult, even with today's technology, to have the computer scan the graph and alert the decision maker to problems in the data. Since the graph conveys information not communicated by the statistics, it is useful to provide a way for decision makers to get to the graph easily. If the decision makers can be relied on to look at the information, simply providing the ability to view the graph through a click of a button is sufficient. An alternative is to have the graph be part of the screen, as shown in Figure 4.15.

Model-Management Support Tools

The kinds of issues associated with model-generated questions like those in the two examples will, of course, depend on what model is being used. For example, if the decision maker is using linear programming to determine a mix of products

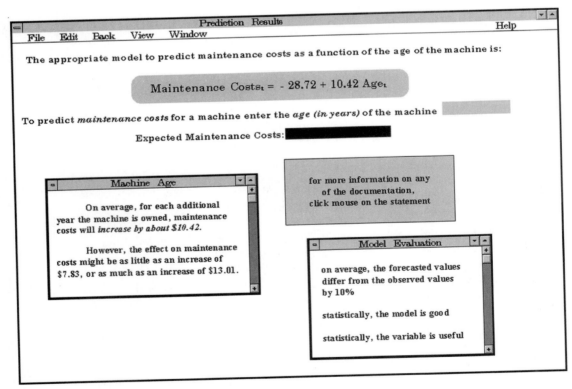

Figure 4.13   Modeling results with some interpretative support.

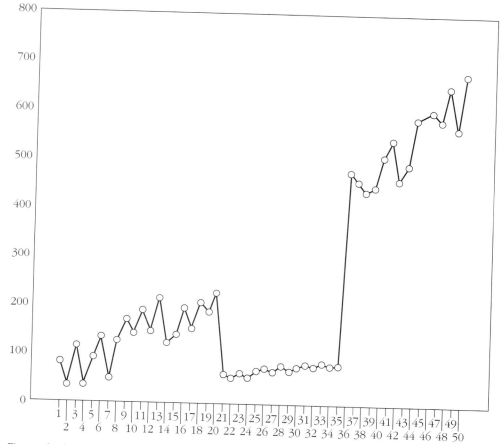

Figure 4.14 Plot of maintenance data.

to produce with a limited set of inputs, then sensitivity analyses will include questions such as (a) What if the company has more of a particular input than specified? (b) What if the company has less of a particular input than specified? (c) What is the impact on production policies if the price of an input changes? (d) What is the impact on production policies if the selling price is changed? and (e) What is the impact if we change the relative input needs of the possible products? Alternatively, if we are using a financial analysis, the questions might be about how present value is affected by discount rate, tax rates, or depreciation.

Further analyses also might be prompted by a particular result of an analysis. For example, suppose that the decision support system has been created to support marketing research for a clothing manufacturer. Suppose further that someone found a result that the demand for high-end trousers was declining in some states but increasing in other states. This might prompt the decision maker to ask questions, such as What do the states where sales are increasing have in common?

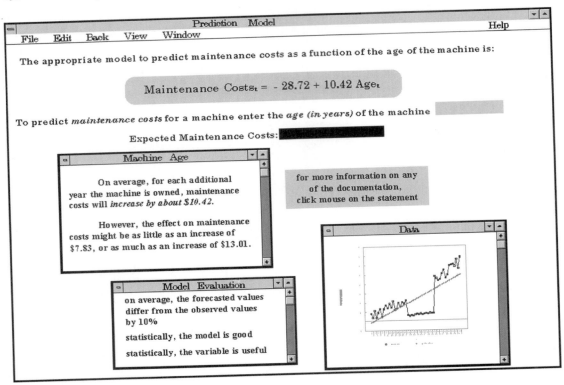

Figure 4.15   Model results with better interpretative support.

and What do the states where sales are decreasing have in common? In particular, the decision maker might be interested in the demographic distribution of the states, the distribution of competitors in the states, and the similarities in income, population, industry, or metropolitan areas in the states. Hence, for the system to be effective, the decision maker should be able to query it about each of these facts. Suppose that in these queries the decision maker finds that the average age of white collar workers is higher in the states where the trousers are selling well than in the states where the trousers are selling poorly. This provides the decision maker with some information. Perhaps the company officials already know that their product appeals to more mature clientele. Then the results probably will not be investigated. However, if decision makers perceive that the product appeals more to younger clientele, this information would suggest a need for further modeling to test the underlying assumptions of the market research efforts.

Perhaps upon receiving the information regarding declining sales, the decision maker who is new has no theories about what could be happening. A good decision support system should be able to help this type of decision maker work through the analyses. For example, it should be able to prompt the decision maker to consider issues such as demographic changes in the area, employment trends, costs of living, and other factors specific to that particular product as shown in Figure 4.16.

Such help might come in terms of a simple "Why?" button available onscreen, as shown in Figure 4.17. Or it might allow appropriate information boxes to appear, such as those shown in Figure 4.17. Alternatively, the decision maker might want to know how the trends are expected to change over the next five years. Another screen might provide information about expected trends.

The important aspect of this kind of support is to provide enough of the appropriate information for the decision maker to understand the phenomenon of interest. The "Why?" button might provide information about automatic analyses among predefined options and display them onscreen. In this way, the decision maker could click the mouse on a particular statement and identify the appropriate analyses that generated it. The result of this action might be the display of all related analyses or it might simply be the display of all significant related analyses. Although each option is appropriate in some cases, a general rule for selecting between these options is the higher in management or the less statistically trained the person, the fewer nonsignificant analytical results the DSS should show.

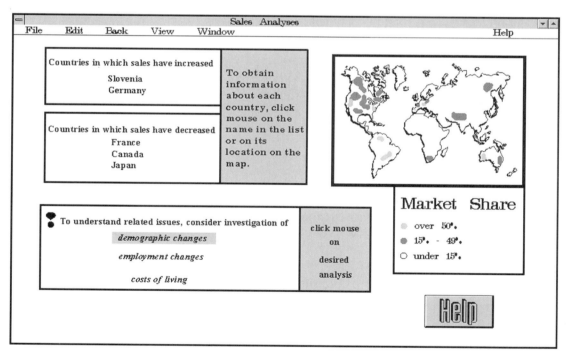

Figure 4.16   Passive prompting for further analyses.

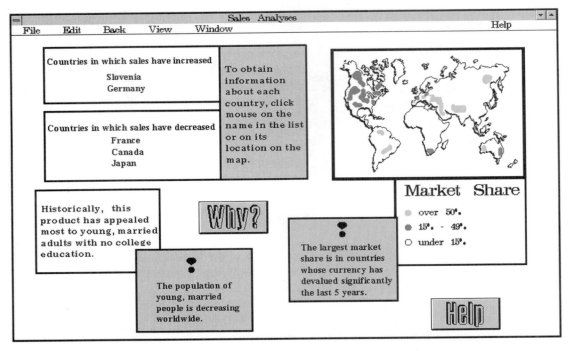

Figure 4.17   Active prompting for further analyses.

Or the Help button might provide information about the kinds of analyses that might be accomplished to further investigate the topic. This differs from the "Why?" button in that it allows the decision maker to explore the relationships through whatever analyses are deemed appropriate. With the "Why?" button, the user is provided "canned" analyses to consider. Alternatively, with this option, the system recommends analyses, but allows the user to select either one of the recommended or a user-defined analyses. Such an option can allow an unknowledgable decision maker to learn more about the decision environment. It can also allow the very knowledgable decision maker to pursue some subtle clue that is suggested by some earlier result.

◆ THE CAR EXAMPLE

A careful consideration of models for the DSS could result in a system that allows users to make truly informed decisions. Models should provide support for all phases of decision making, from the initial generation of alternatives to the final questions of how to finance. In addition, the model-management component should include assistance in the appropriate use of models and intelligence that reviews model use for errors. Finally, where possible, the model-management system should implement heuristics to automate choices where decision makers cannot or do not implement choices.

Brainstorming and Alternative Generation

One important model-management operation is to help users generate alternatives. At the simplest level, alternative generation could include searching for options that meet some criterion specified by the user. Some users will want a car that looks "cool" and goes fast. Others will want a car that will facilitate their car pooling activities or that will be good for trips. Still others will want to consider fuel efficiency or safety in their analysis. Others will just want a car they can afford. The search process is straightforward and was illustrated in Chapter 3.

More likely scenarios, however, are that the user is not sure about the criteria he or she wants to employ or that the user has a general idea of the criteria, but does not understand the specific factors to employ. The DSS should allow users to select any criterion or set of criteria. However, if we put all possible criteria on a screen, users will find the interface both difficult to read and overwhelming to use. If we show only a subset of the possible criteria for consideration, though, we are making choices about the criteria that the decision maker *should* use—this is an inappropriate function for a designer of a DSS. Even if we list all possible criteria but use multiple screens to display them, we are suggesting a relative importance of the criteria by the order in which they are listed.

Hence, the goal is to summarize and guide, while still allowing a great deal of flexibility. One possibility is to categorize criteria and ask users first to specify the *category* of criteria that they want to emphasize. For example, one could provide a menu choice that includes categories, such as comfort, convenience, financial, mechanical, and safety. Using this method, we could ask users to declare their criteria groups under the "Criteria menu," as shown in Figure 4.18. If a user selected "Performance criteria" (as is highlighted), he or she would next select from factors that might be considered performance criteria. This list might include items such as acceleration rates, horsepower, or engine size since these items are clearly linked to performance. Others, however, might consider factors such as fuel efficiency to be a performance characteristic, and so they would be listed, as well. At this screen, decision makers should be able to elect several factors in a category. In this way, decision makers can continue to refine their choice processes.

It is important to help users understand the implications of choices they select. One part of such help is ensuring that the users comprehend the meaning of the terms used in the questions. For example, suppose the user selected safety criteria from the screen shown in Figure 4.18. The next screen to appear would be Figure 4.19. Notice in this figure that there is a question mark icon next to *each* criterion the users are asked to rate. So if the user did not know of the NHTSA or any of its ranking procedures, he or she could click on the question mark icon next to NHTSA, and the system would respond with a pop-up box such as that

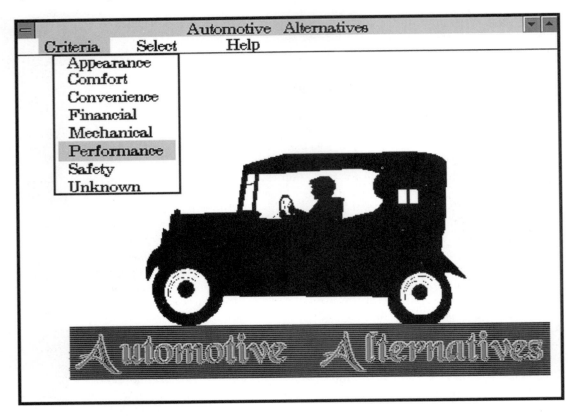

Figure 4.18   Assistance for defining criteria.

shown in Figure 4.20. This box would explain the NHTSA, document the rankings it performs, and discuss the reliability and meaningfulness of its tests.

Another part of the model-management function is to provide users with intelligent help as they proceed through the system. For example, suppose a user selected *none* of the factors listed in Figure 4.19. Since the system would be monitoring these selections, this inaction would trigger the system to fire a demon (daemon) that warns the user of inconsistency in his or her choice of safety as an important criterion without selecting any individual criteria against which the criteria would be evaluated. The kind of result one might get is shown in Figure 4.21 and the Level 5 Object code to achieve it is shown in Figure 4.22.

Rules such as these could be used in an evaluative manner as well. In this way, if users select criteria that are likely to cause them problems, intelligent agents can give them warning. For example, young, unmarried males tend to have very high insurance rates. So, if such a person selected acceleration rate and engine size as the two most important criteria (under the category "Performance"), the system should respond with a warning about the cost of such a decision. This warning would be generated because the following rule would be executed.

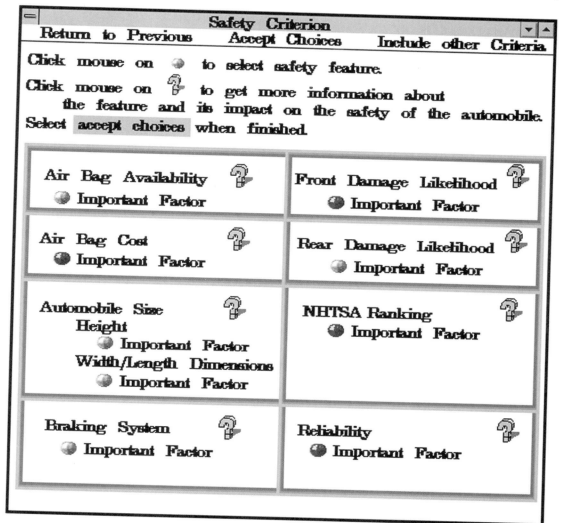

Figure 4.19   Finer detailed definition of criteria.

IF sex IS male AND age ≤ 27 AND marital status IS single
AND Performance Criterion IS acceleration rate AND Performance Criterion
IS engine size
THEN ASK warning display

This would cause a window such as that shown in Figure 4.23 to be displayed.

After the initial evaluations are completed, we might create a scratch sheet onto which users could keep track of automobiles under consideration. A sample of a screen of this type is shown in Figure 4.24; this figure illustrates an actual screen

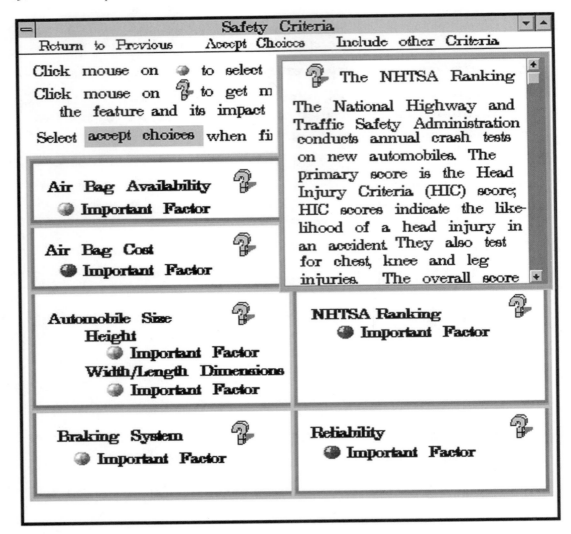

Figure 4.20   Content-dependent assistance of criteria selection.

from the commercial product *Which & Why*. The goal is to have a scratch pad onto which users can keep notes and the system can keep statistics.

Flexibility Concerns

Three possible problems are suggested with this plan. First, users who already know the models of automobiles they want to consider will find this option difficult. It is inappropriate to have these users go through the process of selecting

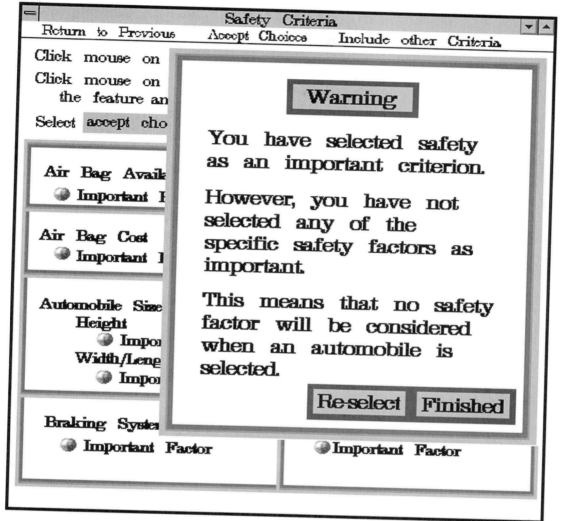

Figure 4.21   Support for criteria definition.

general criteria and specific factors and consider multiple automobiles so as to screen them down to a conclusion at which they have already arrived. Since they know what automobile or automobiles they want to consider, the process should be straightforward. These users can use the "Select" menu to choose one or more automobiles directly and proceed in the analysis from there.

A second problem is the user who wants to select a mixed strategy. This user wants some characteristics specified under multiple categories. For example, the

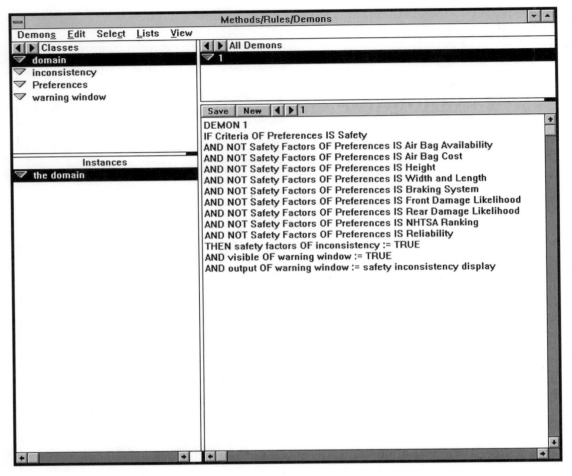

Figure 4.22   Level 5 Object code to generate assistance.

user might want an automobile that has a high fuel efficiency as well as a good safety record. This type of user also can be accommodated if the system allows the user to move into other criteria categories from the secondary screens. So when the user has selected issues of importance under the safety criterion, for example, he or she can then select the option "Identify other Criteria" and be given the list of criteria not yet selected, including Appearance, Comfort, Convenience, Financial, Mechanical, and Performance, as shown in Figure 4.25.

The third problem is the user who has absolutely no idea how to select an automobile. In this case, the model-management system should help users brainstorm criteria with intelligent agents. Specifically, the system should invoke an expert system that focuses on lifestyle questions and generates a set of criteria based on the

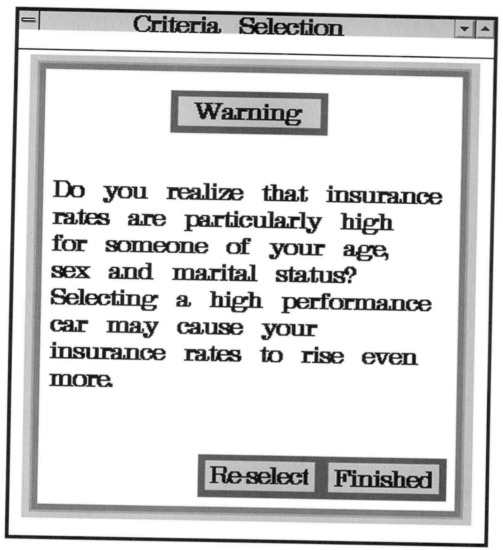

Figure 4.23 Intelligent support in a DSS.

user's answers. The system would ask users questions and process the answers based on rules developed by designers. For example, a rule such as

IF monthly disposable income < 200 THEN Criteria OF Preferences IS Financial

would tell the system to select financial criteria as paramount for those users who would have difficulty making car payments, especially when coupled with maintenance, insurance, and upkeep costs. However, another rule

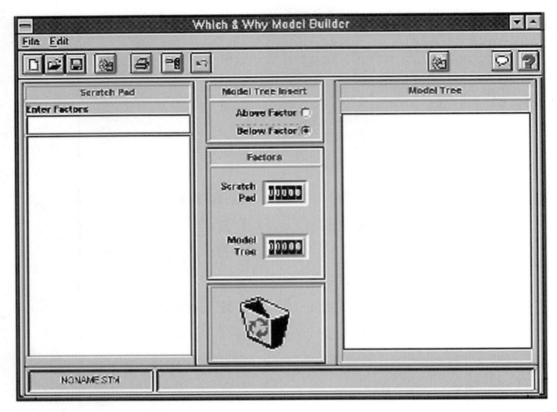

Figure 4.24   Brainstorming support tools.

IF monthly disposable income > 1200 AND number of children ≥ 3
AND primary usage IS car pooling THEN Criteria OF Preferences IS Convenience

would tell the system to consider convenience criteria instead. While there is nothing prohibiting these users from considering cost as a factor, the system would indicate that it is not the primary criterion to be considered. In addition, the system should recommend criteria that should not be applied to the selection of automobiles.

Evaluating Alternatives

As decision makers consider various automobiles, they compare the benefits and costs associated with owning each of them. How they compare them depends on the criteria selected. For example, some decision makers might select the automobile that has the greatest number of desirable features available at the lowest

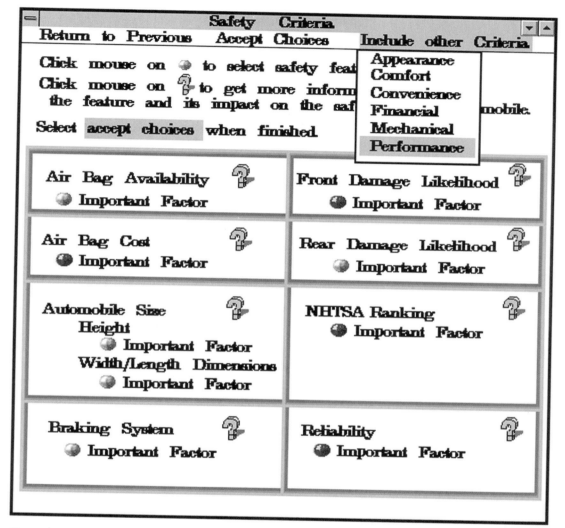

Figure 4.25 Support for multi-criterion choices.

cost. Others may rely heavily on the performance statistics and feel of the drive. Still others may select the automobile that comes most highly recommended by a trusted source.

Part of the modeling function of an automobile DSS is helping the decision maker to compare the functions he or she thinks are important. As with the original definition of the criteria, it is important to view these a limited number at a time. For example, consider the screen taken from the commercial package *AutoAnswers*, shown in Figure 4.26. A very limited number of items is shown in this screen, all under the category "General." As you can see in Figure 4.27, a drop-down menu allows users to select information from a variety of categories. Each category gives information on a limited number of features so as not to overwhelm the user. Of course, an improvement on this approach would be to list the information for multiple alternatives in charts such as these. In that way, users could *compare* the automobiles on the criteria of importance and see how they relate. A system might, in addition, provide a relative score for each automobile in each category, or a highlighting of that automobile that seems to provide better values on the factors, so the user can easily see if there is a dominant alternative among the cars under consideration.

Users might also want the opinion of trusted sources in the evaluation. Publications such as *Consumer Reports*, *Kiplinger's Reports*, *Car and Driver*, and *Edmund's Guides* conduct tests and rate automobiles in various areas. Tables such

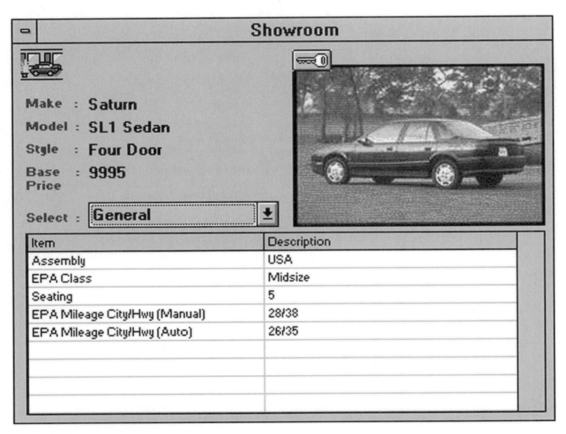

Figure 4.26   Results from analysis using *AutoAnswers*.

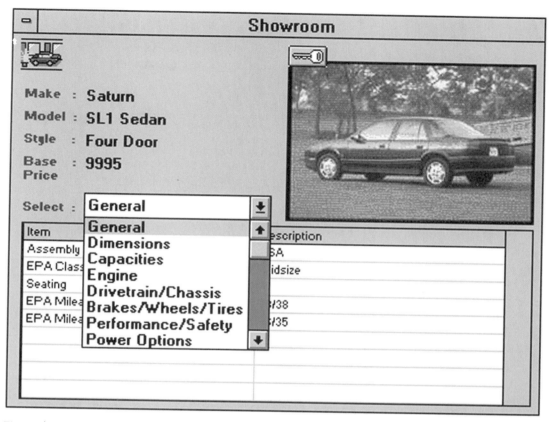

Figure 4.27   *AutoAnswers* menu for examination of other criteria.

as that shown in Figure 4.28 could be incorporated into the system. Users might want to couple this with raw access to text files with reports on automobiles. An example is shown in Figure 4.29, which illustrates part of the *Edmund's Guide* available on the Internet.

Another task for which the DSS could be helpful is in the estimation of the real costs associated with the automobile. Generally, novice users who have not owned a car previously examine only the car payments in an estimation of the cost. Consider Figure 4.30, through which the user is asked about his or her driving tendencies. Once the user responds about the amount of driving completed in a month, the system computes the operation costs, as shown in Figure 4.31. In order to complete these computations, the system must query the system databases regarding the fuel efficiency on the highway as well as in the city and use those with the approximate number of miles driven to compute the amount of gasoline the user could be expected to consume; this multiplied by the cost per gallon of gasoline results in expenditures for gasoline. This result is added to the average monthly maintenance costs that are derived by dividing annual maintenance costs found in the database by the 12 months in a year. The result of these operations is shown in Figure 4.32. The DSS would serve the user considering multiple au-

Test judgments

Performance

Acceleration .... ◑
Transmission .... ◑
Routine handling .... ◗
Emergency handling .... ◗
Braking .... ◗

Comfort

Ride, normal load .... ○
Ride, full load .... ○
Noise .... ◗
Driving position .... ◗
Front-seat comfort .... ◑
Rear-seat comfort .... ◗
Climate-control system .... ◑

Convenience

Access .... ◗
Controls and displays .... ◗
Trunk .... ◗

Other

Fuel economy .... ●
Predicted reliability .... ○

Reliability history

Pontiac Bonneville

TROUBLE
SPOTS   '88 '89 '90 '91 '92 '93

Engine
Engine cooling
Fuel system
Ignition system
Auto. transmission
Man. transmission
Clutch
Driveline
Electrical system
Steering/suspension
Brakes
Exhaust system
Body rust
Pain and trim
Body integrity
Body hardware
Air-conditioning

Safety Information

Driver air bag .... Standard
Passenger air bag .... Standard
Antilock brakes .... Standard
Traction control .... Optional
Side-impact protection claimed .... No
Drive crash protection .... ◑
Passenger crash protection .... ○
Injury claim rate compared with all cars .... ◗
Injury claim rate compared with large
    cars .... ◗
Comprehensive and collision insurance
    cost .... Low

Figure 4.28 *Consumer Reports* data that could be accessed from a DSS. Adapted from *Consumer Reports* 1995 New Car Yearbook, Yonkers, NY: Consumers Union, 1995, p. 102.

tomobiles by providing the information in tabular form coupled with historical information, such as that shown in Figure 4.33.

Models could also help the user with one of the most confusing aspects of purchasing an automobile: financing. For example, they could be built to evaluate car prices under a variety of financing alternatives. Consider the model shown in Figure 4.34. This system allows users to explore the impact of various time periods for loans and various interest rates on the payment schedule. The choice of both time period and interest rate would be left for the user to specify. Once these are selected, the loan payment schedule table (bottom right) would be populated. If the user requests advice by pressing the "Recommend Values" button, the system would respond with information about current interest rates and loan periods at local financing institutions. In addition, the DSS could provide historical trends and forecasts of future values. In this way, users can evaluate the impact of different

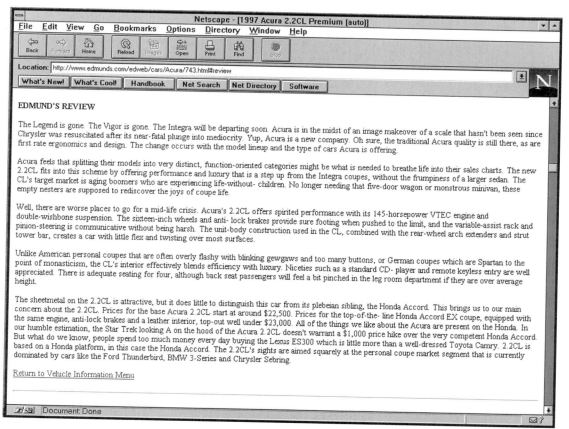

Figure 4.29 Edmund's car review available on the Internet.

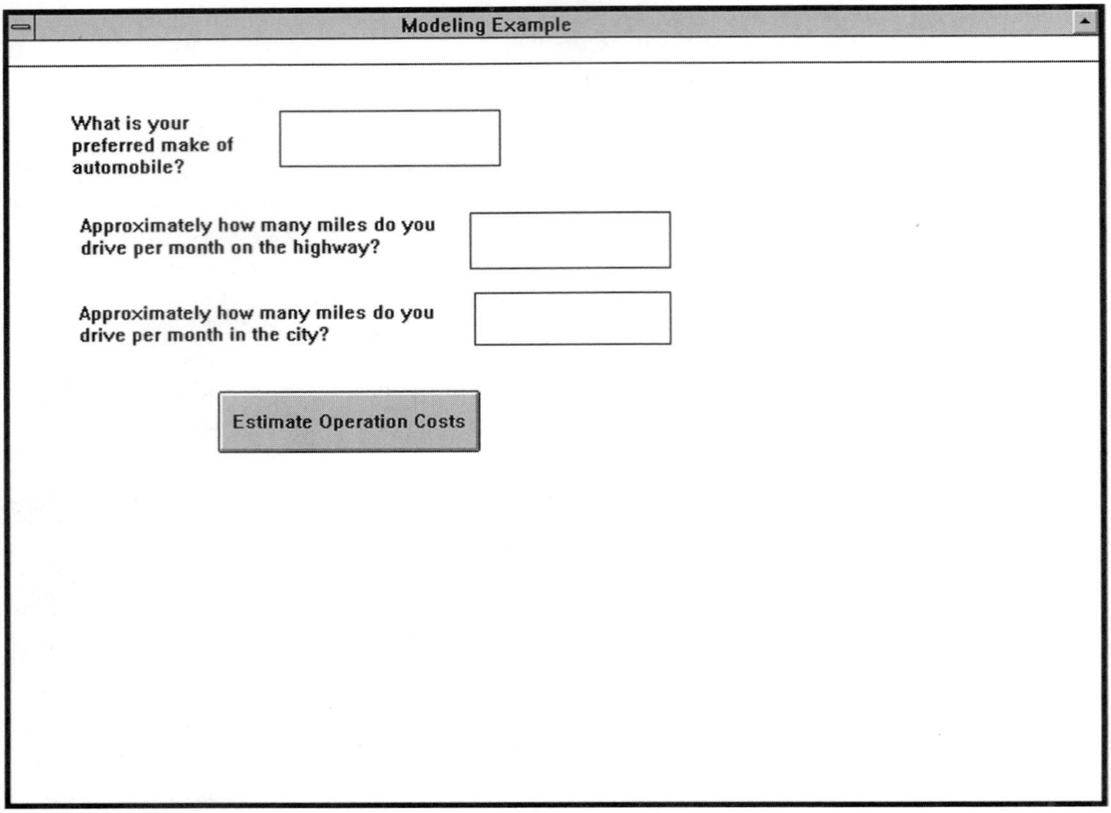

Figure 4.30 Queries like these are designed to help the user better understand his or her choices.

interest rates for different term loans, special rebates, free add-ons, low down payment, or no down payment.

The DSS should also provide intelligent assistance for these experiments by guiding the user. For example, it could recommend sound sensitivity procedures such as maintaining some variables constant from one experiment to the next. Since altering too many variables results in confusing analyses, the system should warn when such comparisons are being conducted. For example, the user should be warned about comparing a four-year loan at 7 percent to a five-year loan at 7.75 percent with a different down payment.

The ability to take into account the time value of money may provide a key tool to some users. Some users' decisions may weigh heavily on the net present value (NPV) of a purchase rather than on the financing specifics of a purchase. Given this need, users should be able to compare NPV results under a variety of purchase options.

Note that in Figure 4.34, the left side of the screen provides information about the cost of the automobile. The information is a function of the automobile se-

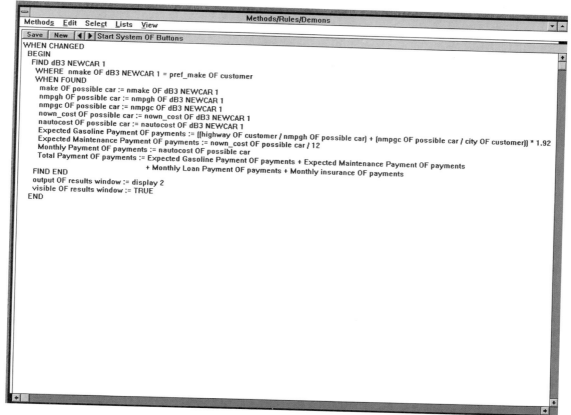

Figure 4.31 Level 5 Object code to support analysis in Figures 4.30 and 4.32.

lected and the options selected for that make and model of automobile. Since these selections were made by the user on previous screens, it is important for the system to carry the values through to this screen *automatically*; the user should not need to re-enter the values or even remember what they were. If the user wants to change the options or review the reasons for the cost, he or she could select the "Review" button on the screen in Figure 4.34 and return to those screens from which the selections are made. Similarly, the system should bring the information about likely dealer discount from the database automatically as well as the information about taxes and license. If the system facilitates the trade-in of used automobiles, that information should be brought forward as well.

The system might also help the user compare purchase with a lease agreement. It could help the user evaluate the options for lease most appropriate for his or her specific needs. The user may be faced with options such as low or no interest, given a particular down payment, or cash back instead of the special interest rates.

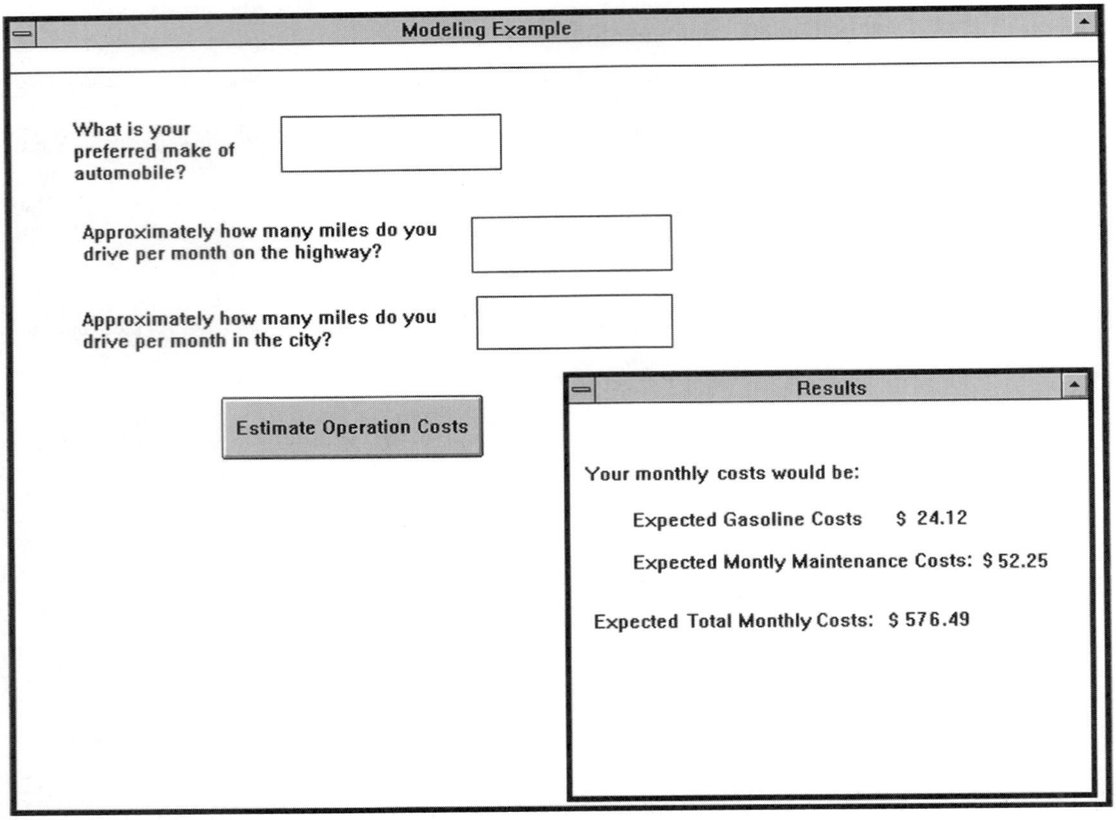

Figure 4.32 Decision support results.

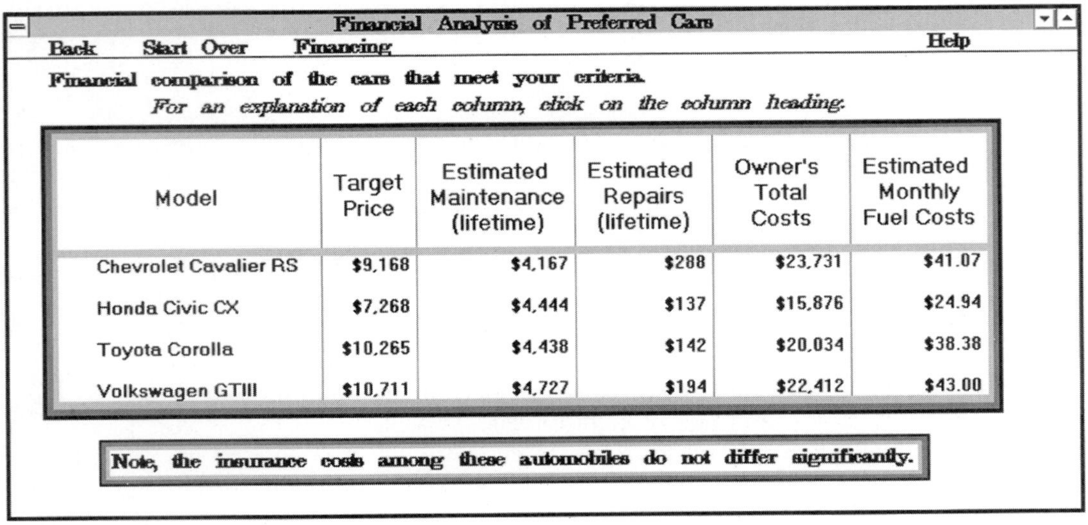

Model	Target Price	Estimated Maintenance (lifetime)	Estimated Repairs (lifetime)	Owner's Total Costs	Estimated Monthly Fuel Costs
Chevrolet Cavalier RS	$9,168	$4,167	$288	$23,731	$41.07
Honda Civic CX	$7,268	$4,444	$137	$15,876	$24.94
Toyota Corolla	$10,265	$4,438	$142	$20,034	$38.38
Volkswagen GTIII	$10,711	$4,727	$194	$22,412	$43.00

Figure 4.33 Historical information to facilitate support.

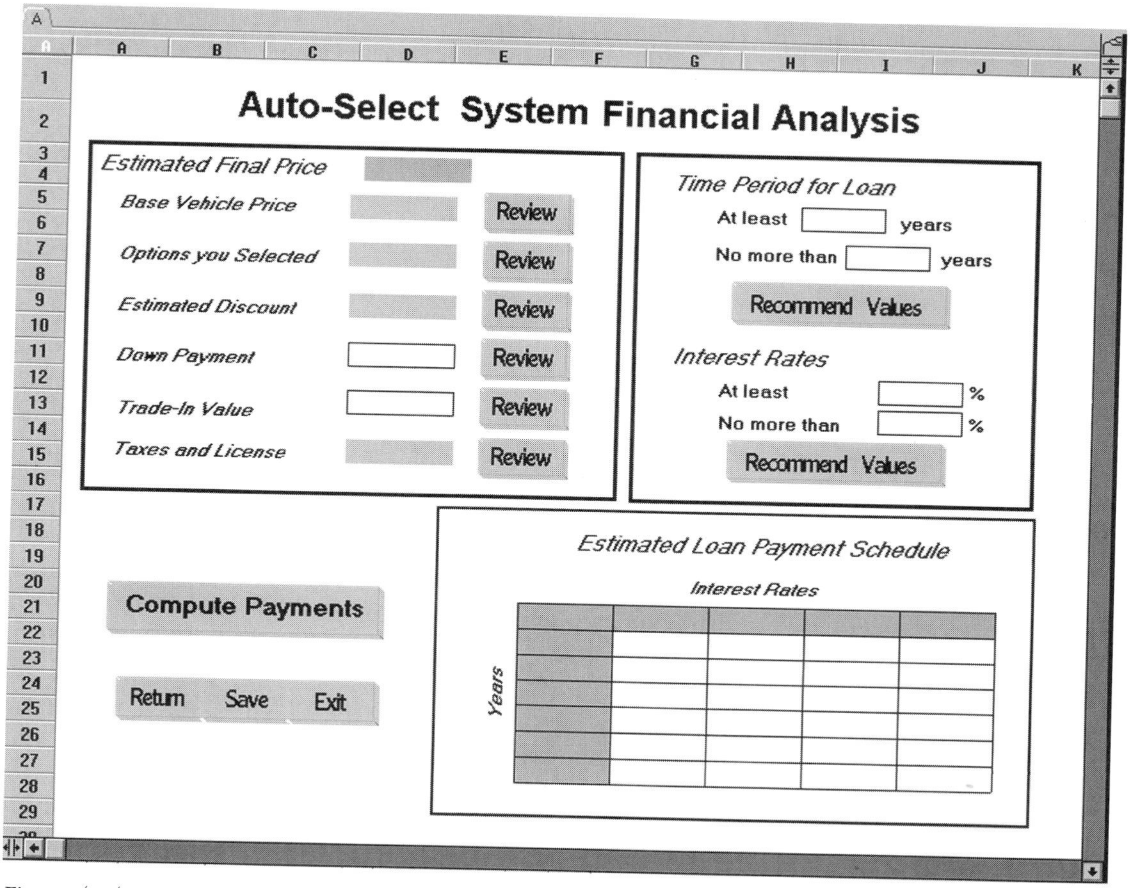

Figure 4.34 Support for users when exploring assumptions.

Running External Models

Often we use external programs to obtain all the modeling support we need. There are a variety of ways of implementing models depending on the environment in which one is operating. On one hand, integration may be simply facilitating the user's access to external modeling packages. For example, suppose decision makers needed access to the package *Lotus 1-2-3* to facilitate financial modeling. Using Level 5 Object, designers could create a push button that invoked the following code:

```
WHEN CHANGED
 BEGIN
  ACTIVATE "IPU,EXTERN,123.exe"
 END
```

This code would cause a batch file that sets the appropriate environment settings to allow the package *Lotus 1-2-3* to run. If *Lotus* were invoked with macros running, the user could be led through particular analyses and shielded from the normal menu options. Of course, the code does not pass parameters to the program or back to the DSS. Furthermore, the code does not provide any of the model-management functions discussed earlier in the book. Hence, it is not a desirable option. It would be preferable to have models and their management a part of the DSS.

DISCUSSION

The goal of the model management component of a DSS is to help decision makers understand the phenomenon about which they are making a choice. This understanding helps decision makers generate alternatives, measure the worth of those alternatives and make a choice. Additionally, the model management component should have tools that help the decision maker use the models and evaluate the results effectively. Designers need to include both passive and active assistance for the decision makers. Context-specific help for using and interpreting models needs to be available for the user. In addition, the system should monitor violations in the assumptions of models, the irregularities of their use, and make the user aware. Finally, all of this support should be easy for the decision maker to understand and not threatening from a technical point of view.

QUESTIONS

1. What is a model and why would a manager use one?

2. Does a CASE tool use models? Describe them. Is it a decision support system? If not, explain why it does not have the attributes of a DSS. If so, explain how we might design CASE tools better by considering DSS technology?

3. Suppose you are developing a DSS to aid an MIS manager in deciding how to acquire computers and computer components for her company. What kinds of models would you provide in such a system? How would these models need to be integrated? What kinds of model-management support do we need to facilitate model understandability and/or sensitivity of a decision?

4. What are the long-term implications for business when too much intelligence is included in a DSS?

5. How can a designer improve the users' understanding of results of a model in a DSS?

6. Suppose you were using a DSS to decide what courses to take for the next semester. What kinds of models would you need? What kinds of sensitivity analyses would you do?

7. How can a designer ensure models in a DSS are integrated?

8. How can a DSS decrease a manager's anxiety about using models?

◆ O N   T H E   W E B ◆

On the Web for this chapter provides additional information about models, model base management systems, and related tools. Links can provide access to demonstration packages, general overview information, applications, software providers, tutorials, and more. Additional discussion questions and new applications will also be added as they become available.

- *Links provide access to information about model and model management products.* Links provide access to product information, product comparisons and reviews, and general information about both models and the tools that support the models. Users can try the models and determine the factors that facilitate and inhibit decision making.

- *Links provide access to descriptions of applications and insights for applications.* In addition to information about the tools themselves, the Web provides links to worldwide applications of those products. You can access chronicles of users' successes and failures as well as innovative applications.

- *Links provide access to hints about how to use models.* These links provide real world insights into the use *and misuse* of models. These are descriptive, and help users to better formulate model management needs.

- *Links provide access to models regarding automobile purchase and leasing.* Several tools to help users purchase or lease an automobile are available on the Web. You can scan links to determine what kinds of models are most useful under what circumstances. Further, you can determine what kinds of impediments and what kinds of model support are introduced by various modeling management tools. Finally, the links can provide evaluations for model management capabilities.

You can access material for this chapter from the general WWW Page for the book, or directly from the following URL.
http://www.umsl.edu/~sauter/DSS/mbms.html

SUGGESTED READINGS

Baldwin, A.A., D. Baldwin, and T.K. Sen, "The evolution and problems of model management research," *Omega: Int. J. of Mgmt. Sci.*, 19(6), 1991, pp. 511–528.

Betts, M., "Efficiency einsteins," *ComputerWorld*, 27(12), March 22, 1993, pp. 63–64.

Bhargava, H.K. and S.O. Kimbrough, "Model management: An embedded languages approach," *Decision Support Systems*, 1993.

Bonczek, R.H., C.W. Holsapple, and A.B. Whinston, "The evolving roles of models in decision support systems," *Decision Sciences*, 11(2), 1980, pp. 616–631.

Brightman, H.J., *Statistics in Plain English*, Cincinnati, OH: Southwestern Publishing Company, 1986.

Fedorowicz, J. and G.B. Williams, "Representing modeling knowledge in an intelligent decision support system," *Decision Support Systems*, 2(1), pp. 3–14.

Geoffrion, A.M., "Computer-based modeling environments," *European Journal of Operational Research* 41, 1989, pp. 33–45.

Hillier, F.S. and G.J. Lieberman, *Introduction to Operations Research, Fourth Edition*, Oakland, CA: Holden-Day, Inc., 1986.

Holsapple, C.W. and A.B. Winston, *Decision support systems: A knowledge-based approach*, St. Paul, MN: West Publishing Company, 1996.

Huff, D., *How to Lie with Statistics*, New York: W.W. Norton and Company, 1954.

Huh, S.Y., "Modelbase construction with object-oriented constructs," *Decision Sciences*, 24(2), Spring, 1993, pp. 409–434.

King, D.L., "Intelligent support systems: art, augumentation and agents," in Sprague, R.H., Jr. and H.J. Watson (eds.), *Decision Support Systems: Putting Theory into Practice Third Edition*, Englewood Cliffs, NJ: Prentice-Hall, 1993, pp. 137–160.

Konsynski, B., and D. Dolk, "Knowledge abstractions in model management," in Gray P. (ed.), *Decision Support and Executive Information Systems*, Englewood Cliffs, NJ: Prentice-Hall, 1994, pp. 420–437.

Le Blanc, L.A. and M.T. Jelassi, "DSS Software Selection: A multiple criteria decision Methodology," in Sprague R.H., Jr. and H.J. Watson, (eds.), *Decision Support Systems: Putting Theory into Practice Third Edition*, Englewood Cliffs, NJ: Prentice-Hall, 1993, pp. 100–114.

Nord, R. and E. Schmitz, "A decision support system for personnel allocation in the U.S.

Army," in Gray P. (ed.), *Decision Support and Executive Information Systems*, Englewood Cliffs, NJ: Prentice-Hall, 1994, pp. 191–201.

Port, O., "Smart programs go to work," *Business Week*, March 2, 1995, pp. 97–99.

Sauter, V.L., "The Effect of 'Experience' upon Information Preferences," *Omega*, Volume 13, Number 4, June, 1985, pp. 277–284.

Sauter, V.L., "A framework for studying the mergers of public organizations," *Socioeconomic Planning Sciences*, Volume 19, Number 2, 1985, pp. 137–144.

Sauter, V.L. and M.B. Mandell, "Using decision support concepts to increase the utilization of social science information in policy-making," *Evaluation and Program Planning*, 13, 1990, pp. 349–358.

Sprague, R.H. and H.J. Watson, *Decision Support for Management*, Upper Saddle River, NJ: Prentice-Hall, 1996.

Star, J. and J. Estes, *Geographic Information Systems*, Englewood Cliffs, NJ: Prentice-Hall, 1990.

Sullivan, G. and K. Fordyce, "Decision simulation: one outcome of combining artificial intelligence and decision support systems," in Gray P. (ed.), *Decision Support and Executive Information Systems*, Englewood Cliffs, NJ: Prentice-Hall, 1994, pp. 409–419.

Wonnacott, T.H. and R.J. Wonnacott, *Introductory Statistics for Business and Economics, Second Edition*, New York: John Wiley & Sons, 1977.

Intelligence and Decision Support Systems

◆ ◆ ◆

Since the establishment of computers as business tools, designers have planned for the day when systems could work on their own, either as decision makers or as partners in the decision making context. Computers such as these would use *artificial intelligence*, which is the emulation of human expertise by the computer through the encapsulation of knowledge *in a particular domain* and procedures for acting on that knowledge. The advantage of artificial intelligence is that the computers would not be prone to the forgetfulness, bias, or distractions that plague human decision makers. Such systems would help us make better decisions, protect us from unanticipated events, and even provide companionship of a sort as the computer played games such as chess with us. Unfortunately, many factors ranging from unreasonable expectations to insufficient developments in hardware once stood in the way of this goal.

During the 1980s, when smaller, faster processors and storage media were first becoming available, many thought the area of "expert systems" would provide a focused use of artificial intelligence and solve problems that usually could be tamed only by an expert or a group of experts, because they required a human reasoning process. This required computers to use symbols in the analysis and to understand, interpret, and manipulate the symbols just as humans do. Such systems would address problems normally requiring an individual to amass large amounts of data and knowledge about a field and process those data using sophisticated reasoning as well as accepted rules of thumb.

For example, early uses of expert systems provided diagnostic assistance to physicians. *CADUCEUS*, developed at Carnegie-Mellon University, provided medical diagnosis of internal medicine problems, and *MYCIN*, developed at Stanford University, provided diagnostics regarding blood diseases. As design and implementation technologies improved, expert systems moved to business applications. Digital Equipment Corporation deployed *XCON*, an expert system to construct systems by determining the set of wires, cabinets, and parts necessary to meet the user's computing needs. Similarly, Peat Marwick developed *Loan Probe* to assist auditors in assessing commercial banks' loan losses and reserves in order to help auditors determine whether the banks could cover bad debt. American Express used *Authorizer's Assistant* to facilitate quick and consistent credit authorization. *Oxiscan*, developed by Oxicron Systems Corp., analyzed market data for product managers by performing statistical analyses on scanner data and then interpreting the results.

Although expert systems were successful from a technological perspective, they were not accepted from a managerial perspective. The proof managers needed about the effectiveness of the systems was not available. In addition, many such

---

◆ **DDS Design Insights** ◆

The acceptance of artificial intelligence has not been universal. Some managers just do not trust the computers to understand all the interworkings of the choice context. Other managers have concerns about the legal ramifications of a wrong choice.

Still other decision makers just do not believe in the reasoning process of computers. One example of this disbelief was expressed by Garry Kasparov when he defended his World Chess Champion position against Deep Blue, an IBM computer programmed to play chess. In the first game of the match, the computer made a move that Kasparov judged to be "a wonderful and extremely human move." However, Kasparov had difficulty responding to the move because a computer "would never make such a move." Kasparov judged that although humans regularly see the impact, "a computer can't 'see' the long-term consequences of structural changes in the position or understand how changes in pawn formations may be good or bad."

In fact, he was so sure that the computer could not reason that he was "stunned" by the move. While he had played chess against many computers before Deep Blue, this move caused him to "feel—I could *smell*—a new kind of intelligence across the table." Unfortunately for Kasparov, the computer had, in fact, psyched him out with the move and actually won the game.

Kasparov, however, showed that the human's intelligence was still superior because the experience forced him to think of the shortcomings of computers througout the remainder of the match and use that information strategically in his play development. For example, he changed moves in a well-known opening sequence in one game. Since the new opening was not stored in the database, Deep Blue could not find an appropriate plan to respond to it. Neither could Deep Blue reason that Kasparov's change from the well-known sequence was meaningless and respond with a known response. In the end, Kasparov won the tournament and kept his title.

Kasparov, G., "The day that I sensed a new kind of intelligence," *Time Magazine*, March 25, 1996, p. 55.

systems were developed on specialized, standalone hardware that did not interface with any existing data or applications. As a result, they never were integrated into the business plan.

The technology was established, however. The current trend (expected to continue to the next millennium) is to embed artificial intelligence and expert systems tools into decision support systems. For example, the U.S. Army uses embedded expert systems in its logistics planning. Similarly, Putnam has embedded intelligence into its trading software to monitor for compliance with regulations. In fact, a 1995 survey by the Commerce Department indicated that more than 70 percent of the top 500 U.S. companies use some form of artificial intelligence in their operations. The intelligence might be embedded in the DSS to help select what data should be analyzed or how the data should be analyzed. Similarly, artificial intelligence might help decision makers to complete sensitivity analyses to ensure that all aspects of the problem have been examined. It might identify aspects of the problem that have been overlooked and relate the current findings to previous analyses or data. Instead of replacing the decision maker, the artificial intelligence is built into the DSS to help the decision maker exploit the tools and the data more fully.

Many DSS include features that facilitate data mining. Through the help of artificial intelligence and statistical analyses, these features find information from existing data. In addition, the system determines how to present that new knowledge so that it is understandable to humans. Other DSSs use embedded neural networks that are trained by examples to recognize patterns and aberrations. For example, changes in purchasing patterns might identify credit cards that are stolen. In fact, MasterCard International uses such systems. "The software is so effective that it regularly notices that a card is stolen before the owner does." (Port, 1995). Still other systems provide hybrid applications of a variety of artificial intelligence tools. For example, combinations of tools that derive conclusions from data and perform inductive reasoning facilitate DSS that provide support for the convertible-bond market.

Over time, almost all DSS will include some kind of artificial intelligence. At present, artificial intelligence tends to be associated with choices needing some expertise where the expert is not always available or is expensive, where decisions are made quickly, and where there are too many possibilities for an individual to consider at one time and there is a high penalty associated with missing one or more factors. Artificial intelligence is helpful, too, when consistency and reliability in judgments—not creativity in the choice process—are the paramount goals.

Currently, the greatest promise lies in hybrid systems that combine both expert systems and neural nets. The capture and preservation of human expertise is best done by expert systems, but they, like humans, do not adjust to changes readily. Neural nets, on the other hand, are not good repositories for human expertise, but they are trained to continue to learn. They can examine large amounts of data and find causal relationships that help them adapt to changes in their environment. Together, the two technologies can provide ongoing support within a DSS.

To build artificial intelligence into the system, two primary topics need to be addressed: how to program "reasoning" and what to do with uncertainty in the decision making context. These will be addressed in the next two sections.

◆ PROGRAMMING REASONING

The reasoning process in humans is often automatic or implicit, and hence it is difficult to see how it might be programmed in a set of deliberate steps for a computer. If, however, we examine the reasoning process slowly and deliberately through its individual steps, we can see how the computer completes the reasoning process. Actually, reasoning by both humans and computers must take one of two basic approaches. Either we begin with a goal and try to prove that it is true with the facts we have available, or we begin with all the "known facts" and try to prove as much as we can. In computer terms, these are referred to as *backward reasoning* and *forward reasoning*, respectively. The following examples demonstrate deliberate examples of backward and forward reasoning and the manner in which intelligence can be built into DSS. Both examples use the same information to illustrate the differences in the processes.

Suppose there is a set of facts, known as Fact A, Fact B, Fact C, Fact D, Fact E, Fact F, Fact G, and Fact H. All these facts are logical facts, and they can be set either to *true* or *false*. In addition, there are certain known relationships among the facts. These are listed in the order in which they might appear in the code:

R1: ➤ IF Fact E and Fact M and Fact G are all true, THEN Fact F is true;
R2: ➤ IF Fact K and Fact E are both true, THEN Fact D is true;
R3: ➤ IF Fact N is true, THEN Fact Y is true;
R4: ➤ IF Fact Y is true, THEN Fact H is true;
R5: ➤ IF Fact B and Fact G are both true, THEN Fact M is true;
R6: ➤ IF Fact K and Fact F are both true, THEN Fact Y is true;
R7: ➤ IF Fact K is true, THEN Fact B is true.

The ways these relationships are processed are quite different with backward and forward chaining.

Backward Chaining Reasoning

In backward chaining, we begin with a goal and attempt to prove it. For example, suppose the goal is to prove that Fact H is true. The system will process the relationships, beginning with the first one it encounters that proves the goal (in this case, Fact H) to be true.

R1: ➤ IF Fact E and Fact M and Fact G are all true, THEN Fact F is true;
R2: ➤ IF Fact K and Fact E are both true, THEN Fact D is true;

R3: ➤ IF Fact N is true, THEN Fact Y is true;
R4: ➤ IF Fact Y is true, THEN Fact H is true;
R5: ➤ IF Fact B and Fact G are both true, THEN Fact M is true;
R6: ➤ IF Fact K and Fact F are both true, THEN Fact Y is true;
R7: ➤ IF Fact K is true, THEN Fact B is true.

In order to prove Relationship 4, it is necessary to prove that Fact Y is true. Hence, proving that Fact Y is true is now the goal of the system. It will again process rules.

R1: ➤ IF Fact E and Fact M and Fact G are all true, THEN Fact F is true;
R2: ➤ IF Fact K and Fact E are both true, THEN Fact D is true;
R3: ➤ IF Fact N is true, THEN Fact Y is true;
R4: ➤ IF Fact Y is true, THEN Fact H is true;
R5: ➤ IF Fact B and Fact G are both true, THEN Fact M is true;
R6: ➤ IF Fact K and Fact F are both true, THEN Fact Y is true;
R7: ➤ IF Fact K is true, THEN Fact B is true.

To prove Relationship 3, it is necessary to prove that Fact N is true. We can see from the seven relationships that there is nothing from which the system can infer whether Fact N is true. Hence, the system is forced either to use a default value (if one is specified) or ask the user. Suppose there is no default value given and the user does not know whether Fact N is true. Under these circumstances, the system is *unable* to infer that Fact N is true, so it assumes *nothing* about the validity of Fact N. However, it must locate another relationship in order to infer that Fact Y is true.

R1: ➤ IF Fact E and Fact M and Fact G are all true, THEN Fact F is true;
R2: ➤ IF Fact K and Fact E are both true, THEN Fact D is true;
R3: ➤ IF Fact N is true, THEN Fact Y is true;
R4: ➤ IF Fact Y is true, THEN Fact H is true;
R5: ➤ IF Fact B and Fact G are both true, THEN Fact M is true;
R6: ➤ IF Fact K and Fact F are both true, THEN Fact Y is true;
R7: ➤ IF Fact K is true, THEN Fact B is true.

To prove Relationship 6, it is necessary to prove that Fact K and Fact F are true. The system begins with trying to prove Fact K. As with Fact N, there are no relationships from which one can infer that Fact K is known. The system then must use a default value (if one is specified) or ask the user. Suppose in this case that the user knows that Fact K is true, and hence the system attempts to prove that Fact F is true.

R1: ➤ IF Fact E and Fact M and Fact G are all true, THEN Fact F is true;
R2: ➤ IF Fact K and Fact E are both true, THEN Fact D is true;
R3: ➤ IF Fact N is true, THEN Fact Y is true;

R4: ➤ IF Fact Y is true, THEN Fact H is true;
R5: ➤ IF Fact B and Fact G are both true, THEN Fact M is true;
R6: ➤ IF Fact K and Fact F are both true, THEN Fact Y is true;
R7: ➤ IF Fact K is true, THEN Fact B is true.

As with Fact N, there are no relationships from which one can infer the value of Fact E (whether or not it is true). The system then must use a default value (if one is specified) or ask the user. Suppose in this case that the user knows that the value of Fact E is known as true, and hence the system attempts to prove that Fact M is true.

R1: ➤ IF Fact E and Fact M and Fact G are all true, THEN Fact F is true;
R2: ➤ IF Fact K and Fact E are both true, THEN Fact D is true;
R3: ➤ IF Fact N is true, THEN Fact Y is true;
R4: ➤ IF Fact Y is true, THEN Fact H is true;
R5: ➤ IF Fact B and Fact G are both true, THEN Fact M is true;
R6: ➤ IF Fact K and Fact F are both true, THEN Fact Y is true;
R7: ➤ IF Fact K is true, THEN Fact B is true.

The first step in that process is to establish that Fact B is true.

R1: ➤ IF Fact E and Fact M and Fact G are all true, THEN Fact F is true;
R2: ➤ IF Fact K and Fact E are both true, THEN Fact D is true;
R3: ➤ IF Fact N is true, THEN Fact Y is true;
R4: ➤ IF Fact Y is true, THEN Fact H is true;
R5: ➤ IF Fact B and Fact G are both true, THEN Fact M is true;
R6: ➤ IF Fact K and Fact F are both true, THEN Fact Y is true;
R7: ➤ IF Fact K is true, THEN Fact B is true.

Relationship 7 states that Fact B is true if Fact K is true. Earlier, the system asked the user and determined that Fact K is true. At that time the value was stored, and hence the system need not query the user again. Therefore, Fact B is true and the system can proceed to attempt to determine whether Fact G is true. As was true with Fact N, there are no relationships from which we can infer the value of Fact G (whether or not it is true). The system then must use a default value (if one is specified) or ask the user. Suppose in this case that the user knows that Fact G is known. Hence, the system now establishes that Fact M is true, since Facts B and G have been established as true. The system again returns to processing Relationship 1.

R1: ➤ IF Fact E and Fact M and Fact G are all true, THEN Fact F is true;
R2: ➤ IF Fact K and Fact E are both true, THEN Fact D is true;
R3: ➤ IF Fact N is true, THEN Fact Y is true;
R4: ➤ IF Fact Y is true, THEN Fact H is true;

R5: ➤ IF Fact B and Fact G are both true, THEN Fact M is true;
R6: ➤ IF Fact K and Fact F are both true, THEN Fact Y is true;
R7: ➤ IF Fact K is true, THEN Fact B is true.

It establishes that Fact F is true. With this information, the system returns to processing Relationship 6.

R1: ➤ IF Fact E and Fact M and Fact G are all true, THEN Fact F is true;
R2: ➤ IF Fact K and Fact E are both true, THEN Fact D is true;
R3: ➤ IF Fact N is true, THEN Fact Y is true;
R4: ➤ IF Fact Y is true, THEN Fact H is true;
R5: ➤ IF Fact B and Fact G are both true, THEN Fact M is true;
R6: ➤ IF Fact K and Fact F are both true, THEN Fact Y is true;
R7: ➤ IF Fact K is true, THEN Fact B is true.

It establishes that Fact Y is true. Since Fact Y is true, the system can establish that Fact H is true through Relationship 4.

R1: ➤ IF Fact E and Fact M and Fact G are all true, THEN Fact F is true;
R2: ➤ IF Fact K and Fact E are both true, THEN Fact D is true;
R3: ➤ IF Fact N is true, THEN Fact Y is true;
R4: ➤ IF Fact Y is true, THEN Fact H is true;
R5: ➤ IF Fact B and Fact G are both true, THEN Fact M is true;
R6: ➤ IF Fact K and Fact F are both true, THEN Fact Y is true;
R7: ➤ IF Fact K is true, THEN Fact B is true.

Since establishing that Fact H is true is the goal of the system, it would stop processing at this point and find no additional information. This process is illustrated in Figure 4S.1.

Forward Chaining Reasoning Process

Consider, now, the path that is followed using forward chaining. Using this system, we begin with information and attempt to learn as much as possible. For example, suppose we begin by knowing that Fact K and Fact E are both true. The system will look to prove any relationship possible given these two facts and hence process Relationships 2 and 7 (sequentially in the order in which they appear in the code).

R1: ➤ IF Fact E and Fact M and Fact G are all true, THEN Fact F is true;
R2: ➤ IF Fact K and Fact E are both true, THEN Fact D is true;
R3: ➤ IF Fact N is true, THEN Fact Y is true;
R4: ➤ IF Fact Y is true, THEN Fact H is true;
R5: ➤ IF Fact B and Fact G are both true, THEN Fact M is true;

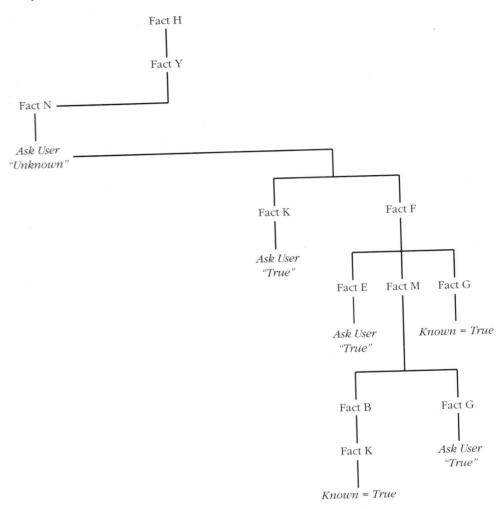

Figure 4S.1 Hierarchy of logic—backward chaining.

R6: ➤ IF Fact K and Fact F are both true, THEN Fact Y is true;
R7: ➤ IF Fact K is true, THEN Fact B is true.

The environment changes as a result of this processing, and the system now knows that Fact D and Fact B are also true. Hence, the system considers all relationships again to determine whether more information can be gleaned. However, there are no additional relationships that can be processed. Unlike the case in backward chaining, the system does not begin to prompt the user for information that might allow it to go further, and hence it would stop and learn no additional facts.

Some software lets developers use hybrid approaches to programming by allowing procedural programming, access programming, and/or object-oriented programming, in addition to forward and/or backward chaining pathways. Consider the preceding forward chaining example. Suppose that the access programming code specified that users should be queried or a database should be searched or a default value should be set if the status of Fact G is not known by this point of processing. If the user or database indicated that Fact G were true, the system would again invoke the forward chaining component and it would process Relationship 5.

R1: ➤ IF Fact E and Fact M and Fact G are all true, THEN Fact F is true;
R2: ➤ IF Fact K and Fact E are both true, THEN Fact D is true;
R3: ➤ IF Fact N is true, THEN Fact Y is true;
R4: ➤ IF Fact Y is true, THEN Fact H is true;
R5: ➤ IF Fact B and Fact G are both true, THEN Fact M is true;
R6: ➤ IF Fact K and Fact F are both true, THEN Fact Y is true;
R7: ➤ IF Fact K is true, THEN Fact B is true.

The information regarding Fact M would cause the system to evaluate all relationships that require some or all of Facts K, E, N, B, or M to be true, and hence it would process Relationship 1.

R1: ➤ IF Fact E and Fact M and Fact G are all true, THEN Fact F is true;
R2: ➤ IF Fact K and Fact E are both true, THEN Fact D is true;
R3: ➤ IF Fact N is true, THEN Fact Y is true;
R4: ➤ IF Fact Y is true, THEN Fact H is true;
R5: ➤ IF Fact B and Fact G are both true, THEN Fact M is true;
R6: ➤ IF Fact K and Fact F are both true, THEN Fact Y is true;
R7: ➤ IF Fact K is true, THEN Fact B is true.

The new information about Fact F requires the system to reevaluate the relationships to determine whether more information can be learned, and hence it will seek any relationship that includes Fact F and some subset of the other facts known at this time, as in Relationship 6.

R1: ➤ IF Fact E and Fact M and Fact G are all true, THEN Fact F is true;
R2: ➤ IF Fact K and Fact E are both true, THEN Fact D is true;
R3: ➤ IF Fact N is true, THEN Fact Y is true;
R4: ➤ IF Fact Y is true, THEN Fact H is true;
R5: ➤ IF Fact B and Fact G are both true, THEN Fact M is true;
R6: ➤ IF Fact K and Fact F are both true, THEN Fact Y is true;
R7: ➤ IF Fact K is true, THEN Fact B is true.

The process proceeds in a similar fashion now that Fact Y is known. Hence, the system will process Relationship 4.

R1: ➤ IF Fact E and Fact M and Fact G are all true, THEN Fact F is true;
R2: ➤ IF Fact K and Fact E are both true, THEN Fact D is true;
R3: ➤ IF Fact N is true, THEN Fact Y is true;
R4: ➤ IF Fact Y is true, THEN Fact H is true;
R5: ➤ IF Fact B and Fact G are both true, THEN Fact M is true;
R6: ➤ IF Fact K and Fact F are both true, THEN Fact Y is true;
R7: ➤ IF Fact K is true, THEN Fact B is true.

Since none of the relationships indicate that any new knowledge can be gained by knowing that Fact H is true, the system would stop with this knowledge. This process is illustrated in Figure 4S.2.

Comparison of the Reasoning Processes

In this example, the system "learned" the same ultimate fact (Fact H is true) with backward chaining and forward chaining *only when* forward chaining was supplemented by access programming. However, the forward chaining with access programming and the pure forward chaining process the relationships in quite dif-

Initial Known Facts: Fact K and Fact E Are True

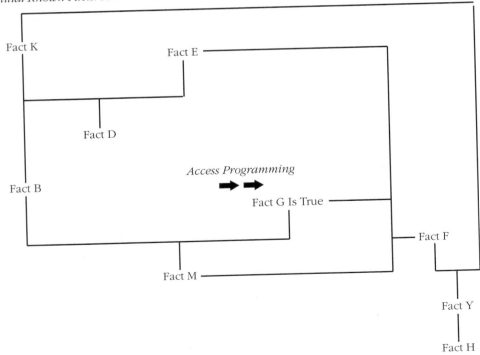

Figure 4S.2   Hierarchy of logic—forward chaining.

ferent order. It is important to note this for two reasons. First, the designer could find himself or herself with a dormant analysis system unless information is sought in a particular manner. For example, suppose the last example were done completely as a forward chaining example (no access programming interrupt). In this case, the system would quit processing after it learned that Fact B was true, and there would be no way to push it to do more. The system would not perform as the designers had envisioned nor as the decision makers need.

Second, we should be concerned about the way the system seeks information from the user for the sake of sustaining the confidence of the decision maker (sometimes referred to as *face validity*). Decision makers expect information to be sought in a particular order. If there are vast deviations from such a logical order, decision makers may question the underlying logic of the system. If the logic can be defended, such questioning helps the decision maker to reason more effectively. On the other hand, if decision makers cannot establish why such reasoning has occurred, they might choose to drop the DSS.

◆ CERTAINTY FACTORS

Decisions are difficult to make because of uncertainty. Decision makers are uncertain about how outside entities will change their environments and thus influence the success of their choices. In addition, sometimes decision makers are uncertain about the reliability of the information they use as the basis for their choices. Finally, decision makers are uncertain about the validity of the relationships they believe govern the choice situation.

Often decision makers also need to interact with "fuzzy logic." The term *fuzzy logic* does not apply to a muddled thought process. Rather it means a method of addressing data and relationships that are inexact. Humans address fuzzy logic regularly whenever they do not treat decisions as totally black-and-white choices. The gradations of gray provide flexibility in approaching problems that forces us to consider all possible options.

Consider, for example, whether a person is tall. The term *tall* is a vague term that means different things to different people. If in the choice process one selection procedure required the machine to select only applicants who were tall, it would be difficult for the DSS to do. Even in a sport such as basketball, where being tall really matters, the term tall depends on the position one is playing. A particular individual might be tall if playing guard but not if playing center, because the requirements of the positions are so different. Even if the discussion is limited to the position of guard, what is considered "tall enough" is dependent on other factors. In 1994 Mugsy Boggs, a basketball guard, was only 5'4", which even I[1] do not consider tall. However, because he had fabulous technique, he was considered tall enough to play that position.

---

[1]That which is considered tall also depends on how tall an individual is. Since I fall into a category generally referred to as "short," I have a more liberal definition of tall than do many people.

Similarly, when trying to select among employment opportunities, we might employ fuzzy logic. There is not one opportunity that is "good" and another that is "bad." Generally, they are all somewhat good on some dimensions and somewhat bad on other dimensions. It is difficult for most people to define what dimensions are most important in a reliable way, but they can tell which opportunities are better than others. This illustrates the historic problem that humans could make better decisions than computers because they could address uncertainty in their reasoning processes.

So, if DSS are to have "intelligence" that facilitates the choice processes, they must also be able to address uncertainty from a variety of perspectives. There are two major processes by which uncertainty is addressed in intelligent systems, with probability theory and with certainty factors. These will be introduced in the following sections.

Representing Uncertainty with Probability Theory

Probability theory, which is the foundation of most of the statistical techniques used in business applications, is based on the belief that the likelihood that something could happen is essentially the ratio of the number of successes to the number of possible trials. So, for example, if we flip a coin 100 times, we expect 50 of those times to show heads, and hence we estimate the probability of heads as being one-half. Since few business situations are as simple as flipping a coin, there are a variety of rules for combining probabilistic information for complicated events. Furthermore, since we may update our estimates of probabilities based on seeing additional evidence, probabilists provide systematic methods for making those changes in the estimates. This is referred to as *Bayesian updating*.

Consider the following example. Let us define three events, which we will call Event A, Event B, and Event C:

Event A:	the act of being a good writer
Event B:	receipt of an "A" in a writing course
Event C:	receipt of an "A" in a systems analysis course

Suppose the following:

$$P(A) = .5 \quad P(A') = .5 \quad P(A \cap B) = .24 \quad P(A \cap B \cap C) = .015$$
$$P(B) = .3 \quad P(B') = .7 \quad P(A \cap C) = .06$$
$$P(C) = .1 \quad P(C') = .9 \quad P(B \cap C) = .02$$

Without any new information, we believe that the likelihood of being a good writer (Event A) is 0.50. If, however, we know the person received an "A" in his or her writing class (Event B), we could update the probability that the person is a good writer by applying Bayes' Rule:

$$P(A|B) = \frac{P(A \cap B)}{P(B)} = \frac{.24}{.30} = .80$$

That is, given this new information, we now believe fairly strongly that the person is a good writer.

If, instead, the probability of the intersection between Events A and B (that is, the probability that the person is *both* a good writer and received an "A" in a writing course) were quite low, such as .01, the conditional probability, P(A|B), would be reduced substantially from the initial estimate to a value of .033. That means we can update an initial estimate after we get new information by either increasing or decreasing our certainty in the likelihood of an event, depending on the new information provided.

A more generalized form of the equation is

$$P(A|B) = \frac{P(A \cap B)}{P(A \cap B) + P(A' \cap B)} = \frac{P(B|A)}{P(B|A)P(A) + P(B|A')P(A')}$$

Suppose we now have the information that the person also received an "A" in his/her Systems Analysis class. Based on our earlier information, we could now update the probability further:

$$P(A|B \cap C) = \frac{P(A \cap (B \cap C))}{P(B \cap C)} = \frac{P(A \cap B \cap C)}{P(B \cap C)} = \frac{P(B \cap C|A)P(A)}{P(B \cap C|A)P(A) + P(B \cap C|A')P(A')}$$

Hence, given all the information available, we believe the likelihood that the person is a good writer is 0.75.

Updating the rules using a Bayesian approach is similar to this process.

Representing Uncertainty with Certainty Factors

A popular alternative for addressing uncertainty is to use certainty factors. Instead of measuring the likelihood as one function, we need to estimate of a measure of "belief" separate from a measure of "disbelief." New evidence could increase (decrease) our measure of belief, increase (decrease) our measure of disbelief, or have some impact on our measure of both belief and disbelief. The effect of the evidence is a function of whether the information is confirmatory, disconfirmatory, or both confirmatory of one and disconfirmatory of the other. Consider the previous example. Suppose you believe the subject to be a good writer. You know the person waived his or her writing course. This information would cause you to increase your measure of belief that the person was a good writer but would have no impact on your measure of disbelief. However, if you knew that the person received a "C" in the writing class, and almost everyone waived the writing class, this would have two effects. First, it would increase your disbelief that the person was a good writer because he or she received a grade of "C" in a class that most people waived. In addition, it would decrease your belief that the person was a good writer. Through this separation of measures of belief and disbelief, it is possible to present evidence (facts or rules) and measure their impact more directly.

Certainty factors have a range between −1 and 1 and are defined by the difference between measures of belief and measures of disbelief as shown below.

$$CF[h,e] := MB[h,e] - MD[h,e]$$

Where:

MB[h,e] := The measure of increased belief in hypothesis "h" given evidence "e"

MD[h,e] := The measure of increased disbelief in hypothesis "h" given evidence "e"

Increments associated with new evidence are made as follows:

$$MB[h,e] = \begin{cases} 1 & \text{If } P(h) = 1 \\ \dfrac{\max(P(h|e),P(h)) - P(h)}{\max(1,0) - P(h)} & \text{otherwise} \end{cases}$$

$$MD[h,e] = \begin{cases} 1 & \text{If } P(h) = 0 \\ \dfrac{\max(P(h|e),P(h)) - P(h)}{\min(1,0) - P(h)} & \text{otherwise} \end{cases}$$

If $P(h|e) > P(h)$, there is increased confidence in the hypothesis. However, the paradox that results is

$$CF(h,e) + CF(h',e) \neq 1$$

Hence, the confidence that a hypothesis is true given particular evidence, and the confidence that the hypothesis is wrong given the evidence does not sum to 1 as it might in probability theory.

Incrementally acquired evidence is used to update the measures of belief and measures of disbelief separately.

$$MB[h,e_1 \ \& \ e_2] = \begin{cases} 0 & \text{if } MD[h,e_1 \ \& \ e_2] = 1 \\ \\ MB(h,s_1) + MB(h,s_2) \cdot [1 - MB(h,s_1)] & \text{otherwise} \end{cases}$$

$$MD[h,e_1 \ \& \ e_2] = \begin{cases} 0 & MB[h,e_1 \ \& \ e_2] = 1 \\ \\ MD(h,s_1) + MD(h,s_2) \cdot [1 - MD(h,s_1)] & \text{otherwise} \end{cases}$$

Furthermore, measures of belief of conjunctions of hypotheses are determined by taking the minimum value of the measures of belief of the individual hypotheses, while measures of disbelief of conjunctions are determined by taking the maximum value of the measures of disbelief of the individual hypotheses. Further corrections are taken if there is uncertainty regarding the certainty of a particular piece of information.

DISCUSSION

Artificial intelligence (AI) has two roles in a decision support system. First, artificial intelligence can serve as a model type. In particular, it is an heuristic modeling technique that manipulates symbols rather than numbers. This kind of modeling replicates the human reasoning process making it particularly useful when addressing poorly structured problems or problems for which data are not complete. A second application of artificial intelligence in a DSS is to provide intelligent assistance to the users. With the use of AI, designers can build into the DSS expertise in modeling, evaluation of alternatives or in post-modeling analysis to improve the quality of decisions for all users of the system. In order to implement it, designers must codify the information that experts would use, build procedures for processing that information and address the manner both uncertainty of information and relationships will be addressed.

SUPPLEMENT QUESTIONS

1. What are certainty factors? What are risks and advantages of their use?

2. Discuss the difference between the concepts of "disbelief" and "the lack of belief" in decision making and the role these concepts play in selecting an automobile. What is the implication for building certainty factors into the system?

3. Historically, what were the differences between decision support and expert systems? What factors led to the narrowing of those differences? What implication does this have for the model-management feature in DSS?

4. How do you know when you have included enough "intelligence" in a decision support system?

5. Compare and contrast symbolic processing and numerical processing. Why is the former referred to as "intelligence"?

6. What factors would lead you to recommend selecting a project that is appropriate for expert systems development?

7. Consider preparing a DSS for which certainty factors are relevant. This may be a class project, an example with which you are familiar, or a hypothetical example. What issues need to be tracked with certainty factors?

◆ O N   T H E   W E B ◆

On the Web for this supplement to Chapter 4 Supplement provides additional information about artificial intelligence and how it applies to DSS design. Links can provide access to demonstration packages, general overview information, applications, software providers, tutorials, and more. Additional discussion questions and new applications will also be added as they become available.

- *Links to applications are provided.* Since artificial intelligence can be nebulous until actual applications are addressed, there are links that can provide descriptions of applications. Information is available regarding stand-alone applications, integrated tools, business-related systems, such as intelligent agents, and general interest applications, such as chess programs

- *Links to press accounts of the use of intelligence are available.* These links provide general overviews of uses in business, industry areas, government, and society as a whole. Furthermore, links can be made to interviews with experts and their forecasts about future use.

- *Links provide access to examples of artificial intelligence tools.* Links provide access to product information, product comparisons and reviews, as well as general information about both artificial intelligence and expert systems tools.

- *Links provide access to more examples of how to build intelligence into a DSS.* Both conceptual examples and actual code are available to add to the material in the chapter supplement.

You can access material for this supplement to Chapter 4 Supplement from the general WWW Page for the book, or, directly from the following URL.

http://www.umsl.edu/~sauter/DSS/mbms_sup.html

SUGGESTED READINGS

Gale, W.A. (ed.), *Artificial Intelligence and Statistics*, Reading, MA: Addison-Wesley Publishing Company, 1986.

Gallagher, J.P., *Knowledge Systems for Business: Integrating Expert Systems and MIS*, Englewood Cliffs, NJ: Prentice Hall, 1988.

Harmon, P. and C. Hall, *Intelligent Software Systems Development: An IS Manager's Guide*, New York: Wiley Professional Computing, 1993.

Klahr, P. and D.A. Waterman (eds.), *Expert Systems: Techniques, Tools and Applications*, Reading, MA: Addison–Wesley Publishing Company, 1986.

Rauch-Hindin, *A Guide to Commercial Artificial Intelligence*, Englewood Cliffs, NJ: Prentice Hall, 1988.

Sauter, V.L. and L.A. Madeo, "Using statistics to make expert systems user-acquainted," *Annals of Mathematics and Artificial Intelligence*, 2, 1990, pp. 309–326.

Turban, E. and H.J. Watson, "Integrating expert systems, executive information systems and decision support systems," in P. Gray (ed.), *Decision Support and Executive Information Systems*, Englewood Cliffs, NJ: Prentice-Hall, 1994, pp. 399–408.

Waterman, D.A., *A Guide to Expert Systems*, Reading, MA: Addison–Wesley Publishing Company, 1985.

Chapter 5

User-Interface Components

◆ ◆ ◆

To the decision maker, the user interface *is* the decision support system. The user interface includes all the mechanisms by which commands, requests, and data are entered into the decision support system, as well as all the methods by which results and information are output by the system. It does not matter how well the system performs; if the decision maker cannot access models and data and peruse results easily, the system cannot provide decision *support*. In fact, if the interface does not meet their needs and expectations, decision makers often will abandon use of the system entirely regardless of its modeling power or data availability.

The key to good user interface design is to present information in such a way that users can avail themselves of the full potential of the system. Today, this is more an art than a science. With experience, designers become more attuned to what users want and need and can better provide it through good color combinations, appropriate placement of input and output windows, and generally good composition of the work environment.

Fortunately, there is an emerging literature explaining how to design user interfaces. The key to making the most of it is knowing when to apply it. Some of the material is pertinent for all user-interface design. Other material applies only in certain circumstances. This chapter will help you know how to apply what is available and how to develop the "art" of design.

To paraphrase Dickens, it is the most exciting of times for designing user interfaces, and it is the most frustrating of times for designing user interfaces. It is an exciting time because graphical user interfaces (GUI), advances in database storage, and client/server technologies have opened a wide range of opportunities for making more useful, more easily used, and more aesthetically pleasing representations of options, data, and information. It is a frustrating time because legacy systems still exist. Some DSS must be built using technologies that actually limit the development of user interfaces. Others must at least interact with such legacy systems and are therefore limited in the range of options available. In this chapter, the focus will be on the future. However, remember that "the future" may take a long time to get to some installations.

User interfaces are changing. Even the keyboards are beginning to look different.

Increasingly, designers have other user interface devices available. One increasingly popular device is a pen-based system that allows users a more natural input capability. Of course, such systems require the DSS to incorporate handwriting recognition as part of the system.

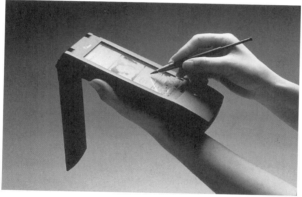

As the virtual reality becomes more practical for DSS incorporation, we will see additional user interface devices becoming popular (for example, the head gear or the glove).

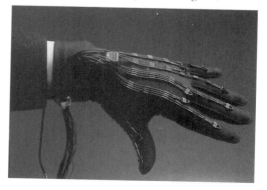

◆ USER-INTERFACE COMPONENTS

We must describe the user interface in terms of its components as well as its mode of communication, as in Figure 5.1. The components are not independent of the modes of communication. However, since they each highlight different design issues, we present them separately; components first.

The Action Language

The *action language* identifies the form of input used by decision makers to enter requests into the decision support system. This includes the way decision makers request information, ask for new data, invoke models, perform sensitivity analyses, and even request mail. Historically, five main types of action languages have been used, as shown in Figure 5.2.

The Menu Format

Menus, the most common action language today, display one or more lists of alternatives, commands, or results from which decision makers can select. Menus often are called *user-friendly* because they help guide users through the steps of processing data. In this way, the designer can illustrate for the user the full range of analyses the DSS can perform and the data that can be used for analysis. The

---

Components

- ■ Action language
- ■ Display or presentation language
- ■ Knowledge base

Modes of Communication

- ■ Metaphor
- ■ Mental model
- ■ Navigation of model
- ■ Look

Figure 5.1   User interface descriptions.

- The menu format
- The question/answer format
- The command language format
- The input/output structured format
- The free-form natural language format

Figure 5.2 Basic action language types.

advantage of these user-friendly systems is clear. If the menus are understandable, the DSS is very easy to use; the decision maker is not required to remember how it works and only needs to make selections on the screen. The designer can allow users keyboard control (either arrow keys or letter/key combinations), mouse control, light pen control, or touch screen control.

Menus are particularly appealing to inexperienced users, who can thereby use the system immediately. They may not fully understand the complexity of the system or the range of modeling they can accomplish, but they can get some results. Clearly, this provides an advantage. In the same way, menu formats are useful to decision makers who use a DSS only occasionally, especially if there are long intervals between uses. Like the inexperienced user, these decision makers can forget the commands necessary to accomplish a task, and hence profit by the guidance the menus can provide.

Menu formats tend *not* to be an optimal action language choice for experienced users, however, especially if these decision makers use the system frequently. Such users can become frustrated with the time and keystrokes needed to process a request when other action language formats can allow them access to more complex analyses and more flexibility. This will be discussed in more depth in the "Command Language" section.

The advantage of the menu system hinges on the *understandability* of the menus. A poorly conceived menu system can make the DSS unusable and frustrating. To avoid such problems, designers must consider several features. First, menu choices should be clearly stated. The names of the options or the data should coincide with those used by the decision makers. For example, if a DSS is being created for computer sales and the decision makers refer to CRTs as "screens," then the option on the menu ought to be screen *not* CRT. The latter may be equivalent and even more nearly correct, but if it is not the jargon used by decision makers, it may not be clear. Likewise, stating a graphing option as HLCO, even with the descriptor "high-low-close-open," does not convey sufficient information to the user, especially not novice or inexperienced users.

A second feature of a well-conceived menu is that the options are listed in a *logical* sequence. *Logical*, of course, is defined by the environment of the users. Sometimes the logical sequence is alphabetical or numerical. Other times it is more reasonable to group similar entries together. Some designers like to order the entries in a menu according to the frequency with which they are selected. While that can be a convenience for experienced users, it can be confusing to the novice user who *is* after all the target of the menu and may not be aware of the frequency of responses. A better approach is to preselect a frequently chosen option so that users can simply press Return or click the mouse on a button to accept that particular answer. Improvements in software platforms make such preselection easier to implement, as we will discuss later in the chapter.

When creating a menu, designers need to be concerned about how they group items together. Generally, the commands are in one list, and the objects of the commands[1] are in another list, as shown in Figure 5.3. Of course, with careful planning, we can list the commands and objects together in the same list as shown in Figure 5.4 and allow users to select all attributes that are appropriate.

In today's programming environment, designers tend not to combine command and object menus. The primary reason to combine them in the past was to save input time for the user since each menu represented a different screen that needed to be displayed. Display changes could be terribly slow, especially on highly utilized, old mainframes. The tradeoff between processing time and grouping options together seemed reasonable. For most programming languages and environments, that restriction no longer holds. Several menus on the same screen can all be accessed by the user. Furthermore, most modeling packages allow a user several options, depending on earlier selections. If these were all displayed in a menu, the screen could become cluttered and not easy for the decision maker to use.

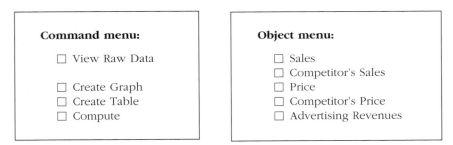

Figure 5.3 Independent command and object menus.

---

[1]The "objects of the commands" typically refer to the *data* that should be selected for the particular command invoked.

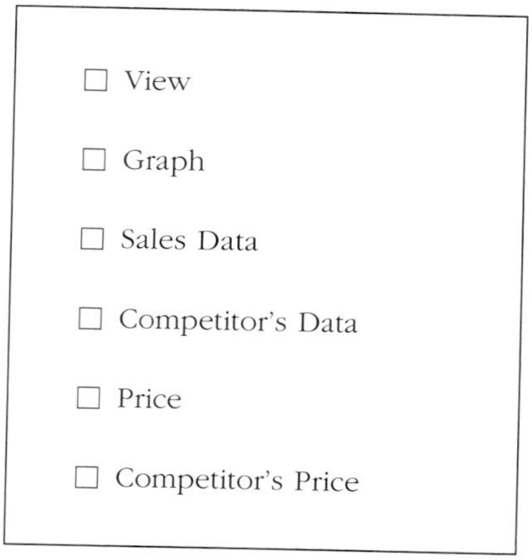

Figure 5.4 Combined command and object.

An alternative is to provide menus that are nested in a logical sequence. For example, Figure 5.5 demonstrates a nested menu that might appear in a decision support system. All users would begin the system use on the first-level menu. Since the user selected "Create Graph" as the option, the system displays the two options for aggregating data for a graph: annually and quarterly. Note that this choice is provided *prior to* and *independent of* the selection of the variables to be graphed so that the user cannot inadvertently select the x-axis as annual and the y-axis as quarterly data (or vice versa).

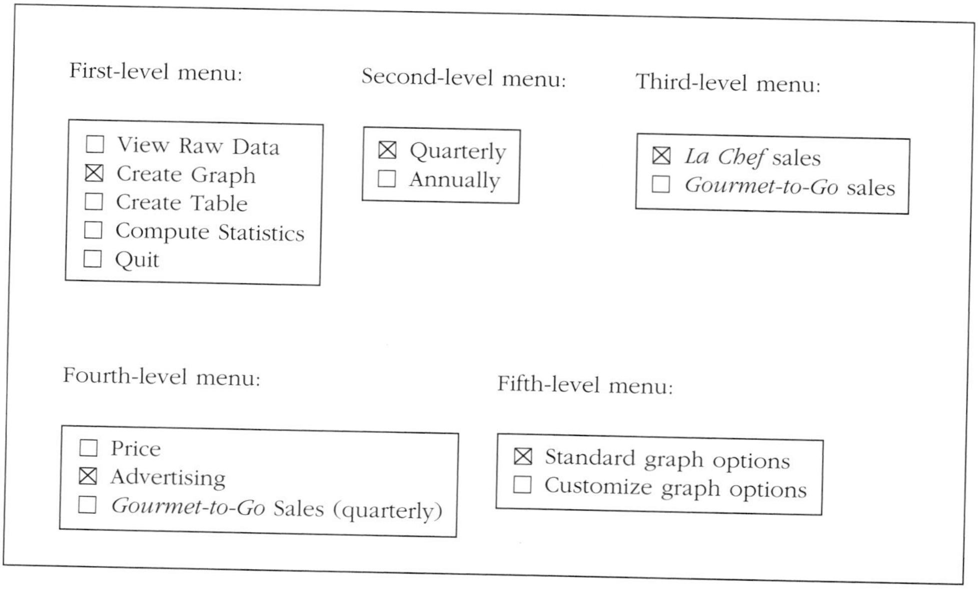

Figure 5.5 Nested menu structure.

The third-level menu item allows the users to specify what they want displayed on the y-axis. While this limits the flexibility of the system, if carefully designed, it can represent all options *needed* by the user. Furthermore, it forces the user to declare what should be the dependent variable, or the variable plotted on the y-axis, *without* using traditional jargon. This decreases the likelihood of mis-specification of the graph.

The fourth-level menu is presented as a direct response to the selection of the dependent variable selection. That is, because the decision maker selected *La Chef* sales, the system "knows" that the only available and appropriate variables to present on the x-axis are price, advertising, and the competitor's sales. In addition, the system knows that the time dimension for the data on the x-axis must be consistent with that on the y-axis and hence displays Quarterly after the only selection that could be affected. Note that the system does not need to ask how users want the graph displayed because it has been specified *without* the use of jargon.

Finally, the last menu level allows the users the option of customizing the labeling and other visual characteristics of their graphs. Since the first option, "Standard graph options," was selected, the system knows not to display the variety of options available for change. Had the user selected "Customize graph options," the system would have moved to another menu that allows users to specify what should be changed.

In early systems, designers needed to provide menu systems that made sense in a fairly linear fashion. While they could display screens as a function of the options selected to that point, such systems typically did not have the ability to provide "intelligent" steps through the process. Today's environments, which typically provide some meta-logic and hypertext functionality as well as some intelligent expertise integrated into the rules, can provide paths through the menu options that relieve users of unnecessary stops along the way.

Depending on the programming environment, the menu choices might have the boxes (□), as illustrated in Figure 5.3, radio buttons (○), underscores (_____), or simply a blank space (   ). Indeed, in some systems, users can click the mouse on an iconic representation of the option. These icons are picture symbols of familiar objects that can make the system appear friendlier, such as a picture of a graph (◐) for selecting the graphing option.

Ideally, the choice from among these options is a function of the preferences of the system's designers and users. In some cases, the choice will be easy because the programming environment will support only some of the options. In still other cases, multiple options are allowed, but the software restricts the meaning and uses of the individual options. For example, in some languages, the check box (□) will support users selecting more than one of the options, whereas the radio button (○) will allow users to select only one at a time. Before designing the menus, designers need to be familiar with the implications of their choices.

Any way the options are displayed on the screen, users might also have a variety of ways of selecting them. In most systems, the user would always have the arrow keys and the Enter key to register options. Similarly, most systems support pressing a character (typically the first letter of the command) to select an option. Many systems also support the use of a mouse in a "move and click" selection of options. Less often, systems include touch screens—where the user literally selects an option by touching the word or the icon on the screen—or light pens—with which the user touches the screen. In a voice input system, the user selects an option by speaking into a microphone connected to the computer. The computer must then translate the sound into a known command and invoke the command. This option is still rare. Voice systems can accept only limited vocabulary and must be calibrated to the speech patterns of each user, and hence are not used much for DSS today.

Question/Answer Format

A second option for the action language is to provide users questions they must answer. This is actually a precursor to modern menus and tends to be found only in legacy systems. An example of computer questions and user answers is shown in Figure 5.6.

One attribute of the question/answer format in some environments is the opportunity to embed information into the questions. Such information might be the name of the user, the project of interest, or other information regarding the use of the system. For example, Figure 5.6 could be redefined as shown in Figure 5.7. While some users respond favorably to the use of their name in these questions, others find it annoying. Furthermore, the use of the personalized questions tends to slow down the processing and make the questions appear much longer and more difficult to read.

Q.   Do you want to request a report?
A.   *Yes*

Q.   Which report?
A.   *First Quarter, 1993, Sales by Representative.*

Q.   Do you want the report on the screen or in hard copy?
A.   *Screen.*

Q.   Do you want a special heading?
A.   *No.*

Q.   Do you want a special format?
A.   *No.*

Figure 5.6   Question-answer format.

Q. Do you want to request a report, Ms. Jones?
A. *Yes.*

Q. Which report would you like, Ms. Jones?
A. *First Quarter, 1993, Sales by Representative.*

Q. Do you want the First Quarter, 1993, Sales by
    Representative report on the screen or in hard copy?
A. *Screen.*

Q. Do you want a special heading on the First Quarter, 1993,
    Sales by Representative report?
A. *No.*

Figure 5.7   The personalized question-answer format.

The goal of the question/answer approach is to give the appearance of flexibility in proceeding through the options of the system. Indeed, its usefulness is optimized when it is most flexible. The question/answer format works best when the user has more control over the system and its options. However, coding such flexibility can be infeasible in many programming environments. Thus, this type of action language is generally implemented as a fixed sequence and format, which is very rigid and often limiting to the user.

The Command Language Format

The command language format allows user-constructed statements to be selected from a predefined set of verbs or noun–verb pairings. It is similar to a programming language that has been focused on the task of the decision support system. An example of command language format is shown in Figure 5.8.

The command language format allows the user to control the systems operations *directly*, thereby *providing* greater latitude in choosing the order of the commands. In this way, the user is not bound by the predetermined sequencing of a menu system, and can ignore the use of options that are not pertinent to a specific inquiry. It can be structured hierarchically, however, so that one major command will control all auxiliary commands unless specific alterations are required. Notice in the example in Figure 5.8 that the user *must* specify only the columns and rows to be able to display a menu. In the event that the user wants more control over the report, he or she can have it, as shown in the latter parts of Figure 5.8.

More importantly, command language gives the user complete access to all the options available. Hence, users can employ the full range of commands and the full variety of subcommands. Since the combinations and the ways in which they

```
NEW REPORT  Break Product Sales

COLUMNS  1991 thru 1994

ROWS  Sales Force, Summary by Region, DISPLAY

DOUBLE SPACE

DISPLAY

NEW ROW  Summary by State

HEADER  Productivity of Sales Force 1991–1994

DISPLAY COLUMNWIDTH 30
```

Figure 5.8 Command language format.

are used are unlimited, the user has greater *power* than is available with any other action language format. The command language format is thus appreciated by the *power user*, or the experienced and frequent user who wants to push the system to its full capability.

However, such a format is a problem for the infrequent user and a nightmare to the inexperienced user, who is likely to forget the commands or the syntax of their use. Such problems can be mitigated with the use of help menus, especially those that are context sensitive.

Generally, decision support systems do not support *only* command language formats because of their inaccessibility. However, good design typically allows both a menu format and a command language format. In this way, the user has the ability to make the tradeoffs between flexibility (or power) and ease of use.

The I/O Structured Format

The I/O structured format presents users with displays resembling a series of forms, with certain areas already completed. Users can move through the form and add, change, or delete prespecified information as if completing the form by hand. Like the question/answer format, this kind of user interface tends to be associated primarily with legacy systems.

Consider a decision support system used by builders or designers of homes. Once they are satisfied with their design requirements, they need to place an order to acquire the necessary materials. While ordering is not the *primary* function of the DSS, it might be very useful if users could simply take the information from their design specifications and move it to an order form like the form shown in Figure 5.9. Once the users are satisfied with the completed form, they can fax it directly from the computer to the wholesaler.

It is not surprising that such I/O structured formats are not commonly seen in decision support systems, because they replicate a repeated, structured, manual process. They should *not* be a primary action language option in a DSS, however, they can be used as a supplement. It makes sense to include an order form as a part of the DSS in our example because its function is integrated with the primary

HOMES UNLIMITED
12345 Designer Lane
Interesting Place, MO 63121
(314) IDESIGN
FAX: (314) 555-IFAX

Purchase Order Number:

Press F5 for automatic PO Number request

DATE:

TO:

Press F2 for a list of current suppliers and addresses

Customer Number:

Number	Item Description	Due Date

Press F3 for a list of materials used in this job

? Check here if you want to combine this with other orders. ☐
? Check here if you want to hold this order. ☐

Figure 5.9   The I/O structured format.

function of the system. Since the completion of the form is integrated with the development of the design, as design features change, the form will be updated immediately. For example, if the designer later finds a need for three items, rather than the two items first entered into the form, the order form will be updated immediately. Or, if the designer decides a conventional widget will not suffice and substitutes an oblique widget, the form will be updated automatically.

The question that should be troubling you are Why have the designer complete the order form at all? Why not have a clerk place the order? Under some circumstances, that might be reasonable. However, a designer tends to have preferences for styles, workmanship, and other factors of particular manufacturers. Part of the actual design is in fact the selection of the manufacturer. Or, the designer might want to complete some cost-sensitivity analyses on a particular design in order to make tradeoffs among various options that could have differential impact on the total cost. Hence, the costing function must be part of the decision support system. However, part of the functionality of the system might be to send information to clerks about parts *not* specified by the designer so they can actually place the orders.

The Free-Form Natural Language Format

The final action language option is the one most like conventional human communication. "Free-form" implies that there is no preconceived structure in the way commands should be entered. "Natural language" implies that the terms used in the commands are not specified by the system but rather are chosen by the users themselves. Hence, the system cannot rely on finding "key terms" in the midst of other language (as it might with the question/answer format), because they may not be present. For example, rather than requesting a "report," users might request a "summary" or a "synopsis" of the information. The system must be able to scan a request, parse the language, and determine that the requested "summary" is actually a report. So the same request that was presented in Figure 5.5 (in the question/answer format) might now be presented as in Figure 5.10.

While parsing of this request can be accomplished, it takes extra computer power and extra processing time. Under conditions of limited possibilities for the requests, such systems have been shown to perform adequately. However, this approach might produce an inappropriate result, especially if the user has particularly unusual terminology (as might be the case if the system serves users transnationally).

> I would like to see a summary of the sales of each sales associate for January, February, and March of 1993, aggregated.
> I want it to appear up by my clock and have an appropriate scaling factor.

Figure 5.10   The free-form natural language format.

The possibility is troubling because the requested information might be *close* to the intended result and the error might not be noticed.

If the input medium is voice, a free-form natural language format can become particularly difficult to implement because of the implications of intonation and the confusion of homonyms. On the other hand, it is with voice input that natural language makes the most sense, especially for addressing special circumstances or needs. Such systems have their greatest contribution in serving physically challenged users who cannot use other input mechanisms. Under these conditions, the extra programming and computer needs are justified because they provide empowerment to users.

The Display or Presentation Language

While the action language describes how the user communicates *to* the computer, the second aspect, the presentation language, describes how the computer provides information back to the user.

Of course, such an interface must convey the analysis in a fashion that is meaningful to the user. This applies not only to the results at the *end* of an analysis, but also to the intermediate steps that support all phases of decision making. Furthermore, the presentation must provide a sense of human control of the process *and* of the results. All this must be accomplished in a pleasing and understandable fashion without unduly cluttering the screen.

Windowing

How one accomplishes the task of organizing information depends on the kind of models, the kind of decision maker, and the kind of environment in which one is working. For example, in the Manhattan Court DSS example illustrated in Chapter 1,[2] (see Figure 1.1) designers faced the problem of how to profile defendants in

---

◆   DSS in Action   ◆

The FRIEND system is an emergency dispatch system in the Bellevue Borough north of Pittsburgh, PA. This system, known as the First Responder Interactive Emergency Navigational Database (FRIEND), dispatches information to Police using handheld computers in the field. The handheld devices are too small to support keyboards or mice. Rather, police use a special pen to write on the screen or even draw pictures. These responses are transmitted immediately to the station for sharing. Police at the station can use a graphical interface or even speech commands to facilitate the sharing of information to members in the field.

Krushenisky, C., "Technology news," *PC Novice*, 9, p. 6.

---

[2]Assael, S., "Moving justice from expert witnesses to expert systems," *Wired*, 2.03, March 1994, pp. 106–111.

a manner that would help judges see the entire perspective of the case. Their solution to the enormity of information available about each defendant is to use a four-grid display in a Windows environment. The top half of the screen displays information about the infractions in which the defendant may have been involved; the left portion provides information about the complaint in question, while the right portion summarizes the defendant's prior criminal history. The bottom-left quadrant summarizes the interview data about the defendant's socioeconomic and health conditions. Finally, the bottom right is reserved for the judge's comments. The software lets the user focus on any of the quadrants through screen maximization and the use of more detailed subroutines. For instance, in its normal state, the bottom-left interview screen displays the defendant's education level (ReadingProb: Y), Housing Status (Can Return Home: N, Homeless: Y) and drug habit (Requests Treatment: N). Maximized, it details everything from what drugs the person uses, to whom he or she lives with and where. In addition, problematic answers are displayed in red so as to highlight them for users.

The underlying tenet of presentation language is that the display should be "clean" and easy to read. Today, the use of the windows standard for many products makes the design of an uncluttered display easier. In particular, this standard brings with it the analogy of a desktop consisting of files. On the screen, we see windows, each representing a different kind of output. One window might include

---

◆ DSS in Action ◆

Since 1992, IBM has worked with the Olympic Committee to create the *Olympic Technology Solution*. This tool was written in object code for use in future Olympic games.

A major challenge in this development effort was the user interface. As Maria Battaglia, IBM's Manager of Worldwide Communications for the Olympic Games noted in *PC Week*,* "With 40,000 volunteers, you have to make sure [the systems] are really human-centric and accessible."

Part of the secret in achieving clarity of the user interface is to separate the various components of the system into separately accessed modules. Hence, users can focus on the Results System, the Press Information System, the Commentator Information System or the Games Management System. The Results System will deliver times to the 31 Olympic venues, pagers, and the Internet. Hence, scoreboards and a Web page will obtain their information from the same source at approximately the same time. The Press Information System and the Commentator Information System get not only the game results, but also personalized athlete profiles and other statistical information. The Games Management System handles all the operational information for the games.

*Moore, M., "IBM pumps up the Olympics," *PC Week*, 13(3), January 22, 1996, pp. 1, 113.

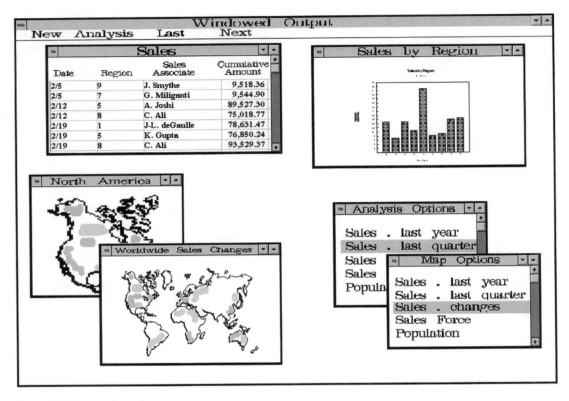

Figure 5.11   Windowed output.

graphs of the output while another includes a spreadsheet and still another holds help descriptions that encourage sensitivity analyses. An example is shown in Figure 5.11. The use of different windows for different kinds of information separates different kinds of results so users can focus their attention on the different components; the windows give order to the items at which the user is looking.

Of course, everyone has seen desktops that are totally cluttered because there are so many aspects of the problem one needs to consider. Layering options allow the various windows to overlap in many applications. Designers should, however, refrain from putting too much on the screen at once for the same reason decision makers are discouraged from having cluttered desks—too many things get lost, and it becomes hard to get perspective on the problem. Instead, if the application allows it, the designer should use icons to indicate various options, as illustrated in Figure 5.12. When the users want to examine that particular aspect of the problem, they can simply click on an icon to enlarge it so it can be viewed in its entirety.

Windows can be sized and placed by the users so they can customize their analysis of the information. Hence, users can have cluttered desktops if they choose, but clutter should not be inherent in the design of the DSS.

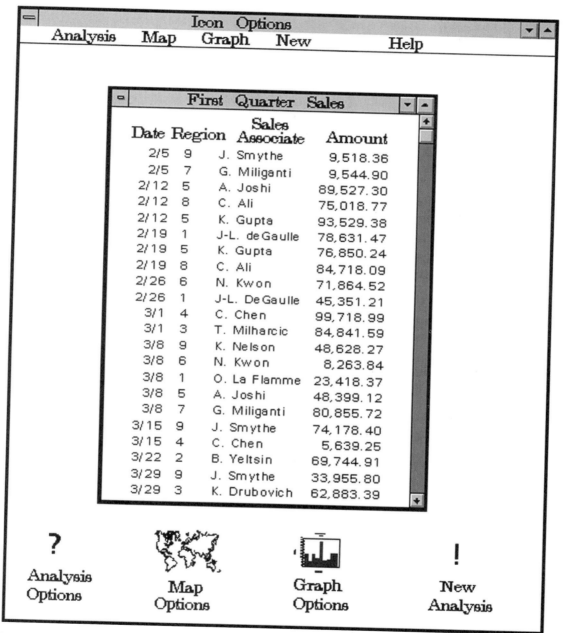

Figure 5.12   Icon options.

Representations

The most common form of output is to show the results of some analysis. Suppose, for example, that the goal were to show the sales of the various divisions for the last year. The appropriateness of the output depends on what the decision maker expects to do with the information. If the decision makers simply wanted to know if the various regions were meeting their goals, they might appreciate the use of images to represent information called *metri-glyphs*, such as those shown in Figure 5.13. Those with "smiling faces" show sales that met the goals, while those with "sad faces" did not. Further, the larger the smile, the more sales exceeded objectives, and the larger the grimaces, the more seriously they missed. We can even illustrate one set of results with the "smile" and another with the "eyes" of the face. For example, if the smile represented the profit level, the eyes might represent the dividend level. Closed eyes would represent no dividends, while the size of the open eyes would represent the magnitude of the dividends. Of course, not all decision makers (or all cultures) appreciate the cute use of metri-glyphs as output.

Alternatively, if the goal of the analysis were to determine where sales were largest, we might display those on a map with different shadings or colors as codes to show the range of results. Or we might draw the map to scale in proportion to the sales of the region, as shown in Figure 5.14.

If the goal were to determine trends over several years, the most appropriate output is a graph of the results, as shown in Figure 5.15. It is easy to see that some regions increased sales while others decreased, and to read off the relative amounts (such as "a lot" or " a little").

On the other hand, if the decision maker wanted the actual numbers (to do some hand calculation, for example), then the graph in Figure 5.15 is inappropriate because it is difficult to glean the actual sales figures from it. In this case, a table of numbers, such as Figure 5.16, is more useful.

Of course, the appropriate output might be animation and/or video rather than a display on a screen. For example, if the model is a simulation of a bank and varies the number of clerks, the types of services handled by each clerk, and number of queues, and the impact of each factor on queue length, then an animation of the queues might be more illustrative than the aggregated summary statistics.

Perceived Ownership of Analyses

In addition to providing the appropriate type of output for the results under consideration, designers should remind the users that they control the analyses and

Figure 5.13   Metri-glyphs.

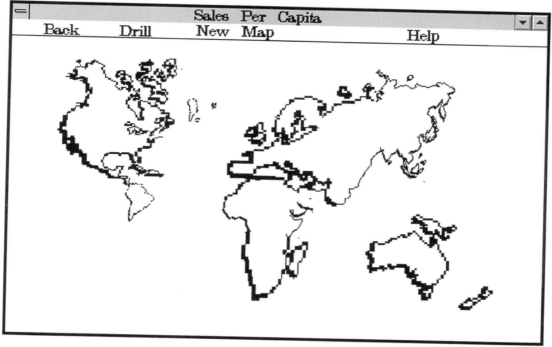

Figure 5.14 Maps drawn to scale of sales volume.

therefore the decision making authority. Computer novices may not feel "ownership" of the answer because it was something "done by the computer," not really by them. One way of counteracting this tendency is to provide users an easy way of changing the analyses if the results do not answer the question appropriately or completely. For example, consider Figure 5.17. Note that in this analysis we can compute profitability either with discounting or without it. The decision maker has chosen discounting (that box is checked). However, the results without discounting are easy to obtain given the onscreen keys. Similarly, Figure 5.18 encourages users to experiment with the model (by providing different estimates for key variables) by prompting the user with the "Revise" button and by making it easy to do. Note in Figure 5.18 that the user has the option to revise both the decision variables under consideration—Number of Clerks and Number of queues. Similarly, the user has the ability to affect the value of the environment variable—Expected Number of Customers Per Hour.[3] However, relevant statistics (in this case, aver-

---

[3]While an average would have been provided automatically, the user may want to test the sensitivity of the model to the parameter. Users should not expect to complete such testing blindly. Hence, there is a button that allows them to review the relevant statistics over different time horizons and during different times of the day.

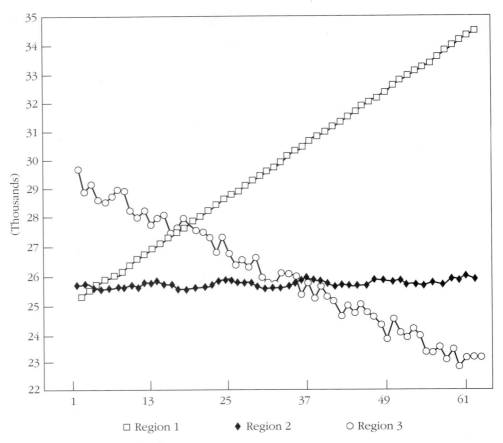

Figure 5.15 A graphical representation.

age waiting time) are only recomputed after the user selects the "Re-Run Simulation" button. This provides the users the ability not only to acquire new values, but also to validate that the entered value is the one intended. Similarly, the simulation is only re-run for the user when requested.

Graphs and Bias

Just as it is important to provide users unbiased use of models, it is also important to provide them unbiased output. What and how designers provide information can affect how that information is perceived by the decision maker. Of course, we assume the designer will not *intentionally* rig the system to provide biased results. However, the more dangerous problem is when the rigging is done unintentionally.

Date	Region	Sales Associate	Sales Amount
2/5	9	J. Smythe	9,518.36
2/5	7	G. Miliganti	9,544.90
2/12	5	A. Joshi	89,527.30
2/12	8	C. Ali	75,018.77
2/19	1	J-L. deGaulle	78,631.47
2/19	5	K. Gupta	76,850.24
2/19	8	C. Ali	84,718.09
2/26	6	N. Kwon	71,864.52
3/1	4	C. Chen	99,718.99
3/1	3	T. Milharcic	84,841.59
3/8	6	N. Kwon	8,263.84
3/8	1	O. La Flamme	23,418.37
3/8	7	G. Miliganti	80,855.72
3/15	9	K. Nelson	74,178.40

Figure 5.16   Disaggregate posting of results.

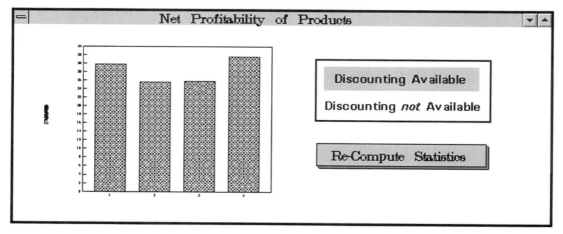

Figure 5.17   Onscreen analysis change prompting.

◆ **DSS in Action** ◆

One of the most widely publicized examples of VR used by the public is a setup created by Matsushita in Japan. This is a retail application set up in Japan to help people choose appliances and furnishings for the relatively small kitchen apartment spaces in Tokyo. Users bring their architectural plans to the Matsushita store, and a virtual copy of their home kitchen is programmed into the computer system. Buyers can then mix and match appliances, cabinets, colors, and sizes to see what their complete kitchen will look like—without installing a single item in the actual location.

Suppose, for example, that the user is considering a decision regarding the management of two plants and examines average daily productivity in those plants. If it provides *only* the average values, the system could be giving biased output because it does not help the user see the meaningfulness of those numbers. Average productivity at plant one could be 5,000, while that at plant two it could be 7,000. This *appears* to be a big difference. However, if we know that the standard deviation in daily productivity is 2,000, the difference no longer looks so significant. Hence, simply providing the appropriate supplementary information, as described in Chapter 4, will help provide unbiased results.

Another place where designers inadvertently provide bias in the results is in the display of graphs. Since most decision makers look at graphs to obtain a quick impression of the meaning of the data, they might not take the time to determine that their impression is affected by the way the graph is displayed. For example, consider the effect of the difference in scaling of the axes in Figure 5.19.

In the first (lefthand) version of this graph, the axes were determined so that the graph would fill the total space. Clearly this graph demonstrates a fairly high rate of revenue growth. However, by simply increasing the range of the x-axis, the second graph gives the impression of a considerably higher rate of growth over

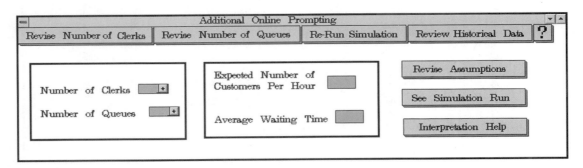

Figure 5.18   Additional onscreen prompting.

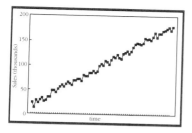 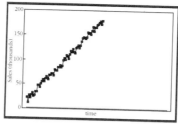 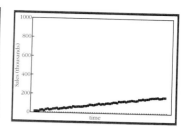

Figure 5.19 Scaling deception.

the same time period. Similarly, increasing the range of the y-axis makes the rate of growth appear much smaller in the last graph. The designer must ensure that this misrepresentation does not occur by correctly choosing and labeling the scale.

The use of icons on bar charts can leave inappropriate impressions, too. Consider Figure 5.20, which presents a histogram of the revenues for three different regions using the symbol for the British pound sterling. It appears that revenues are greatest in Region 2 and least in Region 3. However, the magnitude of the differences in revenues is distorted by the appearance of the symbol. To increase the height of the symbol and maintain the appropriate proportions, we must also increase the width. Hence, the taller the symbol, the wider it becomes. As both dimensions increase, the symbol's presence increases at the square of the increased revenues, thereby exaggerating the magnitude of the increase. Instead, a better op-

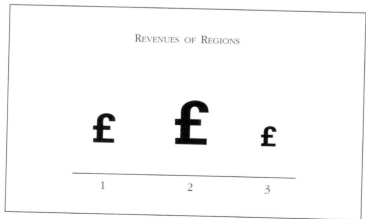

Figure 5.20 Distortion in histogram.

tion is to stack the icon to get the appropriate magnitude represented, as shown in Figure 5.21.

Another factor that can provide perceptual bias for decision makers is the absence of aggregation of subjects when creating a histogram or pie chart. Consider Figure 5.22, which displays the maintenance costs for 16 machines as a function of the age of the machine. Costs increase as the machines get older. However, because the data are not aggregated, it is impossible to obtain a true view of the pattern itself. The eye is directed toward the outliers, such as the second machine, which had high costs as a one-year-old, and the 10th and 14th machines, which had relatively low costs (given their ages). The problem is exacerbated, of course, as the number of subjects increases. Consider, instead, Figure 5.23, in which machines are aggregated by age.

Figure 5.23 makes the pattern in the data much clearer and we are not inappropriately distracted by outlier observations. There is a leveling off of the costs around years 3–5 and again at years 6–7. Furthermore, year 8 seems to be a typically good year with relatively low maintenance costs.

On the other hand, aggregated data can allow decision makers to generalize inappropriately from the data. Specifically, Figure 5.23 does not identify how many of each type of machine exist in each of the age groups. Suppose the maintenance costs for the single 9-year-old machine were exceptionally high. There is no way for decision makers to know they are generalizing from one observation. A better design would identify the number of cases, either as a legend or on the graph.

We cannot enumerate here all the distortion and bias that can be represented in a graph. However, awareness of the problems can help to avoid bias problems in DSS design.

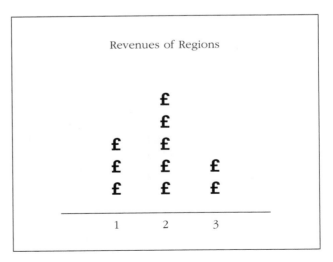

Figure 5.21   Stacked icon histogram.

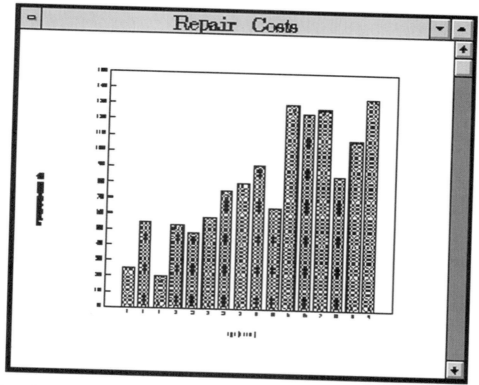

Figure 5.22   Individual histogram.

Support for All Phases of Decision Making

Displays must be constructed so as to help decision makers through all the phases in decision making. According to Simon's model discussed in Chapter 2, this means there must be displays to help users with the intelligence phase, the design phase, and the choice phase.

In the first of these phases, intelligence, the decision maker is looking for problems or opportunities. The DSS should help by continually scanning relevant records. For an operations manager, these records might be productivity and absenteeism levels for all the plants. For a CEO, there might be news reports about similar companies or about the economy as a whole. Decision support is the creation and *automatic* presentation of exception reports or news stories that need the decision maker's attention. Hence, when the operations decision maker turns on the computers, he or she could automatically be notified that productivity is low in a particular plant or absenteeism is high in another as an *indicator* of a problem needing attention. When the CEO turns on the computer, automatic notification of changes in economic indicators might suggest the consideration of a

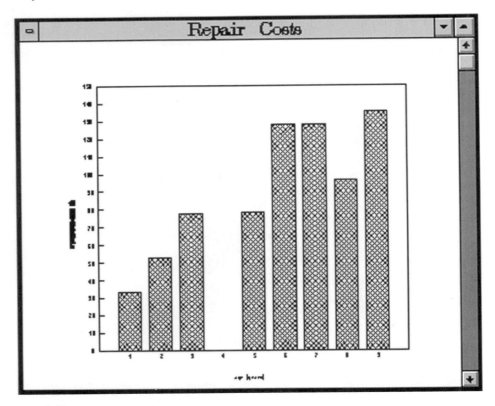

Figure 5.23   Aggregated histogram.

new product. The system does not make the decision; rather, it brings the information to the user's attention. What must be scanned and how it is displayed for it to highlight problems or opportunities is a function of the specific DSS.

In the second phase of decision making, users are developing and analyzing possible courses of action. Typically they are building and running models and considering their sensitivity to assumptions. Displays must be created that will help users generate alternatives. This might be as easy as providing an outlining template on which to brainstorm or the ability to teleconference with employees at a remote plant to initiate ideas.

Displays must also be created to help in the building, analysis, and linking of models. This includes the formulation of the model, its development, and refinement and analysis. This means displays should be able to prompt users for information necessary to run the model that has not been provided. The system should provide suggestions for improvements to the models as well as alert the user to violations of the model's assumptions. Finally, displays must provide diagnostic help when the model does not work appropriately.

In the choice phase, the decision maker must select a course of action from those available. Hence, the displays should help users compare the various options. In addition, the displays should prompt users to complete sensitivity of the models to assumptions and scenarios of problems.

Regardless of what phase of decision making is being supported, the goal of the display is to provide information to the user in the most natural and understandable way. It is critical that any display be coherent and understandable and provide context-sensitive help. Since no one can anticipate all the ideas that might be generated from any particular display, the system must be flexible enough to allow nonlinear movement. For example, the user should be able to transfer to a new topic or model, display a reference, seek auxiliary information, activate a video or audio clip, run a program, or send for help.

The Knowledge Base

The knowledge base, as it refers to a user interface, includes all the information users must know about the system to use it effectively. We might think of this as the instructions for system operation, including how to initiate it, how to select options, and how to change options. These instructions are presented to the users in different ways. Preliminary training for system use might be individual or group training and hands-on or conceptual training. To supplement this training, there is typically some onscreen prompting and help screens with additional information.

In the DSS context, there are additional ways of delivering the knowledge base. One popular mechanism is training by example. The user is taken through a complete decision scenario and shown all the options used and why. The system also can provide diagnostic information when the user is at an impasse, such as additional steps in an analysis. Or it can offer suggestions for additional data use or analyses. For example, the system might recommend to users of mathematical programming techniques that they consider post-optimality analyses.

The goal is to make the system as effortless as possible in order to encourage users to actually use the software to its fullest. This means there must be ways for experienced users *and* inexperienced users to obtain the kind of help they need, and that the training and help must be for specific techniques and models. Users typically are not experts in statistical modeling, financial modeling, mathematical programming, and the like. They need help in formulating their models and using them properly. This help must be included in the system.

Knowing how the users will employ the system is important to understanding what one can assume of them. Historically, users have used decision support systems in three modes: subscription mode, chauffeured mode, and terminal mode.[4]

---

[4]The classical definition of *modes* also includes the clerk mode. This mode differs from the terminal mode only in that decision makers prepare their requests offline and submit them in batch mode. While once common, such batch processing of decision support systems is rarely seen today.

Subscription mode means that the decision maker receives reports, analyses, or other aggregated information on a regular basis, without request. This mode does not allow for any special requests or user-oriented manipulation or modification. Reports might be generated on paper or sent directly to the user's computer for display. Clearly, there is very little involvement of the user with the system and hence users expect the computer requests to be trivial.

Chauffeured mode implies that the decision maker does not use the system directly, but rather makes requests through an assistant or other intermediary, who actually performs and interprets the analysis and reports the results to the decision maker. Since these "chauffeurs" are often technical experts, the system's designer can provide more "power use" instructions and less help with interpretation instructions.

Finally, terminal mode implies that the decision maker actually sits at the computer, requests the data and analyses, and interprets results. These users are often high-level executives who should not be expected to remember a lot of commands and rules for usage. It is especially important for them to have easy navigation through the system, accessible help options for both navigation and content, and recommendations regarding better analyses. Touch screens, mouse entry, and pull-down menus have made many sophisticated systems seem easy.

◆ MODES OF COMMUNICATION

In a listserv discussion group regarding the use of computers in education, one teacher wrote that her class requested information about "what it was like before computers." The answers they obtained with regard to communication included discussion of voice inflections, gestures, and other forms of nonverbal communication that helped people understand what others were trying to convey. Many of us can remember when neatness in written work was another aspect of communication.

In any kind of communication, there is significant room for misinterpretation. The fact that computers do not understand nuances, nonverbal communications, or voice inflections, designers should regard the user interface design with care. As user interfaces become more sophisticated, as technology allows for greater variation in the kind of interfaces designed, and as decisions become more global, our concern about the appropriateness of every kind of communication is increased.

Four basic elements of communication need attention: *mental models, metaphors, navigation of the model*, and *look*. The mental model refers to the organization and representation of data and functions. It is common today to use a desktop as a representation of computer activity. Information might be kept in file folders, access to messages might be through a telephone icon, the delete function might be represented by a garbage can, and so on. This way of representing specific operations makes sense because it brings with it all the shared meaning of these objects. However, if your place of business is *not* an office, this way of organizing

---

◆ DSS Designs Insights ◆

When we emulate speech in a computer, designers need to worry about more than speech recognition and synthesis. Researchers have found three important aspects of speech that need to be incorporated. First, speech is interactive. Few of us can actually hold our part of the conversation without hearing something in return. Without some form of feedback, our speech will probably increase in speed and probably even in tone. Research teams at MIT found that these changes in speech can actually cause the computer to reject commands it would otherwise adopt.[*] Hence, they incorporated phrases such as "ah ha" that would be uttered at judicious times, and found that it helped the human keep his or her speech in a normal range. In other words, some utterances in speech are protocols such as those found in networking handshaking.

A second important aspect of speech is that meaning can be expressed in short-hand language that probably would be meaningless to others *if* the participants know each other well. Over time, shared experiences lead to shared meanings in phrases. For example, occasionally one of my colleagues will utter "1-4-3-2" in a conversation. Those of us who know him well know this is shorthand for "I told you so" (the numbers reflect the number of letters in each of the words). To others, it makes no sense. Another colleague, when discussing the potential problems of a strategy I was about to adopt for a meeting, warned me to remember Pickett's Charge. Now, to those who know nothing about the American Civil War, this warning tells us nothing. Those who know about the war, and the Gettysburg confrontation in particular, know that he was telling me that we all face decisions with incomplete information and that we should not become too confident in our abilities in light of that incomplete information. In fact, he was warning me to (a) check my assumptions and (b) look for indications of crucial information that could suggest a need to my strategy. Many historians believe that had Pickett's charge been successful, the American Civil War might have had a different outcome.

A third important aspect of speech is that it is contextual. A phrase or sentence in context might be totally understandable, but quite baffling out of context. For this reason, we generally have redundant signals in human interactions. Somehow that same redundancy needs to be incorporated into human–computer interactions to ensure understandability.

[*]Negroponte, N., "Talking with computers," *Wired*, 2.03, March 1994, p. 144.

---

your computer probably would not make sense. For example, if your task is in an operating room of a hospital, you need your user interface to resemble the functions you are accustomed to performing. Your screen should look more like a medical chart because it groups together processes and information in the way medical personnel are accustomed to reading it. Understanding how users think about their job is crucial to making the system work for them.

Metaphors are used every day to represent fundamental images and concepts that are easily recognized, understood, or remembered. The desktop image, for example, helps us understand how applications are launched and controlled by using those technologies. Similarly, the classroom metaphor brings with it not only an expectation of how furniture is arranged, but also the general operating rules of the group. In the design of DSS user interfaces, metaphors refer to the substitution of a symbol for information or procedures; the substitution of an associated symbol with the item itself, such as a red cross with medical care; the personification of an inanimate object; or the substitution of a part of a group for the whole, such as the use of one number to indicate data. Before building metaphors into a system, we need to be sure they will convey the intended meaning by being intuitive, accurate, and easily understood. Whether icons, pictorial representation of results (such as in animations or in graphics), or terminology (such as the difference between browse mode and edit mode), metaphors ease and shorten communication but *only* if all parties share the meaning. Consider Figure 5.24, which provides metaphors for type specification. While many people would understand the symbols at the right of this screen, not everyone would.

The *navigation* of the model refers to the movement among the data and functions and how it can be designed to provide quick access and easy understanding. In one environment, it might make sense to group together all the models and to create subgroups of, say, specific statistical functions, because users differentiate them from mathematical programming functions. However, in another environment, users think of the kind of question, not the kind of technique when moving among the options in the DSS. Here, it would be appropriate to group certain statistical tests with financial data and analyses, and certain mathematical models with production planning.

◆ DSS in Action ◆

Often the benefit of user interfaces is in simplicity. For example, in one DSS used for supplier selection,* users are required to enter information only into a limited number of cells in a matrix. To them, this provides complete flexibility because they can still get decision support even in the face of incomplete information. Once the data entry is complete, the DSS ranks the criteria by importance and presents a model that displays only those factors that ranked highly. This facilitates comparison of alternatives among important dimensions. In addition, if a decision maker notices the absence of a particular criterion that he or she believes is important, he or she is warned of a problem immediately.

*Evans-Correia, K., "Putting decisions through the software wringer: Intel uses decision support software for supplier selection," *Purchasing*, 110, March 21, 1991, pp. 62–64.

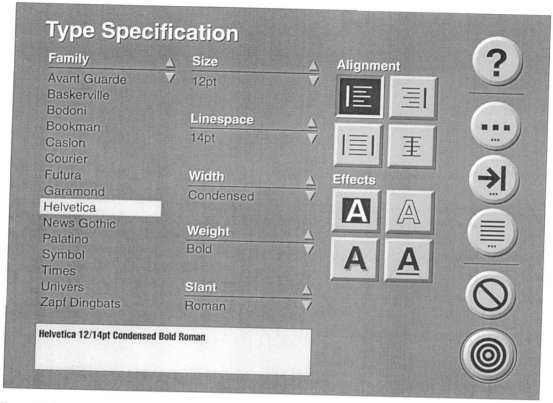

Figure 5.24 Use of international symbols.

Finally, the look of a system refers to its appearance. No one who knows computer company culture would expect to see the same dress code at IBM that was observed at Apple Computer Corporation. By extension, then, we would not expect to find preferences for the same user interface at the two corporations. Just as corporate culture can affect preferences for the user interface, other cultural influences associated with national origin, sex, race, age, employment level, and the interaction among all of those influences will affect the way a person responds to particular user interfaces. However, designers have assumed that all users will respond similarly.

For example, color metaphors mean different things in different cultures. While a red flashing light might be interpreted as an indicator of something important to one culture, it might suggest users stop all processing in another. Similarly, it is believed that the size of the image can affect how we respond to it. A group of researchers at Stanford is studying how different cultures respond to "little people" (as good luck? or as a curse?) to help understand how large human images need

◆   DSS Designs Insights   ◆

Often designers of DSS and other computer systems do not attend to questions of the impact of the screen design on the use of the technology well enough. Studies have shown that some factors heighten emotional response while others calm it. In fact, the literature, taken as a whole, suggests that individuals' interactions with computers and other communication technologies are fundamentally social and natural. One of the current projects of the Social Responses to Communication Technology Consortium is an examination of the effect of the size of the image of a human displayed on a computer for teleconferencing on individuals' responses to that image. Stanford Professor Byron Reeves was quoted as saying "many cultures around the world assign magical properties to people who are small. . . . These small people grant wishes, they monitor behavior and they keep people safe. But they also can punish or be bad just for the hell of it." Professor Clifford Nass further elaborates in that same article, "We want to know, when you see a small face on a screen, do you respond to it as if it were magical? Is it perceived as powerful or capable?"* So, the question is Do you have a different response to the two screens below?

 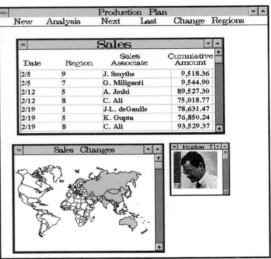

*Morkes, J., "The leprechaun effect," *Wired*, 2.01, January 1994, p. 28.

to be for effective teleconferencing in a DSS framework. Others believe that the linear, restrained treatment of menus is received differently in different cultures. They suggest that a menu that is more curvilinear and less aggressive, such as that in Figure 5.25, might be received better by some cultures.

While we do not have many guidelines for user interface today, it is important to reflect on possible differences in needs and use them in our development efforts. Research is being conducted now that will be used in the future to guide in the development effort.

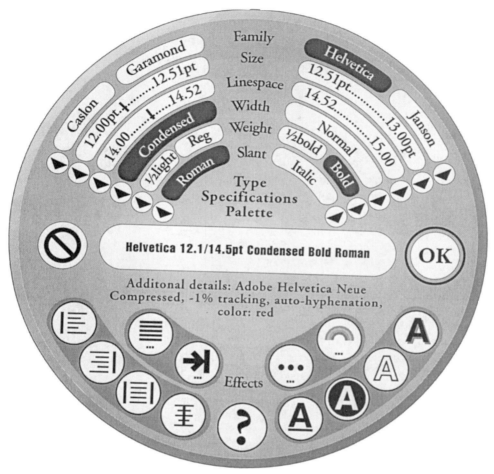

Figure 5.25 An alternative menu format.

◆ THE CAR EXAMPLE

The expected user of the car-selection DSS we have been discussing is a consumer who intends to purchase or lease an automobile. It may be the first automobile the user has ever selected, or the user may have purchased new automobiles every year for the last 20 years. In addition, the user may never have touched a computer before or may be an expert computer user. This leads to a wide range of user capabilities and user needs for the system, which, in turn, leads to complications in the design of the user interface.

It is crucial that system designers provide multiple paths through the system to accommodate the needs of all kinds of users. For example, some users may have no idea what kind of automobile to acquire and need guidance at every step of the process. Other users may have a particular manufacturer from which to select, while other users have particular criteria that are important to them. Still others may have a small number of automobiles they want to compare on specific functions. The system must be able to accommodate all these decision styles, and the user interface needs to facilitate that process. Examples of commercial systems are shown in Figure 5.26.

Early screens should guide users to the part of the system that will meet their needs. The temptation exists to use the first few screens to gain some insight into the user's needs and his or her preferences for information, but the temptation should be resisted. Users want to see information on these first few screens that convinces them the system will facilitate their choice process; background information about themselves will not do that. Rather, it is important to use some simple mechanism for screening users and deciding what part of the system will be most appropriate to use. Some designers simply ask whether the user wants "no support," "partial support," or "total support" from the system. While this may be appropriate in some circumstances, it can be very confusing unless the user can query the system and find what kinds of analyses and access each of those levels provide. An alternative is to ask whether the user knows the set of automobiles from which a selection will be made, whether the user knows the criteria that should be applied to the choice process, or whether the user needs full support in understanding the dimensions that should be evaluated. Further, if the user selects known criteria and specifies financial information, the choice process should follow a financial model selection. That does not mean that the system can not pop up warning messages or help screens that suggest consideration of other criteria. Rather, it means that the *focus* of the process must have face validity and seem relevant to the user.

The first few screens also set the tone for the system, and hence particular attention must be given to their design. The screens need to be simple, clean, and easy to follow. There should be sufficient instructions to help the novice user to move through the system easily while not slowing down the more proficient user. In addition, users will want to see information that moves quickly but is easily discerned.

One way to accomplish this is to provide a menuing system through which it is easy for the user to maneuver. Consider, for example, the three options demonstrated in Figure 5.27. Note that a designer would *not* place all three of these options on the same screen. They are presented here for the purposes of discussion.

The first option (labeled 5.27a) allows the user to enter the manufacturer of automobiles that is preferred. After this the user can select the option to start the search. From a programming point of view, this is the easiest of the searches to accomplish; the Level 5 Object code shown in Figure 5.28 illustrates the process that must be used to accomplish the search. While it appears user friendly at the outset, it actually is not a particularly useful user interface. One problem is that the user is restricted to searching for only one manufacturer of automobile. Many

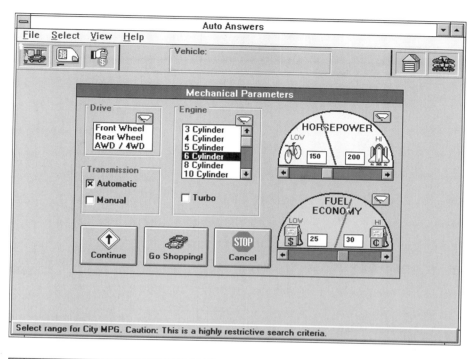

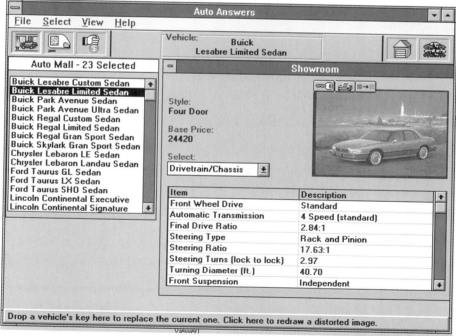

Figure 5.26 Initial screens from commercial automobile purchasing systems.

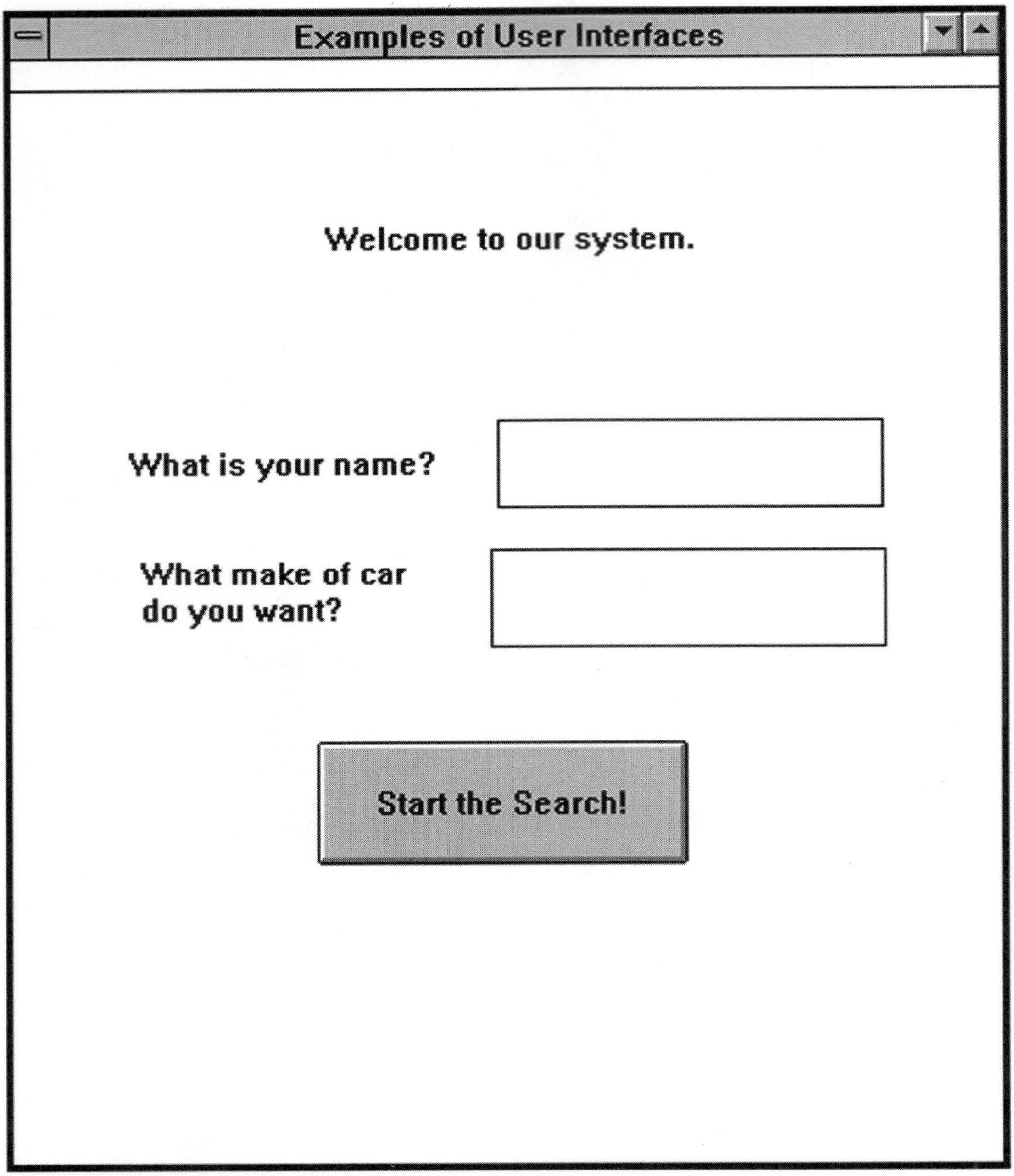

Figure 5.27a   Menu options.

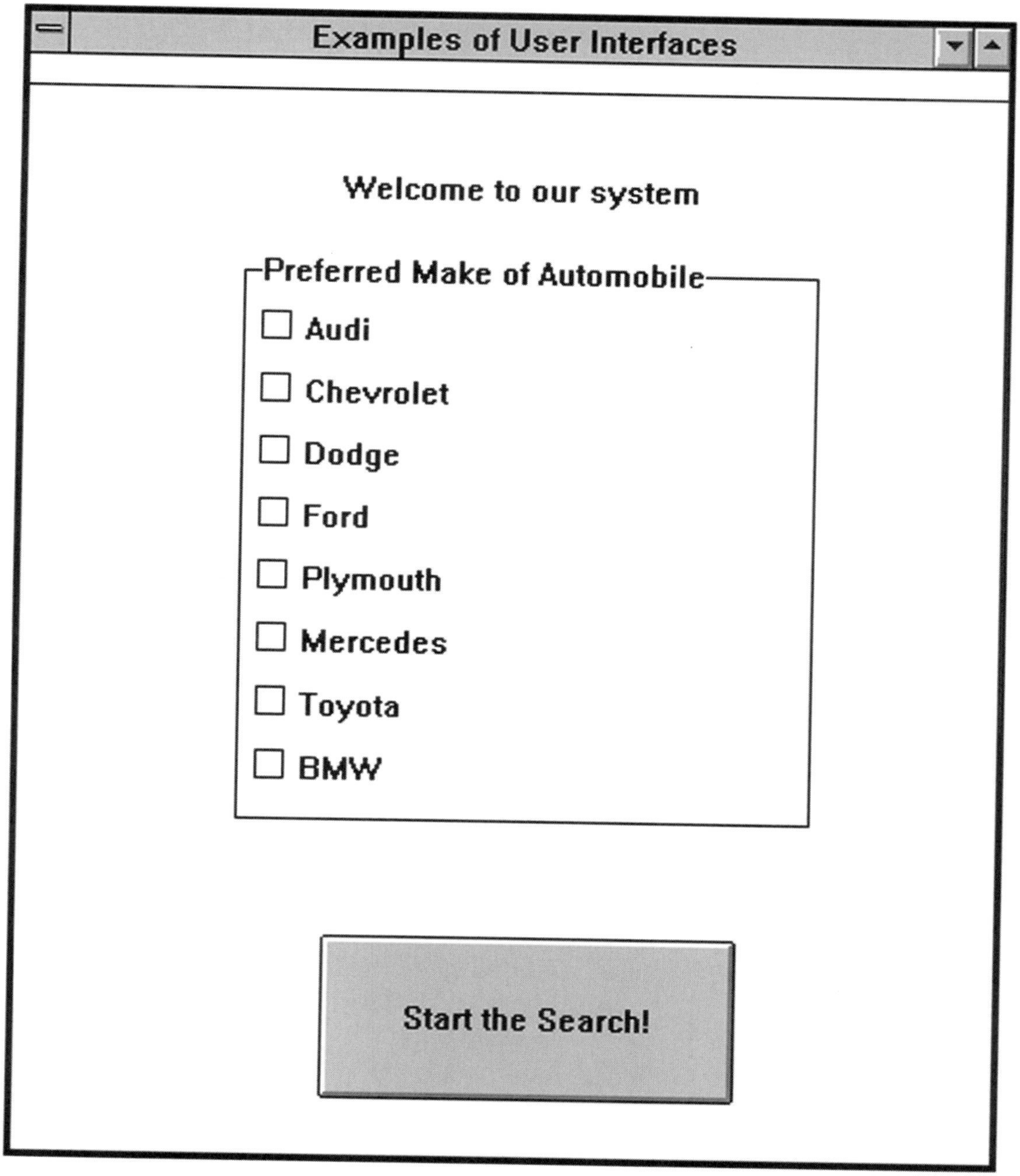

Figure 5.27b   Continued.

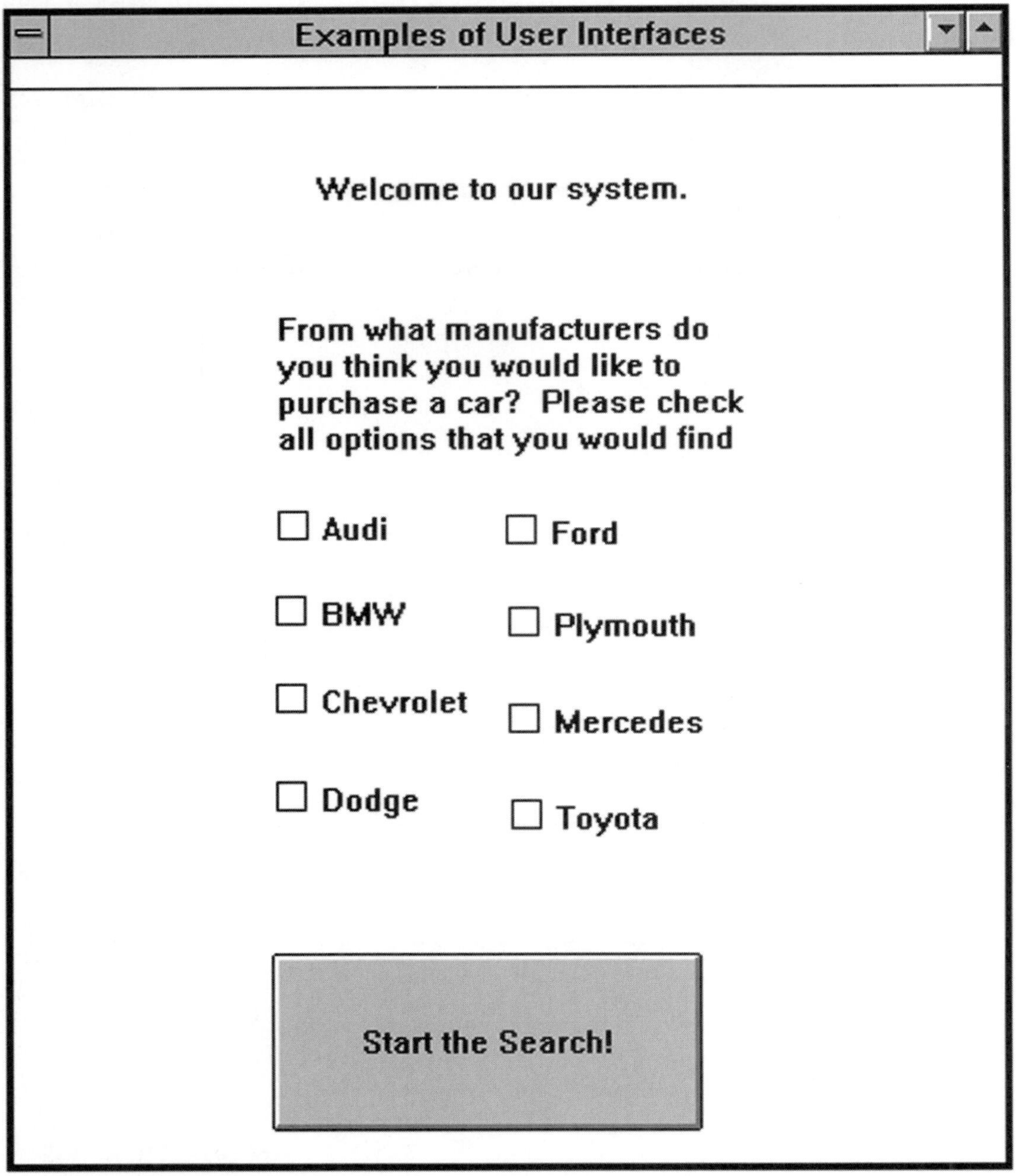

Figure 5.27c Continued.

people want to search on multiple manufacturers; they would have to make several trips through the system and would have more difficulty comparing the results. A second problem is that this method requires users to be able to remember all the manufacturers they might consider. This may cause them to neglect some options, either because they forgot about them or because they did not know they existed. While it is acceptable for the user to narrow his or her search, it is not acceptable for the system to do it on the user's behalf. A third problem is that this method requires the user to spell the name of the manufacturer correctly. Often users do not know the correct spelling, or they make typographic errors, or they use a variation on the name (such as Chevy for Chevrolet). Unless the search corrects for these possible problems, no relevant matches will be made.

Consider instead the option in Figure 5.27b, where the user is given check boxes from which to select automobiles. Users can select as many models as they desire, and since they only need to click the mouse, the designer does not need to worry about spelling, typing, and nickname problems. The Level 5 Object code is somewhat more difficult to write, as shown in Figure 5.29, but not so much more difficult that it outweighs the benefits from a user's perspective. However, by electing to use a check box group, we have limited the label to the name of the variable

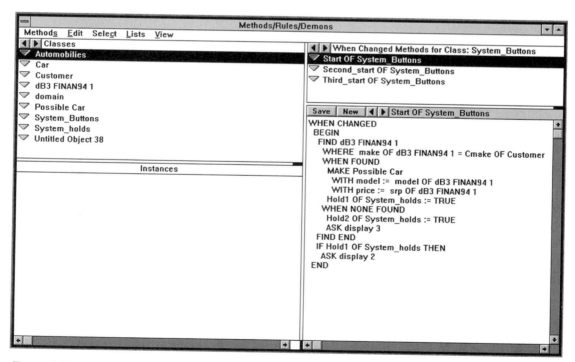

Figure 5.28 Level 5 Object code to perform the search shown in Figure 5.27—lefthand example.

that is specified in the system (in this case, to "preferred make of automobile"). This might not provide the best guidance to the user.

The alternative is to define individual check boxes, such as shown on Figure 5.27c. This method provides all the benefits of the second method and the supporting code is identical. In addition, it allows designers to include a more natural explanation (in terms of a text box) for users to follow. Finally, the individual check boxes allow the designer to order the options differently from the manner in which they were defined (notice, for example, that the third group is entirely in alphabetical order). This allows flexibility to change the order in different screens, as well as to add new manufacturers to the database after the system is deployed.

Another concern in designing a user interface is to keep it simple and easy to use. We know that people work best with seven plus or minus two individual data items. Hence, menus should not overwhelm users with too much information at

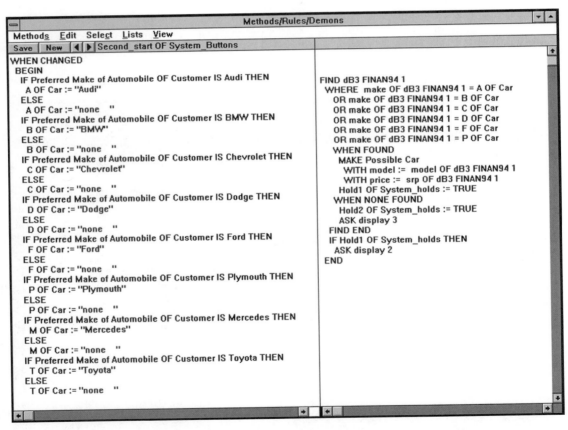

Figure 5.29   Level 5 Object code to perform the search shown in Figure 5.27b and Figure 5.27c.

one time. On the other hand, loading new displays can take time and therefore detract from the system. Another option available with GUI systems such as Level 5 Object is to make options visible only after they become relevant. For example, consider the screen shown in Figure 5.30. The user has two primary questions to address, the length of time that the automobile will be kept and whether it will be new or used. After the user selects a new car to be kept a relatively short period of time, the system determines that this user is eligible to consider leasing a car. Hence, the option of leasing appears on the *same screen*, as shown in Figure 5.31. If the user had selected a used car, then he or she would not be interested in leasing an automobile and hence that option would not be displayed. The underlying code simply notes that another option is added to the screen when these conditions are found to be true:

> IF Type of Automobile OF Automobile Preferences IS New Car
> AND Expected Length of Ownership OF Customer IS Short Time Period
> THEN items OF display 1 := radiobutton group 3

where, radio button group 3 is, of course, defined as an object elsewhere.

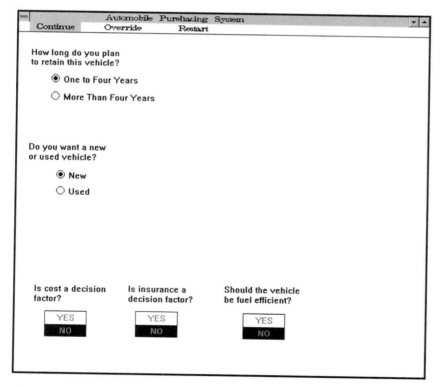

Figure 5.30   Change in menus after other selections.

It is important that the user interface provide a standard and uniform look and feel in the system. One way to do this is to provide consistent windows for the different kinds of information that you might want to provide. For example, consider Figure 5.32, in which some possible windows are defined. In this example, warning messages are displayed in the upper-left corner while help messages are displayed in the lower-right corner. Similarly, graphics may appear in the upper-right corner while technical assistance, such as help in modeling or generating alternatives, appears in the lower-left corner. These windows should have consistent titles, colors, sizes, and other characteristics. In this way, users will develop intuition about the information being displayed and act accordingly.

Generally, these windows will not appear until needed. In Figure 5.33, users can request technical assistance by pressing the "Help" button on the main screen. When they do, the technical assistance window (shown open in this figure) appears. This kind of passive assistance is an alternative to the automatic response that was demonstrated in Figure 5.31 (where the system determines that the additional information is necessary). You can allow the window to be closable using

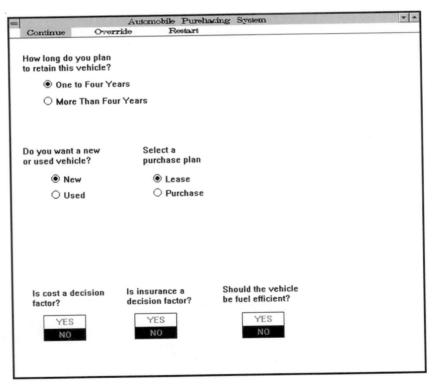

Figure 5.31   Result of the code shown above.

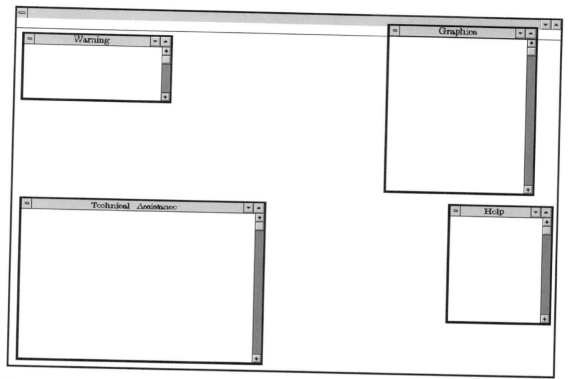

Figure 5.32   Possible window definitions.

standard window tools, through a menu item, or through a push button, as shown in this figure. If you need to ensure that the user reads the information, you can make it impossible for him or her to continue without acknowledgment. If there is a need for additional processing after the window has been displayed, then you must have a mechanism for alerting the system after it has been read. Both those purposes are served best by the push button.

The Level 5 Object code to access the window and to close the window are shown in Figure 5.34. The method at the top, *Help 1 OF Assistance*, shows the simple process for accessing the help. When the user presses the button, the system causes these lines of code to be run. The process is an easy one: First the appropriate display is assigned to the window, and then the window is made visible. In this way, the user can access whatever technical assistance is appropriate for the process being undertaken. Similarly, to close the window, the method at the bottom, *close help OF discontinue*, the designer simply needs to set the visibility of the window to false and then to reset the display that is assigned to that window.

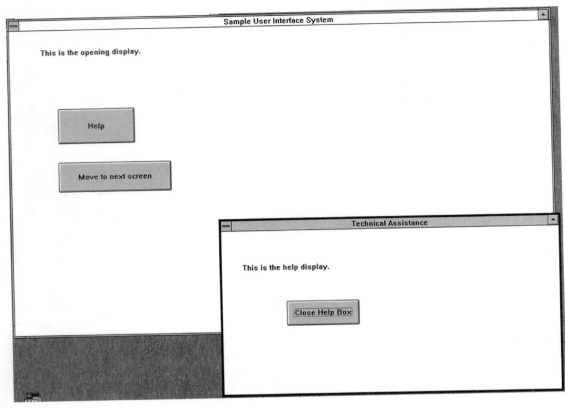

Figure 5.33 Mechanisms for introducing specialized windows.

In Level 5 Object, that is accomplished with the FORGET command. Of course, if the system wanted to maintain a record of what has been accessed, or if the designer wanted other code to be processed as a result of this information being seen, then the additional code would accompany these two commands.

Another way in which additional information might be displayed is shown in Figure 5.35. Here, the user wants to control both the image and the text shown in the "Graphics" Window so that it relates to the same automobile about which the user is asking. Since the user does not require additional functions, the designer elected to allow the user simply to close the screen through typical Windows functions.

The Level 5 Object code used to generate this functionality is shown in Figure 5.36. One might notice that before the window becomes visible, the user has assigned a specific display to the window and then populated that display. The object graphics window has an attribute called "output" that refers to the display that is to appear when the graphics window is made visible, in this case, display 12.

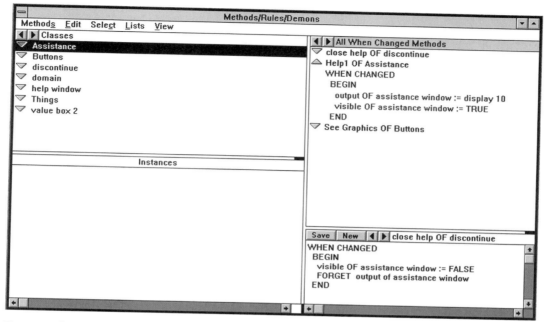

Figure 5.34 Level 5 Object code to control the windows in Figure 5.33.

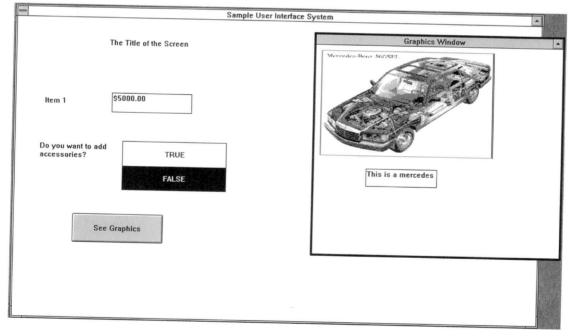

Figure 5.35 Alternate mechanism for introducing specialized windows.

It is possible that display 12 is completely designed, in which case the designer is finished. More likely, however, the designer needs to determine what should appear in the window as a function of that which the user is requesting. In this case, the designer uses an attribute of the display called "item to" identify the items that should appear on the display. The middle lines tell the system that it should place two items, one with a picture (picturebox 1) and one with text (textbox 12) on that window. Of course, these two items could be defined elsewhere. For example, since there is no additional mention of the picturebox, it must be defined already. However, we do define here the attribute text of textbox 14. Similarly, we can define other functions, such as the location factors that complete the method in this example.

Formatting is important for the environment. Sometimes designers use icons or pictures, such as those on the lower side of Figure 5.37, for menu options. These can be helpful *if* they are understandable to the user, *and* if they are used consistently. Since these icons are to elicit the intuition of the user, it is important that they be meaningful to the user, and hence the user needs to be involved in their selection. One way to supplement these is to provide either permanent or transient wording near the icon to help the user build intuition.

Features should be built into the system to lessen the chance of user confusion. Only available options should appear in normal text, and others should be dimmed. Also, when a user selects a specific car, standard options should appear in one box, with add-on options in another.

Another way to help the user is to provide sensitive hyperregions on the screen instead of menu options, buttons, or icons. In the lower-left side of Figure 5.37, a map is illustrated. When the user moves his or her mouse to different continents, they are highlighted (as Asia is in this example). If the user double-clicks the mouse,

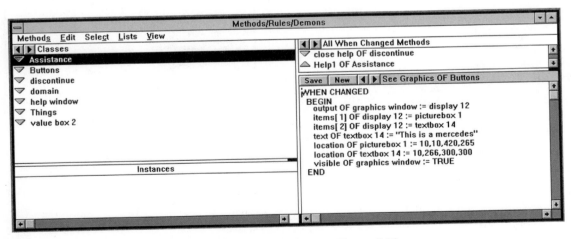

Figure 5.36 Level 5 Object code to control the windows in Figure 5.35.

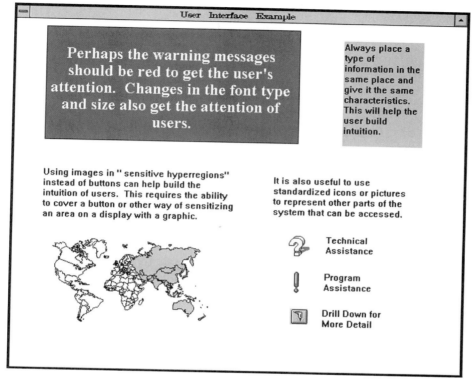

Figure 5.37   Some user interface design concerns.

more information about Asian operations is provided. This requires the designer to have defined the locations *a priori* and to have the appropriate regions linked to the appropriate additional screens.

While consistency helps the user develop intuition regarding the system, changes help gain the user's attention. Consider the warning message in the upper-left side of Figure 5.37. Rather than using the standard appearance of the windows, the designer has elected a different background color, font, font size, and font color for the message to catch the user's attention. Selective use of such changes can help increase the likelihood that information will not be lost.

If the users access the system frequently, alternative information retrieval techniques should be made available. In this way, the user who accesses it frequently can increase the speed of retrieval and hence improve its performance value. The system should be tailored to acquire information in as few steps as possible while still maintaining clarity.

Finally, the format of the output of the system needs to be tailored to specific uses. If the user is comparing the prices for a type of vehicle from several makers, a simple histogram may be an easy way to display the comparison. The actual numeric value should also be displayed in some proximity to the bar that it represents or next to the legend. If, however, the user wishes to compare the available options, a table display may be more appropriate. If an option is available, the system could display the option highlighted, or in a different color from those that are not available. This would allow for an easier comparison since the difference will be more noticeable.

DISCUSSION

The user interface is the most important part of a DSS because it is what the user thinks of as being the DSS. The best access to models and data is irrelevant if the decision makers cannot make the system understand their specific needs for information, or if the system cannot provide the answers in a manner that decision makers can understand and use. As tools become more sophisticated, designers will be able to select input devices that are touch, motion, or voice sensitive and output devices that are graphical, motion, or virtual reality based. All this can bring a richness to the choice context if used appropriately.

QUESTIONS

1. Many computer products now have something called "online documentation." Depending on the product, this can include a text manual available electronically, a passive request system that accesses the text manual, bubble help on menus, and so on. Discuss what formats of online documentation are appropriate for a DSS.

2. Identify how your features of a user interface should be affected by the decision making literature covered in Chapter 2.

3. Andersen Consulting uses a technique described as "low-fidelity prototyping" when designing user interfaces. This method has designers and users design screens together using *paper* template items. Hence, if the user indicates that another item should be added to the screen, such as a button, the designer picks up a paper object shaped like a button and allows the user to place it on the paper designated as the screen. Compare and contrast the advantages and disadvantages of using "low-fidelity prototyping" in the design of a DSS to those associated with using "high-fidelity prototyping" of designing screens with a product on the computer.

4. How should the design of a user interface be influenced by the corporate environment? How should its design be influenced by the national environment?

5. Discuss how you might provide a user interface through which to compare multiple automobiles. Would users' modeling preferences influence this decision?

6. Discuss how virtual reality devices might be used as a user interface in a DSS intended to help users select automobiles.

7. The fact that windows can be sized by the user can be both a problem and an opportunity in the design of DSSs. Discuss the advantages and disadvantages of sizing of windows. How might the disadvantages be overcome?

8. What kinds of problems are introduced if designers use standalone prototyping packages to design screens and interact with users?

9. Discuss how the process for establishing the user interface requirements for a 1-person system would differ from the process for a 25-person system.

10. By what process would you evaluate the user interface of a DSS?

◆ O N   T H E   W E B ◆

On the Web for this chapter provides additional information about user interfaces and the tools used to develop them. Links can provide access to demonstration packages, general overview information, applications, software providers, tutorials and more. Additional discussion questions and new applications will also be added as they become available.

- *Links provide access to information about user interface products.* Links can provide access to information, comparisons, reviews, and general information about software products and tools for user interface design. Users can use the tools to determine the factors that facilitate and inhibit DSS use.

- *Links provide access to descriptions of applications and development hints.* In addition to information about the software itself, the Web provides links to applications of the tools worldwide. You will have access to chronicles of users' successes and failures as well as innovative applications.

- *Links provide access to different user-interface methodologies.* Specifically, users can access currently unconventional user interfaces, such as virtual reality or voice-activated menus.

- *Links provide access to systems regarding automobile purchase and leasing.* Several tools to help users purchase or lease an automobile are available on the Web. Users have the opportunity to access the tools and gain insights of the kinds of options that facilitate and those that inhibit the use of the DSS.

You can access material for this chapter from the general WWW Page for the book, or, directly from the following URL.
http://www.umsl.edu/~sauter/DSS/ui.html

SUGGESTED READINGS

Alter, S.L., *Decision Support Systems: Current Practices and Continuing Challenges*, Reading, MA: Addison-Wesley, 1980.

Bennett, J., "User-oriented graphics," in *User-Oriented Design of Interactive Graphic Systems*, S. Treu (ed.), New York: ACM, 1977.

Donovan, J.J. and S.E. Madnick, "Institutional and ad hoc decision support systems and their effective use," *DataBase*, 8(3), Winter 1977.

Frenkel, K.A., "The art and science of visualizing data," *Communications of the ACM*, 31(2), 1988, pp. 110-121.

Marcus, A., "Human communications issues in advanced user interfaces," *Communications of the ACM*, 36(4), April 1993, pp. 101-109.

Marcus, A. and A. vanDam, "User interface developments for the nineties," *IEEE Computing*, 24(9), September 1991, pp. 49-57.

Miller, G.A., "The magical number seven plus or minus two: Some limits on our capacity for processing information," *Psychology Review*, 63, 1956, pp. 81-97.

Nielsen, J., "Noncommand user interfaces," *Communications of the ACM*, 36(4), April 1993, pp. 82-99.

Norman, D.A., *The Design of Everyday Things*, New York: Doubleday, 1990.

Robertson, G.G., S.K. Card, and J.D. Mackinlay, "Information visualization using 3D interactive animation," *Communications of the ACM*, 36(4), April 1993, pp. 56-71.

Shneiderman, B., *Designing the User Interface: Strategies for Effective Human-Computer Interaction*, Reading, MA: Addison-Wesley, 1993.

Steiger, D., R. Sharda, and B. LeClaire, "Graphical interfaces for network modeling: A model management system perspective," *ORSA Journal on Computing*, 5(3), Summer 1993, pp. 275-291.

Stohr, E.A. and N.H. White, "User interfaces for decision support systems: An overview," *International Journal of Policy Analysis and Information Systems*, 6(4), 1982.

Tannen, D., *You Just Don't Understand: Women and Men in Conversation*, New York: William Morrow and Company, Inc., 1990.

Turban, E., *Decision Support and Expert Systems*, New York: Macmillan Publishing Company, 1990.

Chapter 6

Mail Components

◆ ◆ ◆

Historically, we have thought of the mail system, even the electronic mail (e-mail) system, as an auxiliary function. That is, as developers of decision support systems, we have recognized that a decision maker would probably have electronic mail delivery systems, but ignored such systems when designing and implementing a DSS. To use electronic mail, decision makers would first need to stop processing the DSS. Even when the technology brought "windowing" of applications, thereby allowing the user to move to the e-mail application easily, the two were still independent applications. That is, although it might be easier to get to the e-mail system, the decision maker could not easily send documents, graphics, or text from the DSS or receive such to use within the DSS.

In today's electronic environment, not seamlessly integrating the DSS with an e-mail system means a serious limitation to the information and analyses available to the decision maker. Increasing numbers of managers are finding e-mail to be a productivity-enhancement tool. The Electronic Messaging Association estimates that between 30 and 50 million people use e-mail today and that the number of users will quintuple in the next decade. International Data Corporation estimates that some component of *every* Fortune 500 company uses e-mail and the Electronic Messaging Association estimates that more than half of the 2,000 largest corporations in North America use e-mail. These statistics should be evaluated in light of the fact that only 80% of Fortune 500 companies have installed voice mail systems. Finally, in their book *Re-engineering the Corporation: A Manifesto for Business Revolution,* Hammer and Champy called for all corporations to restructure the functions of the organization around information technology, with e-mail at its core.

◆ INTEGRATION OF MAIL MANAGEMENT

An interface with the e-mail system allows the decision maker greater access to discussion groups, Internet databases, other electronic data, and tools for decision making. These resources can extend the range of available information and can, in some cases, provide access to more timely data. Further, the use of e-mail can help decision makers to communicate with colleagues to clarify information and analyses as well as to establish a shared perspective of solutions. This can, in turn, improve decision makers' communication and credibility with subordinates and build support for choices. These are all important steps in the decision making process.

Consider the options that access to electronic mail can provide to decision makers. First, e-mail can allow decision makers to seek information from colleagues easily. Rather than needing to find a mutually agreeable time for discussion, the decision maker can send a question to a colleague, who can respond to it when time permits. Such flexibility is especially important when decision makers need to communicate with those in other countries. Otherwise, decision makers have a very small window each day during which to contact transnational colleagues, and they cannot use their expertise optimally.

Communication among decision makers is typically more complex than simple questions and answers that fit on a simple mail template. Frequently, they need to build documents and analyses from the analysis effort, or from related records. If the e-mail is integrated into the DSS, they both can easily include documents, spreadsheets, and even graphics in the transmission to enrich the communication. Many of today's commercial e-mail products have the capability to include docu-

---

◆ DSS in Action ◆

Richard Jurek, an officer and international market research analyst for corporate and institutional services at Northern Trust Bank Co. in Chicago wrote of his experiences using the Internet at work in an article in *Internet World.** An example of his use of e-mail is provided here:

Recently, a consultant in Australia sent me e-mail requesting information on gold prices. I forwarded the Australian's message to another analyst and asked if he could help me.

In the meantime, I went to lunch. When I got back to my desk, there was a detailed answer from the analyst waiting in my mailbox. Total elapsed time between request and answer was a little over an hour.

*Before the Net, such a request would have taken several days of intense library research to complete. I let the power of the Net connect me to an expert in the field who was able to find what I needed without me having to miss my lunch. Now **that** is power.*

*Jurek, R., "Surfing Agent Man," *Internet World*, October 1995, pp. 93–94.

ments and records in the e-mail. Figure 6.1 illustrates how *cc:Mail* embeds existing word processing documents in the e-mail. If the user frequently embeds particular documents or kinds of documents, he or she can customize the toolbar to complete those tasks.

Corporate use of e-mail for day-to-day communications that might have traditionally been accomplished by meetings, telephone calls, or postal service gets individuals in the habit of using this means of communication. For reasons that are not readily apparent, most people tend to answer their e-mail more readily and quickly than they do other modes of communication. Similarly, people are more likely to use e-mail to convey information that might not otherwise be shared, especially with superiors or those of superior rank. E-mail provides a link among these individuals that is not represented in their typical interactions. In addition, many people provide more of a personal character to their e-mail messages than to memos. This, in turn, sets the tone of

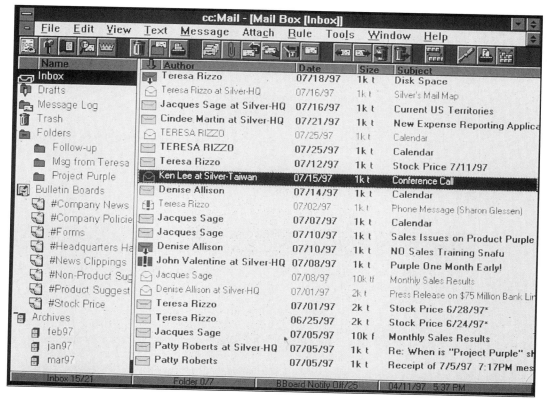

Figure 6.1 Mail from e-mail system.

◆ DSS in Action ◆

PalmVue is a mobile computer system from Hewlett-Packard that facilitates communication between hospitals and physicians, even when the physician is not physically located at the hospital or office. This system transmits patients' vital signs and
test results to a hand-held computer that is accessed similarly to a pager. In this
manner, physicians can alter regimens in response to results or changes in patient
condition.

---

dialogue about a problem or opportunity that can lead to earlier identification
of opportunities viable for strategic changes and/or symptoms of problems in
early stages of the difficulties. So lower-level managers might be willing to
e-mail a supervisor regarding recent changes in absenteeism among employees
and seek advice on how to address the problem or determine if other plants
are experiencing similar phenomena. These same managers tend to wait until
determining whether the problem is severe before writing a memo or seeking
out the supervisor.

In addition to using direct e-mail, decision makers can make use of electronic
discussion groups to gain information or insights from an extended group of colleagues. Open-access discussion groups are available on the Internet on almost
any imaginable topic. For example, decision makers who are trying to find information regarding planning in urban areas can access:

- a general discussion group on urban planning;
- several location-specific discussions, such as one from the Dublin metro
  area;
- some tool-specific discussions, such as on geographic information systems
  or statistics;

◆ DSS in Action ◆

The following is an example of the effective use of e-mail as a medium for discussion in support of a decision:

> A company faced a suddenly announced hostile takeover attempt while its exec-
> utives were scattered about the globe. Since the bid was announced on a Fri-
> day, the executives had until Monday morning to construct an effective counter-
> strategy. Lacking time to return to the home office for a meeting, they
> collaborated by e-mail and succeeded in fending off the bid.*

*Leslie, J., "Mail Bonding," *Wired*, 2.03, March 1994, pp. 42–48.

◆ DSS in Action ◆

E-mail can link co-workers easily, regardless of distances between them. A few years ago, a computer analyst working for Witco, a chemical and petroleum firm, experienced chest pains and severe shortness of breath while working in his cubicle at the firm. Unfortunately, because of his difficulty breathing, he was unable to call for help. However, he could type the words "HELP. FEEL SICK. NEED AID." and, with one keystroke, e-mail the message to all the members of his department. Co-workers received the message almost immediately and came to the rescue. One person trained in CPR began work immediately, while others called for the ambulance.

- some data-specific discussions, such as on using census data;
- several topic-specific discussions, such as ones on disaster planning and preparadeness, transit issues, or tourism.

Similarly, decision makers in human resource departments might find help on the industrial relations, the safety, the drug abuse management, or the training and development discussion groups.

Some of the discussion groups involve industry topics, such as the music industry, hotel and restaurant management, or even automated milking systems groups. There are also discussion groups of interest to decision makers available to support specific kinds of tasks, such as the network administrators, the chemical engineers', or the technical standards discussion groups. Finally, there are some general decision making discussion groups, such as the total quality management (TQM), managed health care, and executive groups. Some of the general topic headings shown on one list are shown in Figure 6.2.

These discussion groups are, for the most part, open to anyone who is interested in the topic. Users generally post their questions through e-mail submission. The question is, in turn, sent to all subscribers of the discussion group. When subscribers know an answer, or a reference, they might respond to the discussion group or to the individual making a query. Users are, of course,

◆ DSS Design Insights ◆

International Discount Communications (IDT) has devised a system whereby blind and visually handicapped individuals will be able to receive e-mail over the telephone. IDT provides each user an Internet address. E-mail sent to that address is automatically converted to voice messages. The user is then called on the telephone and the message is read to the user aloud. Thus, these individuals can experience all the benefits of e-mail.

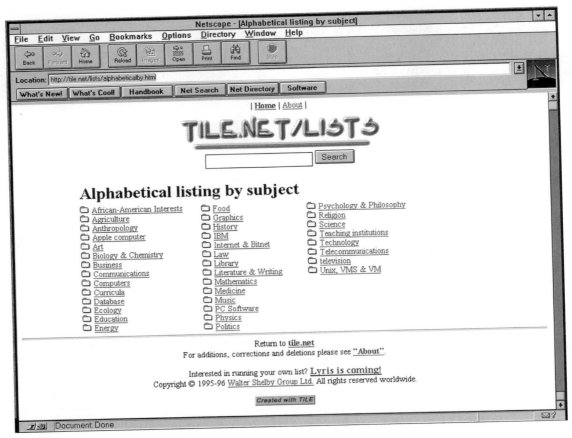

Figure 6.2 Categories for electronic discussion groups.

dependent on other users to check their e-mail regularly and to be willing to respond to questions. Many of the discussion groups work quite well and individuals find much helpful information. Only experimentation with the systems can provide accurate information about what discussion groups will and will not be useful.

Decision makers can also initiate discussion groups composed of employees of their corporation, a department and a project team, or colleagues of similar interests and responsibilities at other corporations. Similarly, discussion groups could be used to suggest procedural or policy changes and/or to identify issues of importance to one's clients or subordinates. Users in these closed discussion groups may be more forthcoming with information and support because they are certain who will read their messages and they do not need to worry about exposing proprietary information or corporate strategic plans. Furthermore, the closed discussion groups share a common goal, and answering queries will help move closer to that common goal.

Some e-mail packages available today actually facilitate such discussions. For example, *DaVinci e-mail*, shown in Figure 6.3, includes a bulletin board for group-wide messaging. Using such a facility, decision makers can build group discussions easily and quickly to respond to questions or queries as they occur. More important, packages such as *DaVinci* have the ability to follow e-mail message threads intelligently. As the decision maker wants to follow the conversation on a particular topic, he or she can find the original message, the replies to the message, and even the replies to the replies to the messages easily, even if there were many other e-mail messages in the meanwhile. Hence, the decision maker is not distracted by other topics and can focus on the issue under consideration.

A third way of using e-mail is as a way of scanning one's environment to identify problems and opportunities. For example, discussion groups or newsgroups

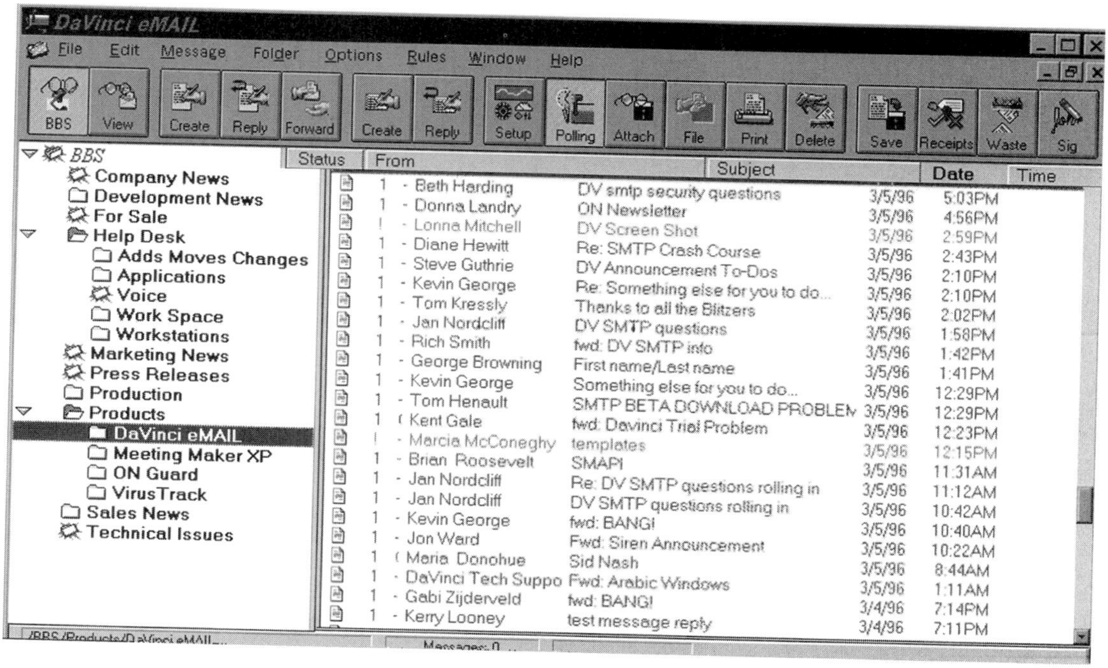

Figure 6.3   DaVinci e-mail system.

◆ **DSS in Action** ◆

Johnson & Higgins is a large insurance broker in New York City. The Information Systems Department at Johnson & Higgins created a *Lotus Notes* system that they call *S&H InfoEdge*. The purpose of this system is to track critical insurance broker-age information, including insurance company profiles, marketing information, live news, technical expertise, and corporate profiles. The *S&H InfoEdge* application al-lows teams to provide customized, filtered information to clients based on their individual user requirements.

A *Datamation* article* cites William Wilson, Vice President of MIS at Johnson & Higgins, as saying, "Our teams span many different cities and countries around the world, yet they can communicate easily. Individual brokers can draw on a world-wide knowledge base that represents the combined resources of all the other bro-kers. . . . With *Notes*, every time you update something on one server, it ripples out to all the other servers, no matter where you started from." This connectivity brings together almost 2,000 users who send an average of 9,000 e-mail messages and 800 faxes each day. As any of the teams get additional information, all teams get the additional information, regardless of their location.

*Baum, D., "Developing Serious Apps with Notes," *Datamation,* 40 (8), April 15, 1994, pp. 28–32.

such as those identified here could help decision makers discover new ideas. For example, questions posed by other users about new techniques or procedures might bring them to the attention of decision makers, who might see them as a strategic opportunity or use the ideas to solve an existing problem. Similarly, de-cision makers from multinational corporations, or who are participating in multi-national negotiations, could monitor recent events in specific countries, such as China, India, Ukraine, and Muslim countries, to look for changes that might re-quire alterations in policies or plans. Similarly, internal discussion groups could be monitored for indicators of problems or ideas.

Discussion groups are not the only ways in which decision makers can utilize electronic communication. There are a variety of news services to which one can subscribe on the Internet. For example, Clarinet News provides timely industry news and technology-related wire stories. From these, the decision makers can stay abreast of the news as it relates to the choices under consideration. This service also provides financial information, stock quotes, and other materials that could be of interest to decision makers. Similarly, Scientific Technical Information Systems (STIS) provides science and technology information from the National Science Foun-dation, and the University of Maryland provides information on a variety of top-ics. Several industry-specific news services also exist. For example, both Pennsyl-vania State University and Clemson University support agriculturally based news services, and OCEANIC provides information on all aspects of marine research. Finally, some services, such as that provided by the Colorado Alliance of Research Libraries, provide indices of current articles, searches of government periodicals, and other library resources.

One does not need to subscribe to all services in order to use them. Recent advancements in Internet protocol have significantly increased the opportunities for obtaining and searching electronic databases. It is simple to find weather information that might affect testing plans at a remote plant or to access the U.S. Department of State Travel Advisories. Similarly, decision makers can search all electronic databases for a particular topic, say managed health care plans, with negligible effort. They can peruse corporate telephone books, press releases, and annual reports from around the world.

Consider, for example, the *infoSage* system from IBM. This system provides intelligent filtering of e-mail as it enters the system. After intercepting and reading messages, *infoSage* attempts to classify the message based on predefined rules. These rules may reflect the importance of the sender of the information, the message, or the source of the message. The actions could be to display the message with a priority rating, save the message in a folder, discard the message, forward the message, or take other actions. Figure 6.4 illustrates how *infoSage* can be used

Figure 6.4   Member profile in *infoSage.*

to filter news or discussion group mail. In particular, the user must select from a listing terms that best describe his or her needs. The user can elect to supplement that list with particular keywords that might appear in the news. Finally, the user can prioritize the topics in the list to reflect her relative interests. At regular intervals, then, the system will scan newswire services and find stories that reflect the user's interests. The articles will then be organized by subject headings and will be prioritized to reflect the interests of the user. An example is provided in Figure 6.5.

This search effort is managed through client/server technology and an Internet browser, such as *Netscape Navigator*. Using such tools, decision makers can access data distributed and maintained on machines throughout the world by navigating through a hierarchy of directories and documents. Alternatively, they can focus their search by probing an index to find all directories using a particular keyword. For example, when trying to find information regarding managed health care plans, a decision maker could create a listing of all entries including the term "managed health care" or "insurance plans." This list would be more focused than the entire Internet and would be more efficient to search. Similarly, decision makers can use a search facility to run a full text search on *all* documents and list those that contain particular keywords. Census data, legal decisions, and pending federal legislation are available for searching and downloading. Similarly, many libraries can be searched via the Internet to determine where a particular reference can

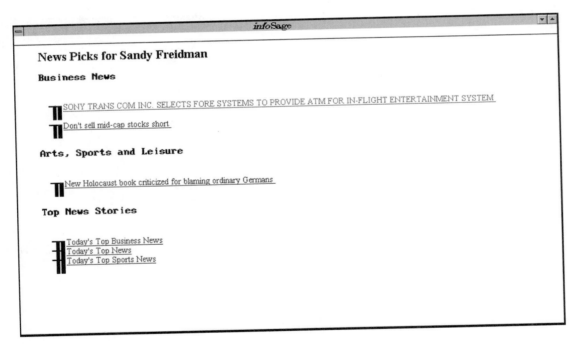

Figure 6.5   Results of a news search using profile.

be found. Many libraries are beginning to provide electronic full-text versions of reference materials and printed material that can be accessed via the World Wide Web. Finally, some professional groups are beginning to provide online access to journals or article summaries. In the long run, the possibilities are endless for those who know how to access the system.

◆ EXAMPLES OF USE

Consider the following example of how decision makers might use these Internet resources and e-mail capabilities in concert with a decision support system. Suppose the decision makers are contemplating where to locate a new plant. The DSS available to them provides information about availability of raw materials, distances to suppliers and clients, and costs of building and taxes. Further, suppose that the analysis of options has identified several equally desirable locations for the plant. So the decision makers need to look for other information to support the choice.

For those locations that are within the United States, decision makers could search census data over the Internet to determine the number of citizens, their average education and income, and the unemployment rate to gain insight into the types of workers available locally. They could also access *Gopher* servers of universities in the region to scan the types of academic programs and experiences available to the citizens to determine if the appropriate skilled workers would be available locally. For those locations outside the United States, decision makers could monitor discussion groups for symptoms of problems that might inhibit success of the plant.

The decision makers might also search industry news services for information that might affect the desirability of locations and/or criteria for making a selection. For example, decision makers could examine recent articles from the wire services for information about any tax changes or other significant legislation that has been passed recently that might affect the desirability of a particular location. Similarly, a newswire feature about a particular community might present previously unidentified features that might make that location more desirable. Decision makers could also use a discussion group of company employees in different locations about local issues that might affect the desirability of a given plant. Similarly, the decision maker might pose a question to managers of existing plants regarding critical success factors that relate to location.

◆ IMPLICATIONS FOR DSS DESIGN

The methods for addressing the design of the mail management system are similar to those of the data management and model management components. In particular, if the decision makers have access to an *adequate* e-mail system, the designers of the DSS should *not* redesign the system, but rather provide links between that e-mail system and the DSS. If, however, the decision makers do not have access to an adequate e-mail system, it would be prudent to include this feature in the overall design.

In the preceding paragraph, the term *adequate e-mail system* was used. This does not mean that availability of *any* e-mail system precludes including this feature in the design. Rather, if the e-mail system is not adequate as defined below, then one should include these functions in the design of a decision support system.

An adequate e-mail system is one that has features that make it useful for decision making. Such systems should have available the conventional e-mail features, such as the ability to index the messages and display that index, as well as the ability to log the messages, delete the messages, forward the messages to other interested individuals, and reply to the messages. In addition, they should have an easily and automatically accessible notebook of individuals and their e-mail address.

To be useful in a DSS environment, the e-mail system needs additional features that facilitate, or at least do not inhibit, the use of the e-mail system as decision *support*. One such enhancement is that the system automatically notify the user that e-mail is available, regardless of what application is being run. If the automatic notification is not provided, the users are required to stop what they are doing on a regular basis to check electronic mail. Under these conditions, the decision makers will probably not use e-mail, or at least not use it effectively. Of course, decision makers should be able to disable this automatic notification function when they do not want to be interrupted in a current task.

Associated with this feature is the need to provide a message filtering system since automatic notification without a filtering mechanism can make the e-mail system more annoying than helpful. Anyone who has subscribed to discussion groups knows that some forward significant amounts of mail. At some times, depending on the number of discussion groups to which one subscribes, as well as other e-mail traffic, decision makers might be notified as often as 100 each hour that mail is available. Clearly, being notified immediately of nonurgent, or perhaps junk mail, is no better than not being notified at all. However, if the e-mail system notified the user only when messages were received from specific individuals or discussion groups, then it would be *useful* information. Similarly, if the filtering system could read the topic of the message (using the "subject" key line), and interrupt only when e-mail regarding a specified topic or set of topics arrived, it would be more useful to decision makers. Furthermore, such a filtering system might discern between messages that are replies to decision maker inquiries and those that are new messages, in order to give notification priority to answers to user-posed questions. That is, if the e-mail were capable of discerning the source of the e-mail message and could compare it to a *user-defined* set of sources and/or determine the topic of the message and could compare it to a *user-defined* set of topics, then it would "know" when messages were important to the decision maker and interrupt accordingly. Such a system could be made even more useful if these three levels of filtering could be specified in a Boolean fashion. For example, suppose one could allow filtering such as the following.

- Allow interrupt for messages that meet any of these criteria;
- Any message from my supervisor;
- Any response to my query regarding desirability of plant location;
- Any new message from a plant supervisor;
- Any message regarding business opportunities in Croatia;
- Log any other messages, but do not send automatic interrupt for them.

Many commercially available e-mail message systems include the ability to build rules such as these. For example, *BeyondMail* has a sophisticated rules-based

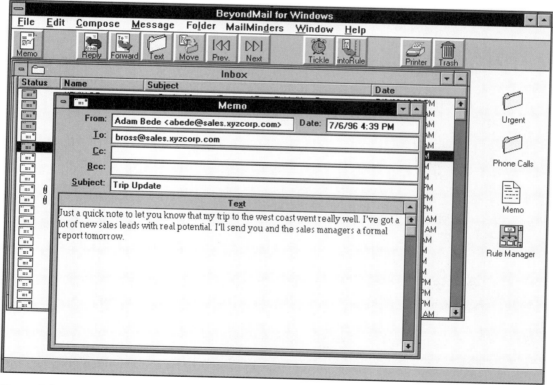

Figure 6.6   BeyondMail e-mail system.

There are both USENET groups and electronic discussion groups addressing the needs of purchasers and owners of automobiles.

In both the "recreation" and "alternative" regions of USENET, there are mailgroups addressing automobiles. Among the ones that can be found there are the following:

Antique and special interest collector cars
    rec.autos.antique
    alt.autos.antique
    rec.autos.misc

Specific manufacturers
    alt.autos.camaro.firebird
    rec.autos.makers.chrysler
    rec.autos.makers.ford.explorer
    alt.autos.ferrari
    rec.autos.makers.ford.mustang
    alt.cars.Ford-Probe
    alt.auto.mercedes
    rec.autos.vw
    rec.autos.makers.vw.aircooled
    rec.autos.makers.vw.watercooled

In addition, there are a variety of electronic discussion groups to which one can subscribe. Among them are lists that specialize in the following topics:

    BMW Digest
    British Cars
    British Pre-War
    Ferrari
    German Marques
    Italian Cars
    Jaguar
    Mercedes
    Sunbeam Alpines
    VW(Aircooled)

Figure 6.7 USENET and electronic discussion groups relating to automobiles.

message-management system (Fig. 6.6). For example, some decision makers might not want any messages interrupting their work on an as-received basis. These decision makers should be allowed to specify how they would like the automatic notification to work to meet their needs. For example, one decision maker might want to receive messages only on an hourly basis, while another might want to know about messages after 10 messages have been received (or even after 10 messages on the same topic). *BeyondMail* allows the user to develop and change rules that process in this manner.

◆ THE CAR SYSTEM

The implications of the mail management system are obvious for an automobile purchasing system. Newsgroups and discussion groups are available for individuals to ask questions about automobiles. Both Usenet groups and electronic discussion groups exist for the purpose of discussing the purchase and ownership of automobiles; an example list is shown in Figure 6.7. Those who are considering a particular automobile might browse the archives of one or more of these lists to determine the types of problems and opportunities that exist with a particular car. Or, if they have a specific question, they could pose it to the group to solicit a wide variety of viewpoints. If the designers of the automobile system wanted, they could provide their own discussion group that could be accessed by dealers, car owners, and others.

There are other opportunities for using electronic mail in the process of purchasing or leasing an automobile. Currently, there are a variety of Web page "advertising centers" for used automobiles, such as the one shown in Figure 6.8.

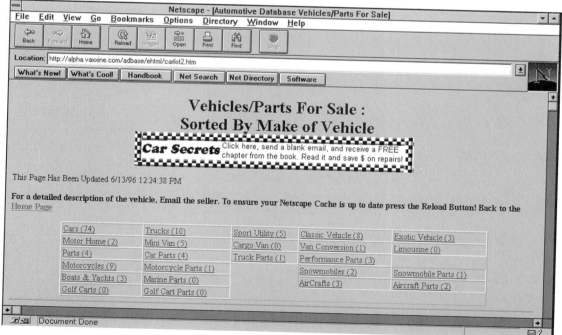

Figure 6.8 Web-based automobile advertising center.

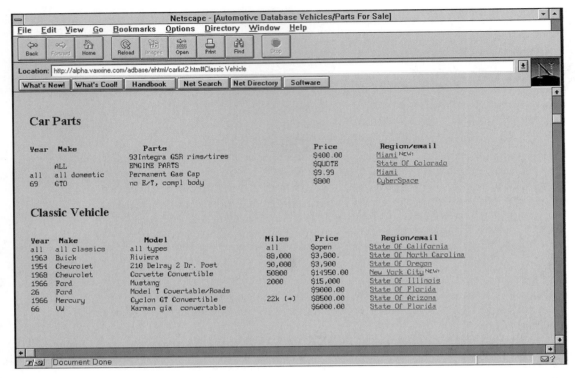

Figure 6.9   Results from a web-based search.

In this case, the Web page provides a medium for bringing together individuals who would like to sell automobiles with those who would like to purchase pre-owned automobiles. The data are provided in categories. If one clicks the mouse on Classic Vehicle, the Web page moves down, and you see the information shown in Figure 6.9. To contact one of those individuals, you need only to click on the line, and an automatic e-mail template appears on the screen for you to complete. Hence, the parties would begin negotiations to purchase the car via e-mail.

Finally, some services are now available to facilitate the negotiation process to get the best possible price on the automobile. These services do the "shopping around" and negotiation for the purchaser. Users must already know what kind of automobile they would like to purchase and the area in which they would like to purchase it. Using e-mail, the customer specifies the necessary information to the service; the dealers respond via telephone. One example of such a system is shown in Figure 6.10.

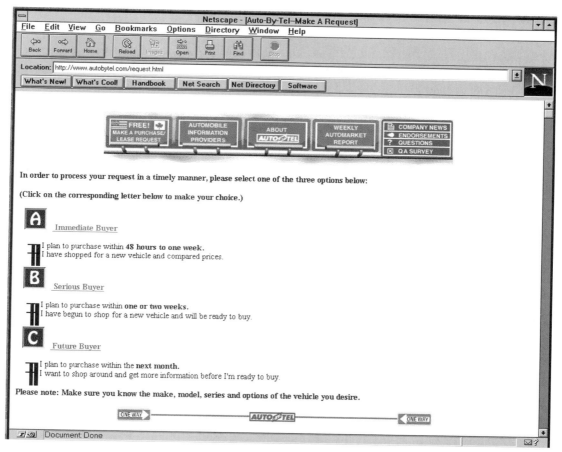

Figure 6.10 Web-based automobile purchasing aids.

DISCUSSION

Electronic mail is quickly becoming an important medium for communication. The value comes in being able to communicate richly, yet asynchronously. E-mail provides a rich medium through which users can have substantive communication on a particular topic and can include documents, graphics, and spreadsheets. However, the person sending the e-mail and the person(s) receiving the e-mail do not need to be engaged simultaneously. Rather, the receiver can wait until a convenient and appropriate time to respond.

With the advent of newsgroups and electronic discussion groups, groups can participate in the discussion. Hence, groups of executives or experts can discuss opportunities and problems. With more open groups, users can get opinions from a wide spectrum of individuals, even those whom users do not know. While this method of collecting information can give the users access to expertise that they might not otherwise have, there is no guarantee that the data being communicated are accurate or relevant to the decision under consideration.

As with the other portions of the decision support system, the mail management system works best if it is well integrated with the other components of the system. Many good commercial products are available that provide the necessary functionality. However, if they can be launched from the DSS and made to have the same feel as the DSS, they will be accepted better and therefore used more.

QUESTIONS

1. Explain why a mail management system of a DSS must have a filtering system for e-mail. What would be the minimum set of factors on which it should filter?

2. What are "mail threads," and why might it be useful to have a system that traces them?

3. Provide three examples of rules one might create for filtering e-mail.

4. Why is it important that the mail management system be well integrated with the DSS?

5. Discuss how a designer would know what Usenet groups or electronic discussion groups are relevant for a particular DSS. How would a designer automate the selection of a list?

6. How can the use of e-mail develop greater support for the acceptance of an alternative?

7. Go to the library or a recent issue of a computer magazine or newspaper and research commercial electronic mail systems available. Which would be useful for integration into a DSS? Why?

8. In Box 6.1, Jurek says that e-mail provides "power" to the decision maker. Explain what he means by power in a manner that you might use to convince an executive.

9. Would the availability of a mail management system increase or decrease the likelihood of acceptance of a DSS by a senior executive? Explain your position.

10. How is DSS usage by transcultural corporations affected by the availability of a mail management system?

◆ O N   T H E   W E B ◆

On the Web for this chapter provides more information about electronic mail, including commercial products, and desirable features and ways these features might be incorporated into decision support systems. Links can provide access to demonstration packages, general overview information, applications, software providers, tutorials, and more. Additional discussion questions and new applications will also be added as they become available.

• *Links provide examples of how e-mail systems are used to facilitate decision making.* For example, one link provides evidence of how groupware is being used at General Motors and has revolutionized how automobile dealers communicate.
• *Links provide examples of different e-mail systems available commercially.* Ex-

amples of and reviews of the leading e-mail systems are provided through these links.
• *Links provide access to information about specific automobile models and opportunities for purchase that are available via e-mail.* Some links parallel traditional operations, such as searching for vehicle parts or making offers for automobiles. Others exploit the communications of the Internet, and allow for centralized queries about products or lowest prices in a region.

You can access material for this chapter from the general WWW Page for the book, or, directly from the following URL.
http://www.umsl.edu/~sauter/DSS/mail.html

SUGGESTED READINGS

Baum, D., "Developing Serious Apps with Notes," *Datamation*, 40 (8), April 15, 1994, pp. 28–32.

Boone, M.E., *Leadership and the Computer*, Rocklin, CA: Prima Publishing, 1991.

Fedorowicz, J., "Evolving Technology for Document-Based DSS," in Sprague, R.H., Jr., and Watson, H.J. *Decision Support Systems: Putting Theory into Practice, Third Edition*, Englewood Cliffs, NJ: Prentice-Hall, 1993, pp. 125–136.

Garnto, C. and Watson, H.J., "An Investigation of Database Requirements for Institutional and ad hoc DSS," in Sprague, R.H., Jr., and Watson, H.J. *Decision Support Systems: Putting Theory into Practice, Third Edition*, Englewood Cliffs, NJ: Prentice-Hall, 1993, pp. 111–124.

Hammer, M. and J. Champy, *Reengineering the Corporation: A Manifesto for Business Revolution*, New York: HarperCollins, 1993.

Jurek, R., "Surfing Agent Man," *Internet World*, October 1995, pp. 93–94.

Kantrowitz, B., "Live Wires," *Newsweek,* September 6, 1993, pp. 42–49.

Kehoe, B.P., *Zen and the Art of the Internet*, 1992.

Krol, E., "*The Whole Internet Catalog and User's Guide*," O'Reilly and Associates.

Leslie, J., "Mail Bonding," *Wired*, 2.03, March 1994, pp. 42–48.

"Making High Tech Work for You," *Fortune, Special Issue*, Autumn 1993.

◆ ◆ ◆

PART III

Issues of Design

Chapter 7

International Decision Support Systems

◆ ◆ ◆

Many executives are choosing to internationalize operations to avail the corporation of larger and more fruitful markets, competition among labor forces, and economical location and distribution incentives. With internationalization comes geographical dispersion, increased industrial and market competition, and increased access to labor pools and natural resources. However, it also brings variations in the technical, legal, economic, and cultural forces affecting the operations and decision making of the enterprise, the impact of which is affected by the form of internationalization.

Transnational corporations can take a variety of forms. For example, it is possible that offices in the various countries produce different products and are essentially separate. On the other hand, it is possible that the products are manufactured or created in one country and marketed in another. Or there can be some combination of the two, such as that described in Figure 7.1. Another form of internationalization is shown in Figure 7.2, where it did not involve the production process, but rather the sharing of data.

◆ MULTINATIONAL DECISION MAKING

Decision support systems have the potential to provide great assistance in multinational decision making because technical variability, legal innuendos, cultural differences, economic pressures, and their coordination exacerbate the turmoil associated with the poorly defined choice processes generally supported by DSS.[1]

---

[1] A team at the University of California at Irvine's Center for Research on Information Technology and Organizations studied the role of information technology in the economies of eleven Asia-Pacific nations. In countries where the investment in information technology exceeded other investments, such as plants and equipment, productivity was the highest. "This means IT investment is more productive than other investments," says one researcher. (*Information Week*, September 19, 1994, p. 74.)

A good description of the complexities of transnational operations, and its suggestion for the importance of decision support systems has been suggested by Dyment.

The global corporation may have a product that was designed in a European country, with components manufactured in Taiwan and Korea. It may be assembled in Canada and sold as a standard model in Brazil, and, as a model fully loaded with options, in the United States. Transfer pricing of the components and assembled product may be determined with an eye to minimizing tax legality. Freight and insurance may be contracted for relet through a Swiss subsidiary, which earns a profit subject only to cantonal taxes. The principal financing may be provided from the Eurodollar market based in London. Add the complexities of having the transactions in different countries, with foreign exchange hedges and contract gains and losses that sometimes offset trading losses or gains, and one has a marvelously complex management control problem.

Figure 7.1   Activities of a Transnational Corporation. Dyment, J., "Strategies of Management Controls for Global Corporations", *The Journal of Business Strategy,* 7(4), 1987, pp. 20–26.

Another example of the complexity of transnational activities illustrating global data transfer, and its implications for DSS is adapted from Sankar and Prabhakar.

Consider the development of a decision support system that could support stock transactions for transnational brokerages with offices in New York, Rome, and Frankfurt. Such a DSS must monitor the activity on multiple exchanges and in multiple markets to help the analyst determine what stocks to trade, when to trade them, and how to trade them. If the stock broker in New York wants to initiate a particular stock transaction, and if that company is listed on multiple exchanges, he or she needs to decide trading on which exchange is most profitable. If, for example, the decision is made to trade on the Rome Stock Exchange, the transaction is sent to a front-end processor in New York, which then transmits it to Rome using a private line. The Rome office sends a confirmation message to New York and sends a duplicate copy of the transaction to the head office. Further, the database used by brokers at all offices needs to be updated immediately so that models tracking trades and prices will be accurate. The coordination among these systems, while still providing decision support, is challenging.

Figure 7.2   Activities of a Transnational Corporation. Sankar, C.S., and P.K. Prabhakar, "Key Technological Components and Issues of Global Information Systems," in Palvia, S., P. Palvia, and R. Zigli (eds), *Global Issues of Information Technology Management,* Harrisburg, PA: The Idea Group, 1992, pp. 332–355.

However, if not implemented properly, DSS can add to the problems of transnational decision making. In order to exploit the benefits, designers need to be sensitive to a wider variety of issues and problems than those considered in the design of domestic systems.

For example, there is good reason to believe that there would be differences in preferences for user interface options for transnational systems. Understanding the preferences and their implications is crucial. Since the user interface is the only way one can interact with the computer, its acceptance by users limits the usefulness of the system as a whole.

The user interface can communicate the importance of information and modeling within a system. Different colors, size of representation (and relative size of representation), spatiality, and contrast provide the "nonverbal cues" for the user interface. Even the way in which one moves from screen to screen or accesses information carries some significance. That is, the user interface can convey what is important to the organization, how the "power" in the organization is controlled, or the corporate norms and expectations.

Consider the screen shown in Figure 7.3. In this screen, the financial implication of a proposed transnational corporate change *to the United States* is emphasized. The message is carried in two ways. First, the implications for the United States are the only ones that default as open to the screen. Users of the system are, in a sense, forced to at least see them (if not use them). However, the implication is that information regarding all other countries is "optional" to the decision because the user needs to take explicit action to cause those results to appear on the screen. The second way in which the United States is emphasized is through

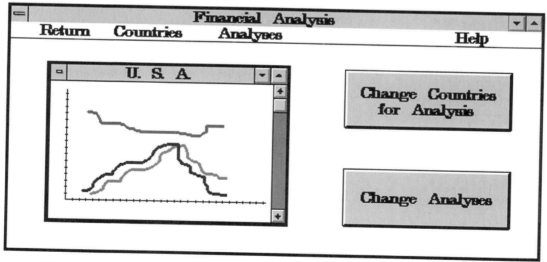

Figure 7.3   User-interface implications

the size of the windows. Even after one has opened the windows for other countries, they are considerably smaller than the window containing the U.S. financial data, hence conveying the idea that non-U.S. data are less important. A similar effect could have been obtained by displaying financial data *only* in U.S. dollars, and not in local currencies. The implications of these differences is, of course, only a problem if the message they convey is *unintended.*

A second problem also is illustrated in Figure 7.3. In this case, instead of emphasizing a specific country, the size and default open options suggest the relative importance of particular analyses. As in the previous example, this screen design suggests that financial implications are the most crucial, whereas all other analyses are secondary. This suggestion of the importance of particular steps in a typical analysis is also conveyed in Figure 5.18. In that screen, the system provides explicit encouragement for the user to attempt to change values and re-run the simulation. The availability of the option is making a statement about the importance of sensitivity analyses; the subtle recommendation would not be apparent without those automatic re-run buttons. This apparent support for particular options can present a problem for a transnational DSS when there are clear cultural differences in the modeling preferences across the cultures. Such differences will be discussed in later sections of this chapter.

Better user interfaces would have given non-U.S. countries greater representation on the screen. Perhaps no analyses would be open as a default, but rather the world as a whole is shown, and users can click on the country—or countries—of interest. Similarly, it would send less of a message if users needed to actually *request* all options.

Language and Custom Differences

The relative sizing and location of objects on the screen is not the only aspect needing attention in a transnational DSS. Since the user interface may be the basis for interaction with other managers using the system, users become totally dependent on this interface for prompts that would otherwise come from "nonverbal cues" and other tempering cues in communication. Hence, words lose their intonation and the user becomes totally dependent on symbols and icons to convey more information. These new ways of affecting patterns of communication are fine as long as everyone agrees to the meaning of the various cues. Problems occur, however, if there is a difference between the codes meant by the creators of the cues and the codes used by the consumers of the cues.

In addition, the user interface may have a variety of problems associated with the use of multiple languages. People in many cultures, such as the French,[2] are

---

[2]To protect their culture, the French are planning to fine anyone caught adulterating the French language with commercial or official English, *including computer terms.* Such terms would now have to be transformed into a French equivalent "when a French term or expression of the same meaning exists." (*Atlanta Journal-Constitution,* March 11, 1994, p. A14.)

adamant about maintaining their language as an active part of their culture, not just some quaint aspect of the small towns in the country. Hence, if one of the nations involved with the system is a country such as France,[3] providing a single language transnational DSS may be impossible; translation of files, commands, databases, and so on may be necessary. Translations can be tricky. Not only do the words need to be translated, but also the *meaning* of the words *as a whole*. For example, the Japanese interpret the word "pragmatic" to mean "tool user." The meaning conveyed by referring to someone as "pragmatic" and that associated with "tool user" are quite different. Without an understanding of the language *and* the culture, the meaning of information used for decision making might be lost. As a result, translations can be time-consuming and people-consuming. Although there are automated translators, they cannot be relied on in such an unstructured setting; they rarely reflect the nuances associated with data. For example, consider the computer-generated translation on the next page. Even without having the original Italian version, it is clear that the *meaning* of the communication has been lost through the translation of the words.[4]

Even when the text is translated properly, its meaningfulness can be affected by the technology associated with data transmission if the language requires special characters. Often, if messages are not sent using an appropriate gateway, encodings become damaged or changed, and hence the message becomes garbled. Some trans-network software strips off control characters, making the reading of text impossible. So, for example, rather than receiving Japanese characters, one might simply receive the following on the screen:

$$\$NJ8 > O\$NNC\$G!"\$ = \$l\$OEnglish\$B\$NJ8 > 0\$9l\#J$$

To be able to salvage the message, the user needs to know how to replace the special characters either manually or with special software tools. Hence, the designers of the transnational decision support system need to concern themselves about the way data are retrieved from corporate databases and transmitted to all users. In addition, designers need to be concerned about the way data from external databases, such as network news services, are retrieved and transmitted.

Translations can also affect the user interface in terms of its appearance. One primary problem is the orientation of the text. For example, in the United States, most users feel comfortable with menus that appear at the top of a screen that

---

[3]Even a system shared with Canada, a country quite similar to the United States, might require a DSS to employ multiple languages, depending on its application. Since the French-speaking population in Canada is so numerous (especially in the province Quebec), Canadian law requires the use of both English and French in many circumstances. For example, even candy wrappers in Canada must provide all information, including the ingredients and nutritional information, in both English and French.

[4]Much work on language translation is in progress. For example, CompuServe is experimenting with software that would translate messages posted in French and German into English. (*Tampa Tribune*, November 7, 1994, pp B9, F9.)

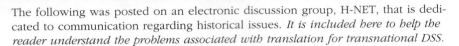

◆ DSS Design Insights ◆

The following was posted on an electronic discussion group, H-NET, that is dedicated to communication regarding historical issues. *It is included here to help the reader understand the problems associated with translation for transnational DSS.*

[Note from H-NET: Professor Andreucci, the moderator of H-ITALY, is fluent in Italian and English. H-NET asked him to review one of the new automatic language translation programs. His review appeared in Italian on H-ITALY. What follows is the automatic machine translation into English of his review. It gives a strikingly clear picture of the strengths and weaknesses of the program.]

From: Franco Andreucci ⟨fran@vm.cnuce.cnr.it⟩
Subject: Italian Assistant Software—Automatic translation of my review

This is the automatic translation—done by the Italian Assistant (*MicroTac Software*)—of the text I posted last week. I didn't intervene in any word or phrase. Unfortunately, the texts intentionally written in Italian in order to be automatically translated as examples in my review are translated. For instance, if you don't control the original Italian text, you'll miss the meaning of the sentence where "leader" is translated with "leader." My criticism was that "leader" is translated with "duce." Some words are not translated because the accents are missing. In this case, the responsibility is totally mine.

"Babele . . . [la'] the Mr. confused the tongue of all the earth" (Genesis, 11) [by] FRANCO ANDREUCCI

The old man dreams of returning to speak the universal tongue of the Genesis and of annul the chastisement of Babele, hard [e'] to die. In the XIX century he engages the character of the artful idiom and then, in our century, that of the automatic translator. Tied hope a time to the legends of the [positivismo], contradicted from the bankruptcy of the introduction of the [esperanto], she becomes alive anchor in a fascinating and modern way from the protection of the computer. Studied in the Soviet Union in the years '30 and then, after the Second world war, in the United States, the [possibilita'] of the automatic tied translation to the action of a computer has done in the last years of the footsteps from giant. If you/he/she/it are thought that the dimension of an electronic dictionary in line [e'] passed from the 250 words of the 1954 to the actual [centinaia] of [migliaia], we one [puo'] make account that at least a problem [e'] having faced in acceptable way.

Borne from the numerous experiences scientific [svoltesi] in the linguistic field for the automatic translation, the idea has found a recent commercial realization in the programs "Language Assistant Series" of the MicroTac Software. The programs—that they are called Italian Assistant, German Assistant, French Assistant, Spanish Assistant and they cost 99.95 $ each—they foresee the translation in the two senses between the English from a part and the Italian, the French, the German and the

Spanish from the other. They represent an enormous footstep in ahead (respect to the by now "old" dictionaries electronic [tascabili] or to the automatic translators of phrases) for their [elasticita'] and their [capacita'] of answer complex challenges. This critique concerns the Italian part of the program in his release for Windows entirely (MicroTac Software Assistant Windows [for], [ver]. 1.00a).

---

orient from left to right because that is the way we read. Lotus 1-2-3's menuing system in the United States uses such an orientation, and it has been very popular. However, when the product was marketed in Japan, not only did Lotus need to translate the words in the menus, it needed to change the orientation to a vertical one because the accepted orientation in Japan is from top to bottom (associated with their reading and writing conventions).

In addition, many languages are considerably more verbose than English. Or, if the language requires special characters, they may assume more space than standard Roman characters. For example, since Chinese and Japanese characters assume twice the width of a standard Roman character, the standard screen holds only 40 Japanese characters (rather than the standard 80 Roman characters). Hence, translation of elementary aspects of the system design, including prompts and labels, may require an entire screen redesign in order to accommodate the translated terms. For example, consider Figure 7.2, which provides a screen design for a simple system developed for use in the United States, Japan, and Israel. Notice how the screen needed to be re-engineered to accommodate the vertical orientation of the Japanese, the right-to-left orientation of Hebrew, and the range of special characters needed for each.

Even when the users can select one language for the system, they may use it quite differently. Researchers in the area of communication long have known that cultures communicate distinctively. Berger (1984, p.43) notes that "even when they speak the same language, there are problems as a result of differences in education, class, level, and cultural backgrounds." Hence, even though the individuals themselves are providing the translations, they may miss the meaning of information, especially if it contains slang or colloquialisms. For example, the British use the term "billion" for what Americans call "trillion." That is, the British use "thousand million" when referring to what Americans call a "billion" and thus a "billion" is not encountered until one increases another order of magnitude (hence, the American's "trillion"). If one were not careful when translating the American version of the English language into the British version of the English language, one might miss the significant implications of size difference.

Languages have different rules for pronunciation, and, therefore, meaning that need to be accommodated. For example, a character with an umlaut will have different impacts in Finnish than in German, even though they may look the same to an English-speaking audience. Similarly, different languages and cultures have

◆   DSS Design Insights   ◆

Japanese text requires special attention in the design of DSS because of the complexity of the language. Some of the issues that contribute to difficulty for a transnational DSS are highlighted here.

In Japanese, one cannot assume that one byte is equivalent to one character, because Japanese characters generally require multiple bytes for representation.

The Japanese character set contains more than 10,000 characters.

The Japanese writing system is a mixture of four different writing systems: Roman characters; Hiragana; Katakana; and Kanji.

Roman characters correspond to the 52 characters (including both uppercase and lowercase) of the English language. In addition, there are Roman characters associated with the 10 numerals. Japanese use the Roman characters primarily in the construction of tables and in the creation of acronyms.

Hiragana characters are ones that represent sounds, such as syllables. Generally, these characters are used to create suffixes for some words, or to write native Japanese words. The Hiragana characters appear to have a calligraphic look. For example, the character ま represents the sound made by the letters "ma" whereas, the character み represents the sound made by the combination of letters, "mi."

Katakana characters represent a phonetic alphabet as well. However, they are used to represent words of foreign origin, such as bread— パ ン (pronounced "pan"), which was derived from the Portuguese word for bread, pão (pronounced "pown"). In addition, they are used for emphasis, similar to the way we use italics in English. The Katakana characters have a squared, rigid look in comparison to the Hiragana characters. For example, the character マ represents the sound made by the combination of "ma" while the character ク represents the sound made by the combination of letters "ku."

Kanji characters were borrowed from the Chinese over 1500 years ago. There are tens of thousands of these characters in use by the Japanese. These characters represent specific words or combinations of words. For example, 木 when used alone indicates a tree, while two of the characters, 林 , indicates woods and three of the characters, 森 , means a forest.

There is no recognized character set for Japanese similar to ASCII for English. Nor is there a universally recognized encoding method for Japanese.

different ways of representing dates, currency, and other units of measurement.[5] For example, 3/1/97 means March 1, 1997, in the United States, but means January 3, 1997, in most of Europe. Finally, different languages and different cultures treat the concept of uppercase and lowercase characters differently. For example, the Hebrew language uses lowercase letters only when the text is handwritten, and uses uppercase letters only when the text is printed. In this case, if the system designer using a combination of uppercase and lowercase characters in English to convey information would not be able to have the same message sent on the Hebrew screen.

There is every reason to believe that other less obvious problems of user interface would be different among cultures as well. Unfortunately, if the user interface is unacceptable to users, they will not use the DSS. Hence, it has an important and direct influence on the ability of the user to realize the full potential of the system. The impact of culture on the database management system and the model-management system in transnational DSS is even less intuitive. The remainder of this chapter will highlight some of the legal, cultural, and economic issues that need to be addressed when defining DSS for transnational corporations.

◆ INFORMATION AVAILABILITY STANDARDS

One of the assumptions regarding transnational decision support systems is that the company can, in fact, *share* the desired information in all relevant venues. This includes the ability to collect information on a micro level, to assemble information selectively, to correlate information or in any way create new information from the original data, and to share that information across borders. This implies that the cultures and the laws of the countries are consistent on the view of information, its privacy, and its shareability. In addition, the goal implies that the manner in which those views of privacy and shareability are *enforced* is consistent among the venues. This often is related to how they approach the relative openness of their borders, investment, business, and commercial innovations—and hence can be quite different, even between two cultures that appear to share a similar "social" culture, such as the United States and Canada.

Data Privacy

Data privacy addresses the question of what information can be accumulated about individuals, corporations, or enterprises, and how that information can be processed and shared. In the United States, we have high expectations for privacy and citi-

---

[5] "The difference between the *almost* right word and the right word is really a large matter—'tis the difference between the lightning bug and the lightning." Mark Twain, U.S. author.

zens *believe* their privacy is quite protected. After all, the Fourth Amendment to the U.S. Constitution states

> *The right of people to be secure in their persons, houses, papers and effects against unreasonable searches and seizures, shall not be violated, and no Warrants shall issue, but upon probable cause, supported by Oath or affirmation, and particularly describing the place to be searched and the person or things to be seized.*

In 1967 a panel on Privacy and Behavioral Research reporting to the Office of Science and Technology stated

> *The right to privacy is the right of the individual to decide for himself how much he will share with others his thoughts, his feelings and the facts of his personal life. . . . Actually what is private varies from day to day and setting to setting.* (Rowe, 1972).

In other words, we generally believe the protection of the right to privacy of individual, personal information is protected. Not all countries share this perception of privacy. For example, totalitarian governments are known for neglecting the rights of citizens' privacy.

However, even in America, where citizens believe their privacy is protected, the enforcement of the privacy regulations is not extensive. In 1977 the Federal Privacy Protection Study Commission found an "imbalance between individuals and record keeping organizations." Specifically, it suggested a variance between the need for information and the requests for disclose. In particular, it suggests that many record keeping organizations are intrusive to the individual, and that the extent and nature of record-keeping needs better delineation, and enforceable expectations of confidentiality by law or statute need to be established.

As a result, Congress passed the Computer Security Act of 1987, which attempts to define the information in need of protection. It defines "sensitive information" as that which if lost, misused, accessed, or modified without authorization could adversely affect the privacy of individuals and be a violation of the Privacy Act. However, each citizen differs with regard to precisely *what* he or she considers sensitive under that definition. Further, while mandated to require "informed consent" prior to data collection, disclosure is permitted *without* consent to those within an agency who have a "need for the record in the performance of their duties," or to agencies in connection with "routine uses" for purposes "compatible with the purposes for which it was collected."

While this sounds as if no one can get access to data without individuals knowing about it, the reality is far different. First, these statements only apply to data collected by government agencies and some specified private agencies, such as banks. Second, few individuals read or understand the "informed consent" clause provided on most application forms. Even fewer individuals would understand quite how far the consent actually applies.

In a recent Harris-Equifax Poll,

- 76% of Americans believe they have lost all control over how personal information about them is circulated;
- 89% believe that computers have made it easier for someone to improperly obtain personal and confidential information on them;
- 68% believe that computers represent a threat to their personal privacy;
- 66% believe there are not adequate safeguards to protect the privacy of personal information stored in computers; and
- 67% believe that if privacy is to be preserved, the use of computers must be restricted.

"Informed consent" also implies that the individual enters into the agreement freely and openly. However, the reality is that the failure to provide this consent results in not getting licenses, credit, or other privileges in society. In other words, you must provide it, or not have full rights. And, if the data are collected by most private enterprises, they can be released or sold to other organizations unless specific statements prohibiting it are signed.

Once collected, the data may be kept in a database *forever*. This is particularly problematic if an error is originally entered and if the customer has no way of knowing that the error was entered. Furthermore, the statutes in the United States put the responsibility for examining the data to ensure its accuracy on the *consumer*, not on the group collecting the data. A small percentage of individuals understand the number of ways errors occur in the transcription of data, the possibility for erroneously merging data, or the wide possibility of errors in the data-processing capabilities. Hence, few individuals check those records to which they have access; and so errors can multiply.

Other cultures take a much stronger stand on the protection of citizens' rights to privacy. For example, in Canada, data collection companies must publish their policies, such as those shown on the next page. It has been suggested that European countries and others occupied during World War II have a strong recollection of the problems that can accrue if data are made available too freely. Hence, they have developed stronger regulations and enforcements. The European Community (EC) provides the following fair use policy:

- Data use is prohibited without authorization of the subject.
- Data subjects must be *personally* notified of who information has been passed on to and for what purpose.
- The data subject can claim compensation if data is misused and caused damage.
- EC data can only be transferred out of the EC *if* the receiving country can guarantee the same level of protection. (diTalamo, 1991)

In these cases, the burden of ensuring that the data are really relevant and accurate is kept on the organization collecting the data. In fact, in Sweden, organizations wanting to collect data on individuals must apply to the Data Inspection Board and be granted a license to do so. In France, organizations are required to destroy data after the specific application for which they were collected is completed. Further, in Italy, most labor unions have agreements with organizations that give them the right to approve any data maintained about individuals in corporate databases.

In early 1995, the Council of Ministers of the European Community adopted a common position on the European data protection directive. The directive is significant for European privacy because it necessitates the adoption of privacy safe-

◆ **DSS Design Insights** ◆

Some provinces have enacted consumer reporting legislation which regulates the conduct of our business. Others have not. However, as a matter of corporate policy, Equifax Canada complies in all provinces of Canada with the regulations of the province which is most strict in each area of our business. Noncompliance by a client with this legislation could result in Equifax Canada severing the client relationship.

Consumer reporting laws provide the basic framework for our information practices, but in many instances, and particularly in provinces which do not regulate consumer reporting, Equifax Canada goes beyond legal requirements to set additional standards and procedures in the interest of consumer service and protection of privacy. For example, even where not required by law, it is our practice to furnish to consumers, regardless of whether they have been denied credit, insurance, or employment, detailed disclosure of all information in our files in easy-to-understand formats and with a system of toll-free access. Our consumer service consultants are trained to provide quick and courteous service, and whenever a recheck or verification of information is requested, we follow up on the process with a new complete report.

Consumer reporting laws permit us to furnish consumer reports only to those businesses having permissible purposes—credit evaluation, insurance underwriting, employment decisions, the granting of a license, or other business needs involving a transaction with a consumer. Euifax Canada applies these permissible purpose standards even in provinces where no consumer reporting legislation exists. To ensure that consumer report information is kept strictly confidential and is used only for permissible purposes, we carefully screen applicants from businesses who want to receive consumer reports. We visit each applicant's premises to confirm identity and purpose of use, and we require every user to certify that reports will be requested in compliance with the aforementioned legal requirements.

"Statement of Policies about Information use" from *Consumer Information and Privacy: The Equifax Canada Perspective,* October 1993.

guards in the European countries that do not yet have legislation. In addition, it requires changes in countries with existing privacy laws because the directive takes a stronger position on data protection than existing national laws. It is believed that the directive will result in greater scrutiny of countries without a data protection commission and/or adequate legislative protections.

So how do these laws and customs affect the use of transnational decision support systems? Many uses of decision support systems technology in the United States could be crippled by these regulations.[6] In general, businesses that depend on the manipulation of computer data lists, such as direct-mail companies, credit-reference agencies, or marketing researchers, would be hampered by these EC directives. First, no data about an individual could be processed or transmitted without that person's "informed consent." This means a database could not include a person's name unless that person *specifically authorized it.* Many individuals would not return an authorization form; still others would reject the corporation's need to keep information about them, fearing computer tracking.[7] Second, the rules limit "profiling" people who share particular characteristics. Finally, since the EC position results in greater scrutiny of countries without a data protection commission and/or adequate legislative protections, such as the United States, it may even affect the basic information sharing among companies, or even among divisions of the same company.

Data Availability

Not all information that is of interest in a decision support system is about individuals in society. Some of the information is about governments, corporations, competitors, statutes and legal precedents, and so on. In order for the technology to be used to its fullest, there is a need for the various cultures to share views on how

---

[6]Big credit card companies, banks, airlines, and insurers use massively parallel processing in an effort to divine which consumers are likely to buy what products when. Marketing managers believe this is a great contribution to their efforts. However, one business professor warns that the fallout could be that nasty ID companies begin abusing their newfound information: "The companies doing this have a big responsibility. Otherwise there will be an information Chernobyl." (*Wall Street Journal*, August 16, 1994, p. B1.) In addition, as these efforts spread to international marketing, other cultures will affect what is defined as responsible behavior.

[7]George Orwell's book *1984* summarizes his prediction (which was shared by many others) of the impact computers, and technology as a whole, would have on daily life. Many citizens were outraged at the thought that they could be "tracked" as Orwell suggested. Orwell was correct in his prediction of the ability of computers to track our activities. Of course, Orwell was generally wrong in his other predictions regarding the impact of computers. Instead of enforcing uniformity as he had expected, they promote heterogeneity and autonomy. Many believe that because computers provide flexibility and adaptability to our activities, we have become more human, not less so, when we use them. (Kelly, "Embrace it," *Harper's*, May 1994.)

such "public" information should be shared. In the United States, the culture has taken from the First Amendment its right to all public information. However, not all countries share this right. Even a country as similar in culture as Canada does not protect this right. This can present a problem if all parties using a DSS cannot have access to the same information. Further, it presents questions as to how the statutes and customs apply. For example, if a DSS user is physically in Country A, accessing a computer and database in Country B, do the laws and precedents of Country A hold, or do those of Country B hold? In other words, is it the individual's physical location or logical location that dictates which statutes apply?

Data Flow

Even if there is agreement among all cultures affected by a particular transnational DSS regarding the privacy or protection of data and the availability of data, there can still be problems. There may be restrictions about where data can reside, where they can be processed, and how access can be maintained. Some countries, such as Canada, maintain that allowing data to be processed outside its borders would reduce Canadian control over disruptions in service, reduce Canada's ability to ensure protection against personal privacy violations and computer crime, jeopardize Canada's jurisdiction over companies operating in Canada, undermine the telecommunications system, and emphasize foreign values, goods, and services. In addition, Canadian officials recognize both the potential for release of information that is vital to Canada and the potential to facilitate the loss of independence and autonomy to other countries [*Telecommunications and Canada*, 1979]. Similarly, advisory groups to the British Cabinet suggest only the government can assess the national interest of information or the UK's vulnerability to disruptions in the availability of that information [HMSO, 1983].

Reports in both Latin America [Latin America Informatics, 1979] and Africa [African Informatics, 1979] recommend that

- data affecting national sovereignty, cultural identity, and technological progress should be protected against processing in other countries;
- data should remain in the country of origin; and
- external information should be screened.

The three messages that are guiding all these concerns about transborder data flows are the following.

- It is imperative that the data-processing industry of the country is preserved. If transborder processing of data is allowed, the data-processing industry would be threatened and potentially eliminated. Since much of the hope for long-term economic survival for most countries depends on the ability to participate in the "information technology race" successfully, it is imperative that the data-processing industry be maintained and bolstered. For example, the Brazilian government is concerned that if data are taken *from* Brazil for processing, both the software and hardware markets will suffer. Hence, they only allow "processed" data to leave its borders. Furthermore, data flowing across borders potentially affects the transfer of payments. For example, information sales (that is, "fees and royalties) was about $5.8 billion in 1980—doubled since 1970.

- National security can be jeopardized if a country becomes too dependent on other countries for vital data and services. This can provide a bargaining chip for political hostage behavior.
- Cultural integrity is threatened as we allow greater amounts of the information we view and the format in which we view it to be from another culture.

While these issues are not threatened by any *individual* use of data in a transnational DSS, they can be threatened by significant use in DSS, as well as other data-processing jobs. Since the regulations tend to be written in terms of data flows, not the purpose of those flows, we as designers of DSS need to be aware of the prevailing laws, customs, and expectations surrounding transborder data flows, and build our systems to accommodate them efficiently.

◆ MODELING ACROSS CULTURES

The model management component of a DSS, as defined in Chapter 4, consists of analytical tools, such as statistical models, financial models, artificial intelligence heuristics, and operations research models, as well as a function for managing those tools. Some of the tools consist of prepackaged analyses, while others provide the users the opportunity to build their own models. The value of this component results from providing easily implemented access to a wide variety of tools and assistance in using the tools, so the users can and will investigate relevant patterns

---

◆ DSS Design Insights ◆

Microsoft is moving to repair its blunder earlier this year when it introduced a Chinese version of *Windows 3.1* that was developed in Taiwan rather than the mainland. This time, its Chinese *Windows 95* will incorporate input from the Chinese government and vendors. Microsoft's biggest challenge remains rampant software piracy—while *Windows* and *MS-DOS* software are marketed through Chinese manufacturers who sell it with their PCs, virtually all applications software sold in China is counterfeit, according to Microsoft's VP for Asia. ("Mending Fences and Windows in China," *Wall Street Journal* November 9, 1994, p. B9.)

and issues in their data. Hence, the goal is to enable users to select the models that they perceive are most appropriate to assist with the particular question under consideration. This goal is only achieved, however, if decision support systems are designed appropriately for the individuals or groups that will be using them.

This is not a problem if all questions and all data have a unique modeling opportunity associated with them. That is, if one believes there is only one way to analyze data correctly, the transnational nature of a DSS should not affect the design of the model-management system. However, that assumption is rarely correct. Even if one simply acknowledges that different divisions will have different perspectives that will affect their approach to decision making, it becomes obvious that they will need to consider different data in different ways to address those differences in perspectives. Hence, the various divisions will require different (and perhaps vastly different) models to support those decisions. In addition, since management style is at least partially a function of the state of development and technology, the variations in these factors will increase the heterogeneity of models required of a successful system.

In addition, there is some evidence that cultural differences exacerbate the problem. There is literature available regarding international management that addresses "management practices" and cross-cultural differences, including the use of analytical tools, measurements, planning, and control. (Kobayshi, 1982) For example, some researchers have found that the use of models is influenced by culture and its norms of the decision maker (Evans *et al*, 1989; Hofstede, 1980). Different traditions and different values alter the variables that are reasonable to consider, the need to optimize, and the methods by which to evaluate alternatives. The parameters of the problem to consider, in turn, will influence the choice of relevant models.

Some researchers have found that *formalized* approaches to decision making may not differ as a function of culture (see, for example, Al-Jafaray and Hollingsworth, 1983, or Negandhi, 1979). However, few would deny that *formal* mechanisms of decision making, such as the reports, forms, and other formal communications regarding the choice process are quite *different* from the actual process one used to get to the decision, such as the searches necessary in a DSS. Furthermore, few researchers would deny that effective ways of leading individuals and organizations can differ as a function of the environment in which they work. Consider, for example, Figure 7.5, which illustrates the cultural assumptions of work ethics in the United States and in Asian countries. These differences affect how people work, how incentives can be established, and what will guide in their management. The process by which one could encourage or convince individuals or groups is also affected by those assumptions.[8] As such, it is clear that the decision

---

[8]Circa 1700, Pascal noted, "There are truths in one country which are falsehoods in another." Such differences affect criteria and other decision processes.

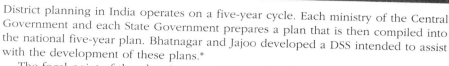

◆ DSS in Actions ◆

District planning in India operates on a five-year cycle. Each ministry of the Central Government and each State Government prepares a plan that is then compiled into the national five-year plan. Bhatnagar and Jajoo developed a DSS intended to assist with the development of these plans.*

The focal point of the planning is a district, which has a population of about 1 million. District-level plans for each sector are passed upward to the state level, where they are consolidated for all districts. Prior to the development of the DSS, the exercise of communications between and among state headquarters and the district to finalize a plan may have taken seven to eight months.

In addition, two key decisions in these five-year plans are made arbitrarily due to the unavailability of the necessary information. These are (a) a districtwise allocation of the total available budget for the department and (b) selecting a specific location choice for a particular facility.

An earlier version of the DSS was developed. Overall, it was considered a success. Almost everyone who saw it recognized its potential to serve as an aid to planning within a district. However, it was recognized that such applications could be developed only if computers supporting graphic facilities were available within the state and district. At that time such graphics facilities were not accessible.

Because today's microcomputers offer reasonable graphic facilities, a second version was created with vastly improved interaction capabilities. This second system provided more general data structures and improved command language structure to simplify interaction. The commands allowed selection of villages from a table on the basis of their attributes, like the existence of a particular type of facility or the distance from it. Other sets of commands display a set of villages on a map, allow interaction with the displayed map, and produce a printed report on the selected villages. The software was table driven, offering the flexibility of carrying out various types of analysis by using the commands in an appropriate sequence.

This DSS was accepted because five key benefits were provided by the system: (a) the graphics and maps created a level of understanding that went above and beyond the level that could be achieved without a DSS; (b) the illustrative graphics helped to create integration across government departments; (c) the quality of decisions were enhanced and the time taken to create the plans was reduced greatly; (d) the integrated data offered an easy tool to determine relative allocations among departments on the basis of existing facilities rather than on the basis of the national norm, thereby creating a better balance of distribution; and (e) it provided an accurate assessment of a district's "backwardness indicator," which is often used for allocating funds. Overall, it was determined that the extensive graphical interface was the biggest selling feature for the users.

The District Planning DSS example provided insight into the user interface issues when designing a DSS for India. In particular, it suggested that the graphical images help to cross cultural and communication barriers in India to make the system more usable.

*Bhatnagar, S.C. and B.H. Jajoo, "A DSS generator for district planning," *Information and Management*, 13(1), 1987, pp. 43–49.

support provided to individuals or groups in those different cultures will also differ. In fact, Hofstede (1994) notes that any system of leading and coordinating the work of employed persons should be geared to their "collective mental programs . . . that is their culture." These collective mental programs cannot be identified as superior or inferior to one another. Rather, the culture is a response to the environment from which it evolved.

From this perspective, it is not useful to debate whether culture will affect the model-management needs, but rather *how* will culture affect the model-management needs. To answer this, first it is necessary to define what is meant by the term *culture*. While there is not universal agreement on how to define a culture, we can rely on the cultural anthropological literature to find a variety of measures for defining and evaluating culture. A culture cannot be defined solely in terms of the nation in which it exists. Many national boundaries are historically artificial. Some nations contain multiple distinct cultures, while other nations share a culture with geographically adjacent nations. Examination of only cross-national differences misses a wide range of characteristics that distinguish among cultures. Hence, this chapter will attempt to discuss culture in terms of the *dimensions* that define it, not generalizations about specific countries. While we will discuss what some of these issues mean in terms of the choice process and DSS for specific countries, in general, we need to look at the individual dimensions to help guide the DSS development process. Figure 7.4 provides a summary of dimensions noted in the cultural anthropology literature.

Uncertainty avoidance is one measure that several researchers have identified as a measure of culture. For example, Hofstede (1983) noted that cultures differ in their patterns of coping with ambiguity and uncertainty. Cultures that accept uncertainty will take risks easily. As a result, they are also more able to accept differences in others, such as in their opinions or behaviors. These cultures accept "relative truths" and evaluate options in terms of the current environment, not compared to a rigid standard. Cultures in which uncertainty is less well accepted try to shield individuals from the unknown. Such cultures tend to adopt laws and procedures that facilitate similarity of thought and behavior. As a result, the cultures are aggressively intolerant of deviant behaviors and opinions, as well as of any action or individual that threatens their view of the world.

This attitude toward uncertainty affects decision making needs. For example, individuals in cultures with high uncertainty avoidance will be more likely to conduct highly structured analyses and fewer *ad hoc* analyses. Since they will want to be prepared for all possible contingencies, they will be likely to evaluate greater numbers of alternatives and more facets of those alternatives. Further, if they have employed optimization, they will be likely to seek postoptimality analyses prior to selecting an alternative for implementation.

The *person–nature orientation* is the second dimension of culture. This measures the individual's or group's view of their relative dominance over fate. At the one end of this dimension, individuals believe they have no affect on the future.

These individuals perceive that they must accept the inevitable, and hence there is no planning for contingencies. In the middle of the dimension are individuals who believe that there is a balance between people and nature. At the other end of the dimension are those who believe in mastery of their fates, if they have the ability to overcome obstacles.

This dimension is likely to affect an individual's basic likelihood of accepting technology as a decision making tool. Those who feel in control of their fate encourage the use of technology as a way of meeting their goals, while those who perceive they have no control are unlikely to adopt technology readily.

In addition, one's perception of one's ability to dominate fate will affect the attitude toward planning. Populations in cultures that do not accept one's ability to influence the future do not participate in long-range planning activities. Evan (1975) associates this with their belief in "luck" as the major influencing factor. Since luck cannot, in their view of the world, be planned, they do not practice much long-range or strategic planning. Rather, it is better to wait and respond as best one can. Hence, these decision makers emphasize reactive decision making. On the other hand, individuals who believe they can master their fates are more likely to conduct strategic and contingency planning. Their goal is to improve their relative position (either individually or as a group) to influence destiny.

Many of the cultures in the middle area of this dimension focus on maintaining a "harmony" with nature. For example, they believe that the more harmonious a social structure and/or organizational structure, the more likely they are to attract luck for the organization. In these cultures, the top executives are likely to attempt to create harmony through meetings, gatherings, and so on. This implies, in turn, that more of their responsibilities are delegated to lower levels in the organization. Hence, broader informational needs and greater authority are likely to be of less importance to those organizations.

Evan (1975) and Negandhi (1983) hypothesize that this orientation affects the formality in an organization, the directions of communication, and the output of the organization. In particular, they note that cultures with strong mastery of destiny attitudes tend to have quite formal methods of socialization, multidirectional communication, and high levels of output. With these factors come well-established and structured conventions for decision making procedures, criteria, and models. In addition, these cultures will require decision making analyses and review of analyses at various levels in an organization.

Societies with a lower confidence of their ability to master fate would be more likely to have informal methods of socialization, unidirectional communication, and low levels of output. Hence, they tend to have strong control over the types of information available at each level of the organization and the kinds of analyses that might be constructed.

The third dimension, the *power distance*, is a related concept. Like uncertainty avoidance, power distance refers to the manner in which people are organized.

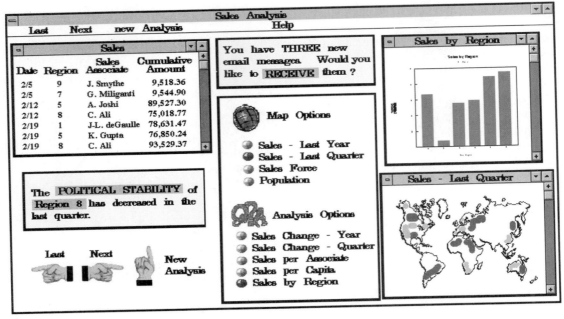

Figure 7.4a Language effects on screen design. Screen in English.

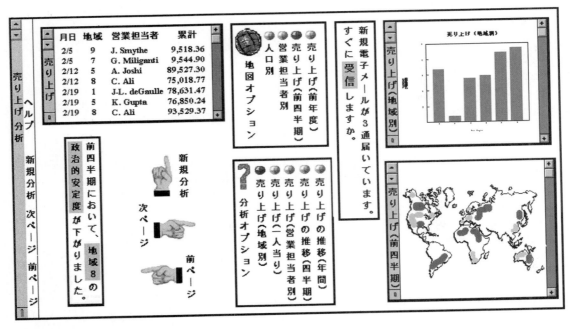

Figure 7.4b Screen in Japanese.

262

Figure 7.4c Language effects on screen design. Screen in Hebrew.

Power distance refers to those aspects of how differences or questions are resolved. In particular, it refers to the question of who is empowered to make those decisions. In a high-power-distance culture, few people are empowered to decide differences of opinion or to make decisions on the best path to follow when experiencing uncertainty. These few are the "bosses" whose choice is adopted and not questioned. On the other hand, in a low-power-distance culture, individuals are empowered to make decisions under uncertainty and to work things out for themselves. This aspect of decision making is operationalized in terms of the level of centralization of decision making in a department or an organization, as well as in terms of the freedom with which information flows in an organization.

The fourth dimension, *activity orientation*, represents the manner in which people evaluate activity and accomplishments. In particular, it is a description of the mode of expression and hence the mechanism by which activity should be evaluated (see, for example, Kluckhohn and Strodtbeck, 1961). At one end of the spectrum is a culture that adopts a spontaneous activity and expression of attitudes. They do not accept planning or development of activities, and hence believe it is inappropriate to evaluate activities against some planned agenda. Instead, they evaluate the worth of an alternative by what it "is," not what it can do. At the other end of the spectrum

Cultural Assumptions Underlying Culture in the USA

- Work is good for people.

- People's capacities should be maximally utilized.

- There are "organizational objectives" that exist apart from people.

- People in organizations behave as unattached individuals.

Cultural Assumptions Underlying Culture in Asian Countries

- Work is a necessity, but not a goal in itself.

- People should find their rightful place, in peace and harmony with their environment.

- Absolute objectives exist only with God. In the world, persons in authority positions represent God, so their objectives should be followed.

- People behave as members of a family and/or group. Those who do not are rejected by society.

Figure 7.5   Comparison of cultural assumptions. Adopted from Hofstede, G., "Management scientists are human," *Management Science,* 40(1), January 1994, pp. 4–13. It is reprinted from *Management Science* with permission from the Institute for Operations Research and the Management Sciences and the author. No further reproduction is permitted without the consent of the copyright owner.

is a culture that emphasizes "getting the job done." These individuals prefer activities with measurable outcomes that can be judged against objective standards.

This orientation significantly affects one's goal orientation and one's willingness to adopt standards. Cultures that regard getting a task completed are more likely to adopt standards for evaluation and therefore submit alternatives to a more uniform evaluation. Associated with this is a stronger tendency to depend on optimization techniques of analysis. Cultures that emphasize the other end of the spectrum are more likely to rely on descriptive measures of analysis to provide evidence of the relative worth of the alternative. These individuals are more likely to be interested in current, static

Long-term orientation

Attitude about uncertainty

Person–nature relation

Activity index

Human–nature attitudes

Power distance

Individualism

Masculinity index

Figure 7.6 Possible dimensions of culture.

measures of worth, while individuals requiring standardized evaluations are more likely to prefer historical data rating the development of the alternative.

Evans, Hau, and Sculli (1989) believe this orientation is associated with a culture's relative levels of aggressiveness in management and decision making. At one end, the decision makers are seen as more aggressive. Since they adopt standards for evaluation, and since they want to select the "best" alternative, they tend to adopt efficiency as an important criterion. Decision makers at the other end are more passive and defensive. They tend to adopt "social harmony"—and the absence of public disagreement—as an important factor to consider in decision making. Therefore, they are likely to allow greater flexibility in the alternative generation and evaluation, especially at the early stages of decision making.

The fifth dimension is the *human–nature orientation*, as proposed by Kluckhohn and Strodtbeck (1961). This dimension measures the likelihood of finding innate "goodness" in human nature, and hence identifies what motivates people in their actions. If one adopts an attitude that people are intrinsically bad, then one needs to adopt planning and management mechanisms that constantly control and discipline workers and departments in order to obtain good results from the organization. Decision makers need to be able to observe people and projects carefully and frequently in order to detect problems as soon as possible. The more strongly held the philosophy, the tighter such monitoring would be.

On the other hand, if one adopts a view of society that is basically good, then the goal of monitoring systems changes dramatically. Instead of designing such systems to identify problems, monitoring systems are created to detect opportunities for development, growth, and/or strategic advantage.

Evans, Hau, and Sculli (1989) claim that the human–nature orientation also influences the flexibility exhibited toward managerial communication. The more a culture adopts an "evil" view of society, the less likely superiors would want alternative opinions, especially from subordinates. Cultures that adopt a "good" view of society are more likely to tolerate conflict situations associated with debates of the relative merits of alternatives and methods for evaluating alternatives. In this latter case, decision makers through more levels of the organization need support from greater use of analytical tools, more alternative-generation capabilities, and greater information retrieval.

The sixth dimension is *individualism*. At one end of the spectrum are cultures that emphasize the continuity of the group, and hence the group goals are paramount in the decision making efforts. These groups are generally homogeneous in some fashion, and want to stay that way. At the other end of the spectrum are cultures in which the value of autonomy of the members of the group is seen as the only important criterion for decision making. Obviously, there are many points between these two on the spectrum.

Cultures that hold the individualistic view emphasize achieving the goals of the individual above all others. These people may accept and pursue group goals, but only if they do not conflict with their own. Collateral societies, on the other hand, emphasize the goals and welfare of the extended group, such as an organization. Cultures at the extreme point of this dimension stress the importance of continuity of the group through time and ordered progression of individuals within the group.

Clearly then, the level of individualism associated with a culture will affect the goals adopted and pursued in decision making, as well as decision makers' general compliance with authority in considering alternatives. Evan (1975) and Negandhi (1983) postulate that this orientation will affect the formalization of the socialization function and the direction of communication within an organization. They suggest that cultures that emphasize the individualistic component will have formal means of socialization within the organization and strong multidirectional communication among decision makers. Cultures that emphasize the group component, on the other hand, will have informal means of socialization within the organization and unidirectional communication. As stated previously, this will affect the types of analyses and standards of alternatives considered, the need for controls on information within the organization, and the need for sharing of analyses among levels within the organization.

The last dimension is the *masculinity index* of a culture. This dimension reflects the association of specific attributes such as assertiveness, performance, competition, and success with the role of men in society. In addition, it reflects the association of more commonly accepted feminine attributes, such as quality of life, strong personal relationships, and care for the weak with the role of men in society. In whole, the dimension relates to how much difference exists in the culture between "men's roles in societies" and "women's roles in society," or, said differently, how much gender equality exists in a culture. This, in turn, results in the culture's calibration of the worth of "masculine" values and "feminine" values in society.

Consider Figure 7.7, in which Hofstede summarizes his measurement of several countries with regard to each of these dimensions. It is difficult to discuss such differences without resulting to stereotypes. What is most important to note at this

Country	Power Distance	Uncertainty Avoidance	Individualism	Masculinity Index	Long-Term Orientation
Arab Countries	80	68	38	53	
France	68	86	71	43	
Germany	35	65	67	66	31
Great Britain	35	35	89	66	25
Netherlands	38	53	80	14	44
Hong Kong	68	29	25	57	96
Indonesia	78	48	14	46	
Japan	54	92	46	95	80
Brazil	69	76	38	49	65
Mexico	81	82	30	69	
U.S.A.	40	46	91	65	29
West Africa	77	54	20	46	16

Figure 7.7   Culture scores for 12 countries. Adopted from Hofstede, G., "Management scientists are human," *Management Science,* 40(1), January 1994, pp. 4–13. It is reprinted from *Management Science* with permission from the Institute for Operations Research and the Management Sciences and the author. No further reproduction is permitted without the consent of the copyright owner.

point is that there are definite differences in culture that can be paired with differences in how comfortable people adopting those cultures will feel making decisions. Where there are differences in how people make decisions, there must be differences in the kind of support provided by decision support systems for those people. Hence, there must be transnational factors considered in the design of decision support systems.

◆ EFFECTS OF CULTURE ON A DECISION SUPPORT SYSTEM

Based on the anthropological definitions of cultures described in the previous section, one would expect observable differences in the preferences for design of decision support systems across cultures. There are five general aspects of the system on which one would expect differences, as listed in Figure 7.8. Figure 7.9 summarizes the discussion of the previous section, illustrating the effects of the various cultural factors on DSS design.

Choice of Model
  Descriptive versus optimization
  Need for strategic planning
  Use of standards
  Variables used
  Need for monitoring
  Variety needs for models

Premodeling Need
  Alternative generation

Postmodeling Needs
  Sensitivity analyses

Temporal Aspects
  Orientation of data
  Static versus dynamic

Desired access
  Scope of access
  Individual versus joint use

Figure 7.8   Cultural differences and their effects on DSS design.

Cultural Indicator groups: **Time Orientation** (Past, Pres, Futre); **Uncertainty** (avoid, tolernt); **Person-Nature** (subj, hrmny, master); **Activity being** (being, bcmng, doing); **Human-Nature** (evil, mix, good); **Relational** (lin'l, coll, indiv).

DSS Characteristics	Past	Pres	Futre	avoid	tolernt	subj	hrmny	master	being	bcmng	doing	evil	mix	good	lin'l	coll	indiv
Choice of Models																	
Descript v. Optimiz									desc		optim			desc	desc	desc	
Need for Strat Plng			high	high		no		high	no	high							high
Use of Standards						no		high	no	high	high		high				
Variables used			*														
Need for Monitoring	some	high	high			**			"is"		"done"	high	high	more	soc	grp	self
Variety needs for models			less		high			high			effcy			high			high
Pre-modeling Needs																	
Alternative Generation			high	high				low			high			high			
Post-Modeling Needs																	
Sensitivity Analyses				high				high			high						
Temporal Aspects																	
Orientation of Data	past	curr	futre						curr	hist	futre	curr	hist	all	hist	hist	fut
Static v. Dynamic		some	high						stat	dynam	dynam	sta	dyn	dyn			
Desired Access																	
Scope of Access						limit	broader	low		high	low			high	low		high
Indiv v. Joint use						indiv		high	indiv	joint	indiv			joint	indiv		joint

* more structured, less ad hoc

** some monitoring: emphasize monitoring for reactive purposes

Figure 7.9 Cultural differences and their effects on DSS design.

First, there are differences in preferences for descriptive models versus optimization models associated with the activity orientation and uncertainty avoidance of the culture. Related to this is the differential need for contingency and planning models depending on the person–nature orientation, the uncertainty avoidance, and the activity orientation. For example, cultures in which people believe they can master their destiny are more likely to emphasize strategic and contingency planning than are other cultures. Furthermore, these attributes affect the decision to adopt standards; the more the culture adopts a "doing" value, the more likely it is to adopt standards for evaluation of actions. Finally, these dimensions affect the flexibility of the decision makers to select from a menu of appropriate analyses to support their choice process. The need for flexibility is associated with cultures that perceive mastery of their destinies, with low uncertainty avoidance tendencies, a positive human–nature orientation, and a highly individualistic orientation of the culture.

From Figure 7.9, it is clear that the literature regarding the impact of culture on decision making suggests that culture will affect the kinds of models required, the premodeling and postmodeling support, the temporal aspects of the model, and the level of access desired. Hence, if one is building a transnational decision support system, one must pay special attention to differences in needs *and* preferences among decision makers in these areas. Such special attention might mean providing more flexibility than one would otherwise provide. Or the special attention might mean providing greater training in the use, more online support, or greater emphasis of the capabilities in those areas.

Of course, being able to determine which of these attributes is important hinges on the ability to identify where the culture of interest falls on each of the dimensions. Some authors have already provided some of this information, such as the ratings represented in Figure 7.7 (see, for example, Hofstede, 1994). These ratings help provide clues to how various cultures fall on the various dimensions, and hence can provide guidance for how to balance the needs of multiple cultures.

As long as the DSS is isolated to a given culture, these differences in the preferences in decision making behavior are of little consequence. However, if the DSS is designed to support decision makers who represent two or more of these cultures, then it must be sufficiently flexible to accommodate the wide range of needs. Knowing these decision making preferences, the designer must balance those preferences in the DSS capabilities. For example, suppose the DSS is designed to support both a culture valuing identification of the best alternative (optimization models) and a culture valuing the identification of a wide range of information about the phenomenon, so as to make a good, but not necessarily the best, decision (descriptive models). The best answer is to develop a DSS that can accommodate both

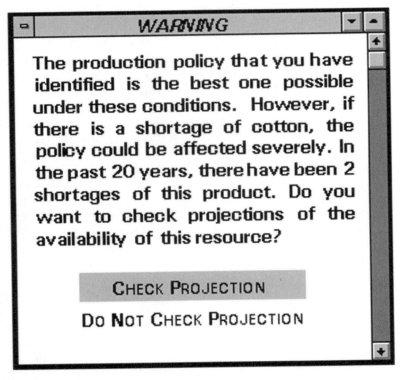

Figure 7.10   Prompting the user to consider postmodeling support.

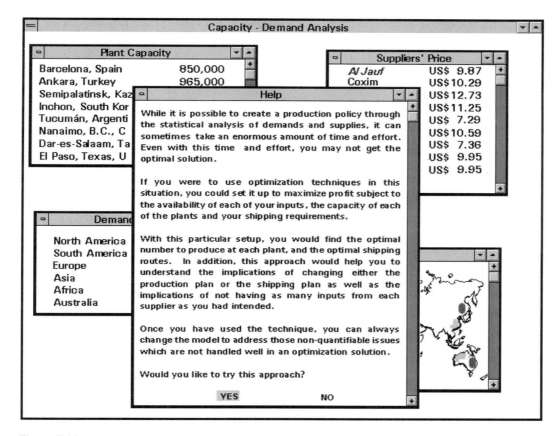

Figure 7.11 Prompting the user to consider an alternative modeling approach.

types of modeling. This may mean more than simply providing both kinds of models to the decision makers. It may also mean providing automated intelligent assistance, which helps the decision makers better use models and which helps them better understand the reasoning behind the use of the model.

Consider the examples of such intelligent assistance shown in Figures 7.10 and 7.11. In Figure 7.10, the system examines the solution elected by the decision maker and helps to identify problems with it. In this example, the production policy is evaluated to determine if it will meet the needs of the customers. The system determines that the user has not elected to examine forecasts of availability of raw materials. In addition, the system scans available databases to determine if any of the raw materials have had significant shortages in the recent past. When one is found, the system brings this information to the attention of the user, thus prompting the user to modify the prepared analysis.

In Figure 7.11, the system examines the process used by the decision maker. By noting the tasks completed by the decision maker, the system can determine that the user is electing to attempt to create a production plan manually. Since the system knows that such problems can be solved using operations research techniques, the system interrupts the user to suggest this alternative modeling structure. Note that the system does not force the user to abandon the current task. Rather, the system notes that it is an alternative, and attempts to explain why. Further, note that the system reassures the user that the final decision is in the hands of the user since it can be altered to include the "nonquantifiable" issues not handled well by optimization. In this way, the system reassures the user that there is a place for his or her analysis.

If the user asked for more information, it might be useful to help him or her understand where the suggested approaches were superior and why. Consider, for example, Figure 7.12. In this screen, the system is comparing the plans developed by the decision maker's approach and those developed by the alternative modeling approach. This provides the user with the evidence he or she needs to believe that the model might work, as well as to determine what flaws exist in his or her analyses. In addition, such objective analyses help the user understand why years of experience might not be substitutable for an appropriate model.

Second, consider a situation in which the cultural differences among users of the DSS suggest a need for broader access to data and models. For example, where organizational goals differ, the need for information will differ. Consider two cultures, one in which organizational goals such as efficiency, productivity, and profit are optimized and the other in which organizational goals such as organizational stability, growth, industry leadership, and organizational efficiency are optimized. This difference in goals suggests a difference in the focus of statistical data. The manager from the first culture will need information regarding issues such as profit, margin on sales, return on total assets, and the time to produce a single item. That is, this manager needs statistics that suggest how profitable the company is in its current state and how profitable it would be if a change were implemented. The focus of this manager is on the size of the profit differential resulting from the change. The manager in the second culture would also be concerned with the difference in productivity, but would focus on the impact of the change on the stability of the company. This manager would consider statistics such as industry ranking and market value, especially with regard to how the change will affect each of those statistics. Hence, both sets of statistics should be available to the decision makers. In addition, screens such as those previously noted that help the user to understand why someone might look at the other statistics could be useful. An example is shown in Figure 7.13.

The options for a DSS designer are somewhat more complicated when the preferences are in conflict with one another. For example, consider a situation in which one culture adopts standards for performance whereas the other culture does not adopt standards and is more likely to focus on the importance of being (rather than an outcome measure). These two cultures conflict both in terms of where to focus (the activity or the outcome) as well as whether to provide standards in the evaluation. One approach to addressing the standards problem is to provide a module that will facilitate the understanding and development of standards. Such a

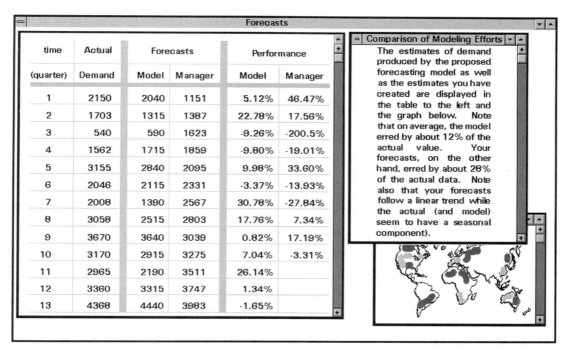

time	Actual	Forecasts		Performance	
(quarter)	Demand	Model	Manager	Model	Manager
1	2150	2040	1151	5.12%	46.47%
2	1703	1315	1387	22.78%	17.56%
3	540	590	1623	-9.26%	-200.5%
4	1562	1715	1859	-9.80%	-19.01%
5	3155	2840	2095	9.98%	33.60%
6	2046	2115	2331	-3.37%	-13.93%
7	2008	1390	2567	30.78%	-27.84%
8	3058	2515	2803	17.76%	7.34%
9	3670	3640	3039	0.82%	17.19%
10	3170	2915	3275	7.04%	-3.31%
11	2965	2190	3511	26.14%	
12	3360	3315	3747	1.34%	
13	4368	4440	3983	-1.65%	

Comparison of Modeling Efforts

The estimates of demand produced by the proposed forecasting model as well as the estimates you have created are displayed in the table to the left and the graph below. Note that on average, the model erred by about 12% of the actual value. Your forecasts, on the other hand, erred by about 28% of the actual data. Note also that your forecasts follow a linear trend while the actual (and model) seem to have a seasonal component).

Figure 7.12 Helping the user to understand the benefits of modeling.

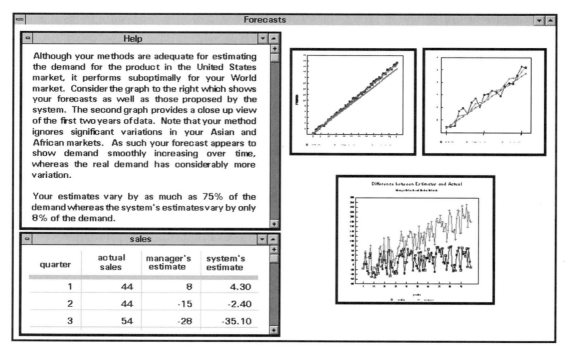

Help

Although your methods are adequate for estimating the demand for the product in the United States market, it performs suboptimally for your World market. Consider the graph to the right which shows your forecasts as well as those proposed by the system. The second graph provides a close up view of the first two years of data. Note that your method ignores significant variations in your Asian and African markets. As such your forecast appears to show demand smoothly increasing over time, whereas the real demand has considerably more variation.

Your estimates vary by as much as 75% of the demand whereas the system's estimates vary by only 8% of the demand.

sales

quarter	actual sales	manager's estimate	system's estimate
1	44	8	4.30
2	44	-15	-2.40
3	54	-28	-35.10

Figure 7.13 Helping the user to see the benefits of an alternative approach.

module could help users see a relationship between the rankings on relevant criteria and alternatives generally accepted as good in order to facilitate the development of standards in the long run. Similarly, the module could help users identify noncompensatory relationships among standards. That is, by examining the standards, the average standard, and actual outcomes, decision makers are more likely to become aware of situations in which acceptable levels on a given standard are as important as (or more important than) meeting an overall standard of performance. This method of providing historical data of outcomes and data allows the decision makers generally to perceive opportunities for improved decision making. If it is important that changes in the process happen quickly, the system can be programmed to encourage decision makers to consider these relationships by providing pop-up screens noting inconsistencies in decision making procedures or the value of alternative information in selecting among alternatives.

The culture will also affect the premodel functions and the postmodel functions in the model-management system. The time orientation of the culture, uncertainty avoidance tendency, and human–nature orientation affect the desirability of methods for generating alternatives to known problems or conditions. Cultures that are future oriented, have high uncertainty avoidance, and/or have a "good" human–nature orientation are likely to want systems that facilitate alternative generation. Similarly, the uncertainty avoidance tendencies and the person nature orientation of the culture are expected to affect the needs for postmodeling support, such as "what if" analyses or postoptimality analyses. In particular, high uncertainty avoidance tendencies and cultures that perceive that they can master their destinies will value such ad hoc queries to determine the sensitivity of their solutions to potential changes in their environments.

In this situation, prompting the user to consider more premodeling and postmodeling functionality is probably best. For example, if the value of a given decision is dependent on the availability of a scarce resource, the system might automatically notify the user. In this case, the system could post a message such as the one in Figure 7.10.

Cultural norms will also affect the temporal orientation of the data that decision makers will expect to find in a DSS. The time orientation and activity orientation of the culture affects the preference for current or historical data in an analysis. Cultures that emphasize the past and/or the being nature will emphasize historical data in the system. In addition, the human–nature orientation, the activity orientation, and the time orientation will affect the desirability of monitoring systems as part of a DSS and the kind of information that should be maintained in such monitoring systems. Furthermore, the activity orientation and the time orientation affect the preference for static measures of merit of an alternative over dynamic measures of historical change. For example, societies that emphasize the value of individuals and their development will require monitoring systems that trace the growth of people, projects, or organizations over time to support their decision making. This is in contrast to societies that emphasize the individual who would need only current performance information.

Another area in the design of DSS affected by culture is the scope of the DSS to which members of the organization have access. In some cases, access to either information, models, or results is expanded (limited) because of the need for more (fewer) people involved in the decision-making process. For example, in cultures that emphasize harmony with nature, lower levels of management need information because upper management's focus is on maintaining harmony. Similarly, in cultures that believe in "good" human–nature orientation, information is available to greater numbers of people so as to generate more innovative solutions to problems. At other times, this access changes to limit the generation of alternatives, the questioning of assumptions, or the direction of communication. The scope of the system seems to be affected by the person–nature orientation, the level of individuality, and the human–nature orientation of the culture.

DISCUSSION

It is important to focus on the differences in culture that could affect decision makers' needs because such features could affect the perceived usefulness of a system substantially. As more companies become transnational *and* as more decision making in those transnational corporations is decentralized, DSS design that allows flexibility in the approach to decision making and that helps decision makers become more comfortable with the styles associated with other cultures will become critical. If the decision makers cannot use the system to be responsive to their own needs and to communicate their analyses to their colleagues, the system will not be used. In the long run, if decision makers do not *use* the system, then even the best designed system is a failure.

QUESTIONS

1. Describe the factors that would influence your design of a decision support system for another country. In particular, describe the cultural factors that are either unique to that country and/or strongly influence the decision making process in that country, as well as the specifications of design that would be affected. Explain why you believe this association exists. Be specific.

2. What guidelines would you provide to a designer of a transnational decision support system to help him or her be more sensitive to the needs of decision makers in all countries? In particular, what aspects of the system are most likely to be affected by the transnational nature of the system? How? Be specific.

3. Suppose you are developing a DSS for a CEO of a U.S. corporation (you may select a specific industry, if you like) for strategic planning. One of the tasks of this CEO is to acquire one or more transnational corporations. Discuss how you would design database access in such a system. Include how you would integrate corporate databases,

how you would provide unique databases for this system, and how you would integrate public databases. Be certain to include databases available via the Internet or other public source.

4. Suppose you propose an Internet-based, *strategic* DSS project at your company (or at some fictitious company) for your (non-IS) department. Discuss the issues that you want included in the feasibility analysis for the project. In particular, discuss the various costs and benefits that would need to be considered and how they would be measured.

5. Suppose you work for a company that has divisions in two countries, e.g., the United States and China. Each division needs information systems for both transaction processing and decision support systems development. Analyze the needs and designing systems for the United States division *first* and then perform similar activities for the division in China. Your communication will be through e-mail. What changes in methodology would you make to ensure other projects are successful?

◆ O N   T H E   W E B ◆

On the Web for this chapter provides additional information about international standards, transnational management, and communications issues as they apply to the design of DSS. Additional discussion questions and new applications will also be added as they become available.

• *Links provide access to information about transnational business.* The Web Page provides links to sites to help the user learn about conducting business in other countries as well as across national boundaries. These links provide directories of businesses and trade associations, news access and information about resources, and restrictions to business.

• *Links provide access to information about transnational communication.*

Communication implies that information can be transferred and understood. These Web links help in translation of languages (including idioms), as well as information about legal and technical issues for concern.

• *Links provide users with multicultural information.* One problem in designing a transnational DSS is the understanding of culture in other parts of the world. The Web Page can provide tours and insights into different cultures to help users gain that information.

You can access material for this chapter from the general WWW Page for the book, or, from the following URL.
http://www.umsl.edu/~sauter/DSS/intl.html

SUGGESTED READINGS

Al-Jafaray, A. and A.T. Hollingsworth, "An exploratory study of managerial practices in the Arabian Gulf Region," *Journal of International Business Studies*, Volume 14, 1983, pp. 143-152.

Baligh, H.H., "Components of culture: Nature, interconnections, and relevance to the decisions on the organization structure, *Management Science*, 40(1), January 1994, pp. 14-27.

Berger, A.A., *Signs in Contemporary Culture*, New York: Longman, 1984.

Bhatnagar, S.C. and B.H. Jajoo, "A DSS generator for district planning," *Information and Management*, 13(1), 1987, pp. 43-49.

Bortnick, "Transborder data flow issues," *Electronic Publishing Review*, 1(4), December 1981.

Bradley, S.P., J.A. Hausman, and R.L. Nolan (eds.), *Globalization, Technology and Competition: The Fusion of Computers and Telecommunications in the 1990's*, Cambridge, MA: Harvard Business School Press, 1994.

Branscomb, A.W.,"Global governance of global networks," in Branscomb, A.W., *Towards a Law of Global Communication Networks*, New York: Longman, 1986.

Chinese Culture Connection (a research team), "Chinese values and the search for culture-free dimensions for culture," *Journal of Cross-Cultural Psychology*, 18(2), 1987, pp. 143-164.

Collier, H., *Information Flow Across Frontiers: The Question of Transborder Data*, Oxford: Learned Information, 1988.

Davis, H.J. and A.S. Rasool, "Values research and management behavior: Implications for devising culturally consistent managerial styles," *Management International Review*, 28(3), 1988, pp. 11-20.

diTalamo, N., "Private secrets," *Direct Marketing*, April 1991, pp. 42-44.

Dyment, J.J., "Strategies of management controls for global corporations," *The Journal of Business Strategy*, 7(4), 1987, pp. 20-26.

Eom, H.B., S.M. Lee, C.A. Snyder, and F.N. Ford, "A multiple criteria decision support system for global financial planning," *Journal of Management Information Systems*, 1987-1988, pp. 94-113.

European Telecommunications: The Information Industry Perspective, London: EUSIDIC (The European Association of Information Services), 1987.

Evans, W.A., K.C. Hau, and D. Sculli, "A cross cultural comparison of managerial styles," *Journal of Management Development*, 8(1), 1989, pp. 5-13.

Fuentes, C., quoted in "To see ourselves as others see us," *Time*, June 16, 1986, p. 52.

Ghoshal, S., H. Korrine, and G. Szulanski, "Interunit communication in multinational corporations," *Management Science,* 40(1), January 1994, pp. 96-110.

Graham, J.L., A.T. Mintu, and W. Rodgers, "Explorations of negotiation behaviors in ten foreign cultures using a model developed in the United States," *Management Science,* 40(1), January 1994, pp. 72-95.

Hofstede, G., *Cultural Consequences: International Differences in Work-related Values,* Beverly Hills: Sage, 1980.

Hofstede, G., "The cultural relativity of organizational practices and theories," *Journal of International Business Studies,* Volume 14, 1983, pp. 75-89.

Hofstede, G. and M.H. Bond, "The Confusius connection: From cultural roots to economic growth," *Organizational Dynamics* 14(4), Spring 1988, pp. 4-21.

Hofstede, G., *Cultures and Organizations: Software of the Mind*, London: McGraw-Hill, 1991.

Hofstede, G., "Management scientists are human," *Management Science,* 40(1), January 1994, pp. 4-10.

Iyer, R.K., "Information and modeling resources for decision support in global environments," *Information and Management,* 14(1), January 1988, pp. 67–73.

King, W.R. and V. Sethi, "A framework for transnational systems," in Palvia, S., P. Palvia, and R. Zigli (eds.), *Global Issues of Information Technology Management,* Harrisburg, PA: The Idea Group, 1992, pp. 214–248.

Kluckhohn, F.R. and F.L. Strodtbeck, *Variations in Value Orientations,* Evanston: Row Patterson and Co., 1961.

Kobayashi, N., "The present and future of Japanese multinational enterprises," *International Study of Management and Organizations,* Volume 12, 1982, pp. 38–58.

Lachman, R., A. Nedd, and B. Hinings, "Analyzing cross-national management and organizations: A theoretical framework," *Management Science,* 40(1), January 1994, pp. 40–55.

Licker, P.S., "The Japanese approach: A better way to manage programmers?" *Communications of the ACM,* 26, 1983, pp. 631–636.

Lunde, K., "Japanese information processing," *ORA.com,* Fall 1993, pp. 19–22.

Lunde, K., *Understanding Japanese Information Processing,* Sebastopol, CA: O'Reilly and Associates, Inc., 1993.

Maisonrouge, J.G., "Regulation of International Information Flows," *The Information Society,* 1(1), 1991, pp. 17–30.

Making a Business of Information, A report to the British Cabinet by the Information Technology Advisory Group, HMSO, 1983.

Mallory, G.R., R.J. Butler, D. Cray, D.J. Hickson, and D.C. Wilson, "Implanted decision-making: American owned firms in Britain," *Journal of Management Studies,* 20, 1983, pp. 191–211.

Ming-Te, L., Q. Youzin, and T. Guimaraes, "A status report of the use of computer-based information systems in PRC," *Information and Management,* 15(5), 1988, pp. 237–242.

Moiri, K. and T. Kawada, "From Kana to Kanji: Word processing in Japan," *IEEE Spectrum,* 20(8), 1990, pp. 46–48.

Moore, S. "Information managers must face the international communication web," *Data Management,* 1984, pp. 30–32.

Neganshi, A.R. "Convergence in organizational practices: An empirical study of industrial enterprises in developing countries," in C.J. Lammers and D.J. Hickson (eds.) *Organizations Alike and Unlike,* London: Routledge and Kegan Paul, 1979.

Negandhi, A.R., "Cross-cultural management research: Trend and future directions," *Journal of International Business Studies,* Volume 14, 1983, pp. 17–28.

O'Reilly, T., "Worlds apart," *ORA.com,* Fall 1993, p. 19.

Report on the *Third Conference of Latin American Informatics Authorities,* Buenos Aires, United Nations Centre on Transnational Corporations, 1979.

Report on the *Conference on African Informatics Integration,* Abidjan, United Nations Centre on Transnational Corporations, 1979.

Report to the Conference on African Informatics Integration, Abidjan, 1979.

Report to the Third Conference of Latin American Informatics Authorities, Buenos Aires, 1979.

Ripper, M.D. and J.L.C. Wanderley, "National telecommunications system," Paper presented at the IBI World Conference on Transborder Data Flow Policies, Rome, 1980.

Rowe, B.C., *Privacy, Computers and You,* Chesire, England: The National Computing Center Ltd., 1972.

Sankar, C.S. and P.K. Prabhakar, "Key Technological Components and Issues of Global Information Systems," in Palvia S., P. Palvia, and R. Zigli (eds.), *Global Issues of Information Technology Management,* Harrisburg, PA: The Idea Group, 1992, pp. 249–275.

Sauter, V.L., "Cross-cultural aspects of model management needs in a transnational decision support system," in Palvia, S., P. Palvia, and R. Zigli (eds.), *Global Issues of Information Technology Management*, Harrisburg, PA: The Idea Group, 1992, pp. 332–355.

Sauvant, K.P., *International Transactions in Services: The Politics of Transborder Data Flows,* New York: Westview Press, Inc., 1986.

Shi, Y. and R. Larson, "Chinese online—Problems and solutions," *Information Technology and Libraries,* 9(2), 1990, pp. 144–154.

Shields, P. and Servaes, J., "The impact of the transfer of information technology on development," *The Information Society,* 6(1), 1989, pp. 47–57.

Stabell, C.B., "Towards a theory of decision support," *DSS-88 Transactions,* Boston, MATIMS 1988, pp. 160–170.

Stabell, C.B. and B.W. Hennestad, "The executive's operational code: Decision style or decision culture?" *Norwegian School of Management Working Paper 1987/5,* Bekkestua, Norway, 1987.

Telecommunications and Canada, Ottawa: Canadian Government Publication Centre, 1979.

Transborder Data Flows and Brazil, New York: United Nations Publication Number ST/CTC40—E.83.II.A.3, 1982.

Wu, Z. and J.D. White, "Computer processing of Chinese characters: An overview of two decades' research and development," *Information Processing and Management* 26(5), pp. 681–692.

Designing a Decision Support System

◆ ◆ ◆

At this point you may be sold on the idea of decision support systems. You believe they are important and you want to include them within the assets of your department or organization. The next logical question is how to start. The answer is a clear and unequivocal, "it depends."

The best approach depends on the kind of systems already in place and the intended focus of the DSS. As with any good systems analysis and design process, it is important to understand the requirements for the application and to select the models, model management system, databases, database management system, mail management system, and user interface in a manner that *best* meet the requirements for that application. Successful DSS can be built on almost any kind of platform with almost any kind of software, but it is crucial that the choices fit the application. Selecting tools and vendors before understanding the problem or forcing tools to meet needs after the fact will certainly lead to failure.

◆ DSS Design Insights ◆

As in any large-scale, important application, the question of *who* should do the development may be critical. Often project teams are hand-picked members of the staff who are pulled together especially for their ability to respond to a particular need. They are thought of as a SWAT team in that they develop the DSS and then return to their separate departments. If they are successful, then they are often called on for the next important application. Especially with the design of decision support systems, there are sometimes subtle elements of group synergy that lead to success for the group in one application, but not in other applications. Unfortunately, the understanding of what leads to such success in high-performance projects is not well understood.

Moad, J., "Can high performance be cloned? Should it be?" *Datamation,* 41(4), March 1, 1995, pp. 44-47.

The physical design of a successful DSS must follow a logical design, which in turn must be *guided by* the decision making process. In particular, designers should ask the same fundamental questions as those on which reporters rely:

- *Who* needs the DSS?
- *What* advantages does the user expect from using the DSS?
- *When* will the DSS be used?
- *Where* does this system fit into the general business process?
- *Why* is a DSS needed?
- *How* will the DSS be used?

While these questions seem obvious, we must keep returning to them as a reality test that the system is providing support for decisions.

Unfortunately, the systems development life cycle (SDLC) approach, which provides a reliable framework in which to design transaction processing systems (TPS), generally does not work for DSS design. Unlike TPS, DSS typically will have fuzzy problem definitions that change substantially over time. In addition, since DSS support decision making, generally that of higher-level managers who have little time and little inclination to attend training sessions, it is necessary to create a system that has lower training needs than those generally associated with TPS. Finally, it is difficult to determine with certainty that a DSS works properly for all applications. Test data sets and problem scenarios can be developed for TPS and run against a system to determine whether it works properly. But, by its very nature—which is to be flexible and allow decision makers to use it as it best fits their decision style—a DSS cannot be "tested" to ensure that it works properly. Therefore, a DSS requires a different approach to design. We will discuss design first in terms of the general business planning, and then with regard to the development of specific systems.

◆ PLANNING FOR DECISION SUPPORT SYSTEMS

In an ideal world, a multilevel plan guides the development of new DSS, such as that described in Figure 8.1. The plan provides specifications for a specific decision support system, in terms of the way it interacts with the rest of the business processes, the kind of information that it will provide, and its relative importance to the growth of the organization.

The specifications for a DSS begin with the corporate strategic or long-range plan. A strategic plan defines where the corporation expects to change its products or processes and during what time line, and provides the direction to the management of the corporation as a whole. The MIS master plan, in turn, inherits its priorities and concerns from this corporate strategic plan. The IS plan provides guidelines for prioritizing requests for maintenance of existing systems and creation of new systems. In particular, it describes the priorities for hardware, soft-

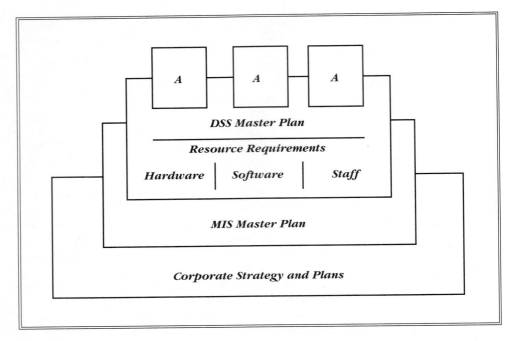

Figure 8.1   Ideal planning.

ware, and staff necessary to respond to corporate strategy plans. The IS master plan specifies modifications and maintenance of legacy systems, creation and implementation of new systems, and diffusion of technology within the organization. It should provide a plan for regular updating and other maintenance. Finally, it should provide specifications for how staff should proceed in the creation of systems.

The DSS plan derives its priorities from the IS plan. Its goal is to coordinate future implementations in the broadest possible way to ensure that all decision making is supported in an appropriate way, while planning for the reuse of code, flexibility for the future, and the greatest potential for growth. In particular, the DSS plan should help answer questions such as those posed by Sprague and Carlson:

- How can current needs susceptible to DSS be recognized?
- How can the likely extent of their growth be assessed?
- What types of DSS are required to support the needs, now and in the future?
- What are the minimum startup capabilities, both organizational and technical, required?
- What kind of plan can be developed to establish the long-term direction, yet respond to unanticipated developments in managerial needs and technical capabilities?

The DSS master plan would provide direction in the selection of hardware and software, and for integration with current systems. In addition, it could include a process for the creation of reusable libraries of code that future designers could embed into similarly operating DSS.

◆ DESIGNING A SPECIFIC DSS

Where DSS master plans exist, there is already some guidance in how to proceed. More often than not, however, such plans do not exist. Then, designers must judge how the DSS will fit into corporate plans and how it will interact with other systems. The methodology described in Figure 8.2 will help designers ensure that they get the best fit. Note that it differs from the traditional SDLC approach in that it puts much more emphasis on determining what information needs to be provided, and in what fashion.

In the first stage, the designer learns the decision needs and environment. Designers must know the key decisions under consideration by the decision maker and the related information needs if the DSS is to be a tool that supports decisions. Then they can begin to examine the parameters needed for consideration. Sometimes these parameters will be easy to identify. For example, one key issue for investment executives is what investments will provide the best returns. Knowing that, we know they need to consider return, relative risk, tax advantages, term of return, and other fiscal parameters. On the other hand, a chief executive officer's key issue might be how to prevent a leveraged buyout or how to strategically acquire a new vertical market. In this situation, knowledge of the key decision reveals information needs.

Requirements Analysis
Interviewing Techniques

Often, designers learn about decision makers' needs by interviewing them. There are many ways of conducting interviews, each of which provides different kinds of information. For example, consider the interviewing styles noted in Figure 8.3 and discussed in the following paragraphs. Interviews can be structured, unstructured, or focused. They can follow case studies or protocol analysis. Finally, they can utilize tools such as card sorting and multidimensional scaling.

The benefit of interviews is that they provide access to information, or a perspective on information, that only the decision maker can provide. In both the structured interview and the focused interview, the designer is interacting with the decision maker to obtain information regarding a prescribed set of topics. This interaction might be in a face-to-face setting, over the telephone, via computer, or on a pen-and-paper questionnaire. Generally, the preferred option is a face-to-face setting in a neutral location (away from the interruptions of the decision maker's normal activities) because the richest information can be gleaned from this situa-

---

INITIAL ANALYSIS

GOALS:
- IDENTIFY KEY DECISIONS
- IDENTIFY KEY INFORMATION NEEDS

GONCERNS:
- THEORETICAL OR CONCEPTUAL NEEDS
- INDUSTRY-BASED NEEDS
- CORPORATION-BASED NEEDS
- DECISION-SPECIFIC PARAMETERS

SITUATION ANALYSIS

GOALS:
- UNDERSTAND THE ORGANIZATIONAL SETTING
- UNDERSTAND THE TASK
- UNDERSTAND THE USER CHARACTERISTICS

SYSTEM DESIGN

GOALS:
- LOGICAL DESIGN
- SYSTEM CONSTRUCTION
- SYSTEM EVALUATION

IMPLEMENTATION

GOALS:
- DEMONSTRATION
- TRAINING
- DEPLOYMENT

Figure 8.2 DSS design methodology.

tion. Good results can be achieved with intelligent computer questionnaires (that move through the questions according to the answers already provided); unfortunately, it is generally too expensive to develop this software for one-time use.

The degree of structure we build into the interview depends on the specificity of information we seek. A structured interview is one in which the questions and the order in which they will be asked are prescribed. The interviewer seeks short answers that provide specific information. A focused interview, on the other hand,

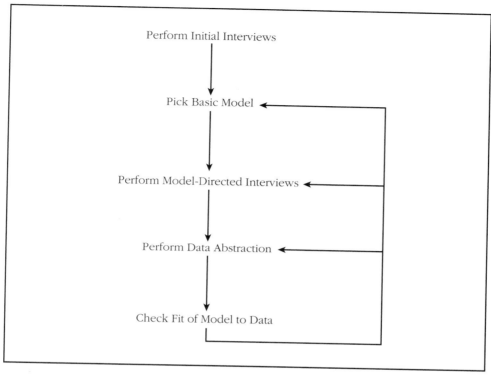

Figure 8.3 Iterative nature of situation analysis.

is relatively unstructured. In this case, the interviewer also has a set of questions and an order for asking the questions. However, the questions are more general, allowing the respondent to drive the direction of the discussion. The interviewer must be prepared with probing questions that help the respondent to focus on salient points.

The more structured the interview, the greater chance the decision maker will provide precisely the information sought. However, the more structured the interview, the less likely the decision maker will provide insights the designer had not considered previously. Therefore, if the designer is relatively uninformed about the choice process or the decision maker's tendencies, the focused interview will allow for greater probing of new avenues, and hence greater understanding of the relationships between tasks and concepts, and why the procedures are sequenced in a particular fashion.

A protocol analysis is a different kind of interview because the interviewer does not set even the basis of the discussion. Instead, respondents complete their typical choice processes (including seeking information, generating alternatives, merging information, modeling, sensitivity analysis, and other tasks included in the process). In order to communicate what is happening and why it is happening, the decision maker verbalizes each task and subtask and how a decision is made to move to another task. Usually, the interviewer does not intervene but just records the descriptions provided. Protocol analysis is a valuable tool because it helps the designer understand what the decision makers actually do in the choice process, not what they *perceive* that they do. This can be important because often the decision maker is not aware of the actual tasks and hence cannot communicate them; this can be a particular problem with very experienced decision makers, as discussed in Chapter 2.

Other Techniques

Both the card-sorting technique and multidimensional scaling require the decision maker to perform some task from which the designer infers the preferred information and models. "Card sorting" refers to any task (whether or not one actually uses cards—even if one uses a computer simulation) in which the decision maker iteratively sorts and combines things or concepts to determine a point of view. For example, if the choice situation involves loan applications, the decision maker would sort a set of loan applications into multiple piles (perhaps "acceptable," "borderline," and "unacceptable"). After the decision maker is comfortable with the similarity of the loan applications in each pile, the designer analyzes the applications, with the help of the decision maker, to determine the bases for the sorting. In other words, by noting the similarities and differences among the applications within piles and between piles, the designer can figure out the set of criteria and standards for applying them. This helps the designer to understand how to provide information and models for the decision maker.

Multidimensional scaling is a similar process in which decision makers are asked to rate items as being similar or dissimilar. It differs from card sorting in that it forces the decision maker to make choices among less complex alternatives. For example, rather than asking whether an entire application is acceptable, the designer would ask the decision maker to compare two candidates with particular incomes or particular debt ratios with regard to their risks as loan candidates. Designers pose a large number of combinations and analyze the data mathematically to determine the criteria being employed by the decision makers. Unfortunately, the factors driving the decision often are not obvious or they lack face validity. Hence, the exercise can result in no useful information.

To identify more information needs, designers research the specific kind of decision under consideration. For example, they can identify some information needs by studying the conceptual and theoretical bases for decisions, such as those covered in business school classes. From such an analysis, designers could identify that investment executives need to consider term of investment, relative risk, tax advantages, and other fiscal parameters in addition to the fundamental question of return on investment. This would provide a starting point for identifying additional needs. Alternatively, designers can gain insight by learning about the industry in general. For example, designers of a DSS for a pharmaceutical firm could gain insights by examining the creation, approval, marketing, and selling processes for drugs. Issues such as testing, purity, reliability, and statistical confidence levels would become evident. Such topics would likely have a home in any DSS in such a firm. Finally, designers could examine copies of reports, memos, transactions, and models to identify additional needs. This is comparable to an archeological analysis of the context from which inferences about needs can be drawn.

Situational Analysis

When an initial analysis of the key decisions and related information needs has been completed, designers must complete a situational analysis to help identify some of the remaining needs. This includes an analysis of the task, the organizational setting, the user characteristics, and how each contributes to the informational requirements of the DSS.

Using either interviewing or other techniques, a designer completes a task analysis to identify the baseline information and models needs. The baseline needs represent the theoretical or conceptual information needs that everyone would have, without consideration of the preferences of the decision maker or external needs imposed by the choice context. These needs are driven by the nature of the tasks—their relative structure, variability, length, and frequency—to identify information needs and sources as well as constraints. Simon's stages of decision making can provide insight into these needs. If the decision maker's goal is "intelligence," the system must monitor and scan data to identify indicators of problems and opportunities, such as trends, patterns, or exceptions to patterns. For example, a financial DSS might continually scan the stock and bond market for investment opportunities that have high potential payoff. On the other hand, if the goal is "design," the system must be able to facilitate the identification and construction of alternative strategies. In this case, the DSS needs to provide opportunities for investment, such as tools for identifying mutual funds with characteristics that will meet the needs of the investor. Finally, if the goal is "choice," the system must facilitate evaluating and testing of the alternatives for sensitivity to assumptions. In this case, the financial DSS might evaluate alternatives for past performance as well as the expected reaction of the financial opportunity to changes in resources, political climates, or other factors that could affect its desirability.

Similarly, the task analysis determines whether there are limitations on the number or types of models appropriate or necessary in the analysis. For example, in the case of the investment executive, task analysis identifies the need to distinguish between deciding when to invest, how much to invest, and for how long to invest, as well as the outcomes of liquidity, rate of return, and total profit. In addition, it reminds us to consider related factors such as the inflation rate, competition, and market stability.

Once we know the main independent, dependent, and interdependent aspects of the choice context, we can begin to understand what the decision maker needs to do, what the decision maker can control, and what constrains the decision maker's actions. Designers must learn what guides and limits the decision maker as well as what measures are appropriate for assessing the quality of the decision and/or outcome. Knowing the facets of the problem and the interdependencies among them will help identify information sources, authority constraints, and co-ordination necessary to provide decision makers what they will need.

The organizational setting analysis describes the forum in which the choice will take place. In this analysis, designers identify informal norms or other relevant practices for analyses, as well as the climate in which the decision maker functions and relevant relationships among the decision makers within their organization. Each of these evaluations results in information and modeling needs for the DSS.

Finally, designers need to examine the user characteristics such as the amount of experience and knowledge possessed by the decision makers and the extent of their skills. As we saw in Chapter 2, this is influenced by the experience and background of the users concerning the problem type under consideration, with the models appropriate for that problem and with DSS or other computer-based tools. Further, this is influenced by information preferences, decision making styles, and approaches to problem identification and evaluation. Knowledge of the user requirements along all of these dimensions will provide insight into the information needs (primarily background needs), as well as into the model management and other user interface requirements.

The entire situation analysis results in a deeper understanding of how the DSS will be used, including the kinds of information, models, support, and intervention the user is likely to employ. To achieve this understanding, designers develop a model of how decision makers will use information. They identify a basic understanding of the model through the identification of baseline needs. This model is refined by interviews and observation of the decision makers. Designers abstract important information from those interviews and compare the expressed needs to those predicted by the model. Differences between the expressed and predicted needs are used to refine the model. Often, these steps are followed in an iterative fashion, with designers forming and refining models of the decision makers' needs between data collection steps, as shown in Figure 8.4.

Designers should be able to understand how the decision maker conceptualizes, analyzes, and communicates problems. For example, at this stage, designers should be able to learn where and how decision makers will employ graphs, lists, charts, and other aids to understand the problem. In addition, designers should know how decision makers analyze and manipulate the information in different contexts. This includes understanding the representations (that is, lists, graphs, charts, and so on), operations (that is, the means of analysis), and the linkages between representations and operations, as well as the model management tools, notepads, or user interface components that facilitate those linkages. Finally, the situation analysis suggests frameworks for making the DSS useful to decision makers. In particular, it suggests characteristics of the user interface, its design, the necessary kinds of intelligent and context-specific assistance, and the relationships be-

		Structured Interviews	Focused Interviews	Case Study Interviews	Protocol Analysis	Card Sorting	Multidimensional Scaling
Concepts	Raw Concepts	✓	✓	✓	✓		
	Concept Definition		✓				
	Concept Structures		✓			✓	✓
Problems (major tasks completed by decision maker)	Problems	✓	✓				
	Problem Types					✓	✓
Solutions (possible outcomes)	Solutions	✓	✓	✓	✓		
	Solution Types					✓	✓
Problem-Solving Steps	General Steps	✓		✓	✓		
	Specific Steps		✓	✓	✓		

Figure 8.4 Interviewing techniques matrix.

tween modeling and database components. Said differently, it would tell the designers how to evaluate the four components of a DSS discussed in earlier chapters.

The end of the situation analysis begins the design phase. As shown in Figure 8.2, the design stage begins with a logical design of the system and ends with the construction of the system. In particular, this includes the identification and/or creation of (a) available databases and a database management system, (b) available models and a model-base management system, (c) user interfaces, and (d) a mail management system. In this step, designers determine how the system will work and what hardware is appropriate. Further, they must identify what software or tools to utilize or create. Finally, they must identify an appropriate design approach. Advantages and disadvantages of different approaches are discussed in the next section.

After the construction of the system, designers must evaluate and then implement the DSS. This stage includes testing and evaluating the system by the designers as well as the users. Implementation includes training, deployment, and demonstration. Of course, the final stage is maintenance and adaptation. Maintenance covers the correction of any defaults in the system that appear after deployment of the system. In adaptation, designers modify the system in response to changing demands on the choice process resulting from new choices or information sources, or they make improvements in usage of the system.

As with the SDLC, there have been several attempts to provide methodologies that specify the various steps in the design of DSS. Among these are *ESPIRIT, KADS* from the University of Amsterdam, and *Model/1* from Andersen Consulting. Each of these follows the basic structure outlined in this chapter, but they provide additional details and specifications for completing the analysis phase.

Systems Design

Table 8.1 outlines the three approaches to design and implementation. These three methods suggest that you either build the whole system from scratch ("one-stage, complete system") or use current technologies to facilitate the development ("quick-hit method" and the "evolutionary method"). In addition, they suggest that you either treat the DSS as a one-time development, with some maintenance over time ("one stage, complete system" and the "quick hit method") or you plan for the system to grow with the demands placed on it ("evolutionary development"). (See Table 8.1)

Systems Built from Scratch

The "one-stage, complete system" approach assumes that nothing, including the models, the model-base management system, the databases, the database management system, and the user interface—or even their components—is available on which to build the desired DSS. As the name suggests, this approach requires the designers to build an entire system and deliver it, in total, to the decision maker. In these cases, designers use the DSS-adapted life-cycle approach, shown in Figure 8.2, with significant emphasis on the design and construction phases. It means that designers code every aspect of the system from one or more languages, without the benefit of available electronic tools or modules. Although all early decision support systems were built in this way, today, the one-stage, complete system approach is implemented only when building a large-scale, multiple-user, or unique system.

This approach is useful when the models are so specific to the problem that modeling software is not available. For example, suppose the purpose of the DSS is to facilitate decisions regarding battlefield logistics and strategy. Or suppose the DSS must simulate human tolerance of toxic wastes. The necessary models are so-

TABLE 8.1   Design Approaches

One-Stage, Complete System Approach
Quick-Hit Method
Evolutionary Development Method

phisticated and unique, libraries of such models do not exist, and the models may be quite complex. Since the model is such an important part of the DSS, it might be easier to build the system around the specialized model than to incorporate it into preexisting tools and modules.

The best generalized example of the use of a one-stage, complete system today is the design of geographic information systems (GIS). These systems provide decision support for a particular class of problems, namely those requiring map-oriented analyses of data. For example, city planning agencies might need to track sewer development, electricity and gas hookups, movement of the population, and housing starts. For some analyses and decisions, it may be most meaningful to model the infrastructure to support housing starts with a map. In this case, the map and the associated analysis tools serve as the model and model management tools. In other words, the GIS is a DSS that uses a specialized set of models and model management capabilities, specialized database files, and a powerful user interface. Since these tools require a unique programming platform at this time, this form of DSS is now designed as a one-stage, complete system, especially because the tools are generally used in isolation.

When using the one-stage, complete system method, designers often prototype as a means of determining system requirements. A prototype is a facsimile system that simulates the user interface as well as the data and modeling activities of the DSS. Designers develop prototypes using fourth-generation languages or other prototyping tools that allow rapid development and easy change of the system. After decision makers specify the basic needs and preferences, designers can quickly produce a prototype that they believe meets those needs and preferences. Users then operate the prototype as they intend to use the ultimate system. In this way, they experience the user interface, data management, model management, and mail management features and capabilities. Since users can demonstrate problems or less preferred options for the designer, they can also respond to specific features or constraints and express their concerns more precisely. Similarly, designers can ask questions in an unambiguous manner.

Designers armed with this feedback can adjust the prototype quickly to respond to the users' needs. Since the elapsed time between the expression of preferences and observation of the effects is so short, and since specific system attributes are identified, users can focus on whether designers understood and implemented their concerns. This cycle is repeated until the user is satisfied with the design of the entire DSS.

The prototype enables designers and users to communicate concretely, reducing the chance of miscommunication. Such a tool is important because the designers and the decision makers have different mental representations of the problem that bias how they respond to new information provided to them about the system. The tangible nature of the prototype allows them to look for disconfirmatory data that identifies when the DSS is not performing adequately. While many seasoned designers prefer an intuitive approach, this empirical way to determine needs will generally provide a better analysis of decision making needs.

After a satisfactory system has been created, the designer could translate the fourth-generation code into more efficient and easily maintained production code. This would have the benefit of providing a system that could be maintained over time, and that could be used by multiple users without magnifying the strain on resources. However, it introduces a time delay in users' access to the real system. Further, since production code may not have the same capabilities as are available in the fourth-generation languages, some important features can be lost. More often, designers leave the DSS in the fourth-generation language and allow users immediate access to the technology. If there are few users, particularly if they do not use a system frequently or intensely, the advantage of improved efficiency in code is not worth the delay.

Although the one-stage, complete system method was once the preferred approach to design, it is unusual to use this approach to DSS design today. The change is associated closely with the move from file processing applications toward database applications in most corporations and organizations. In earlier periods of data processing history, most applications had their own unique data that ran with the system, and hence the need to identify data and control it was associated with the DSS itself. In today's environment, there has been a move toward *shared* databases. Certainly most mainframe users have shared data both to simplify control and access to the data, but make results across applications consistent. Further, this shared view of data allows more types of data to be available for a greater number of applications and therefore make possible richer decision making. Increasing numbers of models are being computerized and easily integrated within a DSS. Since these sophisticated databases, models, and their control mechanisms exist, it would be inefficient to design without them.

Access to the wide range of databases has made the DSS more useful. However, it has also led decision makers to make greater data demands on systems. Fortunately, with the greater connectivity available through the Internet and the capability of "surfing" the Internet, decision makers can get access to broader data in shorter times.

Simultaneously, there has been a change in the capability of hardware and the efficiency of the software provided as DSS generators. Early generators were quite limited in the range of models and data they could reach, were relatively inefficient in their analyses, and provided user interfaces that would be considered archaic today. Today, designers can realize significant economies of scale from centralizing the development of such sophisticated tools. Such centralized tools being implemented properly can result in the development of a very efficient engine and a system that integrates well with other systems.

Furthermore, since tools are substantially more sophisticated today, building them from scratch is likely to be a long, tedious effort, which most corporations cannot tolerate. The resulting system would be both late and technologically obsolete before use. In short, the resources available to DSS designers are substantially better today than they were in the past. Hence, where the resources exist, it makes sense to use them.

Using Technology to Form the Basis of the DSS

The other two approaches to designing a decision support system differ from the first in that both rely on the use of an existing base technology, called a decision support system generator. In the one-stage, complete system approach, designers customize all the components by building them from a language. More often, designers use commercially available, leading edge tools and technologies to construct the system more quickly. These tools and technologies are referred to as "generators" for the DSS, or DSS generators.

Evaluating a DSS Generator

Of course, more quickly is only good if the generator will, in fact, meet the needs of the application. Said differently, it will only be appropriate to use a generator if it allows the uses and functionality that are anticipated for the DSS, such as those described in earlier chapters. These needs must be stated before purchase or lease. Certain issues must be considered for any generator, such as those summarized in Tables 8.2–8.7.

TABLE 8.2   Data and Data Management
Considigerations in Selecting a DSS Generator

- Adequacy
  - Provides common user view of data
  - Links well to corporate database management system
  - Facilitates data warehousing
- Flexibility
  - Offers the creation of "personal" databases
  - Supports a wide range of database formats (text, graphics, audio, video, and so on)
  - Facilitates ad hoc query capability
  - Provides flexible browsers for public databases
- Usability
  - Offers ease in data selection
  - Has data dictionary
  - Handles necessary amount of data
  - Can handle sparse data
- Security
  - Provides data security features
  - Offers multiple levels of security
  - Controls number of users, with what kinds of access, in simultaneous use
  - Creates audit trails

The needs summarized in these tables corresponds to the DSS needs discussed in earlier chapters. For example, Table 8.2 shows some features to consider regarding the database and data management component of the DSS. From a macro perspective, we need to ask whether the generator will simplify or prohibit access to and manipulation of the necessary data. Unfortunately, it is not always easy to determine *what* data will be used or even how the demand for data will expand as the DSS is used. So designers need to take the perspective of the decision maker when asking whether the generator is adequate, flexible, and usable and provides sufficient security to meet the needs of the application.

In particular, the designer needs to consider whether the generator (a) is consistent in providing data (both in raw and processed form) to users—regardless of the source of the data; (b) interfaces well with the corporatewide data management tools; and (c) allows data warehousing. In other words, adequacy reflects whether the generator will provide users access to the necessary data in a seamless and friendly fashion. Further, the generator must be flexible in its use of data to meet the varying needs of decision makers. For example, earlier chapters discussed the importance of allowing development and use of personal databases exclusively by the decision makers. The generator must allow such development and provide full tool use on these data. Similarly, decision makers must have a tool that searches public databases using the full range of query development they use in the corporate databases. An ideal system would provide the same search engine for all databases, thereby making transition from one type to another transparent to the user. In addition, the generator must allow for formats beyond simple text. Depending on the application, decision makers are likely to need graphics, audio, video, and even access to virtual reality files. These alternate-format files can only be effective support mechanisms, however, if they can be indexed, stored, and retrieved easily, and merged with other data.

Usability refers to the system's ability to meet data and decision maker needs. On one hand, the question of usability can refer to the size of databases, the size of resulting tables, or the number of queries that can be made at once. Since size and price are often highly correlated, we need to be sure of buying enough to meet foreseeable needs. On the other hand, the question of usability can refer to the decision maker's ability to find the necessary variables and to make the system understand those variables.

Finally, any company needs to provide security for certain data. Users expect that the DSS will ease the problems of location of information and reports. With this ease, however, comes the requirement that the generator prevent those not employed by the corporation from using the data. It is also true that some data are so important or controversial that only some members can have access to it on a need-to-know basis. Hence, the generator must be able to provide multiple levels of security as well as necessary audit trails to determine who has gained access to what data.

Similarly, designers need to evaluate these issues with regard to the models and the model management system associated with the DSS generator. The generator needs to meet both the modeling and analysis capabilities of the decision makers, such as those described in Table 8.3. In this case, the modeling concerns address whether the generator can handle the kind and size of models that are of interest to the decision maker. In particular, it examines the models that can be accessed, the ease of use, the flexibility (especially with regard to size), and the functionality made available in the system.

The analysis capabilities, on the other hand, question the generator's ability to provide the decision makers with a rich modeling environment. The characteristic of a DSS that distinguishes it from being simply a modeling package is its ability to simplify both the use and the interpretation of the models. For example, the

TABLE 8.3 Models and Model Management Considerations in Selecting a DSS Generator

- Modeling
  - Functionality
    - User-defined functions
    - Procedurability (ability to solve equations independent of their ordering, symbolic reference of data)
    - Mathematical and financial functions
    - Nonprodedurality
    - Time as a possible dimension
  - Flexibility
    - Size restrictions
    - Currency and date conversions
    - Ability to aggregate and disaggregate analyses
    - Ability to link sequential analyses
    - Multidimensionality
    - Links well to available modeling packages
  - Appropriateness of included models
    - Symbolic modeling
    - Statistical ability (descriptive statistics, hypothesis testing, predictive statistics, regression)
    - Project management ability (PERT/CPM, multilevel work breakdown structure)
    - Operations research ability (mathematical programming, stochastic analysis)
    - Forecasting and econometrics ability (time series analysis, causal modeling, seasonalization, smoothing)
  - Ease of use
- Analysis capabilities
  - Sensitivity analysis
  - What-if analysis
  - Impact analysis
  - Symbolic reasoning evaluation
  - Context-sensitive model help

model management component needs to be able to use the output of one analysis as the input to a second analysis, if wanted. In addition, the generator must allow and simplify appropriate sensitivity and what-if analyses associated with the models in its portfolio. Not only must it tolerate review of the assumptions and rerunning of models in light of changes in the assumptions, but it also must encourage the user by providing an easy path to such analyses and a user-friendly interpretation of the output. Finally, the generator needs to provide context-sensitive modeling assistance for the user. This does not refer to the online version of the user manual as exists in many PC-based applications today; rather, this is a level of assistance in how to run the model, including a statement of the assumptions and limitations of the model and even an intelligent intervention when modeling assumptions have been stretched or violated. While most generators will not have such assistance built into the package, a good one will simplify the development of such tools.

Consideration of the user interface capabilities is important as well. Table 8.4 refers to those needs outlined in Chapter 6. In particular, in order for the system to be helpful for the decision maker, it must be user friendly (whatever the level of user expertise and experience); support a wide range of output and input devices; provide graphical, video, and audio interpretation of the results; and provide a reporting format that can be customized for the specific application and/or user under consideration. From the designer's point of view, this means that the generator must either provide such functionality itself or make it easy to design.

As with any software adoption, we need to be concerned that the system will work in our environment and will be affordable and can be upgraded over time. Tables 8.6–8.8 summarize criteria to consider for ensuring that the selection of the generator makes good business sense.

Table 8.6 illustrates the issues associated with compatibility. It is important to ensure that the generator will work with the equipment available and with the operating systems and networking options available. In addition, it must be able to work with any additional resources acquired, including input, output, and storage devices.

Table 8.7 illustrates the cost issues associated with the use of the generator. Today, software can be purchased or leased using a variety of options. Designers must examine these costs carefully to ensure that they are in line with the usage patterns of decision makers. For example, it is not appropriate to deploy a product across many occasional users of a system if the cost is based on each installation of a developed product, especially if it is not possible to deploy those copies via a network. On the other hand, it would be appropriate if the cost were a function of the number of simultaneous users of the product.

Finally, Table 8.8 illustrates issues that should be considered to ensure that the vendor is reputable and is likely to provide the kinds and level of support needed for your application. Such support will be important not only during the development stage, but also as users begin to find undocumented features needing explanation.

TABLE 8.4 User Interface Considerations in Selecting a DSS Generator

- ■ User friendliness
  - ■ Novice and expert modes
  - ■ Menus and prompts
  - ■ Consistent, natural language commands
  - ■ Command abbreviations
  - ■ Context-sensitive help
  - ■ Clear, end-user–oriented error messages
  - ■ "Undo" command support
  - ■ Meaningful identifiers
  - ■ Documentation
  - ■ User-defined commands
  - ■ Context-sensitive warnings
- ■ Support of modeling and data needs
  - ■ Wide range of graphics support
  - ■ Windowing support
  - ■ Multitasking support
  - ■ Support for a variety of input and output devices
  - ■ Color and functional control over user interface
  - ■ Support for individual customization
- ■ Graphics
  - ■ Quality and resolution of the output
  - ■ Multicolor support
  - ■ Range of output control
  - ■ Support for dynamic graphics and video and audio enhancements
  - ■ Basic plots and charts
  - ■ Complex charts
  - ■ Format and layout control
  - ■ Spacing of graphs
  - ■ Compatibility with available graphics devices
  - ■ Preview ability
  - ■ Modification ability
  - ■ Ease of use
- ■ Reporting formats
  - ■ Flexibility of reporting formats
  - ■ Standard formats
  - ■ Ease of customization

Using a DSS Generator

If a DSS generator forms the basis of a decision support system, a designer has two possibilities for development, the quick-hit approach or the evolutionary approach. The difference between the two is in the staging of development and the basic involvement of decision makers in the design process.

The goal of the quick-hit method is to design a system *quickly* in response to some well-understood and usually immediate need that is expected to have a high

TABLE 8.5   Connectivity Considerations in Selecting a DSS Generator

- Compatibility with available electronic mail system
- Document sharing
- Data sharing
- Communications
- Mail handling and priority setting code
- Connectivity to Internet resources, including news services, gopher services, and Web pages
- Electronic searching devices for Internet resources
- Firewall availability

payoff. Furthermore, the system is likely to reside on a microcomputer and be used by either one person or a small group. The goals and procedures are clear, the data are available, the system can stand independently, and there is little need to address conflicting concerns. Hence, much of the analysis component of design can be done quickly. Further, because the system is discarded after the choice is made, it is not necessary to employ many of the procedures necessary that ensure the long-term viability of a DSS.

We might use this approach to design a DSS for a problem such as a high-level personnel decision. In some industries, many of the criteria needing evaluation are well known. Furthermore, selecting the right person for the job can save corporations significant money and provide significant opportunities for growth. However, it is a decision that is not made often. Hence, a DSS to support a choice would be a good candidate for use of the quick-hit design process.

TABLE 8.6   Hardware and Software Considerations in Selecting a DSS Generator

- Compatibility with available equipment
- Compatibility with available operating system
- Compatibility with available networking configuration
- Printer and plotter support
- Preferred hardware/operating system/networking configuration
- Time-sharing option
- Disk and other resource requirements

TABLE 8.7   Cost Considerations in Selecting a DSS Generator

- Initial purchase/license cost
- Per capita fee
- Maintenance costs
- Documentation
  - Paper version
  - Online version
- Resource utilization
- Conversion costs
- Upgrade frequency and costs

To achieve the goal of fast deployment, designers rely heavily on already available tools and packages, existing data and model sources, and existing data, model, and mail management systems. Such systems work well in the short run because designers can rely on tested components that use the current technology. However, over the long run, designers only may be able to update, maintain, or enhance the system when the vendor provides updates to the generator. In addition, the vendor dictates the kinds of enhancements provided in the system. Alternatively, if the system is composed of a makeshift combination of existing tools and systems, the processing efficiency may not be as good as it can be with more structured systems. Of course, in the long run, it may be difficult to bridge such systems to other existing systems or to systems introduced later.

TABLE 8.8   Vendor Considerations in Selecting a DSS Generator

- Financial stability and viability
- Length of time in business
- Size of installed base
- Growth in customer base
- Quality and size of staff
- Activity of research and development staff
- Ongoing commitment to this product
- Technical support personnel
- Availability of support hotline
- Availability of Internet-based support
- Time horizon for support
- Internet user discussion group
- Organized user group
- Product target market
- User perceptions

The quick-hit process relies heavily on the use of a generator and other tools so that the designers can focus their energies on the analysis and user interface components. Such a process is reasonable if the system can stand independently and if the data are already available. However, it becomes difficult if there is a long-term need for the system, or a need to tie it to existing systems. The approach only works if users know what kinds of data and models to use and do not need significant levels of "support" in either the data selection or modeling phases. In fact, it works best if the need is so domain specific that a particular modeling package can be used as the core of the system.

The third approach, evolutionary development, is similar to the quick-hit approach in that it is dependent on the use of DSS generators, which allow for quick development and quick changes. Further, DSS generators allow the designer to focus on analysis of the needs rather than on construction of the software. Evolutionary development differs from the quick-hit approach in that designers expect that the system design will mature as decision makers gain experience with the system and the information access.

Evolutionary development begins when the designer selects an important subproblem of the choice process. Through focus on this subproblem, the designer learns about the information needs, modeling needs, and user interface needs of the decision maker. This subproblem must be small enough to be unambiguous to both the designer and the decision maker, but large enough to require computer support. In addition, the problem must be important to the decision makers so that they will participate closely in the development process and adopt the process after design.

The process of design is heavily dependent on the use of prototyping, discussed earlier in this chapter. Designers begin by seeking user needs. From this information, they design a "quick and dirty," but working, mock-up of the system. Decision makers test and evaluate the prototype and refine their information needs. Designers then fine-tune the system and provide it to decision makers again for testing and evaluation. This process is repeated until the evaluation calls for no substantive changes and an acceptable and stable product is available to the decision maker.

The key to this being different from the one-stage, complete system process defined is two-fold. First, it builds all components from scratch. Therefore, there is often a delay between the agreement of specifications and the provision of the product. The evolutionary approach, on the other hand, provides decision makers with a working system quickly. However, rather than providing the entire system at once, the evolutionary system provides only a small component of the eventual DSS at the outset. This allows users to experience using the system with the agreed upon specifications and to be able to change those specifications as the system matures.

In addition, when prototyping is used in the one-stage, complete system method, it generally is not a working system, but rather a mockup using a shell tool, a limited database, and a stand-alone machine. Often, response is better with these prototypes (both in terms of quality of the response and response time) than the designers can provide with the production language. As a result, users are often disappointed by the final system. In the case of the evolutionary development, designers use generators, not mockup shells, in development. Hence, what the user sees when interacting with the system early is what the user sees with the eventual development system. Furthermore, since designers and decision makers concentrate on one small part of the process in the prototyping effort, it is easier for both parties to concentrate on the implications of features and changes to features. In addition, because the evaluation of the system and changes requires less of the decision makers' time (because it is smaller), the decision makers are able to provide better and more meaningful feedback to the designer, and thus the exercise tends to have better results. By focusing on the small but important component of the process, decision makers can understand the implications of their suggestions better. In the one-stage, complete system process, designers and decision makers dilute the focus by looking at the entire system at once. Since there is so much to look at, decision makers may not consider how many of the functions will actually work in a production system. Decision makers may not commit the amount of time, energy, or attention to understanding the entire system at once.

The problem with the evolutionary development is, of course, where to start. We need to begin with some component of the problem that is important to the decision maker. Once that decision is made, however, the designer still needs to determine what information should be included at the outset. However, information is not a unidimensional concept. Suppose decision makers state that their most important focus is on effectiveness. While "effectiveness" of the alternatives might seem like an unambiguous concept, it can really mean very different things to different people. To the designers, it might mean cost-effectiveness. To the decision maker, it might mean the expected outcome of attracting new clients. Even if there is agreement on the measure "attracting new clients," there might be disagreement about when relevant data are actually information. For example, designers might think of hard numbers of new clients, and thus new sales. However, decision makers might think of an increase in customer satisfaction that will lead, in turn, to acceptance of the product.

Ultimately, all these views might be important to the decision maker. Nevertheless, designers need to know where to start. To define the needed information, designers must look at it from a variety of perspectives: (a) the content; (b) the representation; and (c) the attributes of the data themselves. An understanding of the appropriate content means an understanding of what knowledge needs to be accumulated and maintained, or what issues need to be addressed. Here, for example, the designer determines if the most important issue is the attrition rate, the schedule needs, or the advertising expenditures. In addition, the designer must differentiate the relevant perspective of that content. For example, designers need to determine if decision makers prefer the function or merit associated with the relevant content. If one considers the topic of "advertising expenditures," a "function" perspective would represent how the money was spent, where the money was spent, and so on, whereas a "merit" perspective would represent how the expenditure had an impact on the clientele. Similarly, designers need to determine the focus of the information, or whether the data should be oriented toward how the alternative is structured (an internal focus) or on the service that is provided by the alternative (an external focus). Third, designers need to understand what kinds of measures are most important to the decision makers. This might include cost data, activity data, performance data, or impact data. For example, the data needs are quite different if decision makers simply want to know on what kinds of ads money is spent than if decision makers want to know what market segments are reached and are likely to be influenced by the information. The representation of data has traditionally included the format, or the presentation of what kinds of data in what order. This would include whether graphs or charts, icons or text, and numbers or conclusions are provided. Finally, the attributes of the information are those characteristics discussed in Chapter 3. This includes whether the data are qualitative or quantitative, facts or judgments, specific information or global generalizations, or past performance or expected performance data. In addition, it includes a specification of who provides the data and what kinds of credibility go along with that presentation.

Once one can describe the content in this multidimensional manner, it is possible to provide guidance as to how to start the DSS design and how to let it evolve. Fortunately, the dimensions cluster together, making it easier to determine where information will be most useful. For example, the content and representation of the data required often is a function of the experience level of the decision makers. As decision makers gain greater experience with a particular type of decisions, they move from seeking feasibility information to preferring information regarding the performance of alternatives under consideration; with increasing amounts of experience, they tend to move toward information regarding the efficiency of alternatives. A similar shift occurs with regard to the attributes of the information. Decision makers with little experience tend to seek quantitative, factual data that reflect future economic implications. As decision makers gain more experience, they seek more information regarding the past performance of alternatives, usually in terms of qualitative information and more speculative opinions. Finally, decision makers with significant amounts of experience tend to address process issues. They seek quantitative, factual data, reflecting the operations issues of the adoption of the alternative.

These preference patterns can be useful for guiding the evolution of systems. For example, if it is known that users are primarily inexperienced in a particular category of decisions, it would be wise to emphasize feasibility information with factual data reflecting the economics of the environment in the early stages of development.

In addition, decision makers' preferences for analytical methods evolve over time, as a function of how the decision context changes. For example, decision makers are likely to employ compensatory models, such as optimization models, only when considering tactical decisions in a stable environment for which the user has significant experience. Knowing this suggests a need for including many exploratory and statistical tools in the early stages of DSS development, and can de-emphasize other kinds of tools until later stages of the evolution of the system.

The Design Team

Selecting the appropriate design approach and the appropriate technology are important aspects of DSS design. A third concern is selecting the appropriate project team to meet the needs of the system. This is particularly important for the first DSS in a corporation or group, and/or if the DSS is part of a strategic change to the corporation.

First, the team must include a champion (even if it is simply an *ex officio* position) from among the senior management of the group. Including such a person and keeping him or her updated regularly can help you to get the necessary access to resources, data, and models. In addition, you need a team of developers with the appropriate skills. For most DSS applications today, this team needs to include people trained in graphical and object-oriented technologies who are open-minded and imaginative. However, it is important to include people who understand the issues associated with disaster recovery and security. Planning for problems from the start makes it much easier to solve them. Finally, it is important to include end user decision makers on the team to ensure that the DSS meets their decision making needs.

Whether internal end users or external consultants, team members need to have certain characteristics, such as those outlined in Table 8.9. Notice that the primary team need is a sense of creativity and open-mindedness. If the DSS is to result in better decisions, the team must do something more than simply automate the current procedures. If team members do not have the capacity to see potential opportunities for change, change will not occur.

TABLE 8.9   Characteristics of Good Team Members

- Creativity and openmindedness
- Good communication skills
- An understanding of the decision task and the organization, business, and marketplace
- An understanding of and experience with DSS design and/or use
- An understanding of possible technology
- A willingness to work cooperatively
- Good chemistry between the design team and the use team

DSS Design Insights

Computer people often are guilty of talking only in acronyms. This can be intimidating to the user who may not understand the acronyms and hence cannot fully understand the problems or opportunities that are being presented. However, it can also be confusing when the end user has similar acronyms and does not understand how they are being used differently.

One of the best examples of this was observed when an external consulting team developed a DSS for a large, progressive hospital. Part of the development team met with a committee of the nurses and nursing supervisors to design one component of the system. During this discussion, designers kept referring to the I/O and how it would change. The nurses were obviously becoming more and more confused until one of them asked, *"What do the patient's liquid inputs and liquid outputs have to do with how we can make better nursing decisions?!"* In other words, they were baffled because "I/O" had a meaning to them, but not the same usage as that of the consulting team.

A second need is good communication skills. Later in this chapter, we will discuss the problems associated with putting decision needs into words. In addition, it is difficult to communicate technical requirements or enabling technology. Without good communication, no creative change to the decision process can happen.

Similarly, the team needs to have a good understanding of the decision task, how that task fits within the organization, and how it relates to the business and the marketplace. The goal of the exercise is to provide a value-added service through the DSS.

DSS DESIGN AND REENGINEERING

In today's business environment there is considerable discussion about business process reengineering (BPR). The term was coined by Hammer (1990) to mean the radical redesign of business processes to achieve dramatic performance improvements. The redesign typically uses modern information technology and changes of the focus of decision making so that it crosses functional and departmental lines. BPR requires (a) the organization of activities around outcomes (not tasks); (b) decision making at the point of work performance; and (c) the development of adequate control processes. Finally, it requires that information be captured only once, at its source. Much has been written about the reengineering process and how it is conducted, but it will not be repeated here because that is not the purpose of this text. However, since BPR has an impact on decision making and the use of technology, it is reasonable to question the relationship between the design of DSS and BPR. In particular, we will address three questions:

Is DSS design BPR?
Does DSS design require BPR?
Can DSS design facilitate BPR?

DSS design is *not* the same as BPR. Although technology and its rapid development is the enabler to achieving the goal in both cases, the goals of the analysis and the expected outcomes are quite different. Business process reengineering, by its very nature, focuses on the fundamental activities of a department or organization, the processes necessary for their completion and improvement, and the activities that would improve the flow of work in the organization. This might include an analysis of what information and what models are available to whom, but the more likely focus would be on who makes the decision, how decentralized the decision making becomes, and what controls are established to ensure that it happens well.

DSS design instead focuses on the process by which decisions are made. It does not question whether the individual decision makers *should* be making the decision, does not focus on most of the employees of an organization, and does not necessarily result in a physical product or service being improved. Like business process reengineering, DSS design does not have cost-cutting as its goal. Rather, its goal is a better-thought-out choice process that often has as a natural result a reduction in costs and losses. In addition, good DSS design, like good BPR, can have a side benefit of improvements in corporate performance, because decision making is improved. There are parallels, but they are two substantially different activities.

The second question is: Does DSS design require BPR? Not always. Sometimes, designers and decision makers intend for the DSS only to improve access to data and models, but not to make a fundamental change in how operations are conducted. In these cases, reengineering is not an important component of the DSS design. However, at other times, the decision to move toward a DSS is part of a corporate strategic decision. In such cases, the existence of a DSS *alone* is unlikely to cause a substantial change in the way business is conducted. Just throwing the power of a computer at a problem will not cause expected productivity gains. As Hammer has said (1992), "turning the cowpaths of most business processes into superhighways using the plethora of computer hardware just doesn't work." That is, if all the DSS does is to automate the current decision processes, and the decision makers have only the same data, the same models, and the same charts as they have always had, decision making will not improve.

Instead, the DSS design needs to be coupled with a reengineering of the decision process. The design process allows designers and decision makers alike to rethink the choice process by considering explicitly what decision makers need to know and how they need information presented. It allows an opportunity to take a holistic view of the process, the natural way of considering choices, the neglected opportunities for insight, and possible integration strategies. The technological solution is not as significant as the way the technology is used to implement an organization's strategic vision.

The third question is: Can a well-designed DSS facilitate the BPR? Yes! The DSS can be a resource that simplifies the reengineering effort. One of the major difficulties in reengineering is the absence of necessary data. It is impossible to plan for change or predict the impact of change without appropriate information regarding current operations and current environmental data. Unfortunately, such data are not readily available in most organizations. However, a DSS can provide managers access to the data and means for understanding them. The DSS can help managers to challenge old procedures and create new ones through better alternative generation, more informed decision making, and better use of models. In addition, decision makers can view a given problem from a variety of perspectives and be better able to understand the problem, the assumptions, and the implications of the solutions. With group DSS technology, decision makers across functional areas can collaborate by sharing information, analyses, and models. The use of DSS technologies can actually help the reengineering effort be more effective and productive. (This topic will be discussed in more detail in Chapter 11.)

Although BPR and DSS design are two separate activities, they have similar aspects, and therefore there are some lessons we can learn from BPR that have parallels in DSS design. First and foremost, communication during the process is crucial. Carr and Johansson (1995) indicate that communication is crucial in the beginning of BPR to assess the cultural climate and the barriers to change, and in the later stages for obtaining acceptance of the changes so that the improved processes will not be sabotaged.[1] Furthermore, communication can help us improve the overall design by gaining from the experience of many individuals through their comments and suggestions. This is true with DSS design as well. Without active communication, the designer will implicitly state assumptions of the design process in the following way:

There is one best way to make decisions.
I can understand how your decisions are made easily and quickly.
Little about how you make decisions is worth saving.
You will make decisions in the manner that the designer specifies.[2]

---

[1] For example, Carr and Johansson (1995, p. 51) suggest that Motorola's success with TQM and BPR is due, to a large measure, to its strong communication plan. The company holds "town hall meetings" to review concerns, changes, and the overall state of the business with their employees, and managers hold informal communication sessions with their employees.

[2] This list is adapted from one developed for reengineering as described in Davenport, T., "Don't Forget the Workers," *INFORMATIONWEEK*, August 8, 1994, p. 70.

While managers and other employees might not be as concerned about job loss as they would be during BPR, there are concerns about making the task "too hard" or the perception that managers were just not doing a good enough job. Forcing people into a new decision style may not be productive. Table 8.10 shows some tenets of "good communication" during BPR adapted for DSS design.

This leads to the second similarity between DSS design and BPR: There is likely to be resistance to change. Concerns about uncertainty and additional workload affect both DSS design and BPR. However, perhaps a bigger problem in DSS design (as compared to BPR) is the fear of criticism. Most decision makers consider a specific set of issues when they make choices. Some of those factors may use sophisticated models or grand database mergers. For others, decision rules might be quite simple, coming quite close to "gut feelings" or generalizations from past experiences. Decision makers may be concerned about sharing these procedures, regardless of their reliability, for fear of looking silly or less capable, and regardless of fear that they will need to learn new and harder methods of making decisions. They may be unwilling to share accurate information about choice processes or information and modeling needs. Of course, effective communication is one approach to addressing this resistance to change. Another is the implementation of a planned environment for change.

Finally, the third similarity is that good DSS design, like good BPR, takes place incrementally over a period of time. BPR is best when it is limited to a process or a group of processes at the outset. DSS design works best when a particular focus or type of analysis is prototyped and built, then improved and expanded over time. Both require a multilayered process that must be repeated over time. Fur-

TABLE 8.10   Tenets of Effective Communication

- It is impossible to use too much communication
- Simplify your message, no matter how complex the issue
- Anticipate the issues and communicate your position early
- Don't underestimate the technical requirements of a communications project
- Involve all levels of management where appropriate
- Honesty is the best policy. Tell the truth

Adapted from Carr, D.K. and H.J. Johansson, *Best Practices in Reengineering*, New York: McGraw-Hill, 1995, p. 55.

ther, managers need to become accustomed to them before moving on to change another component of their organization.

DISCUSSION

When DSS have been designed well, they represent tools that add value to the process of making selections among alternatives. Improvements in hardware and design tools release designers to focus on meeting the needs of the decision maker. Regrettably, there is no process the use of which will ensure the resulting system is a value-added product. However, the use of prototypes to discuss specifications, an evolutionary strategy to development, and good communication skills increase the chance of getting a useful and used system.

QUESTIONS

1. Suppose you were designing a DSS to help students make better career decisions. Identify three questions you might use during interviews to determine their decision support needs. How would you alter those questions if the person being interviewed were too talkative? Were uncooperative?

2. Defend the use of the evolutionary development of DSS in a manner that you might for a boss or client of a consulting firm.

3. What kinds of documents would you request to begin the process of understanding users' needs for the development of a DSS for production planning?

4. Should users design their own DSS? Why or why not?

5. Discuss the advantages and disadvantages of using a DSS generator and available tools in the design process.

6. Consider a DSS design project (perhaps a class project). How would this DSS develop if the evolutionary development process were used?

7. Discuss the potential design tradeoffs involved in designing a specific decision support or expert system directly from tools, as compared with using a DSS generator or expert system shell.

8. One of the steps in generally recognized methodologies is the testing of the system to ensure reliability and validity of a system. How would you test a decision support system for reliability and validity? What kinds of tests would you run? What kinds of data would you need?

9. Critique the concept of using a standardized methodology to design decision support systems.

10. Suppose you were attempting to justify the development of a DSS for a corporation. Discuss how you would justify the expenditures.

◆ O N   T H E   W E B ◆

On the Web for this chapter provides additional information about how decision support systems enhance design concepts. The links provide access to case studies and success stories about the design process. In addition, links can provide access to information about methodologies for design, design standards, and reengineering hints. Additional discussion questions and new applications will also be added as they become available.

• *Links give access to information about DSS generators.* The page provides links to corporations and marketing information about generators as well as reviews of products.

• *Links give access to actual decision support systems.* Not only will the pages link you to the DSS, but also to a "behind the scenes" look at the development process.
• *Links provide access to example DSS for automobile purchase and leasing.* Several tools to help users purchase or lease an automobile are available on the Web. In addition, these links provide access to insights regarding how that decision might be accomplished.

You can access material for this chapter from the general WWW Page for the book, or directly from the following URL.

http://www.umsl.edu/~sauter/DSS/design.html

SUGGESTED READINGS

Beyer, H.R. and Holtzblatt, K. "Apprenticing with the client," *Communications of the ACM,* 38(5), May 1995, pp. 45–52.

Carey, T.T., and Mason, R.E.A. "Information system prototyping: Techniques, tools and methodologies," *Canadian Journal of Operational Research and Information Processing*, 21(3), August 1983, pp. 177–191.

Carr, D.K. and Johansson, H.J. *Best Practices in Reengineering,* New York: McGraw–Hill, 1995.

Davenport, T., "Don't forget the workers," *INFORMATIONWEEK*, August 8, 1994, p. 70.

Dickson, G.W., Desanctis, G. and McBride, D.J., "Understanding the effectiveness of computer graphics for decision support: A cumulative experimental approach," *Communications of the ACM*, 29(1), January 1986, pp. 40–47.

Dumas, J. and Parsons, P. "Discovering the way programmers think about new programming environments," *Communications of the ACM,* 38(6), June 1995, pp. 57–64.

Garzotto, F., Mainetti, L. and Paolini, P. "Hypermedia design, analysis and evaluation issues," *Communications of the ACM*, 38(8), August 1995, pp. 74–87.

Hammer, M., "Reengineering work: Don't automate, obliterate," *Harvard Business Review,* 68(4), July–August 1990, pp. 104–112.

Hammer, M. and Champy, J. *Reengineering the Corporation: A Manifesto for Business Revolution*, New York: HarperCollins, 1993.

Hastings, A.F. and Knox, S.T. "Creating products customers demand," *Communications of the ACM*, 38(5), May 1995, pp. 72–80.

Hayne, S.C. and Pendergast, M. "Experiences with object-oriented group support software development," *IBM Systems Journal*, 34(1), 1995, pp. 96–119.

Henderson, J.C. and Schilling, D.A. "Design and implementation of decision support systems in the public sector," *MIS Quarterly*, 9(2), 1985, pp. 157–161.

Isakowitz, T., Stohr, E. and Balasubramanian, P. "RMM: A methodology for structured hypermedia design," *Communications of the ACM*, 38(8), August 1995, pp. 34–48.

Janson, M.A., "Applying a pilot system and prototyping approach to systems development and implementation," *Information and Management*, 10(2), 1986, pp. 209–216.

Janson, M.A. and Smith, L.D. "Prototyping for systems development: A critical appraisal," *MIS Quarterly*, 9(4), December 1985, pp. 305.

Marshall, C.C., and Shipman III, F.M. "Spatial hypertext: Designing for change," *Communications of the ACM*, 38(8), August 1995, pp. 88–98.

Meador, G.L. and Mezger, R.A. "Selecting an end-user programming language for DSS development," *MIS Quarterly*, 8(4) , December 1984, pp. 267–281.

Moad J., "Can high performance be cloned? Should it be?" *Datamation,* 41(4), March 1, 1995, pp. 44–47.

Morris, D.C. and Brandon, J.S. *Re-engineering Your Business,* New York: McGraw-Hill, 1993.

Murray, T.J. and Tanniru, M.R. "Selecting between knowledge-based and traditional systems design," *Journal of Management Information Systems*, 4(1), Winter 1987, pp. 42–58.

Orfali, R. and Harkey, D. "Object component suites: The whole is greater than the parts." *Datamation*, 41(3), February 15, 1995, pp. 44–49.

Petre, M., "Why looking isn't always seeing: Readership skills and graphical programming," *Communications of the ACM*, 38(6), June 1995, pp. 33–44.

Reimann, B.C. and Waren, A.D. "User-oriented criteria for the selection of DSS software," *Communications of the ACM,* 28(2), February 1985, pp. 166–179.

Robey, D. "Implementation and the organizational impacts of information systems," *Interfaces*, 17(1), January 1987, pp. 72–84.

Rockart, J.F., "Chief executives define their own data needs," *Harvard Business Review*, July–August, 1981, pp. 81–93.

Rzevski, G., "Prototypes vs. pilot systems: Strategies for evolutionary information system development," in Buddy, R., K. Kuhlenkamp, L. Mathiassen, and H. Zullinghoven (eds.), *Approaches to Prototyping,* Berlin: Springer-Verlag, 1984, pp. 356–367.

Sauter, V.L., "The effect of 'experience' upon information preferences," *Omega*, 13(2), 1985, pp. 277–284.

Sauter, V.L. and J.L. Schofer, "Evolutionary development of decision support systems: What issues are really important for early phases of design," *Journal of Management Information Systems*, 4(4), 1988, pp. 77–92.

Sauter, V.L. and M.B. Mandell, "Transferring decision support concepts to evaluation," *Evaluation and Program Planning,* 13, 1990, pp. 349–358.

Senge, P.M., *The Fifth Discipline,* New York: Doubleday, 1990.

Sprague Jr., R.H. and E.D. Carlson, *Building Effective Decision Support Systems,* Englewood Cliffs, NJ: Prentice-Hall,1982.

Thuring, M., J. Hannemann, and J.M. Haake, "Hypermedia and cognition: Designing for Comprehension," *Communications of the ACM*, 38(8), August 1995, pp. 57–73.

Walker, W.G., R.S. Barnhardt, W.E. Walker, *Selecting a Decision Support System Generator for the Air Force's Enlisted Force Management System*, RAND Paper P-7149, Santa Monica: The RAND Corporation, 1985.

Webb, S. and J. MacMillian, "Cognitive bias in software engineering," *Communications of the ACM*, 38(6), June 1995, pp. 57–64.

Winograd, T., "From programming environments to environments for designing," *Communications of the ACM*, 38(6), June 1995, pp. 65–74.

Chapter 9

Object-Oriented Technologies and Decision Support Systems Design

◆ ◆ ◆

A popular adage says that *software is not written, it is rewritten*. In other words, software is not static, but rather is updated, modified, or corrected over time. Although the saying refers to standard transaction applications, it is even more applicable to the design of decision support systems. DSS applications need to change over time because the information needs of decision makers change over time. Similarly, the process of evolutionary design of DSS, which recommends building a DSS in stages so that it better fits the needs of decision makers, requires systems to change over time. Hence, it is apparent that whatever product[1] is chosen for the building of a DSS, it must be one that adapts well to change in the databases accessed, the models used and integrated, the way in which mail is used in decision making, and even the user interface. In order to meet decision making needs, especially in a competitive and dynamic environment, such changes need to be implemented quickly with a minimum of flaws. The question is what kind of tool will best meet those changing needs.

Many recent demonstrations suggest that object-oriented programming (OOP) tools provide the best groundwork for systems that will need to be changed over time. The evidence suggests, in particular that it is easier to make needed changes, to prevent unwanted changes, and to program more quickly with than the other forms of systems development. While there is insufficient experience in operational systems to test this theory from a long-term perspective, there are some reasons to believe the hypothesis might be true. This chapter will illustrate the strengths of the object-oriented paradigm, and how it might be used to design DSS.

---

[1]The product may be a programming language or a programming tool. For the purposes of this discussion, no distinction will be made between these two.

◆ KINDS OF DEVELOPMENT TOOLS

The obvious questions are "Why object-oriented tools?" and "Why object-oriented tools *now*?" The fundamental answer is that these tools provide a platform for faster development and maintenance because of the style of programming and the emphasis on reusability of code. To explore that answer fully, however, we need to cover two issues: (a) why other tools are less appropriate and (b) what makes object-oriented tools appropriate.

Non–object-Oriented Tools

Programmers select languages and tools that allow them to leverage scarce resources while best meeting the users' needs. In the early days of computing, programmers used machine code, and later assembler code, to leverage the power of the available hardware. In other words, the available computing power was so minimal (in comparison to today's computers) that programmers chose languages that required the computer to do the least amount of interpretation, thereby allowing maximum computing power to be put on the task at hand. However, programming in this way is difficult, especially if the application is the least bit demanding. Later, as computers gained in capability and corporate computing needs focused on accounting, inventory, and other transaction-based programs, programmers selected tools that excelled in repeated operations on numbers; the preferred software technology was procedural, such as that represented by BASIC or COBOL.

Since these tools represent the foundation of the greatest percentage of operational code, they should be considered for DSS design. Using procedural tools, programmers provide a set of instructions the computer must follow each time the program is invoked. The code might provide points for branching, but the fundamental routine of instructions is the same each time the program is run. A good program is structured, because such programs are easily maintained and more likely to work reliably. This means that there is a primary routine through which data must flow *each* time the program is invoked, which calls all other routines. All the routines in the program must follow one of the three basic control structures: sequence, iteration, or alternation. Hence, all users "enter" the program through the same route, and all users "exit" the program through the same route. Simple programs are quite easy to write using procedural tools, but more complex programs are quite difficult to write. More important, though, is that sophisticated programs (such as those necessary for DSS) are difficult to maintain.

Procedural programming is in use because it has provided an adequate methodology for accomplishing repetitive and straightforward tasks that do not change substantially over time. For example, such programming tools form a reasonable basis for developing payroll systems because there are certain procedures that must be done each time a paycheck is issued. When the tax rules change, some of those procedures change, but even then it is a minor type of change to the system.

Suppose, instead, that we are programming the task of running a major corporation. The task in one meeting might be simple arithmetic, while in another meeting it could be assembling project teams. It is easy for humans to see that the concept of "addition" is the same whether we are adding two numbers to get a sum or adding two employees to make a list. However, in a computer routine, it is difficult to substitute "Jawaharlal Nehru" and "Pocahontas" for the numbers 3 and 5. The result of the computer operation in the first case is a list including the names Jawaharlal Nehru and Pocahontas. The result of the second operation is a number (the sum of 8). To humans, both processes are addition, and it is a minor logical change to process the two examples. For the computer code, on the other hand, this is a major difference in operation, and we must make substantive changes in coding to accommodate the different processes. In fact, even the minor screen changes to display the differences in information can cause major programming needs.

In addition, programmers develop most procedural applications in a vacuum. Each programming effort begins from scratch, with little or no reliance on the other systems that have been developed over the years (unless the new code must interface with existing code). Each designer and programmer has peculiarities to his or her own approach, and so each program provides its own set of problems and own maintenance needs over time. Completed separately, there is no opportunity to fix multiple programs at once and no opportunity to learn from past experiences. Maintenance, including correcting earlier mistakes and making enhancements and changes, takes time and money. Most MIS shops are so overwhelmed with application needs that they cannot respond to needs for changes and updates in a timely fashion, and most procedurally written programs are so complex that end users cannot change them. Such an environment does not provide either the reliability needs or the implementation speed necessary to respond to decision making needs. Furthermore, it contributes to the high cost of systems development and thus of computing costs.

While most existing programs are procedural, other kinds of programming tools might be considered for DSS. For example, declarative programming provides a more fundamental approach to programming, but it is also a much more complex programming environment. The programming effort was to develop a logic base for the problem under consideration in environments such as Prolog and LISP. To run the program, a user provides the system all the information known, and then the system attempts to use its logic base to form a conclusion. Clearly these tools could provide solutions to complex problems. However, when introduced, they required specialized machines or were resource intensive and caused problems in conventional media. The hardware available at that time did not support such languages well and most corporations abandoned them to "special projects."

However, some declarative tools evolved into "access tools." In access-oriented programming, changes in the values of some fields can cause procedures to be invoked. This may mean that some flag or counter has changed value so that expected procedures happen, such as counting the days in a week and issuing paychecks on the last day. Or it may mean that some new information has been made available to the system and that its availability causes programs to run. For example, suppose the system waits to perform an EIS-scheduled analysis until data are available from all plants at an organization. Hence, when the data are sent electronically and retrieved by the system, it automatically "knows" to begin running the reports. Finally, it may mean that a value of some variable has changed unexpectedly, triggering specialized procedures that bring this information to the attention of the human decision maker. For example, a DSS designed to trade stocks and bonds might bring a suggestion of action to the decision maker when unusual or unexpected changes happen in the marketplace.

This access-oriented programming clearly is different from procedural programming, which requires users to begin at the top and move systematically and predictably through the code. Access tools are better suited to DSS needs because they provide exactly the kind of response to changes that managers make and that DSS therefore need to support. Current technologies require such programs to be rewritten each time a new application is created. However, when presented with object-oriented code as hybrid code, access programming provides an excellent medium on which to build a system to provide support for decision making.

To review, there are several problems with using non–object-oriented tools for DSS development. The main ones are that the resulting systems generally take too long to be created, have specialized maintenance needs, and need to be rewritten each time a new application is created. Instead, a good environment is one in which the DSS is created quickly, using known, reliable components of code from other systems where appropriate and that provide a seamless interface among applications. These attributes can be achieved through the use of object-oriented tools.

Object-Oriented Tools

Object-oriented programming, as the name suggests, revolves around the definition of *objects*. Objects, or, as they are sometimes called, *classes of objects,*[2] are components or ingredients that are important to the system. They can be identified by naming all the "real world" things of interest, all the general groups of

---

[2]At this time, the terminology is *not* consistent among authors and among computer package implementations. Some authors and some packages use the terms "object" and "class" interchangeably. However, in some languages, such as C++, class is a description of an entity. For example, the definition of possible attributes of a bicycle being style, manufacturer, number of speeds, color, etc. is referred to as a class, while a specific example of the class, say Larry's bicycle, is referred to as an object. Hence, authors who use C++ (or a similar language) in their examples (or simply who are most familiar with C++) will use terminology consistent with that language. In other languages, such as Level 5 Object, the definition of possible attributes is referred to as a class, but a specific example of the class is referred to as an "instance." Similarly, authors using such packages may use the terms in a manner consistent with that usage. Here, we will use the terms interchangeably. However, the reader is encouraged to be cautious when moving to other authors or packages because they may use the terms differently.

items, or all the abstract nouns describing items of interest to the system. Objects can represent individual items or groups of items.

Defining Objects

As previously stated, we can identify objects by analyzing the characteristics of the problem under consideration. In doing this, designers must recognize all relevant tangible objects. In addition, they need to catalog all roles relevant to the decision task (including the operations performed or the roles played by individuals); interactions (in terms of either personal contact or transactions); important events; specifications; and all incidents of importance to the decision task. It is also useful to identify devices with which the system or its users need to interact, locations, and organization groups.

It is best to begin the identification of classes with the simplest view of the system. For example, in the car-purchasing system discussed earlier in the book, we might define the classes "consumer," "automobile," and "acquisition strategy." There are people who will use the system, automobiles that will be described in the system, and strategies for acquisition that will be recommended by the system. In addition, there is a fourth class of importance, the automobile *database*. While the database itself describes information about the automobiles, the database object describes how the information about cars is maintained, accessed, and updated. Hence, the database needs to be defined as a separate object, with additional attributes in need of identification.

Figure 9.1 illustrates these four basic objects[3] and their relationships within the basic car system. In particular, it notes that consumers acquire automobiles, secure acquisition strategies, and search the automobile database. Similarly, it states that automobiles must qualify for particular acquisition strategies and that the automobile database describes possible automobiles. Hence, Figure 9.1 provides a basic understanding of how the system will work; it provides the basic explanation for the messages that will be sent between pairs of classes.

Complete and accurate object definition is crucial. While it seems simple enough to define all the tangible aspects of a problem in terms of objects, most individuals think about applications procedurally, not as objects, and so it is difficult to find all the relevant objects. This problem is exacerbated for programmers who are not familiar with the business because, as we saw from the literature reviewed in Chapter 2, the tendency to think procedurally is more pronounced for individuals inexperienced with the task at hand. Of course, the system's developer is likely to be inexperienced with the task for which the system is created, and hence the problem is exacerbated. While he or she may identify the major categories of objects, less obvious objects, as well as systems-based objects such as forms, databases, or approvals, may be overlooked.

---

[3]This is meant to be an example of object definition. It is not intended to be an exhaustive search for all relevant objects for the purpose of the system. Similarly, the reader should not assume that the remaining sections on attributes and inheritance provide a complete view of those aspects of objects.

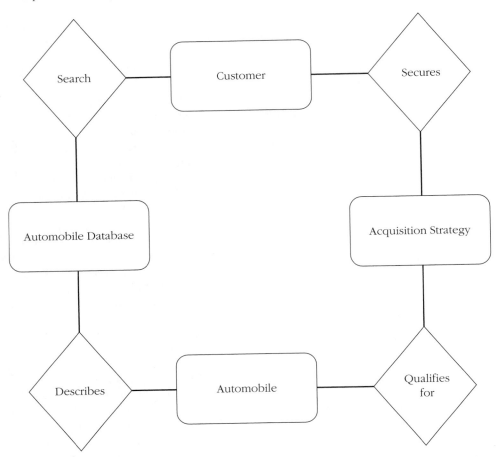

Figure 9.1   Classes and their Relationships.

It is necessary, therefore, to think of other rules that facilitate the identification of objects in a system. First, the object definitions must provide a template for classifying and organizing all information about an application. If all objects are defined properly then DSS designers should be able to define all operations and procedures specified by the decision maker with the defined objects. Relationships that cannot be specified with the available objects highlight the need for new objects. For example, suppose we had not specified "customer" as an object earlier. If the designer tried to explore relationships between the automobile and the customer's preferences for options, financial limitations, or driving history without the "customer" object, he or she would easily confuse characteristics of a given automobile with characteristics preferred by the customer and hence find the resulting analysis and design impossible. Such situations would cause a designer to seek a new object, in this case, a "consumer."

Second, all items that are similar in nature should be grouped together. If there are too many unrelated objects that seem to have similar characteristics, the DSS designer should look for a new "super-class" that joins together such objects. This concept and its implications will be discussed shortly with regard to "inheritance."

Finally, the designer needs to remember that each part of the system framework is in itself an object. For example, consider the Level 5 Object screen shown in Figure 9.2. All items on the left side of the screen are "system" (or built-in) ob-

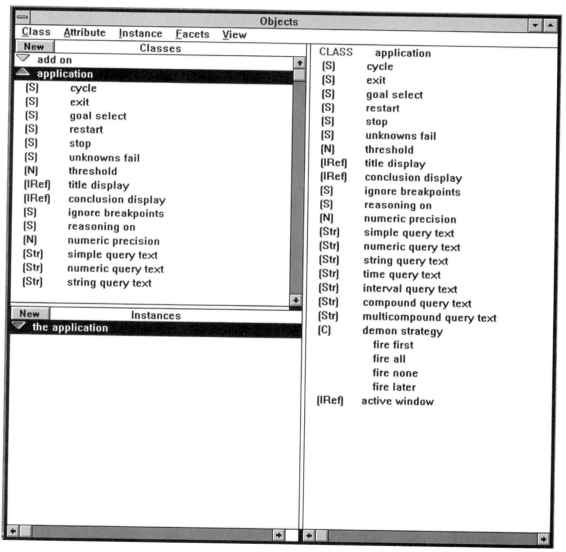

Figure 9.2 Level 5 Object system-defined classes.

jects. Hence, the application, the windows, the displays, the buttons, and all other features of the user interface and the basic DSS generator are objects and must be treated as such. Each example of those objects is a specific condition of the object itself, referred to as an *instance*. Hence, every display designed for a particular DSS is an instance of the system object, "display." Furthermore, every model is an object that has attributes and methods needing specification.

In defining objects, designers use an iterative approach followed by logical system design. When designing becomes difficult, designers return to the stage of object definition. In fact, some object-oriented programming platforms create objects and their attributes automatically as they are used. The beauty of object-oriented programming, however, is that we can add new objects as needed without changing the available objects or code that has been written.

Attributes and Methods

Each class is a receptacle holding both data and instructions for acting on the data. The data provide information through which we can gain a better understanding of the object and its characteristics and behavior. Such information helps the designer understand the necessary specifications for the database management system as well as for the user interface and model management systems. The data must be specified so it is possible to enumerate values, define data types, or outline ranges of values they might assume. For example, the class automobile might have data such as those described in Table 9.1, including the manufacturer, model, size, and performance. These are referred to as *attributes* of the class because they are characteristics of the objects about which information is included in the sys-

TABLE 9.1   Examples of Attributes of the Class Automobile

- Manufacturer
- Model
- Size
  - Number of doors
  - Trunk/cargo capacity
  - Length
  - Width
  - Height
  - Wheelbase
- Performance
  - Engine size
  - Engine type
  - Transmission type
  - Mileage—city
  - Mileage—highway
  - Horsepower

tem. Similarly, Table 9.2 provides the attributes of the class automobile database. Notice that while some of the characteristics, such as those directly related to the specific automobiles, are the same as in Table 9.1 (the automobile attributes), other characteristics are unique to the physical repository in which the data actually reside. For example, the database filename and index filename refer to the actual location in which the DSS can find the data, not to the actual automobiles.

The goal is to define all attributes of interest in the system. As with the definition of objects, the DSS designer needs to ensure that all *relevant* characteristics important in forming relations are identified. If there are problems in addressing important questions, new attributes are needed. One of the advantages of object-oriented programming is that such attributes can be added later as they are needed without affecting the code written to that point.

The class also defines the *methods* of the object. Methods define both the *messages* understood by the object and the action implemented by the object as a result of the message. For example, Montlick defines a particular object, "Dog." The

TABLE 9.2   Examples of Attributes of the Class Automobile Database

- Manufacturer
- Model
- Size
    - Number of doors
    - Trunk/cargo capacity
    - Length
    - Width
    - Height
    - Wheelbase
- Performance
    - Engine size
    - Engine type
    - Transmission type
    - Mileage—city
    - Mileage—highway
    - Horsepower
- Database filename
- Access
- Action
- End of file
- Record number
- Index file
- Active
- Status
- Error message
- Default error handling

Dog class defines messages that "the Dog object understands, such as 'bark,' 'fetch,' and 'roll-over' " [Montlick, 1995, p. 2]. The *method* defines the action taken as a result of the message. The method may be stated simply or may include multiple arguments to convey the requisite information. Montlick continues his example with the message "roll-over," which "could contain one argument to say *how fast*, and a second argument to say *how many times*" (Montlick, 1995, p. 2). Different *instances* (or actual occurrences) of objects may implement methods differently. For example, one instance of an object, say "Spot" may go to sleep after receiving the message "roll-over," while another instance of the object, say "Atlas" may roll-over three times quickly. Similarly, various instances of "automobiles" may implement the attribute manufacturer differently: some have the value Toyota while others have the value Mercedes, for example.

The automobile database definition shown in Table 9.2 provides a similar example of methods being defined as a part of the class definition. The automobile database object "understands" messages to open, to protect, or to close the database. In addition, it can check for the end of file, advance a record, or append a record. The code needed to implement the message is embedded in the automobile database object. Systems do not need to search through code each time the message is referenced because it exists in a fixed place.

This relationship between methods and objects causes the instructions for what to do and how to do it to be part of the object itself, not separate from the object as in a procedural language. For example, the code specifies how to search for the data, who has access to the data, and how errors are handled. Consider the object definition (shown in a Level 5 Object screen) of an automobile database shown in Figure 9.3. The specific generating code would look similar to the Level 5 Object code illustrated in Table 9.3; note that all attributes are in bold. The object definition reports everything necessary to use the database, including the fields, the type of data represented in the fields, the physical location of the database, and the available operators for the database. Since the operations are part of the definition itself, the object definition specifies how to make changes in the database.

Hence, to update the database, we might implement the following code:

```
BEGIN
    action OF dB3 OPTIONS 1 IS bottom
    AND action OF dB3 OPTIONS 1 IS append record
        WITH manufacturer := Toyota
        model := Corolla
        engine_size :=
            ⋮
    AND action OF dB3 OPTIONS 1 IS close
END
```

Specifically, this code tells of three "actions"—(which is an attribute of) dB3 OPTIONS 1 (the database)—to move to the bottom, then to append a record, and then to close.

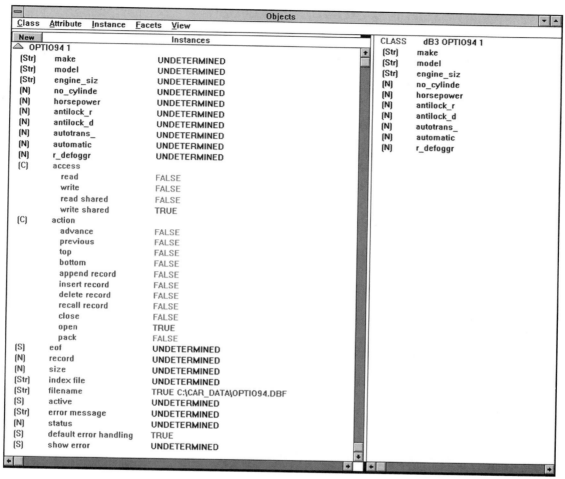

Figure 9.3 Example of a database object definition in Level 5 Object.

Inheritance

Sometimes objects consist of major subcategories of instances that share specific attributes or methods not shared among all instances of the object. Consider again the automobile object defined earlier. While there are certain characteristics for all automobiles, such as those defined as attributes of the automobile class, there are other attributes relevant for only *some* cars. For example, knowing whether the automobile is new or previously owned dictates additional attributes and methods relevant to the object.

Similarly, within the class "acquisition strategy," there are multiple options, including "purchase outright," "purchase with a loan," and "lease." As with the class automobile, there are some characteristics that join all three of these objects to-

TABLE 9.3   Generating Code for Automobile Database

```
CLASS dB3 OPTIONS 1 SINGLE EXTERNAL "dBASEIII"
  WITH make STRING
    SEARCH ORDER CONTEXT
  WITH model STRING
    SEARCH ORDER CONTEXT
  WITH engine_siz STRING
    SEARCH ORDER CONTEXT
  WITH no_cylinde NUMERIC
    SEARCH ORDER CONTEXT
        :   :   :   :   :
        :   :   :   :   :
        :   :   :   :   :
  WITH exhaust_sy STRING
    SEARCH ORDER CONTEXT
  WITH air_bag_av STRING
    SEARCH ORDER CONTEXT
  WITH ac_bag_cost NUMERIC
    SEARCH ORDER CONTEXT
  WITH ac_cost NUMERIC
    SEARCH ORDER CONTEXT
  WITH automatic NUMERIC
    SEARCH ORDER CONTEXT
  WITH r_defoggr NUMERIC
    SEARCH ORDER CONTEXT

INSTANCE OPTIONS 1 ISA dB3 OPTIONS 1
  WITH access IS write shared
  WITH action IS open
  WITH filename := "C:\CAR_DATA\OPTIONS.DBF"
  WITH default error handling := TRUE
```

gether and other characteristics that differentiate them. Finally, within the class "consumer," we can define the objects "first-time consumer," "moderately knowledgeable consumer," and "experienced consumer." There is some information the system will need about all consumers, and some operations that will be done on all consumers. As you will see shortly, much of the art of object-oriented programming is in determining the best way to define classes and objects of those classes.

When examples of major subclasses exist, subobjects are defined with their basic definition *inherited* from the original definition of the object. That is, when the new object is defined, it will contain all attributes and methods from the original object (also known as a *super-object).* Programmers may then add additional attributes, additional methods, or both, but they may not change or delete the original, inherited attributes and methods.

Consider again the class automobile. Table 9.1 outlines some of the attributes that are defined at the class level. All automobiles have those attributes, and so they should be defined when automobiles are defined. However, within the subclasses "new automobile" and "previously owned automobile," there are additional characteristics, which are not relevant in objects in the other subclass. By defining these two categories as subclasses of the object "automobile," they will inherit all attributes of automobile. That is, prior to any other definition, we would know that "new automobiles" and "previously owned automobiles" will both have all of the attributes listed in Table 9.1. If the name of an attribute is changed, added to, or deleted from the definition of automobile, it will be changed, added to, or deleted from the definition of new automobiles and the definition of previously owned automobiles automatically.

In addition, by defining these categories as objects, programmers can define other attributes that have meaning to all instances of the particular class. For example, consumers are interested in attributes such as the suggested retail price, the availability of particular options, and the estimated future value of the automobile for new cars only. The characteristics that vary across automobiles should be included. However, anything that is constant across all these cars should not be included. For example, in 1931 heaters and rear-view mirrors were considered options on new cars, and hence the definition of a 1931 new automobile object would include the availability of a heater and the availability of a rear-view mirror as fields. However, heaters and rear-view mirrors have long since been adopted as standard equipment on all cars, and thus these fields should not be identified in today's new automobile object. An example of the kinds of items needed in the definition of the new automobile object is shown in Table 9.4; the shaded regions represent attributes inherited from the original automobile class.

Similarly, we can define attributes that have meaning to all instances of previously owned automobiles. Table 9.5 illustrates the attributes associated with previously owned automobiles, with the shaded regions representing the inherited attributes of automobiles. This object also inherits the attributes of the automobile object defined earlier. The programmer is allowed to define characteristics unique to the condition of being previously owned, such as information about the car's age, its condition, the previous mileage, and other information that might suggest the automobile's condition.

We continue to decompose objects into smaller objects as the application dictates. If designers can gain some generalized information by decomposing an object, they should do it. For example, suppose there are some major differences among the attributes that are relevant to new automobiles depending on whether the make of the automobile is considered luxury or sports or conventional. In this case, the designer might decompose the object new automobile discussed earlier by defining three subclasses: new luxury automobile, new sports-model automobiles, and new conventional automobiles. Through inheritance, each of these new objects would have all the fields of the original automobile object as well as those added when defining the new automobile object as well as further relevant fields

TABLE 9.4   Examples of Attributes of the Object New Automobile

- Manufacturer
- Model
- Size
    - Number of doors
    - Trunk/cargo capacity
    - Length
    - Width
    - Height
    - Wheelbase
- Performance
    - Engine size
    - Engine type
    - Transmission type
    - Mileage—city
    - Mileage—highway
    - Horsepower
- Options
    - Braking system
    - Steering
    - Exhaust system
    - Radio
- Standard packages/additional costs
    - Wheels
    - Radio
    - Tires
    - Transmission
    - Safety
    - Rear window defogger
- Purchase information
    - Suggested retail price
    - Estimated dealer's cost
    - Consumer's target price
    - Destination charge
    - Options cost
- Estimated future value
    - Expected resale in 5 years
    - Expected maintenance costs—5 years
    - Expected repair costs—5 years
    - Owner's total cost

TABLE 9.5   Examples of Attributes of the Object, Previously Owned Automobile

- Manufacturer
- Model
- Size
  - Number of doors
  - Trunk/cargo capacity
  - Length
  - Width
  - Height
  - Wheelbase
- Performance
  - Engine size
  - Engine type
  - Transmission type
  - Mileage—city
  - Mileage—highway
  - Horsepower
- Age of car
- Condition of car
  - Engine
  - Outside appearance
  - Inside appearance
- Mileage attained on car
- Color
- Expected price
- Recall history
- Price
  - Original price
  - Asking price
  - Current wholesale
  - Average retail

added to each class. Hence, a tree (such as the one in Figure 9.4) describing all the attributes associated with new luxury automobile, including those defined through inheritance, could be created.

Inheritance also allows the designers to avail themselves of the advantages of system-defined and system-based functions. For example, the definition of actions of any database is taken from a system-defined database. Hence, if the system were altered to enable new functionality, such as multiple indexing, it need only be defined in the system-level definition of the object database. Specific instances of databases, such as the automobile database, receive this update automatically because they inherit the system definition of methods *dynamically*. That is, not only do they inherit the characteristics available at the time of creation of the instance,

AUTOMOBILE	NEW AUTOMOBILE	NEW LUXURY AUTOMOBILE	
attribute 1	attribute 1	attribute 1	
attribute 2	attribute 2	attribute 2	
:	:	:	attributes defined by the
:	:	:	"automobile" object
attribute n	attribute n	attribute n	
	attribute n + 1	attribute n + 1	
	attribute n + 2	attribute n + 2	
	:	:	attributes defined by the
	:	:	"new automobile" object
	attribute n + m	attribute n + m	
		attribute n + m + 1	
		attribute n + m + 2	
		:	attributes defined by the
		:	"new luxury automobile"
		attribute n + m + p	object

Figure 9.4   Inheritance tree showing the origin of the attributes of the new luxury automobile object.

but they receive all the changes to the definition of the super-class as they are made over time. For example, consider the definition of a database object in Level 5 Object, which is shown in Figure 9.2. Attributes in the left column are defined by the programmer. All other attributes (those listed in the lefthand column, but not in the righthand column) are inherited from the system class, "database." However, if the "database" class is changed at the system level, the specific instances of databases will be changed automatically and instantaneously.

Another example can be created by considering *windows* in a system. Suppose for a particular application that the designer wants assistance pages that are consistent. However, the designer wants all the statistical assistance pages to appear with the title "STATISTICAL ASSISTANCE," but all the financial assistance pages to appear with the title "FINANCIAL ASSISTANCE." The designer could create a new object called "assistance window," such as that illustrated in Figure 9.5. The "assistance window" would inherit the characteristics of the system-defined class "window." Hence, it would have the attributes of being visible (without calling it), sizable, movable, closeable, and so on, and its location and size. At that level, the designer could specify the size, location, and other characteristics of importance to the application. After said definition, the designer could create two subclasses, "statistical assistance window" and "financial assistance window." Since these are subclasses of the "assistance window" object, they would inherit all the specified

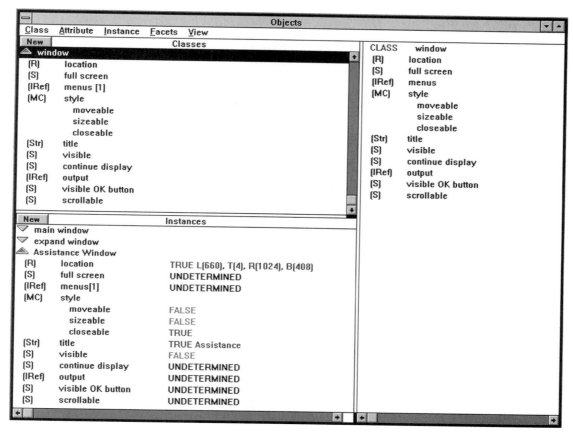

Figure 9.5   Windows definition showing inheritance.

attributes and hence both the "statistical assistance window" and the "financial assistance window" would automatically have the size, location, and other attributes
desired by the designer. The title, display, and functionality could be specified differently for each window. If in a revision of the system the designer decided to
resize or relocate the assistance windows, the change would only need to be done
once, at the "assistance window" object level.

Models and model management functions also are identified as objects in an
object-oriented DSS. These objects, like all objects, have attributes and methods
associated with them, as well as subclasses that inherit the properties of higher-
level classes. For example, we can use Geoffrion's (1987) structured modeling
framework as the kernel of a model management system of a DSS. Designers would
define super-objects of "models" and "solvers" that could be placed into libraries
for use in a specific DSS. These classes would have attributes such as the five defined by Geoffrion: *primitive entity, compound entity, attribute, function,* and *test.*

As Geoffrion defines them, they represent the basic foundation attributes of a model, the specific rules for processing the model, known constants, and ways of testing the models. In addition, the classes could have subclasses that inherit attributes from them. For example, we could trace the attributes of a "linear programming model" to its subclass, the "transportation model," and, in turn, to its subclass the "assignment model." At each level, the messages necessary for model management and solution simplification would be identified as a part of the object definition.

Facets

The attributes, in turn, have *facets*. These facets define the way in which the system should consider the attributes when no additional information has been provided. Of course, the relevant facets are a factor of what attribute of what object is being considered. If the object is a data-oriented object, relevant facets might include (1) the initial value; (2) the default value; (3) the search order for determining the value of the instance; (4) the methods for addressing unknown values; (5) the methods for addressing confidence in the information; (6) the display from which the system queries the user for information; and (7) the information provided when the user requests more information. On the other hand, if the object is a model-oriented object, one might specify the solution procedures or the model initial parameters. These facets allow the designer some control over how information is sought and used in relation to a particular object.

DISCUSSION

As we review the tools available for designing and building DSS, it is important to restate the objectives of the process. In this case, there are two primary ones. First, once DSS are identified, they must be built well, but quickly, so that decision makers can glean the greatest strategic advantage from them. Second, once DSS are in place in an organization, they must be able to change quickly in response to changes in the decision makers' perspectives, tasks, and information preferences.

The previous section illustrates some of the benefits of object-oriented tools and some of the liabilities associated with other kinds of design tools. The argument for the object-oriented tools boils down to the potential to reuse code that can facilitate rapid development of systems as well as rapid adaptation of systems in use. Since objects include necessary code for implementation, programmers can reuse already available objects to perform the same functions across multiple applications. For example, Vayda Consulting Company, on a project for Siemens Industrial Automation, Inc., let "MIS leverage the work of the best specialists," by developing a library of objects that were reused multiple times (Adhikari, 1995, p. 34). Further, object-oriented programming provides a similar but more powerful level of control over procedures. Since object-oriented tools isolate program functions and data characterization, as shown in Figure 9.6, designers and programmers can easily change one function without rewriting multiple aspects of the ap-

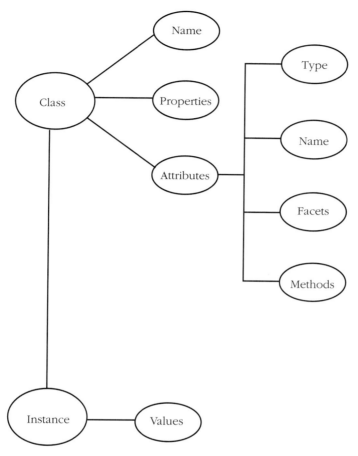

Figure 9.6 Components of an Object-Oriented Program.
Adapted from *Level 5 Object User's Guide*, 1990.

plication. Thus, development and adaptation are made easier and faster. The Zurich Insurance company reduced the amount of time spent on coding and testing by one-half, and the amount of time spent of integration of systems by three-quarters. Similarly, at the Federal Reserve, the designers completed an object-oriented project in two months that had previously taken a year using conventional procedural programming (Adhikari, 1995). If the object-oriented technologies can be married to the "access programming" defined earlier, resulting programs can mimic the decision maker's thought process and thus allow greater flexibility in use of the system.

There are, of course, some problems associated with development in object-oriented programming. These include compatibility of platforms and indexing of objects so others can find them. However, by far the biggest problem is for developers to learn to think in objects. Over time and enough education and experience, however, these problems can be resolved.

QUESTIONS

1. What attributes might be associated with an object class of flower? How would you know if you had appropriate attributes or sufficient attributes?

2. Suppose you were developing a DSS to facilitate advising. Identify object classes and their attributes. Identify at last two instances of each of the object classes.

3. How does a designer know whether to store information about an object as an attribute or to create subclasses?

4. One goal of object-oriented design is to facilitate reusability of code. Discuss how using an object-oriented tool would help to adapt the automobile-purchasing system discussed in the book to a system of *related* use, such as purchasing a home.

5. Discuss how the main features of an object-oriented DSS generator would differ from the main features of a traditional DSS generator.

6. Discuss how using an object-oriented DSS generator would make designing a system easier.

7. Discuss how using an object-oriented tool can facilitate the use of evolutionary development methodologies in the design of DSS.

8. Would the procedures for selecting object-oriented DSS generators differ from selecting conventional DSS generators?

9. Discuss how the use of object-oriented technologies could make applications for transnational corporations easier.

10. How is the user interface design influenced by the use of object-oriented tools?

◆ O N   T H E   W E B ◆

On the Web for this chapter provides additional information about object-oriented programming, especially as it applies to decision support systems. Links can provide access to tutorials, and frequently asked questions (FAQ) pages about object-oriented programming. In addition, they link to object-oriented DSS generators, such as Level 5 Object, guidelines for object oriented analysis, general overview information, applications, and more. Additional discussion questions and new applications will also be added as they become available.

- *Links provide examples of programs written using an object-oriented language.* Examples of how to complete specific tasks in an object-oriented language are available from the web site. These are provided both in outline (non-package specific) and in Level 5 Object code.
- *Links offer success stories illustrating how object-oriented technologies facilitate the design process.*
- *Links provide glossaries.* Access is provided to both glossaries of terms used with object-oriented technologies as well as bibliographies about the topic.
- *Links provide access to information about commercial object-oriented tools.*

You can access material for this chapter from the general WWW Page for the book, or, directly from the following URL.
http://www.umsl.edu/~sauter/DSS/oo.html

SUGGESTED READINGS

Adhikari, R., "Code recycling saves resources," *Software Magazine,* 15(7), July 1995, pp. 31–37.

Coad, P. and E. Yourdon, *Object-Oriented Design*, Englewood Cliffs, NJ: Prentice–Hall, 1991.

Geoffrion, A., "An introduction to structured modeling," *Management Science,* 33(5), May 1987, pp. 547–588.

Harmon, P. and C. Hall, *Intelligent Software Systems Development*, New York: Wiley Professional Computing, 1993.

Hayne, S.C. and M. Pendergast, "Experiences with object-oriented group support software development," *IBM Systems Journal,* 34(1), 1995, pp. 96–119.

Huh, S.Y., "Modelbase construction with object-oriented constructs," *Decision Sciences,* 24(2), Spring 1993, pp. 409–434.

Kim, W., "Object-oriented databases: definition and research dimensions," *IEEE Transactions on Knowledge and Data Engineering,* 2(3), September 1990, pp. 327–341.

Korson, T. and J.D. McGregor, "Understanding object-oriented: A unifying paradigm," *Communications of the ACM,* 33(9), September 1990, pp. 40–60.

Lenard, M.L., "An object-oriented approach to model management," *Decision Support Systems,* 9(1), January 1993, pp. 67–73.

Level 5 Object User's Guide, New York: Information Builders, Inc., 1990.

Montlick, T., *What Is Object-Oriented Software?* Bethlehem, Connecticut: Software Design Consultants, 1995 (http://www.soft-design.com/soft-info/objects.html).

Morrison, K.M., "Warming up to objects," *DEC Professional,* 14(7), July 1995, pp. 20–24.

Muhanna, W.A., "An object-oriented framework for model management and DSS development," *Decision Support Systems,* 9(3), March 1993, pp. 217–229.

Murphy, F. H. and E.A. Stohr, "An intelligent system for formulating linear programs," *Decision Support Systems,* 2(1), January 1986, pp. 39–47.

Nielsen, K., *Object-Oriented Design with Ada,* New York: Bantam Books, 1992.

Turban, E., *Decision Support and Expert Systems: Management Support Systems, Third Edition,* New York: Macmillan Publishing Co., 1993.

Chapter 10

Implementation and Evaluation of Decision Support Systems

◆ ◆ ◆

To implement a DSS is to realize the planned system. Implementation includes interpreting designs into code, but it goes far beyond coding. It also includes creating and populating databases and model bases, and administering the final product, which includes installation, deployment, integration and field testing. Training users and ensuring that they accept the DSS as a useful and reliable tool is yet another aspect of implementation. Finally, evaluation includes all those steps to ensure that the system does what is needed and does it well.

◆ THE IMPLEMENTATION STRATEGY

The success of any implementation effort is highly affected by the process adopted by the implementation team. Unfortunately, there are no standard steps to ensure success; what works well in one implementation might be inappropriate in another. However, Swanson has noted nine key factors in the success or failure of information systems. These include measures that address the system itself (such as design quality and performance level), the process of design (such as user involvement, mutual understanding, and project management), and the organization within which the DSS will be used (such as management commitment, resource adequacy, and situational stability). Table 10.1 lists these factors and provides examples of how they may facilitate or inhibit the implementation process. Throughout this book, specific strategies for addressing these nine factors to result in successful implementation have been noted. The strategies can be summarized in four principles.

Ensure That the System Does What It Is Supposed to Do, the Way It Is Supposed to Do It

The success of a DSS implementation depends to a large measure on the quality of the system and the ease and flexibility of its use. Clearly, if decision makers do not perceive that the DSS facilitates their decisions, they will not use it. The

◆ DSS Design Insights ◆

Three ostriches had a running argument over the best way for an ostrich to defend himself. The youngest brother practiced biting and kicking incessantly, and held the black belt. He asserted that "the best defense is a good offense." The middle brother lived by the maxim that "he who fights and runs away lives to fight another day." Through arduous practice, he had become the fastest ostrich in the desert—which, you must admit, is rather fast. The eldest brother, being wiser and more worldly, adopted the typical attitude of mature ostriches: "What you don't know can't hurt you." He was far and away the best head-burier that any ostrich could recall.

One day a feather hunter came to the desert and started robbing ostriches of their precious tail feathers. Each of the three brothers therefore took on a group of followers for instruction in the proper methods of self-defense—according to each one's separate gospel.

Eventually the feather hunter turned up outside the camp of the youngest brother, where he heard the grunts and snorts of all the disciples who were busily practicing kicking and biting. The hunter was on foot, but armed with an enormous club, which he brandished menacingly. Fearless as he was, the ostrich was no match for the hunter, because the club was much longer than an ostrich's legs or neck. After taking many lumps and bumps and not getting in a single kick or bite, the ostrich fell, exhausted, to the ground. The hunter casually plucked his precious tail feather, after which all his disciples gave up without a fight.

When the youngest ostrich told his brothers how his feather had been lost, they both scoffed at him. "Why didn't you run?" demanded the middle one. "A man cannot catch an ostrich."

"If you had put your head in the sand and ruffled your feathers properly," chimed in the eldest, "he would have thought you were a yucca and passed you by."

The next day the hunter left his club at home and went out hunting on a motorcycle. When he discovered the middle brother's training camp, all the ostriches began to run—the brother in the lead. But the motorcycle was much faster, and the hunter simply sped up alongside each ostrich and plucked his tail feather on the run.

That night the other two brothers had the last word. "Why didn't you turn on him and give him a good kick?" asked the youngest. "One solid kick and he would have fallen off that bike and broken his neck."

"No need to be so violent," added the eldest. "With your head buried and your body held low, he would have gone past you so fast he would have thought you were a sand dune."

A few days later, the hunter was out walking without his club when he came upon the eldest brother's camp. "Eyes under!" the leader ordered and was instantly obeyed. The hunter was unable to believe his luck, for all he had to do was walk slowly among the ostriches and pluck an enormous supply of tail feathers.

When the younger brothers heard this story, the youngest said, "he was unarmed. One good bite on the neck and you'd never have seen him again."

"And he didn't even have that infernal motorcycle," added the middle brother.

"Why, you could have outdistanced him at a half trot."

But the brothers' arguments had no more effect on the eldest that his had had on them, so they all kept practicing their own methods while they patiently grew new tail feathers.

Moral: *It's not know-how that counts; it's know-when.*

In other words: *No single "approach" will suffice in a complex world.*

Adapted from Weinberg, G.M., *Rethinking Systems Analysis and Design,* Boston: Little, Brown & Co., 1982.

more help the system can provide—in terms of accessing information decision makers might not otherwise know, providing insights decision makers might not otherwise have, or combining information that would have otherwise been kept isolated—the more likely the decision makers are to use it. Further, the easier it is for decision makers to access information and models, the more likely they will be to use them. Much of this book is dedicated to describing what kinds of features need to be considered and included and how to make the information support richer.

Prototypes

One of the keys to ensuring that the system will provide the kinds of information desired in an appropriate fashion is to use prototypes of the DSS throughout analysis and design. Unlike with the design of transaction processing systems, designers should not expect to obtain concrete specifications at the initiation of the project. Decision makers often have difficulties abstracting how they might make choices and how they might use a system if they do not have previous experience with DSS. Further, most manual "support systems" are not well documented; decision makers simply implement a process, but are not fully aware of it. Using prototypes, decision makers can discuss specific issues such as movement among screens and windows, kinds of help or other information, layout, and adequacy of information. Decision makers respond better to specific features if they see them in a prototype. Designers and decision makers decrease the likelihood of misunderstanding if they discuss the system in terms of the prototype.

Of course, there are risks associated with using a prototype. First, in order to evaluate a prototype, decision makers must be willing to spend some time using the product. This takes commitment on the part of the decision makers that may be difficult to secure. Second, if only some decision makers participate in the development of a multiuser DSS, designers risk over-specifying design to meet the needs of a subset of the population of users. Designers need to ensure that those decision makers participating in the design process are typical. Third, the final system may not respond in the same manner as did the prototype, particularly in

TABLE 10.1 Key Factors in Implementation Success and Failure*

ISSUES	SUCCESS FACTORS	FAILURE FACTORS
User Involvement	• User involvement and interest • Much user involvement and user-level documentation • User and data processing department cooperation	• Lack of user commitment to application • Lack of end-user involvement • Local user involvement only
Management Commitment	• Full management attention • Top management support	• Insufficient management interest • Lack of top management involvement in key area • Lack of support for required project organization
Value Basis	• Good public reaction to DSS • Value of application • "Second system" based on established value of first	• High risk
Mutual Understanding	• Designer's understanding of user needs	• More attention to technical than to user issues • Lack of user acceptance of information value • Failure to understand the choice process
Design Quality	• Good design • Flexible design	• Nonspecific functional design specifications • Inflexible design
Performance Level		• Poor performance • No performance objectives • Clumsy implementation of key function
Project Management	• Strong project and budget control • Frequent creative project meetings • Use of prototypes • Careful planning and testing • Good planning	• Lack of training package • Excessively complex implementation approach • Implementation too rushed • Poor timing in terms of deadlines
Resource Adequacy		• Excessive use of computing resources • Inadequate or poorly used resources • Project leader's time not fully committed • Lack of resources to make system "friendly" • Insufficient technical skills • Lack of designer's commitment • Bad input data
Situational Stability	• Stability of user requirements	• Departure of designer during implementation

*Adapted from Swanson, E.B., *Information System Implementation*, Homewood, IL: Irwin, 1988.

terms of response time. Since users expect the same kind of response, designers need to manage those expectations to make sure the prototype is realistic. The evolutionary approach to designing DSS is an extension of the prototype philosophy. In this approach, designers start with a small but important part of the problem. As users come to rely on this one portion of the system, and thereby become more knowledgeable about their needs, they can better explain their support needs for future parts of the DSS.

Interviewing

While prototypes will help designers gain this information, they alone are not sufficient; designers must gain much of their information, particularly early in the process, from interviewing. Good interviewing requires preparation. Interviewers must prepare the environment and the opening, gather interview aids, select a strategy, and prepare a closing for the interview.

The goal of preparing the environment is to set a stage where the interviewee will focus on the task at hand and feel sufficiently comfortable to reply usefully. The location must be comfortable, private, and free of distractions and interruptions. A neutral site allows the interviewee and interviewer to work together without interruption from telephone, visitors, or other tasks that need completion (such as piles on one's desk or a calendar). The timing of the interview must also be considered. Generally it is best not to schedule interviews when the interviewee is in the middle of a task or close to lunch or quitting time, because it is hard to get the individual's full attention. Of course, the timing must consider when the interviewer also will be free from distraction and the amount of time necessary to prepare materials. If the interviewee needs to complete a task, or review materials, or bring materials to the interview, allow time for that to be done.

The purpose of preparing the opening is to build rapport with the interviewee. Often it is helpful to consider the interviewee's background and interests, or shared experiences and history Interviewers need to be friendly and sincere and explain the purpose of the interview as well as the benefits associated with being involved. This opening must be consistent with the purpose of the interview and should not be misleading to the individual.

Prior to the interview, the designers should have gathered the relevant and necessary data, documents, checklists, and access to the information system. These materials might be part of the interview, or could provide interviewers with the background necessary to complete a meaningful exchange. Interviewers should complete a checklist or an interview schedule that will guide them through the process. This helps maintain the focus of the interview, while ensuring that important topics will not be missed. For example, initial interviews often focus on support needs. This means that the interviewer must ascertain the scope and boundaries of the tasks in which the decision makers are involved, as well as the tasks in which they are *not* involved. Within particular activities, where possible, interviewers must determine the sequence in which decision makers complete tasks and the factors they need to consider. This includes identifying relationships of importance and the means for identifying them, the heuristics followed, and the process of verifying the outcome of an analysis.

Generally the hardest part of an interview is getting started, so it is particularly important for the interviewer to have ready a series of questions to begin the discussion. These might include the following:

- Could you give me an overview of what you do?
- What initiates your activities and decisions?
- How do you determine when you have examined a problem/opportunity enough to act on it?
- What is the output of your decision making effort? Where does it go when it leaves you?
- Do other individuals contribute to your decision making effort?
- What are the basic components of your decision making effort?
- Can you define terms?

Post-introductory questions are determined by the strategy of the interview. There are three basic choices: directive, nondirective, and hybrid. In a directive interview, the goal is to get specific information from the decision maker. The questions one selects are highly structured, such as multiple choice questions or short answer questions. Where elaboration is allowed, the questions are primarily closed, allowing very little room to deviate from a specific point. When using the directive strategy, one must be very prepared and knowledgeable about the system. Interviewers must ensure that all important issues have been identified and relevant options given.

Nondirective interview strategies, on the other hand, encourage the decision maker to speak freely within a particular domain. The style of interview is highly unstructured and questions are most likely open-ended or probe questions. It is crucial that the interviewer be a good listener and know when to probe appropriately. The hybrid approach allows a mixture of both kinds of questions.

Often decision makers respond better to the nondirective strategy, particularly at the beginning of a project. While some decision makers will talk freely, others require more probing before the important information is obtained. Hence, the interviewer needs to be prepared with probing questions, such as the following:

- Can you think of a typical incident that illustrates how you make decisions?
- What advice would you give to a novice just getting started?
- Have you ever had a situation where . . . ? How did you proceed?
- When you get stuck, what do you do?
- What was the hardest decision you have ever had to make? What did you do?
- What would you recommend if the data . . . ?

If the goal is to elicit heuristics for the choice process, the interviewer might attempt questions such as the following:

- Do you have any rules of thumb for approaching choices such as . . . ?
- In these circumstances [previously described], you seem to. . . . Are there any exceptions to this process?
- Are there solutions that are possible, but not acceptable? How do you proceed in those cases?
- How do you judge the quality of your decision? of the choice process itself?
- How do others judge the quality of your decision? of the choice process itself?
- How do you make a decision? For what outcomes are you looking?

On the other hand, if the goal is to determine relationships between tasks, interviewers might attempt questions such as the following:

- This decision process X and the process Y seem to be similar. How are they alike? How are they different?
- Can you compare the task Z to anything else?
- Does the process that you complete, X, depend on something else? What about Y?

Similarly, if the goal is to verify the interviewer's understanding of a description, questions such as the following are appropriate:

- I understood you to say. . . . Have I misunderstood?
- How would you explain . . . in lay terms?
- Is there anything about your decision process that we have omitted?
- Would it be correct to say that . . . means . . . ?

Keep the Solution Simple

It is important that the DSS provide the support that the users want. This means that the system must provide the necessary tools for the choice task, without making the technology the focus of the decision maker's efforts. Too often, designers lose perspective on users' needs and try instead to provide users with the latest "new technology," or all the "bells and whistles" associated with the available technology. Or designers may computerize parts of the operation just because it is possible, not because it facilitates the choice process. This may be appealing to the designer who wants to experiment with these technologies, but it seems only a diversion to getting "real work done" to the decision maker. Hence, such approaches are likely to impede implementation processes.

Most decision needs are not "simple." In those cases, the DSS cannot be designed to be simple. However, the system *as the decision maker sees it* needs to be simple. Generally, the decision maker does not need to know about the operation of the system. Similarly, the approach to solving a problem, and therefore the steps decision makers need to take, must be intuitive and uncomplicated. For example, users do not need to be aware of all components of determining the system's confidence in particular information; rather, they need to know that the operation exists. Similarly, new or unsophisticated users need not understand all the flexibility in running models the system has afforded; rather, they need to know how to get the base model implemented. Simplicity of use will facilitate decision makers' acceptance and ultimate institutionalization of the system.

Develop a Satisfactory Support Base
User Involvement

Most people do not like change. For decision makers, this dislike maybe well grounded; often they have been successful because they have long operated in a particular fashion—changing it seems counterproductive. Adapting to a new computer system, particularly if one is not particularly comfortable with computers, can be a difficult enterprise. There are many reasons why such concerns exist. For example, decision makers may fear that they will become obsolete with the introduction of technology and that their job responsibilities will change or ultimately they will have no job security. Others may feel a certain possessiveness about information that previously only they could obtain or generate. Still others may view the introduction of the DSS as an invasion of their privacy. Many managers are not secure about all the methods they use in the choice process, and therefore find the analysis phase (where informational and modeling needs are determined) uncomfortable. Finally, the introduction of the DSS may change the balance of power operating within the organization. If information is power, by shifting the availability of information, the introduction of a DSS may threaten the power or influence of a given decision maker or department.

While a fear of change can affect the implementation process, more often it is resistance to having no control in the process that causes the bigger problem. For this reason, most designers will need to involve users throughout the analysis and design process. Users who are involved will better understand the reason for the system, the reason for choices for the design of the system, and the reason why some options were not taken. Their expectations will then be more realistic, which is crucial to effective implementation.

User involvement will also help shape the DSS and its features. Different people approach the same problem with quite different methods, including the manner in which they perceive the problem, the importance of features, and the navigation within the system. If users whose style is likely to be employed with the system participate in the design process, the system will be more usable to them in the long run. If they are involved from the beginning, they can affect the system in a stage where it is inexpensive and easy to do so. Furthermore, others not involved in the design effort might be more willing to accept the needs expressed by their co-workers, but not the word of systems designers who are perceived as "outsiders".

User interaction correlates highly to later use of the system. With some users, however, designers should act on the principle of "small encounters." In other words, the designer and the decision maker will have only brief—and generally informal—interactions during which they address one or two specific issues with regard to the system. In fact, it may seem that these interactions are composed more of nonsystem discussions (or "chit-chat") than of system-relevant material. The goal is to address a specific concern *and* to increase the decision maker's comfort level with the system.

User involvement in the analysis and design processes requires a balance between the influence of the designers from information technology (IT) and influence of the users and decision makers. When the balance is lost, the system suffers. For example, if IT has too much influence on the system design, the DSS may not provide innovative links to resources because of concerns about compliance with other standards in the corporation. On the other hand, if the decision makers have too much influence on the system, standardization may be eliminated, and hence too many resources may be spent on maintenance and integration. Table 10.2 illustrates other examples of imbalances between designers and users of the DSS.

◆ DSS Design Insights ◆

Whenever individuals encounter unknown situations, they build a hypothesis about how their lives will change as a result. Peters [1994, p. 74] notes "the less we know for sure, the more complex the webs of meaning (mythology) we spin." This leads to one of the foremost problems in implementation. If the decision makers and users do not understand what the system will do, how it will do it, or how it will be used, they will tend to create scenarios about the system and its use. The greater the delay between the hint that something about the new system could be undesirable and the explanation of or discussion about the new system, the worse the scenario is drawn.

The lesson to be learned from this is to keep users and decision makers informed about the progress of development. This leads them to perceive greater control over the situation and therefore to less resistance to the implementation.

Further, they are likely to have suggestions that, if introduced early enough in the process, might lead to a better DSS in the long run. If, however, they do not have the opportunity to voice an opinion until the system is complete, the suggestion is likely to be too expensive to implement.

TABLE 10.2 Possible Implications of Excess Dominance*

INFORMATION TECHNOLOGY DOMINANCE	USER DOMINANCE
■ Too much emphasis on database hygiene.	■ Too much emphasis on problem focus.
■ No recent new supplier or new distinct services.	■ Explosive growth in number of new systems and supporting staff.
■ New systems always must fit data structure of existing system.	■ Multiple suppliers delivering services. Frequent change in supplier of specific service.
■ All requests for service require system study with benefit identification.	■ Lack of standardization and control over data hygiene and system.
■ Standardization dominates—few exceptions.	■ Hard evidence of benefits is nonexistent.
■ Benefits of user control over development discussed but never implemented.	■ Soft evidence of benefits is not organized.
■ Information Technology specializing in technical frontiers, not user-oriented markets.	■ Technical advice of Information Technology not sought or, if received, is considered irrelevant.
■ Information Technology thinks it is in control of all.	■ User building networks to own unique needs (not corporate need).
■ Users express unhappiness.	■ While some users are growing rapidly in experience and use, other users feel nothing is relevant because they do not understand.
■ Portfolio of development opportunities firmly under Information Technology control.	■ No coordinated effort for technology transfer or learning from experience between users.
■ General management not involved, but concerned.	■ Growth and duplication of technical staffs.
	■ Communications costs are rising dramatically through redundancy.

*Adapted from Cash, J.I., F.W. McFarlan, J.L. McKenney, and M.R. Vitale, *Corporate Information Systems Management: Text and Cases, Second Edition*, Homewood, IL: Irwin, 1988, p. 320.

Commitment to Change

Commitment to change is also important. It comes only after the users have bought into the system. If they were involved throughout the process, decision makers are probably already committed to it. If not, it is difficult to gain their commitment without a demonstration of the clear benefits of the system. The organization must be committed to changing the way in which people make decisions and how information is made available. It must be committed to the project so that during the phases of development, installation, and use, management understands the problems and develops solutions to them. In addition, management must have commitment to making a good effort and making the system work.

Commitment begins at the top. High-level managers cannot be negative, or even benignly negligent, about the project. Since their priorities set the tone and agenda for an organization, they must support the system if people are to be involved enough to make the system work.

Managing Change

Management of change is important for the successful introduction of a system. It has three basic phases: unfreezing, moving, and refreezing. *Unfreezing*, as the name suggests, is the process of creating a climate favorable to change. This includes recognizing that there is a need for change. Moving is the process of introducing the new system, and refreezing is the process of reinforcing the change that has occurred.

In the first phase, designers must work with the organization to establish a climate that encourages honest discussion of the advantages and disadvantages of the current system and allows brainstorming of possible solutions and opportunities. In terms of DSS acceptance, this phase hinges on the development of objectives for the DSS to affect the decision making process, and hence it is begun early in the analysis phase of the project. Designers want to assess the factors that will encourage and discourage implementation. Some possibilities are noted in Table 10.3. This table highlights that the organizational climate, the role of senior management, and the design process all can affect the success of the implementation process. For example, the organizational climate conducive to new systems implementation, as outlined in Table 10.3, is one in which users can talk openly about their needs and concerns, both because of open communication channels and because of a great amount of knowledge and experience with systems. However, the environment can be affected by other unrelated issues as well. For example, a corporation in the midst of merger or financial difficulties might not be conducive to change regardless of the levels of sophistication and communication available. Employees might be so focused on the survivability of their own employment positions that they cannot focus properly on the DSS under construction or implementation.

Similarly, the role that senior management plays in the process is crucial. As reflected in Table 10.3, senior managers who use systems, provide adequate resources to their use, and have high expectations for the payoff of such systems set an environment that is more conducive to implementation than do senior managers who are not involved. In addition, the greater the parallel between the DSS development and strategic plans for the department or organization, the more likely that the implementation process will be successful because managers and users will see the need for the system.

Designers must focus on the nature of the users' problems as well as the opportunities that a DSS might affect. Decision makers must perceive a real need and must see that a DSS might meet that need. Of course, during this phase, design-

TABLE 10.3 Factors to Assess in Systems Implementation*

- ■ **Organizational Climate**
  - ■ Degree of open communication
  - ■ Level of technical sophistication of users
  - ■ Previous experiences with using DSS and other computer-based systems
  - ■ General attitude about computer-based systems and information technology
  - ■ Other disruptive influences that might parallel the DSS development and implementation
- ■ **Role of Senior Management**
  - ■ Attitudes of senior management toward computer-based products and the Information technology department, both in terms of their actions and their statements
  - ■ Adequacy of the resources devoted to the information technology function in general and the DSS development in particular
  - ■ Amount of time spent on IT-related issues by senior management
  - ■ Expectancies of senior management
  - ■ Integration of information technology personnel in strategic decision making
- ■ **Design Process**
  - ■ Recognition of IT impacts in the organizational planning process
  - ■ Participation of IT management in the organizational planning process
  - ■ Perceived need for IT in the strategic goals

*Adapted from Dickson G.W., and J.C. Wetherbe, *The Management of Information Systems*, New York: McGraw–Hill Book Company, 1985, p. 402.

ers and decision makers must agree on the goals for the DSS and procedures to monitor progress on those goals. In addition, it is desirable to define a person or group of people who will champion the idea, and to gain the commitment of senior management to make the project work. In fact, evidence suggests that implementation success is improved substantially if senior managers demonstrate commitment to the introduction of a DSS. Furthermore, if senior managers initiate the DSS development, implementation success increases substantially. Such commitment may be shown in the amount of resources, time, and people (both the design team and the users) dedicated to the project. For the project to have an impact, though, the commitment must be ongoing and continuous, not simply for the initial development. All DSS need ongoing support for maintenance and operations. However, if a DSS is to become an important tool, the support must come in gaining new databases and models and other enhancements for the system.

One particular difficulty is the difference between real and perceived problems as well as between real and perceived opportunities. These differences can lead to resistance to implementation or to misstatement of system needs. For example, resistance often results from perceptions that the introduction of the DSS will change one's authority, influence, or even job status. While such perceptions may be unwarranted, knowing about them and attempting to get at their causes may lead to important information that will help with the unfreezing stage of change.

The second phase of change is *moving*. During this phase, effort focuses on the development of the DSS. Both technical and managerial resources play a role. Management focuses on involving users, balancing the influence of the designers and the users, responding to resistance, and creating an environment for eventual acceptance of the new tools. A team of users and designers sets priorities for the project and evaluates tradeoffs of possibilities. During the process, the team should provide feedback to the entire community of users and seek their advice. In addition to the technical factors, the team should evaluate how the introduction of a new DSS will change the organizational dynamics associated with decision making. Throughout this phase, the team needs to focus on:

- perceived needs and commitment;
- mutual understanding;
- expectancies;
- power and change needs;
- technical system issues;
- organizational climate; and
- project technical factors.

The final phase of change is *refreezing*. In this phase, designers must work with users to ensure that the system meets needs adequately, and that decision makers understand how to use new procedures. More important, it requires the development of organizational commitment and institutionalization of the system.

Institutionalize the System

With a number of factors acting against successful implementation of the system, the designers, in concert with managers, need to plan to institutionalize the system gradually. For example, the manner in which the system is introduced is crucial. If uninterested individuals are offered the system for voluntary use, the DSS is likely to sit idle. Voluntary use will happen only when individuals have the intellectual curiosity to experiment with the system or when the need for the system and its ability to meet that need are well established. On the other hand, managers who insist on mandatory use of a DSS also face potential failure. It is difficult to legislate decision making styles. Hence, users may not really use the system, but only provide the appearance of doing so.[1]

---

[1]Many students who were taught to program by drawing flowcharts can appreciate this strategy. In most procedural programming language classes, students historically have been taught to draw the flowchart to *facilitate* the development of the logic for writing the code for a program. This is similar to using a DSS to help the decision maker understand all the possible influences of adopting a particular course of action. However, students often write their code and *then* create the flowchart that corresponds to their code. In other words, the flowchart was not an *aid* in their decision-making process, but rather documentation that they followed the appropriate procedures. Similarly, unhappy users over whom use of a DSS has been legislated may form their decisions first, and then use the DSS to try to prove their choice. In other words, the system will not *support* the choice process, only *document* an unaided process.

Others may work harder to find the weaknesses of the system in order to "prove" that it is not worth the time.

A better approach to system institutionalization is to provide incentives to use the system. Appropriate incentives will, of course, differ from application to application and from organization to organization. However, they need not be elaborate or even financial. For example, one incentive is to pique curiosity by providing information *only* on the DSS, or on the DSS *first*. If the system is well designed, it should then sell itself based on its usefulness to the choice process.

When the incentive system has gained the attention of some individuals to the DSS, these individuals can help others to see the advantage of using the DSS. Enthusiasts can demonstrate the benefits of the systems to others in their work or provide informal incentives for the use of the system. In fact, there is much evidence that the word-of-mouth approach to institutionalizing a system is the one that works best. Hence, it is important for developers and managers explicitly to facilitate its use.

Associated with the need for incentives to institutionalize systems is, of course, a need for training. Since *each* potential user cannot be involved in the design process, some users will not know how it operates or why it flows in a particular manner, and hence they need training. However, DSS are used by managers, often senior-level managers. Since managers often cannot make substantial commitments of time to training because they cannot abandon the remainder of their operations for an extended period, training for DSS cannot follow conventional training

---

◆ DSS Design Insights ◆

Many years ago I had a colleague who thought it was time I learned to use electronic mail. Although he often spoke about the benefits, which I as an MIS person should certainly understand, I resisted because I had no immediate need to learn about e-mail and felt my time was better spent addressing other priorities. My colleague disagreed. Hence, for two weeks, he would send me a message every morning with some little "bit" of information he thought I would find amusing, interesting, or helpful. Just to ensure that I knew the bait was available, he would drop by my office to tell me he had sent me e-mail, but not the information contained in the e-mail. Although I found this annoying, it provided just enough incentive to check my e-mail. After a few weeks, it became habit to check my e-mail regularly. Over the years, as more of my colleagues, friends, and students have begun to use e-mail, I have found endless possibilities for its use (as most of my colleagues, friends, and students would tell you). It is a tool I now could not function without. Probably I would have learned to use it anyway, eventually. However, I wonder whether I would have discovered its uses as rapidly or as early without my colleague, who provided just the right incentive to get me started. Such small, subtle, and customized incentives often provide the best motivation to use new systems.

schedules. One approach that works well, especially with senior-level managers, is to train on a one-on-one basis. In that way, the trainer goes to the manager's office (or vice versa) and works through the system with the decision maker. Since there are no other individuals present, the approach and the focus can be customized to the user, and managers experience less discomfort about asking questions and voicing their concerns. Finally, since the meetings do focus on the manager, trainers can provide as little training as is necessary at a given meeting and schedule as many sessions as necessary to gain the appropriate comfort level of the manager.

Not only are one-on-one meetings less uncomfortable for the decision maker, they are more focused from a training perspective, in that they allow the time to be spent on activities relevant to the individual user and the individual situation. Evidence suggests that training is most effective when it considers needs from an individual's, the task's, and the organization's perspectives. Training on a one-on-one basis allows trainers to work with individuals to help them learn specific knowledge and skills necessary for effective performance. This may include a remedial lesson on using a mouse or an overview of the Internet, or other necessary technology not known by a particular decision maker. Trainers can also ensure that the program includes information and skills necessary to complete specific tasks, regardless of the user. For example, this might include guidelines on how to search the new databases or how to merge models. Finally, trainers also can identify how the goals of an individual affect or constrain performance or motivation to learn and develop a training program in response to them.

This method can be particularly effective if it is coupled with some post-implementation tailoring of the system to meet a given user's needs or capabilities. Such a strategy may mean allowing the user access to a command-line level of control or to turn on the assistance menu so that it automatically appears. The value is that the trainer can determine what works best for a given user, help the user to do the necessary tasks as well as possible, and then change the system where the user cannot adapt.

◆ IMPLEMENTATION AND SYSTEM EVALUATION

How does a designer *know* when a DSS and the implementation of that DSS are successful? Scott (1995) characterizes three approaches to identifying success, depending on whether a measure reflects "input," "output," or "process" models of the organization. For example, using an input model of the organization means that the evaluator examines how the DSS affected organizational resources. In particular, the measures of the system's success would focus on how the DSS helped the organization acquire additional resources or the measures of success would reflect improvements in the use of scarce resources. Dickson and Powers (1973) suggest quantitative measures, including (a) ratio of actual project execution time to the estimated time; and (b) ratio of the actual cost to develop the project to the budgeted cost for the project. While these may measure the efficiency of the implementation, they do not reflect the effectiveness of the implementation.

Measuring implementation success with an output view of the organization causes the evaluator to measure the improvement in organizational effectiveness attributable to the DSS. For example, this might include measurement of the success of the implementation by the payoff to the organization, especially in terms of benefits-to-costs ratios. However, DSS by their very nature are associated with difficult decisions, managerial operations, and significant externalities. The system might be effective, but still not change the way operations are conducted or not help to anticipate an unusual external event that strongly affects an outcome.

We must, therefore, separate the issues "good" or "bad" decision from "good" or "bad" outcome. Good decisions, as stated earlier, are well informed. It is not always true that good decisions are linked with good outcomes, or that bad decisions are always linked with bad outcomes. Often that interaction is a function of chance or other factors we do not yet understand. In other words, the DSS might have helped the decision maker make a good decision, or a well-informed decision, but that decision resulted in a bad outcome.

While it might be desirable to evaluate a DSS in terms of input costs or benefits to the organization, neither of these two help designers to make a system better. The third option is the process model, which focuses evaluation on the way in which the system works within an application. In general, the DSS should meet a recognized need, be easy to use, meet even the most sophisticated informational needs, have exploration capabilities, provide intelligent support, and be easy to maintain. As a *support* system, the DSS must also meet the decision making needs and the organizational restrictions, and be accepted by users. Hence, for implementation to be successful, the designer must address (a) technical appropriateness and (b) organizational appropriateness. While many of these aspects were discussed in some detail in earlier chapters, we will review the important issues here.

Technical Appropriateness

If the technical requirements of the decision makers are not achieved, then the system will not be used. If the system is not used, then by definition the implementation has been a failure. Hence, one possible measure for determining implementation success is the extent of use of the DSS, especially compared to the intended use. However, a more pragmatic measure might be the number of features consistent with the user's information needs, especially compared to the number of possible features. Chapter 3 suggested multiple dimensions of information, including those identified in Table 10.4. If the system provides information that is consistent with regard to decision making needs on all these dimensions of information, then it is successful. Similarly, Chapter 4 suggested the need for variability in models and model management features, such as intelligent assistance and model integration. If the system provides appropriate models and model management capabilities, then the DSS can be considered successful.

TABLE 10.4   Successful Database Criteria

Timeliness
Sufficiency
Level of detail and aggregation
Redundancy
Understandability
Freedom from bias
Reliability
Decision relevance
Cost efficiency
Comparability
Quantifiability
Appropriateness of format

To determine whether the system functions properly, we can test it to see whether the system does what it is supposed to do. For example, database calls can be performed to determine if the correct information is called, and models can be tested to determine whether they perform the correct manipulations. The decision aids, such as intelligent help, can be checked by testing a modeling situation in which such assistance should be invoked. Success of these components can be judged by measuring the percentage of cases for which appropriate advice was given and the adequacy of the explanations provided by the system.

It is imperative that such tests be done under client conditions. For example, testing a network-based system in "supervisor" mode does not measure whether the DSS works properly. Supervisor mode allows many privileges not available to the typical user that may be crucial to the system functioning effectively. Nor is testing a system away from the user's station sufficient. Users, particularly managers, are likely to have a variety of programs residing on their machines, each with its own peculiarities; these programs may alter the path by which the operating system will check for programs and/or files. They may have drivers that conflict with the DSS or they may affect the allocation of memory in a way that conflicts with the DSS. It is not sufficient to tell the managers that the DSS would work if only they would quit using other applications. Testing is meant to determine whether the system works from the users' stations under their usual operating conditions.

Many aspects can be tested individually. However, unlike transactional processing systems, DSS can never be completely tested for all possible contingencies. Designers cannot anticipate all the uses to which decision makers will put the system, and so they cannot ensure that the system will work properly in all those applications. Hence, it is also imperative that some tests be done by the potential users themselves. Often minor system flaws are associated with the order in which programs are loaded or the manner in which functions are invoked, which experienced programmers may address instinctively (and hence not detect the malfunction); less experienced users are likely to find such problems early. Even if the problem is not a "bug" *per se*, it might just be a bad or difficult way for the software to function.

To measure the system as a whole, designers must measure its usefulness to the subject and determine if the system facilitates a logical analysis of the problem. This can first be determined by decision maker users testing the system. It is necessary to have experienced decision makers during this phase of testing. They would use the system and determine whether it provides reasonable advice and suggestions for the situation under consideration. If so, it can be judged to be functioning properly. A problem flag can be generated when these decision makers find lapses in the advice or peculiar steps through analyses. Sometimes these are actual problems in the software, which needs maintenance. Other times, these flags denote a non-intuitive approach to analysis that might call for more assistance windows or greater use of artificial intelligence aids.

Another way of testing the system is with a modified Turing Test.[2] The purpose of such a test is to determine whether the system is providing appropriate advice and analyses that are consistent with what an expert analyst might provide. Prior to the test, expert analysts are asked to provide solutions or explanations for situations that a decision maker using the DSS might encounter. These human-based expert solutions or explanations are intermixed with those generated by the DSS. Decision makers are provided two solutions or explanations to a problem and asked to compare them. If the decision makers cannot tell the difference between a human-based answer and a machine-based answer, the DSS is judged to be working properly. Some form of comparison of the outcome of the DSS and that of an expert analyst is necessary.

Measurement Challenges

There are other measures designers consider when evaluating system success. Some designers check the degree to which the system meets its original objectives or the degree of institutionalization of the DSS. Others measure the amount of systems usage as a surrogate of system effectiveness. However, there are problems associated with this measurement. First, how does one actually measure usage? Number of keystrokes and other mechanized measurements only relate the number of times the user invoked particular commands. The number of times a system is invoked tells us very little about how much or how well the system con-

---

[2]The original Turing Test was created by the English computer scientist Alan Turing to measure whether a computer system demonstrated "artificial intelligence." The Turing test required a human interviewer to "converse" with both an unseen human and a computer on a particular topic. If the interviewer could not determine when he or she was conversing with the human or computer, the computer system was said to have artificial intelligence. If it was obvious when the computer responded, then the system failed the test. Many individuals have challenged the Turing Test. It is not appropriate for evaluation of a DSS. However, the modified Turing Test does provide some insight into the adequacy of analyses and advice provided by the system.

Some insights into implementation can be found by considering the procedures implemented by *Edmark*, an educational software company. (Educational software provides the same function for children that a DSS does for managers. Good educational software helps children discover opportunities to learn new concepts, identify how those new concepts are similar to what they have used in the past, determine what they need to know, discover how to apply that information, and help them make appropriate decisions about how to move on to a new topic. Hence, some of the same design principles can be applied to both kinds of effort.)

Of course, the programmers test the software to ensure that it works. However, in addition, the son of the CEO and the CFO, as well as some of their friends, also test the software. In fact the CEO's son, now age 9, has been testing the software for the last 4 years. These software "testers" represent the children who ultimately will be the users of the system. If they cannot use the software, find errors in the functionality, or find the procedures kludgy, it is redesigned before it goes to market.

Similarly, the company employs mothers of young children to spend time in stores explaining its products to clerks and customers. In this way, nonthreatening facilitators can adapt the assistance and information they provide to users appropriately. Since users better understand how to use the product, they are more satisfied with its use.

Yang, D.J., "The pied piper of kids' software," *Business Week*, August 7, 1995, pp. 70–71.

tributed to the choice process. Decision makers might invoke commands multiple times to assure themselves that the command will be read the same way each time, or because they forget they have already done so. In these cases, many observations of usage would not reflect greater importance or usefulness to the decision maker. Similarly, a small number of usages might not reflect lesser importance or usefulness. For example, sometimes simply seeing an analysis *once* might initiate a creative solution to a problem that would not otherwise have been apparent.

While electronic monitoring of usage can have difficulties, so can reported usage. If designers rely on the decision maker to report system usage, they might receive faulty information. Most decision makers are too involved in a decision task to be accurately aware of how much or how little they use the tool. If decision makers were favorable toward the introduction, they might bias their estimates positively; if they were unfavorable toward the introduction, they might bias their estimates negatively. Finally, even if we could measure use reliably, use does not equal usefulness. Studies in the mid-1980s (see, for example, Srinivasan, 1985) showed that system usage did not correlate highly with perceived usefulness of a DSS and thus did not provide reliable measures of system success.

To address such problems, others measure user satisfaction. The logic behind this measurement is that if the DSS is effective, it will make users more satisfied with the system. Many devices have been constructed to determine whether users are satisfied with the system. Ives, Olson, and Baroudi (1983) examined many of the instruments being used to measure satisfaction and found that they could standardize them by examining factors relating to decision makers' satisfaction with regard to about 40 factors. While reliable measurements can be made by asking about users' satisfaction with each individual factor, many decision makers are not willing to take the time to complete such a questionnaire. Furthermore, users tend to generalize these factors (such as ease of use) and may report their first, last, or typical experience rather than an overall experience. However, this approach does work well during the development process if designers are using prototypes. Specifically, if the users are queried with regard to specific technical attributes of the system *iteratively* (rather than only at the end of the design process), decision makers and designers can understand the components that work best and that work most poorly in the system. This then leads to a better design and, in the long term, more satisfaction with the system.

Davis (1989) found that measures of "perceived usefulness" and "perceived ease of use" were easier to obtain and therefore were more reliable measures of DSS success. He used Likert scales to measure attributes of perceived usefulness and attributes of perceived ease of use. To measure perceived usefulness, Davis provided Likert scales that asked users to rate a product (that is, a DSS) on a scale from "extremely likely" to "extremely unlikely" with regard to seven perspectives of usefulness. These have been adapted here with regard to DSS use.

- Enable the decision maker to accomplish analyses more quickly.
- Improve the decision maker's choice performance.
- Increase the user's productivity.
- Enhance the user's effectiveness in making choices.
- Make it easier for decision makers to make choices.
- Help the user to find the DSS useful in making decisions.

Similarly, Davis used the Likert scales to measure perceived ease of use. In the context of a DSS, these measurements might involve the following.

- Learning to use the DSS would be easy for the decision maker.
- The decision maker would find it easy to get the DSS to do what he or she wanted it to do.
- The decision maker's interaction with the DSS would be clear and understandable.
- The DSS would be flexible in interactions.
- It would be easy for the decision maker to become skillful at using the DSS.
- The decision maker would find the DSS easy to use.

Davis and others since him have found these instruments using questions easier-to-use and more reliable indicators of success of the DSS than the more specific and technical issues generally identified in user-satisfaction questionnaires.

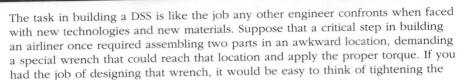

◆   Technical Information   ◆

The task in building a DSS is like the job any other engineer confronts when faced with new technologies and new materials. Suppose that a critical step in building an airliner once required assembling two parts in an awkward location, demanding a special wrench that could reach that location and apply the proper torque. If you had the job of designing that wrench, it would be easy to think of tightening the nut as your goal.

It would take a higher-level view to envision the goal as one of holding those two parts together. As new generations of adhesives became available, the engineer with this view would consider them while the "nut tightener" engineer would not.

But only the highest level of thinking would recall that the goal is to transmit a force or a bending movement through the structure, with the assembly of these two parts being merely a means to that end. If new materials made it practical to make a one-piece part to do the job, the question of how to fasten the two parts would disappear.

Adapted from Coffee, P., "Value tools by their decision making power," *PC Week,* 12(27), July 10, 1995, p. 27.

Organizational Appropriateness

Also in earlier chapters was a discussion of how the system must become a component of the entire system of the organization. To do this, it must support the decision styles of the users and the manner in which those decision styles change over time. In addition, it must behave appropriately for the organization in which it exists. It must provide levels of security and use consistent with corporate policy and provide information consistent with the expectations of the users. Just as new employees must "fit in" to a department and an organization, the system must fit in and meld comfortably with the department. This might include the appropriateness of the user interface, the appropriateness of the data availability, or the appropriateness of the modeling methodologies. If the system does not fit in to the department, it is likely to suffer the same fate as an employee who does not fit in, and hence it will not be implemented.

Dickson and Powers (1973) believe one can capture the behavioral appropriateness of the implementation by measuring (1) managerial attitudes toward the system; (2) how well information needs are satisfied; and (3) the impact of the project on the computer operations of the firm. These measures all reflect perceptions of the system. In addition, they are all measures taken *after* the system is implemented. Hence, they are not in keeping with the philosophy of planning for implementation throughout the project. A better approach would be to evaluate the various types of nontechnical feasibility discussed in Chapter 2.

The DSS must also fit within the constraints placed on it by the organization. For example, Meador and his colleagues concluded that a DSS is successful if it.

- fits with the organization's planning methods;
- helps with decision makers' ways of thinking about problems;
- improves the decision makers' thinking about problems;
- fits well with the "politics" of how decisions are made;
- uses results in choices that are implemented;
- is cost-effective and valuable relative to its cost; and
- is expected to be used for some time.

In other words, DSS need to interface well with other systems within the organization. Even if the DSS does a great job facilitating decisions, it cannot be a success if it does not facilitate mandated decision steps or other activities.

DISCUSSION

Implementation implies realization of the planned system. The purpose of this chapter is to highlight some of the barriers to implementation and some of the strategies that can increase the likelihood of successful implementation. Better the analysis of real needs, greater sensitivity of the designers to organizational climate, greater involvement of users early in the process, and greater commitment of management will improve the likelihood that a technically appropriate DSS is implemented.

QUESTIONS

1. The chapter identifies five principles to successful implementation. Discuss how inattention to each of them could discourage implementation efforts.

2. Compare and contrast the use of interviewing and prototyping during the design process in terms of the impact on the implementation process.

3. Why and how should users be involved in the design process?

4. How can we establish whether a given decision support system is effective?

5. What incentives can one use to encourage users to try the technology?

6. Compare and contrast the use of measures of utilization with measures of user satisfaction in measuring DSS effectiveness.

7. Create an interview schedule for users of a hypothetical DSS design project.

8. What activities would a designer engage in to develop a satisfactory support base?

9. What role does senior management play in the design of a DSS?

10. Compare and contrast technical appropriateness and organizational appropriateness in the DSS evaluation process.

◆ ON THE WEB ◆

On the Web for this chapter provides additional information about the implementation and evaluation processes associated with DSS design. Links can provide access to demonstration packages, general overview information applications, software providers, tutorials, and more. Additional discussion questions and new applications will also be added as they become available.

- *Links provide overview information.* Some links provide access to general information about implementation and evaluation processes.
- *Links provide access to successful implementation and evaluation efforts.* Where available, links can also provide access to unsuccessful efforts that illustrate processes to avoid.

- *Links provide interview and evaluation questionnaire hints.* Information obtained from these links could be incorporated into other applications.
- *Links provide access to prototyping tools.* In addition to providing an access to the tools, the Web provides product reviews, and success stories about their use. The links also provide bibliographies and general information about prototyping as a DSS analysis and design tool.

You can access material for this chapter from the general WWW Page for the book, or, directly from the following URL.
http://www.umsl.edu/~sauter/DSS/impl.html

SUGGESTED READINGS

Adams, D.A., R.R. Nelson, and P.A. Todd, "Perceived usefulness, ease of use and usage of information technology: A replication," *MIS Quarterly*, 16(2), June 1992, pp. 227–247.

Alter, S.L., *Decision Support Systems: Current Practice and Continuing Challenges*, Reading, MA: Addison-Wesley, 1980.

Carmel, E., R.D. Whitaker, and J.F. George, "PD and joint application design: A transatlantic comparison," *Communications of the ACM*, 36(4), June 1993, pp. 40–48.

Cash, J.I., F. W. McFarlan, J.L. McKenney, and M.R. Vitale, *Corporate Information Systems Management: Text and Cases, Second Edition*, Homewood, IL: Irwin, 1988.

Clement, A. and P.C. Den Besselaar, "A retrospective look at PD projects," *Communications of the ACM*, 36(4), June 1993, pp. 29–39.

Davis, F.D., "Perceived usefulness, perceived ease of use and user acceptance of information technology," *MIS Quarterly*, 13(3), September 1989, pp. 319–342.

DeLone, W.H. and E.R. McLean, Information systems success: The quest for the dependent variable," *Information Systems Research*, 3(1), March 1992, pp. 60–95.

Dickson, G. and R. Powers, "MIS project management: Myths, opinions and realities," in McFarlin, W., et al (eds.), *Information Systems Administration*, New York: Holt, Reinhart & Winston, 1973.

Dickson, G.W. and J.C. Whetherbe, *The Management of Information Systems*, New York: McGraw-Hill, 1985.

Dumas, J. and P. Parsons, "Discovering the way programmers think about new programming environments," *Communications of the ACM*, 38(6), June 1995, pp. 45-56.

Galletta, D.F., M. Ahuja, A. Hartman, T. Teo, and A.G. Peace, " *Communications of the ACM*, 38(6), July 1995, pp. 70-79.

Ginzberg, M.J., "Steps towards more effective implementation of MS and MIS," *Interfaces*, 8(3), May 1978.

Ginzberg, M.J., "Key recurrent issues in the MIS implementation process," *MIS Quarterly*, 5(2), June 1981.

Guimataes, T., *et al.*, "The determinants of DSS success: An integrated model," *Decision Sciences*, March/April 1992.

Ives, B., M.H. Olson, and J.J. Baroudi, "The measurement of user information satisfaction," *Communications of the ACM*, 26(10), October 1983, pp. 785-793.

Ives, B. and M.H. Olson, "User involvement in information systems development: A review of research," *Management Science*, 30(5), May 1984, pp. 586-603.

Jenkins, A.M. and J.A. Ricketts, "Development of an instrument to measure user information satisfaction with management information systems," Unpublished Working Paper, Indiana University, Bloomington, 1979.

Keen, P.G.W, "Information systems and organizational change," *Communications of the ACM*, 24(1), January 1981.

Lewin, K., "Group decision and social change," in Newcomb, T.M., and E.L. Hartley (eds.), *Readings in Social Psychology*, New York: Holt, Reinhart & Winston, 1947.

Loofbourrow, T., "Expert systems are still alive," *InformationWeek*, 536, July 17, 1995, pp. 104.

Meador, C.L., M.J. Guyote, and P.G.W. Keen, "Setting priorities for DSS development," *MIS Quarterly*, 8(2), June 1984, p. 117-129.

Nelson, R.R., E.M. Whitener and H.H. Philcox, "The assessment of end-user training needs," *Communications of the ACM*, 38(6), July 1995, pp. 27-39.

Peters, T., *The Pursuit of WOW!* New York: Vintage Books, 1994.

Port, O., "Computers that think are almost here," *Business Week*, July 17, 1995, pp. 68-73.

Raghunathan, B. and T.S. Raghunathan, "Information systems planning and effectiveness—an empirical analysis," *Omega: The International Journal of Management Science*, 19(2-3) 1991, pp. 125-135.

Robey, D., "User attitudes and MIS use," *Academy of Management Journal*, 22(3), September 1979.

Scott, J.E., "The measurement of information systems effectiveness: Evaluating a measuring instrument," *Database: Advances in Information Systems*, 26(1), February 1995, pp. 43-59.

Srinivasan, A., "Alternative measures of system effectiveness: Associations and implications," *MIS Quarterly*, 9(3), September 1985, pp. 243-253.

Swanson, E.B., *Information System Implementation*, Homewood, IL: Richard D. Irwin, 1988.

Wagner, I., "A web of fuzzy problems: Confronting ethical issues," *Communications of the ACM*, 36(4), June 1993, pp. 94-100.

Weinberg, G.M., *Rethinking Systems Analysis and Design*, Boston: Little, Brown and Company, 1982.

Yang, D.J., "The pied piper of kids' software," *Business Week*, August 7, 1995, pp. 70-71.

Zmud, R.W. and J.F. Cox, "The implementation process: A change process," *MIS Quarterly*, 2(2), June 1979.

PART IV

◆ ◆ ◆

Related Systems

Chapter 11

Group Decision
Support Systems

◆ ◆ ◆

Many decisions in an organization are made not by an individual, but by *groups* of individuals. By its very nature, a group enriches the choice process by gathering the knowledge, experience, and probably the different perspectives of several people. The enrichment may, in turn, allow the group to understand the problem better, spark synergy for creative solutions, and identify errors in the information or process. Finally, since more people are involved, they create a deeper commitment to the choice, and thus less resistance to its implementation.

However, groups bring a few drawbacks to the decision process. Most group decisions take longer to reach than individual decisions. Groups tend to spend significant nonproductive time waiting, organizing, or repeating what already has been said. Group dynamics can inappropriately influence the process if there are substantial differences in the rank or temperament of the members. Often, the supporting work may be uncoordinated if completed by multiple individuals, or some people may abdicate their tasks and responsibilities to others. Finally, there is social pressure to conform to a group position. "Groupthink" can exist in any group and may exacerbate incomplete or inappropriate uses of information.

Groupthink is an agreement-at-any-costs mentality that often results in ineffective group decision making and poor decisions (Hellriegel, *et al.*, 1993). It is associated with groups having a high degree of conformity and cohesion that are insulated from outside information sources challenging their decisions, that have excessively directive leadership, and/or that exist in a complex and rapidly changing environment. When groupthink occurs, members ignore limitations or impropriety of their analyses as well as possible consequences of their choice process. In fact, the group collectively rationalizes its choice and process, going so far as to censor itself when group members deviate from the established position, solution, or parameters.

◆   DSS in Action   ◆

Collective rationalization is the characteristic that allowed North American automobile executives to agree on two "facts" about the consumers in the 1970s. In particular, the executives agreed that (a) only a small segment of North American automobile buyers would, in fact, purchase Japanese-manufactured automobiles and (b) North American consumers would be willing to tolerate a per-gallon gas price of over $2.50. It is likely that at least one of those executives had concerns about the validity of these two assumptions and their impact on the automobile design decision-making process. However, he or she may have been hesitant to express concerns in a meeting where others perceived the assumptions to be true. This was groupthink and it had a remarkably negative impact on the North American automobile industry.

The problem with groupthink is obviously that it can lead to poor decision processes. In particular, it is associated with

- incomplete generation of alternatives;
- incomplete understanding of goals;
- failure to examine risks of preferred choices;
- poor search of information;
- bias in the interpretation of information; and
- failure to appraise and reappraise alternatives.

Each of these, in turn, is associated with bad decision making. Unfortunately, DSSs, as they have been defined to this point, do not provide methods for addressing these problems.

Hence, to support *group* decision making, a tool needs to have not only the characteristics of decision support systems discussed throughout this book, but also the hardware, software, and procedures necessary to reveal the positive aspects of the group and inhibit the negative. Group decision support systems (GDSS) represent this hybrid technology; they combine decision support systems *and* groupware technologies. GDSS should have the components of a DSS, including the model management system, database management system, user interface management system, and mail management system, as described previously. The system must be able to support the needs of all the decision makers easily. GDSS must have the range of models and model management functions necessary to meet the choice needs of the participants. Further, they must be able to access and aggregate information from a variety of sources in a variety of formats to meet the group's broad information needs. Finally, GDSS must be easy for all users to operate.

Too often, the group dynamics themselves block active participation by one or more people and discourage innovative thinking. GDSS must therefore include tools that address the group dynamics so that decision makers can gain consensus about a particular problem or opportunity, and include a group dynamic management system to address the special needs of group processes. Group consideration of any problem allows the use of additional information, knowledge, and skills, but only if all participants have equal opportunity to be heard and to have ideas received. Since GDSS use the technologies of groupware, before discussing more about GDSS, we will examine the concept of Groupware in more depth.

◆ GROUPWARE

Groupware or group support systems (GSS) have evolved over time. One definition available in the literature is that GSS are computer-based information systems used to support intellectual, collaborative work (Jessup and Valacich, 1993). This definition is too broad for one discussion because it does not specifically address the role of groups. Another definition is "tools designed to support communications among members of a collaborative work group" (Hosseini, 1995). Another way to describe a GSS is as "the collective of computer-assisted technologies used to aid group efforts directed at identifying and addressing problems, opportunities and issues" (Huber, Valacich, and Jessup, 1993).

Groupware exists to facilitate the movement of messages or documents, so as to enhance the quality of communication among individuals in remote locations. It provides access to shared databases, document handling, electronic messaging, workflow management, and conferencing. In fact, groupware can be thought of as a development environment in which cooperative applications—including decisions—can be built. Groupware achieves this through the integration of eight distinct technologies: messaging, conferencing, group document handling, work flow, utilities/development tools, frameworks, services, and vertical market applications. Hence, it provides the foundation for the easy exchange of data and information among individuals located far apart. Although no currently available product has an integrated and complete set of capabilities, Table 11.1 summarizes the range of functions that may be included in groupware.

There are many examples of successful use of groupware to enhance communications. In fact, it is believed that more than 90% of firms using groupware will receive financial returns of 40% or more, with some as large as 200%. Boeing engineers collaborated with engineers at parts manufacturers as well as maintenance experts and customer airlines while designing the 777. Using groupware technologies, engineers shared ideas through e-mail and specifications through CAD. Similarly, Weaton Industries used desktop videoconferencing to

TABLE 11.1   Functionality of Groupware Products

- ■ Enterprise Needs
    - Cross-vendor support
    - Local/remote servers
    - Integrated networks
    - Executive information systems standards
    - Network operating systems
    - Database
    - Document and image repository
    - Object repository and knowledge ware
- ■ Group Needs
    - GDSS
    - Desktop video and audio conferencing
    - Group application development environment
    - Group editing
    - Work flow management
- ■ Tools
    - E-mail and messaging
    - Calendar management and scheduling
    - Personal productivity applications
    - Models and model management

◆   DSS in Action   ◆

A surprising number of companies are going beyond simple document sharing, deploying such programs on an enterprisewide basis and using repository-based groupware as databases, internal communications networks, and work flow systems. Many companies are using groupware products to spearhead efforts to reengineer the way they do business. For example, a Wall Street investment firm used groupware to help prepare the final details of a merger and acquisition deadline. It became clear to these managers that they could not finish those details without help at 3 P.M. the day before the proposal was due. This company contracted with Coopers & Lybrand to finish the proposal by 9 A.M. the next day.

Using *Lotus Notes,* Coopers & Lybrand met their needs. At the end of the day for the Dallas office of Coopers & Lybrand, management handed the work to the San Francisco office. These employees worked on the project until the end of their work day, when they, in turn, passed the project to the Sydney office. Sydney employees eventually passed the work to the London office, which in turn passed it to the New York office, which eventually returned the work to the Dallas office for presentation to the client at the originally scheduled time (that is, the next morning).

diagnose and repair giant blow-molding machines around the world. Finally, law firms use groupware to gain access to documents for improved efficiency and customer service.

The main groupware competitors at this time are:

- *LinkWorks* from Digital Equipment Corporation;
- *Lotus Notes* from Lotus Development Corporation;
- *Oracle Office 2.0* from Oracle Corporation;
- *Team Office* from TeamWare division of ILC, Inc.; and
- *GroupWise 4.1* from WordPerfect: The Corel Group.

In addition, Microsoft will soon introduce a product, *Exchange*, and IBM is in the process of developing a product. Currently, *Lotus Notes* enjoys the position of market leader among groupware products.

One of the major problems with most groupware products at this time is that they rarely interface with one another. This means that the tools are applicable within only a local workgroup, and rarely on an enterprise level. Furthermore, it means that users must adopt and maintain a single product line regardless of whether it continues to meet their needs because it is expensive for all users to change. Hence, there is a move in the industry to develop a groupware standard including items such as those described in Table 11.2.

TABLE 11.2   Possible Standards for Groupware Products

■ Scheduling capabilities should be provided to all network applications through a well-defined standard.

■ The multivendor scheduling standard should support transparent scheduling for all store-and-forward messaging transports, as well as via real-time network protocols.

■ The standard should include hooks into shared X.500 directory services, as well as proprietary e-mail, groupware, and network operating system directories.

■ The standard should support the calendar synchronization policies maintained by various scheduling tools.

■ The standard should support interfaces to multivendor network-enabled project planning and management tools.

■ The standard should allow users to control who can access their personal calendars, what fields can be viewed and modified, and what types of events can be scheduled without the owner's prior consent.

■ The standard should mediate between the various techniques used by scheduling tools to request meetings, negotiate meeting times and places, and reconcile conflicting schedules.

◆   DSS Design Insights   ◆

In an attempt to stifle current and future competition, Lotus Development Corporation has created *Notes Express*, a scaled-down version of the full-featured *Notes*
(*Notes Express* sells for about 10% of the price of the complete *Notes* product).
Notes Express includes electronic mail and five miniature group applications, such as
a group discussion database, but contains no customization tools, and does not allow access to Notes applications. In addition, Lotus Development Corporation developed *Notes Desktop* as a runtime version of the product that runs with any *Lotus
Notes* application; this product sells for about 30% of the price of the full version.
    Further, Lotus Development Corporation has made it possible for third-party
vendors to connect their products directly to *Lotus Notes*. For example, Marshall
Consulting, Inc., developed applications for project management, personal calendar-
ing, equipment tracking, forum discussion, and contact management. Similarly,
GroupQuest Software developed an administration tool that can add or remove
users and servers from the *Lotus Notes* Name and Address Book, as well as change
user access privileges. Carthage International developed an online newspaper, At-
tack Systems International developed a real estate management system, and
Egghead Software has developed a system to provide corporate customers with
product information and order tracking.

◆ GDSS DEFINITIONS

A *group* decision support system incorporates groupware technology with DSS technology. As such, GDSS consist of hardware, software, and procedures for facilitating the generation and evaluation of alternatives as well as features for facilitating
to improve group dynamics. However, a GDSS is not a reconfiguration of an existing DSS, but a specially designed system that integrates DSS and groupware technologies.
    A typical configuration includes model management, database management, and
group management tools interconnected and managed by a facilitator. The purpose of the facilitator is to coordinate the use of the technology so that the focus
of the decision makers is on the problem under consideration, not on the use of
technology. Often these interconnected machines are located in one room (sometimes called a decision room) to create a *decision conference*, attended by an appropriate group of individuals to consider options and find a solution to the problem. In this configuration, information can be communicated to and from
participants via a network or by use of one or more public screens projecting the
output of a particular computer. Alternatively, participants can use graphic pads to
create sketches and graphs that are to be projected onto the public screen. Finally,
often participants can generate hard-copy versions of the meeting so they can refer to them between meetings.

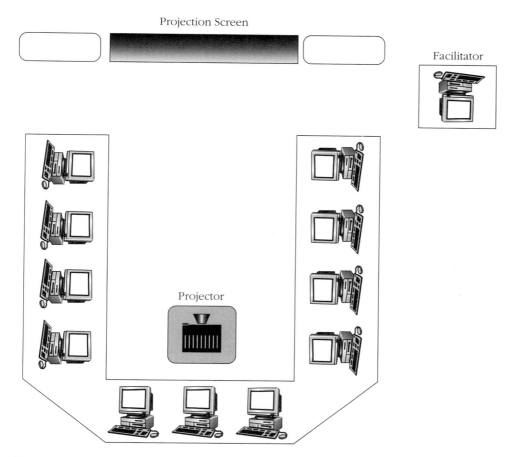

Projection Screen

Facilitator

Projector

Figure 11.1 Decision conferencing configuration, typically a control room and one or more "breakout" rooms are adjacent to this room.

A typical decision making process has several stages. After an introduction by the facilitator, the group is asked to discuss the issues and concerns so that the problem can be detected and defined. Once a set of alternatives is understood, the group attempts to construct a model of the choice context through which to evaluate the several alternatives. The analyst then assists the participants to refine the model and evaluate its results.

An alternative framework is one in which all members of the group are provided with a personal handset providing a two-line display and a numeric keyboard, referred to as a *keypad system*. These keypads are configured like a telephone or hand-held calculator, and are linked to a central microcomputer by cable or radio. Participants use the keypad system to vote on the options available.

The process generally is guided by support staff. There must be a facilitator to help the group focus on the task by addressing and solving the technology issues.

In addition, there is an analyst who provides expertise in developing computer models, and a recorder who chronicles the proceedings by recording the critical issues and syntheses as they occur.

Workstation-centered systems operate with a set of microcomputers linked by a local area network, or LAN, and many public screens on which documents can be projected. These systems allow users to draft ideas at their own workstations. After some consideration of the document, the user may elect to share ideas by sending them as electronic mail or as projection to a public screen. Alternatively, users may elect to hold documents for a later, more appropriate, time or to discard weak results. The display of many ideas on one or more public screens can lead to a more integrated discussion of a topic. Since it is not possible to identify the originator of a particular idea, the opinions of particular individuals can be shared anonymously.

Watson et al. (1988) completed an extensive study of this type of configuration and compared the results to group meetings with other kinds of assistance. Their overall conclusion was that in general the workstation approach seems to provide greater process support than other methodologies. Some examples of systems using this approach are:

- *GroupSystem;*
- *VisionQuest;* and
- *Software-Aided Meeting Management System (SAMM).*

Variations of the workstation methodology include teleconferencing and the remote decision-making approach. In teleconferencing, group support is like that in the decision conference, but participants are geographically separated from one another. In addition to the electronic connection, there is visual and audio communication so users can see and hear one another as if they were in the same location. An example of this setup is shown in Figure 11.2. Remote decision making is similar to the workstation approach, but with offices that are not in close proximity. These sessions might also have videoconferencing support, or they might simply be electronic.

Finally, it is important to note that an organization does not necessarily need to have the GDSS facilities built at its site to avail itself of them. Several universities and commercial vendors provide the use of sites for a fee. Some possible sites are listed in Table 11.3.

◆ FEATURES OF GDSS SUPPORT
Decision Making Support

The GDSS must provide both decision making support and process support. Decision making support begins with the features that have already been addressed with regard to all decision support systems. That is, the GDSS must include access

Figure 11.2 GDSS and Videoconferencing Room. General American MIS Research Laboratory at University of Missouri–St. Louis.

to models and model management tools, data and database management tools, and mail and mail management tools. However, groups generally are created to solve particularly poorly structured problems, often with strategic or long-term implications. Hence, GDSS need to provide particular support for alternative generation and issue interpretation. Alternative generation require an electronic brainstorming tool that records ideas and comments about ideas. Furthermore, the tool needs to facilitate consolidation of ideas by helping either the group members or the facilitator to identify common concerns, common attributes, and/or relationships among ideas. This facility is sometimes known as an *issue analyzer tool*. Finally, the GDSS needs to facilitate the identification of stakeholders, the assumptions that are being made with regard to them, and what role and importance they will play in the process.

Alternative generation, analysis, and categorization can be quite difficult in a group setting because everyone wants to participate at once and because participants follow different thought processes. GDSS tools can provide the distinctive feature of parallel communications, or "the ability . . . [for] group members to communicate information simultaneously"(Bostrom, Anson, and Clawson, 1993). With this in place, members need not wait for others to complete thoughts prior to expressing their own opinions. This keeps an individual's train of thought focused,

TABLE 11.3   GDSS Facilities*

UNIVERSITY-BASED FACILITIES

University of Arizona	New York University
Claremont Graduate School	University of Minnesota
University of Georgia	University of Missouri–St. Louis
University of Indiana	Southern Methodist University
University of Louisville	State University of New York–Albany
	Western Washington University

CORPORATE-BASED FACILITIES

Electronic Data Systems	Gould, Inc.
IBM Corporation	Xerox Palo Alto Research Center

COMMERCIAL FACILITY VENDORS

ICL	Metapraxis

FOR-HIRE COMMERCIAL SYSTEMS: PERMANENT INSTALLATIONS

Decision and Designs, Inc.

FOR-HIRE COMMERCIAL SYSTEMS: PORTABLE INSTALLATIONS

Applied Future, Inc.	Perceptronics, Inc.
K.R. Hammond	Wilson Learning Systems

*Table was adapted from Sprague, R.H., and H.J. Watson, *Decision Support Systems: Putting Theory into Practice*, New York: Prentice-Hall, 1989.

yet prevents time lags between the expression of one idea and another (Wilson and Jessup, 1995). The ability for group members to work in parallel "may account for the increased productivity of GSS idea-generating groups" and the higher satisfaction levels of participants (Dennis and Gallupe, 1993). In addition, parallel communication can lead to time savings. Since there is no competition for "air time," domination by an outspoken member of the group can be reduced (Wilson and Jessup, 1995). Also, since ideas can be contributed simultaneously, the total time to collect information is reduced (Dennis, et al., 1995).

Another way in which the GDSS provides decision support is by acting as a "group memory." In particular, it provides an electronic record of the meeting, both in summarized and raw form. This allows individuals who want to review the process access to the concepts and alternatives that were identified as well as the flow of the information being compiled by the group (Hosseini, 1995). In other words, not only can an individual get the overall impression of the meeting, but he or she can follow the exchanges to determine how final positions were derived. This retracing of the group thought process can help the individual to understand the "why" behind the "what" that resulted from the meeting. It can be defined as "a sharing of interpretations among individuals of a group" (Hoffer and Valacich, 1993) . Some of the components necessary to support group memory are

- access to a wide variety of information both external and internal to the organization as well as internal and external to the group process;
- the ability to capture information easily and to store and integrate information generated by group interactions and about group processes dynamically;
- support for use of both quantitative and qualitative decision models and aids (Hosseini, 1995); and
- the ability to support weighting and ranking of alternatives that have been proposed an stored in group memory.

These features will allow group members to examine information available to the group, whether it was generated by the group itself or prepared externally and presented to the group. For example, members have access to the raw data, the molding of data into information, and the group's implied evaluation of the relevance, accuracy, and importance of data.

This information must be available to group members on an as-needed basis. Members might need to review activities that have occurred since they left the conference and to be brought up to speed easily once they rejoin the group discussion. The group memory should allow group members to peruse the results of prior meetings they were unable to attend (Wilson and Jessup, 1995). Such a feature will be of particular importance to the use of GDSS in reengineering because it will facilitate diverse membership and cross-functional attendees, who might not all be available for meetings simultaneously. The group memory configuration also must allow browsing of what has transpired even while the meeting continues. This means that the individual can leave the conference, digest information at his or her *own pace,* and then rejoin the conference. Such a feature allows for disparity in learning speed and learning style, without biasing the group's opinion of the member (Hosseini, 1995).

There are technical considerations associated with providing an adequate group memory, especially in terms of preserving the richness of the information associated with discussion. However, when accomplished properly, it can assist in increasing task focus, and thereby aid effectiveness.

Process Support

As stated earlier in this chapter, one of the main contributions provided by GDSS technology is support of the process. Research has demonstrated that large groups benefit most from the use of a GDSS. This is the case because in traditional, non-

GDSS settings, the larger the group, the greater the negative aspects of group behavior. Since a GDSS manages the negative aspects of group behavior and makes a group more effective in accomplishing its goals, it therefore has a greater impact on larger groups. This is not to say that it cannot be an effective aid in small groups. Rather, it suggests that because the negative aspects of group behavior are not as prominent, the relative impact is not as great. This includes all features that encourage the positive attributes of group decision making while suppressing the negative group dynamics.

One GDSS process feature is that the technology allows greater flexibility in the definition of meetings. Often, group members cannot attend all the same meetings. This aspect of group meetings is a growing phenomenon as more diverse individuals—who have diverse responsibilities and schedules—are brought together to work on projects. As corporations downsize, it is likely that the expertise necessary to solve a problem or to complete a project will not be available at common locations. Also, if high-level managers are involved in the project, they might need to be away from the group to respond to needs in their own departments. GDSS can be extended for use in different places and at different times. Hence, the discussion and decision making meetings will be populated by "virtual groups." Group members *might* meet at the same time in the same place. Or, as discussed earlier, they might meet at the same time, but in geographically different locations joined through teleconferencing. With GDSS, they might meet in the same *place* but at different *times*. Finally, the GDSS allows the groups to meet at *different times* in *different places*. This extension of the technology will mean that the number of face-to-face meetings will decline, and the meetings will not interfere with other productivity gains.

A second process feature allowed by GDSS is the anonymity feature. In particular, this feature allows group members to pose opinions, provide analyses, or vote without revealing their own identity to other members of the group. The anonymity feature allows for a more democratic exchange of information because individuals must evaluate information on its own merits, not on what seems politically most expedient. If the author of a proposal is not known, then the evaluation of the proposal does not hinge on the status of the author, but rather on the merit of the idea itself. This feature is most important when a group consists of individuals of significant differences in stature. In meetings where pressure to conform is perceived to be high, the anonymity feature allows for the most open contributions, and hence is most highly valued. There is also the possibility that preserving anonymous contributions will eliminate personalities from the process and allow the focus to be on the analysis of the problem on the table.

With a GDSS, an environment can be created in which group members participate equally, vote their conscience, and participate more often than they might in a noncomputerized environment where their contributions are more easily identified. Hence, anonymity can result in more information being generated, better analyses, and hence better decision making.

Of course, the GDSS must also provide facilities for voting and negotiating aids for the group meeting. For example, the GDSS might include an electronic version of *Robert's Rules of Order* or some other parliamentary procedure, or it might provide the facility to develop and call on rules for discussion and voting in the meeting. An "intelligent counselor" is a knowledge-based system that can provide advice on the rules applying to a particular situation. Support for voting might include the provision of numerical and graphical summarization of votes and ideas. GDSS might also include programs for the calculation of weights in multiattribute decision problems and Delphi techniques for progressive movement toward consensus building.

Another resource that can be built into the meeting process is the use of facilitators. Facilitation can be defined as "a set of functions carried out before, during, and after a meeting to help the group achieve its own outcomes" (Bostrom, Anson, and Clawson, 1993). A facilitator can increase the likelihood that a meeting will produce the desired outcomes. In other words, if a facilitator is used, then the meeting will make use of the GDSS tools, but the process will not be driven by the GDSS tools. A facilitator should be adept at exploiting the GDSS technology to achieve the goals of the group; the additional talents that need to be utilized are far too numerous and embrace too many disciplines to be outlined here. Otherwise, the group will either become overly focused on the technology (at the loss of the topic at hand) or will not avail itself of the richness of the tool to address the topic.

◆ GDSS AND REENGINEERING

Reengineering projects draw on employees from diverse areas of the organization. This diversity must be present to ensure that every element of the process is considered carefully (Ziguram and Kozar, 1994). For example, consider three case studies in which GSS were used: U.S. Army Installation Management, Flagstar, and the Department of Defense Battlefield Logistics. A review of these case studies illustrates that the GSS technology facilitated their success (Dennis et al., 1995). The most significant factor to emerge from the analysis was the essential nature of the team concept. Senior managers need to provide support, but a team of middle managers is the core of the process, and they need to work as one. Cross-functional teams, whose members are diverse in style and experience, need to hit the ground running and not waste time establishing ground rules and procedures. A good GDSS handles those problems. The team that "owned" the business process redesign had its skills enhanced by the qualities of the GSS while consulting with some information technology staff for the technical characteristics of making it work.

History is full of problems in implementation because lower-level managers were not part of the discussions, thereby requiring upper-level managers to rely on their memories as to how functions were performed. For example, consider the reengineering effort of Garland Power and Light. Although this company had failed at collaborative projects in the past, the management believed that a reengineering effort was in need. To this end, the strategic plan developed highlighted commonality in purpose and definition; collaboration among the managers of the five divisions; and dissolution of the boundaries between divisions to provide more end-to-end work. Unfortunately, the process at Garland Power and Light failed. An analysis of the failure identified problems of collapsed coordination and lack of communication (Ziguram and Kozar, 1994). The use of a GDSS could have helped avoid the failure. The fundamental processes present in a GDSS would facilitate collaboration and blurring of boundaries. Group memory would help team members converge the purpose and definition of the project.

DISCUSSION

Group decision support systems merge groupware technology with decision support technology. All the characteristics and needs of DSS discussed in earlier chapters need to be fulfilled. In addition, these systems provide tools to help exploit the advantages of group decision making while avoiding some of the problems thereof. There have been many applications of GDSS to problems, and much research has been devoted to understanding how to apply them to solving group choice processes.

QUESTIONS

1. What is the difference between decision support systems with an active mail component and a group decision support system?
2. What is the difference between group decision support systems and groupware? What features would one expect in GDSS, but not in groupware?
3. What are the advantages of having groups consider issues? What attributes of GDSS exploit those advantages?
4. What are the disadvantages of having groups consider issues? What attributes of GDSS help to minimize those disadvantages?
5. How would reengineering efforts be improved by using GDSS?
6. Discuss two decisions in which you have been involved that might have been improved with the use of a GDSS.

◆ O N   T H E   W E B ◆

On the Web for this chapter provides additional information about group decision support systems (GDSS). Links can provide access demonstration packages that operate on the Web, and provide users with the experience of using groupware even if it is not present at their own installation. In addition, they can provide information about teams and collaboration and what works, regardless of the technology. In addition, the page provides links to groupware products, their reviews, and examples of their use. Additional discussion questions and new applications will also be added as they become available.

- *Links to overview information about group decision making.* These links provide bibliographies and overview papers on the topic of group decision making, both with and without GDSS tools.

- *Links to products.* Several groupware and GDSS providers have pages that allow collaborative projects with people in the same room or across the world.
- *Links provide access to GDSS examples in business, government, and research.* Some links provide access to papers on the Web describing GDSS applications and their uses. Others provide descriptions of the process by which the application was developed.
- *Links provide summaries of applications in particular industries.* Examples of how specific business problems have been solved using GDSS are identified and reviewed.

You can access material for this chapter from the general WWW Page for the book, or directly from the following URL. http://www.umsl.edu/~sauter/DSS/gdss.html

SUGGESTED READINGS

Anonymous, "Groupware and the Virtual Enterprise," *Datamation*, March 15, 1995, pp. S4–S8.

Bostrom, R.P., R. Anson, and V.K. Clawson, "Group facilitation and group support systems," *Group Support Systems: New Perspectives*, New York: Macmillian Publishing Co., 1993, pp. 146–168.

Cole, B., "Channel surfing across the groupware seascape," *Network World*, September 5, 1995, pp. 35–38.

DeSanctis, G. and R.B. Gallupe, "A foundation for the study of group decision support systems," *Management Science*, 33(5), May 1987, pp. 589–609.

Dennis, A.R., D. Daniels, G. Hayes, G. Kelly, D. Lange, and L. Massman, "Business process

reengineering with groupware," *Proceedings of the Twenty-Eighth Annual Hawaii International Conference on System Sciences, Volume IV*, Los Alamitos, CA: IEEE Computer Society Press, 1995, pp. 378–387.

Dennis, A.R. and B.R. Gallupe, "A history of group support systems empirical research: Lessons learned and future directions," *Group Support Systems: New Perspectives*, New York: Macmillian Publishing Co., 1993, pp. 59–77.

Heighler, E., "Obstacles block the road to groupware Nirvana," *Inforworld*, October 24, 1994, p. 56.

Hoffer, J.A. and J.S. Valacich, "Group memory in group support systems: A foundation for design," *Group Support Systems: New*

Perspectives, New York: Macmillian Publishing Co., 1993, pp. 215-229.

Hosseini, J., "Business process modeling and organizational memory systems: A case study," *Proceedings of the Twenty-Eighth Annual Hawaii International Conference on System Sciences, Volume IV*, Los Alamitos, CA: IEEE Computer Society Press, 1995, pp. 363-371.

Huber, G.P., "Issues in the design of group decision support systems," *MIS Quarterly*, 8(1), 1984, pp. 195-204.

Huber, G.P., J.S. Valacich, and L.M. Jessup, "A theory of the effects of group support systems on an organization's nature and decisions," *Group Support Systems: New Perspectives*, New York: Macmillian Publishing Co., 1993, pp. 255-269.

Jessup, L.M. and J.S. Valacich, "On the study of group support systems: An introduction to group support system research and development," *Group Support Systems: New Perspectives*, New York: Macmillian Publishing Co., 1993, pp. 3-7.

Kobielus, J. "Scheduling standards are key to groupware strategies," *Network World*, August 29, 1994, pp. 27-29.

Lawton, G. and J. Vaughn, "Groupware vendors jockey for position," *Software Magazine*, September 1994, pp. 23-24.

Schrage, M., "Groupware griping is premature," *Computerworld*, August 29, 1994, 28(35), p. 37.

Simpson, D., "Variations on a theme," *Client/Server Today*, July 1994, pp. 45-47.

Sprague, R.H. and H.J. Watson, *Decision Support Systems: Putting Theory into Practice*, New York: Prentice-Hall, 1989.

Stahl, S., "Groupthink," *Informationweek*, August 22, 1994, pp. 12-13.

Straub, D.W. and R.A. Beauclair, "Current and future uses of group decision support systems technology: Report on a recent empirical study," *Journal of MIS*, 5(1), Summer 1988.

Turoff, M., R.H. Starr, A.N.F. Bahgat, and A.R. Rana, "Distributed group support systems," *MIS Quarterly*, 17(2), December 1993, pp. 399-417.

Watson, R.T., G. DeSanctis, and M.S. Poole, "Using a GDSS to facilitate group consensus: Some intended and some unintended consequences," *MIS Quarterly*, 10(3), September 1988, pp. 463-478.

Watson, R.T., T.H. Ho, and K.S. Raman, "Culture as a fourth dimension of group support systems," *Communications of the ACM*, 37(10), October 1994, pp. 45-54.

Whiting, R., "Not for workgroups only," *Client/Server Today*, July 1994, pp. 58-66.

Wilson, J. and L.M. Jessup, "A field experiment on GSS anonymity and group member status," *Proceedings of the Twenty-Eighth Annual Hawaii International Conference on System Sciences, Volume IV,* Los Alamitos, CA: IEEE Computer Society Press, 1995, pp. 212-221.

Ziguram, I. and K.A. Kozar, "An exploratory study of roles in computer-supported groups," *MIS Quarterly*, 18(3), September 1994, pp. 277-297.

Executive Information Systems

◆ ◆ ◆

Executive information systems (EIS) are specialized decision support systems that help executives analyze critical information and use appropriate tools to address the strategic decision making of an organization. In particular, EIS help executives develop a more accurate and current global view of the organization's operations and performance, as well as that of competitors, suppliers, and customers.

◆ WHAT IS AN EIS

The focus of an EIS is to monitor events *and trends* both internally and externally. Armed with timely and wide-ranging information and appropriate tools, top-level managers are better prepared to make strategic changes to avail the organization of opportunities and eliminate problems. According to a recent article, worldwide sales of executive information systems are rising at a rate of about 18% per year (Korzenlowski, 1994), and EIS are expected to:

- act as a competitive weapon and strategic planning tool;
- improve the quality of top-level decision making;
- reduce the amount of time dedicated to finding problems and opportunities;
- improve the quality of planning performed at top levels in the organization;
- provide mechanisms to improve organization control; and
- provide better and faster access to data and models.

Some believe that EIS have been installed on the desks of between 25% and 50% of senior executives of the largest companies. Others think that the number might be larger, given the significant rate of growth in the EIS industry in the early 1990s.

There are a number of basic requirements for an effective EIS. Tables 12.1 through 12.3 summarize some of the characteristics that were illustrated earlier in this book. The most important characteristic of a successful EIS is that it be simple and easy to use. Well-designed EIS allow the executive to understand the corporate performance after using only a small number of commands. In addition, the

◆   DSS in Action   ◆

Pilot's *Decision Support Suite* is a comprehensive set of client/server OLAP technology used to build business intelligence systems quickly and easily, enabling organizations to respond immediately to rapidly changing business conditions. With the Suite, decision makers can easily display, analyze, and manipulate data from almost any source instantly—delivering better informed decisions and a competitive edge. For example, Ferguson Enterprises, based in Newport News, Virginia, is a billion-dollar supplier of plumbing, heating, and air conditioning equipment. With annual growth of 20%, Ferguson was challenged to maintain its profitability and credibility in a fast-growing marketplace. Prior to building its new application, Ferguson was using an internally developed solution that delivered static, text-based paper reports. This required extensive re-keying to create informative views. Now, to meet market demands, Ferguson is deploying a sales and marketing application using Pilot's *LightShip Suite* (the predecessor of the *Decision Support Suite*) for timely answers to critical business questions. For instance, by choosing geographical views, users can drill up or down from headquarters to region, branch, or satellite locations to determine sales trends by geographic location.

TABLE 12.1   Information Needs to Be Met by an EIS

■ Timeliness: Information needs to be available as soon as possible.
                  Response time should be very short.
■ Sufficiency: Information needs to be complete.
                  Users need extensive external data.
                  Users need historical data as well as the most current data.
■ Aggregation level: Users need access to global information of the organization and
                  its competitors.
                  Information should be provided in a hierarchical fashion.
                  Information needs to be provided at various levels of detail, with
                  "drill down" capability.
                  Users need "exception" reports or problem "flags".
■ Redundancy should be minimized.
■ Understandability: System should save users time.
                  Problem indicators should be highlighted.
                  Written explanations should be available.
                  System should support open-ended problem explanation.
■ Freedom from bias: Information must be correct and complete.
                  Information must be validated.
■ Reliability: Access must be controlled but reliable for those approved to
                  use the system.
■ Decision relevance: System must meet the needs of executives.
■ Comparability: Users need trends, ratios, and deviations to interpret.
■ Appropriateness of format: Flexibility is crucial.
                  Format should reflect user preferences.
                  System should integrate text and graphics appropriately.

TABLE 12.2   Modeling Needs to Be Met by an EIS

- Extensive use of hypertext links and hypermedia
- Easy-to-use *ad hoc* analysis
- Extensive use of exception reports and facility for tracing the reason for the exceptions
- Models are provided that are appropriate to address critical success factors
- Forecasting models are integrated into all components
- User has easy access to filters for data analysis
- Extensive use of what-if facility
- Extensive use of planning models

system anticipates some needs by automatically generating prespecified exception reports and trend analyses that help executives to identify both problems and opportunities. EIS must have user-friendly interfaces that encourage system use. Often this is achieved with the use of color screens and mouse or touch-screen capabilities. Screens such as those represented in Figure 12.1 would appear in "stoplight" colors to illustrate regions that have demonstrated particular characteristics.

Further, the data must be presented in an easy-to-understand format with tools that allow executives to change the format of presentation if necessary. Hence, a related concern is that EIS must be flexible in presentation and graphics capabilities. EIS must allow—and facilitate—the executives to follow paths as they think appropriate with a minimum amount of effort. This includes flexible data browsing, data manipulation, and presentation modes that facilitate executives gaining insights into competitive trends, business opportunities, and emerging problems. Consider, for example, the screens in Figure 12.1 in which the user can investigate the reasons for and patterns in sales by considering only certain regions or certain states. Executives should be able to ask questions relating to forecast projections, inventory status, or budget planning as they feel appropriate.

Third, the EIS must provide the broadest possible base of information. Executives need both qualitative and quantitative information and information from within

TABLE 12.3   User Interface Needs to Be Met by an EIS

- Interface *must* be user friendly.
- Interface must incorporate sophisticated use of graphical user interface.
- Interface should incorporate alternative input/output devices such as mouse, touch pads, touch screens, and so on.
- System must be accessible from a variety of machines in a variety of locations.
- Interface should be intuitive.
- Interface should be tailored to management style of individual executives.
- Interface should contain help menus for function of the EIS.
- Interface should contain content-sensitive help menus.

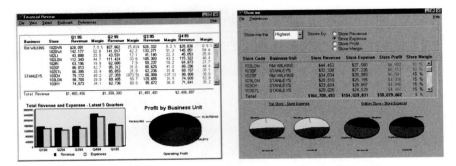

Figure 12.1   EIS Easy-to-Use Interfaces. Screens are from Focus/EIS for Windows.

the firm and without. The internal data must represent corporatewide performance and operations. It must include both current and historical data that support long-term trend analyses. The external data must facilitate the evaluation of external forces affecting the corporation. EIS have a well-organized presentation of data that allows the executive to navigate the system quickly. Often, EIS offer a "snapshot" of the present (or the past) in an easy-to-understand format. In addition, the systems have "drill-down" capabilities that enable the executive to investigate analyses underlying the summary information that might better identify problems and opportunities; an example of such drill-down screens is shown in Figure 12.2. These prepared drill-down screens are supplemented by an *ad hoc* query capability through which executives can investigate unanticipated questions or concerns.

Fourth, EIS must respond quickly. This includes, of course, the time the system takes to respond to a particular request. Executives are busy and are accustomed to fast response from their employees; they expect nothing less from their computer systems. In addition, EIS must facilitate fast reaction to ideas generated from the system. EIS need to provide easy and quick communication and report-generating capabilities to allow executives to react to the information provided.

◆ HOW EIS ARE USED

As a result of these capabilities, an EIS can provide a number of benefits. For example, executives can use their time more effectively. They can reduce search time for information and identify and respond to exceptions as soon as they are recorded. Furthermore, EIS provide information that is more timely, accurate, and relevant. Decision makers also can identify and resolve problems more quickly and can easily make better decisions. In this way, the corporation can treat information as a "strategic resource" and free MIS personnel and other assistants to work on longer-term projects.

The EIS can function only in an environment that is ready for it. Several issues need to be addressed to determine readiness. First, prior to EIS implementation, there must be an *information delivery problem*. In particular, there must be

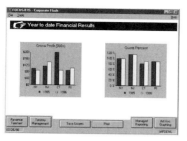 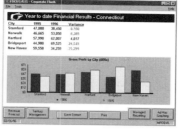 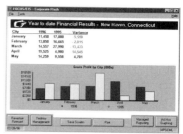

Figure 12.2 EIS Drill-Down Ability. Screens are from Focus/EIS for Windows.

critical information that is not available in a timely fashion, prohibiting executives from making high-quality decisions. Alternatively, there may be a real business problem that cannot be addressed because of information delivery problems. Without a prior problem, the value of the EIS is not apparent to the decision makers and hence they are unlikely to take the time to learn how to use the system.

Second, prior to EIS implementation, there must be some level of *technological maturity* of either the executives or the organization. This means that the organization (or the executives themselves) must have experience with the technology or must be willing to change technology. Some organizations are more resistant to technological change than others or require a more planned approach to evolve to greater use of technology.

◆ DSS in Action ◆

A CEO located in the Northwest was given an EIS created and promoted by the VP of MIS. It had all the right physical interfaces and was implemented on the basis of critical success factors.

Although the EIS was praised initially, the CEO began to observe increasingly that the EIS really was just a toy, and not the key business tool that was promoted. Finally, after eight months, she asked that it be removed.

From discussions following its removal, the real problem emerged. While she found that the insights the system raised were exciting, the CEO had no mechanism for sharing those thoughts with others in the company. "At least before I could communicate the points I was trying to make while the feeling was 'hot.' Now I first have to print it, then wait for delivery, and then comment and send it. It may not sound like much, but after a while, it became frustrating."

Adapted from Burkan, W.C., "Making EIS work," *DSS '88 Transactions,* the College on Information Systems of The Institute of Management Sciences, 1988. Used with permission from the Institute for Operations Research and Management Sciences.

The process of movement to an EIS also needs to be managed. Many executives have a staff that addresses analytical problems for them, monitoring important indicators and bringing them to the attention of the executive when necessary. In addition, these staffs provide analysis when requested. Sometimes the move from this situation to an online EIS is too big for the executives to make. That is, sometimes the move toward their own integration of and focus on information *and* learning a computer system is not successful. In these cases, designers get better results if they decompose the change into two separate components: learning to use the computer and learning to focus on their own information analyses. For example, some move executives to a "query" stage by getting them used to online capabilities first. Others move the executive first to a batch EIS where questions are asked and reports are generated, at the request of the executive using "executive briefing books." After they feel comfortable with half of it, moving to a full EIS is easier.

Of course, not all predesign concerns involve the executive. Prior to EIS implementation, designers need to understand the management process. Since EIS address upper-level management and strategic choices, the system needs to be molded more to management processes than do general decision support systems. In addition, designers need to be creative in their development of incentives to encourage senior managers to use the system.

The design of the EIS must be managed more carefully than other DSS design because of the kind of decision and the kind of user. Several factors need to be considered when implementing an EIS. For example, Volonino and Robinson (1991) offer guidelines for development.

- A prototype of the EIS should be built quickly after a decision is made to implement an EIS. In this way, executives have hands-on experience with a system early, thereby keeping the enthusiasm and momentum at a high level. In addition, the prototype allows the designer to understand upper management's needs better.
- Customization of the EIS and the information it provides must be an ongoing process. The focus of upper-level managers changes over time. If the EIS is to be effective, it needs to adapt to these changes and their associated information requirements.
- Designers must have an executive sponsor to help guide the project in the organization. The person should be a strong advocate, placed as highly as possible in the organization (preferably among the top three people in the organization). Without this kind of support, even the best EIS are likely to fail.
- Avoid assumptions about design needs. Too often designers think they understand the needs or do not want to bother high-level executives with their questions. It is crucial that the EIS reflect *real* information needs, and these needs are most likely to be reflected if the designer and decision makers communicate well from the beginning of the process.
- The EIS must be easy to use. Watson (1995) states that "because of the nature of the executive user, the system has to go beyond user friendly and

be 'user intuitive' or even 'user seductive'." Designers should standardize screens and provide a menu as a gateway to any access to the system. Further, they should use standard definitions for terms so that users do not need to guess what is meant.

- The EIS must contain current information from both within and without the organization.
- The EIS should have fast response time. In fact, some designers suggest that the response time needs to be less than five seconds. Whatever standard is chosen, faster is better because high-level executives are intolerant of waiting for the response. More important, the system must be designed to anticipate increased usage without degradation of response time. System usage is likely to grow over time, sometimes exponentially, and the system needs to be designed to provide similarly fast response time with the greater usage. Watson (1995) cites an unnamed EIS developer as defining "maximum acceptable time to move from screen to screen as 'the time it takes the executive to turn a page of *The Wall Street Journal*.'" However, he noted that executives are more tolerant of response time for *ad hoc* queries than simple scanning of prefabricated, standard analyses.
- The EIS must provide information through a variety of media that are easy to use and provide content quickly. Graphical displays are important to present information quickly. In addition, hypertext and hypermedia allow executives to move through text more quickly. However, even if an EIS has the most up-to-date capabilities, it will be wasted if the executive quits using the system because it is too slow in response.
- Designers must not only provide the technical ability to eliminate paper from the decision process, they must address the political, legal, and organizational implications of doing so. Such an analysis must provide alternatives for addressing those problems.
- Screens need to be designed carefully. They must carry only useful messages. Furthermore, they must be easy to follow and should minimize the designer's influence and bias associated with their design.

◆   **DSS Design Insights**   ◆

Although fast response time is important to the executive, designers need to be aware that a sudden move to fast information on which the executives can act can lead to instabilities in the organization. Consider, for example, the experience seen with database technology, summarized by Chapnic (1989):

Information feedback that is too rapid and not controlled properly is very destabilizing for a system, causing its behavior to oscillate wildly . . . we may inadvertently destabilize large organizations by forcing them to react too quickly to changes.

- The system must be cost-effective. Unfortunately, we cannot justify an EIS using the same terms we would for a transaction processing system because the benefits rarely can be traced directly to a dollar savings for the enterprise. Rather, the key benefit is in providing relevant information quickly and reliably.

Several methodologies have been put forward for designing an EIS. Most fall into the class of traditional systems development life cycle methodologies. Rockart (1979) developed the Critical Success Factors methodology, which allows users to define their own key indicators of performance. These indicators track the most important pieces of company and market information for the executive. Further, the method keeps executives involved with the evolution of their system by periodically requiring them to review and modify their indicators as their needs change.

Another methodology , developed by Volonino and Watson (1991), is the Strategic Business Objectives (SBO) methodology. SBO focuses on the company goals, rather than the executive's views of performance. It requires users to identify and prioritize critical business objectives. These priorities then specify the information identified and captured in the EIS.

The one critical aspect in each methodology is the successful identification, capture, and inclusion of information to meet the requirements of strategic planning. Watson and Frolick (1993) conducted studies to examine the manner in which EIS are developed. Too often, they found, executives were only consulted in the initial design phase or after implementation when modifications are considered. However, they found that more discussions with executives during planning meetings and throughout the project lead to better outcomes. Some of the criteria used to evaluate EIS products found in another project by Watson and his colleagues (1992) are shown in Table 12.4.

Once the framework for implementing an EIS is in place, the next major area of consideration is the hardware. A number of factors affect the appropriateness of the hardware. First, the hardware should be capable of supporting management functions critical to executive tasks, such as deductive reporting, trend analysis, and exception reporting. Second, the hardware must have high-resolution, bitmapped display screens to provide superior output to the paper-based methods. Too small a screen or unclear output will be distracting and unusable for managers. Third, the processor speed must be sufficient to ensure a timely response to a request. Not only must the processor meet the current demand, it must meet future increases in demand. Fourth, the computer hardware must allow input and output by mechanisms other than the traditional keyboard. Executives respond better to media such as voice-activated systems and touchscreens. Fifth, the computer hardware should enable executives without computer skills to enhance their daily work experience. Sixth, the computer must be networked. The executive must be linked to departmental, corporate, and external management information as well as electronically linked to managers who might provide insights into the problems under consideration. Finally, the hardware must be integrated with other technological equipment of importance to the decision maker

TABLE 12.4 Sample EIS Adoption Criteria

1.0 **Ease of Use**

Development
- Applications to be easy and quick to develop
- New users to be easy and quick to add to the system
- Suitability for quick prototyping
- Display alternative output formats quickly

Learning
- Learning time for developers
- Learning time for users
- Availability of appropriate documentation and tutorials

End User
- Menu system
- Customized menus for each user
- Ability to bypass menus not required
- Various modes of use (mouse, touch-screen)
- Minimal number of keystrokes
- Consistent use of functions

Maintenance
- Easy to add and modify data
- Ability to maintain integrity and timeliness of data (handling of frequent updates)
- Easy to add and modify screens, reports, and graphs
- Availability of standard templates
- Ability to copy existing screens, graphs, and so on
- Ability to monitor system usage
- Easy to add additional users
- Ability to incorporate changes to corporate structure

2.0 **Reporting Capability**
- Reports to be presented as both graphs and tables
- Ability to display graphs, tables, and text on a single screen
- Ability to switch between tabular and graphic output
- Ability to color code exceptions on the current screen
- Ability to present a summary screen listing all exceptions throughout the system
- Support analysis of budgeted, actual, and forecast figures
- Effective presentation of time series data
- Ability to highlight variations
- Support interactive user-defined variance criteria
- Retrieval of historical data as required
- Maintain historical data and discard after a user-defined period
- Analysis of historical data and identification of trends
- Built-in restrictions to protect historical data
- Facility for personalized queries (i.e., ability for users to scan the data base according to interactively defined criteria)
- Explanatory notes to be attached to reports

3.0 **Graphic Presentation**
- Quality of graphics
- Speed of presentation
- Effective use of default color coding
- Ability to highlight areas of concern
- Availability of individual color schemes
- Ability to include explanatory notes for each graph
- Ability to produce a variety of graphs (pie, bar, 3D bar, line)
- Automatic generation of simple, default formats which can be customized
- Easy to produce executive defined graphs
- Automatic scaling
- Graph limitations
- Automatic legends

4.0 **General Functionality**
- Drill down capability
- Built-in statistical capabilities
- Lookaside capability for interrupting a process to use another facility
- Screen scrolling (horizontal and vertical)
- Multiple tasks to be operating and displayed concurrently (e.g., windows, split screens)
- Access to notepad facility
- Integration with DSS
- Import data from spreadsheets/word processing

TABLE 12.4   Sample EIS Adoption Criteria (*Continued*)

- Minimal screen repainting
- Ability to display other languages

5.0 **Data Handling**
- Version checking to ensure all users are accessing the same version of software, applications, and data
- Interfaces with external databases and internal WMC systems
- Efficient storage of time series data
- Stored aggregates for rapid access
- Built-in periodicity conversions
- Efficient indexing and retrieval mechanism
- Instantaneous distribution of new data among users
- Ability to consolidate various sources and formats of data into an EIS database via manual input or eletronic data transfer from other systems
- Ability to sort screen data according to user defined criteria

6.0 **Output Options**
- Laser printer, plotter, color printer, transparencies, dot matrix
- Large screen presentations for meetings

7.0 **Performance**
- Response times
- PC-mainframe communications uploading and downloading data
- Efficient resource usage
- Capacity issues (i.e., number of users, volume of data)
- Reliability of software
- Recovery facility

8.0 **Electronic Mail**
- Ability to run VAXMAIL
- Ability to incorporate EIS reports and graphs into mail facility

9.0 **Security**
- Restricted system access
- Restricted function access
- Add/edit/delete restrictions for applications and data

10.0 **Environments and Hardware**
- Local access
- Across networks
- Multi-user access to the same data (only 3 users tested)
- Portability
- PC-mainframe links

11.0 **Documentation**
- Reference manual, introductory guide, tutorials
- Overall style of documentation
- Online, context sensitive help screens
- Meaningful error messages
- Appropriate cross-referencing and indexing
- Stand-alone chapters

12.0 **Vendor Support**
- Training courses for developers
- Technical support
- Local support
- Timeliness and smoothness of initial installation
- Availability of off-the-shelf applications
- Availability of source code
- Hot line support

Adapted from Watson, H.J., B.A. Hesse, C. Copperwaite, and V. Devos, "EIS software: A selection process and the western mining experience." *The Journal of Information Technology Management*, 3(1), 1992, pp. 19–28.

such as electronic mail systems, fax equipment, voice mail, and video conferencing systems.

◆   AVAILABLE PACKAGES

Many EIS are developed using proprietary packaged software; a sample listing is shown in Table 12.5. The three major packages in the market are *Command Center, Commander EIS*, and *Executive Edge. Command Center* was the industry's first

Figure 12.3 Pilot Decision Support Software.

TABLE 12.5   Selected Commercial EIS Software Providers

PRODUCT	VENDOR	DESCRIPTION
CA–Strategem	Computer Associates 711 Stewart Avenue Garden City, N.Y. 11530-4787 (516) 227-3300	A set of products that can be integrated to create an EIS
Command Center	Cognizant Corporation One Canal Park Cambridge, MA (617) 374-9400	A full-capability EIS product
Commander EIS	Comshare 3001 S. State Street Ann Arbor, MI 48108 (313) 994-4800	A full-capability EIS product
EASEL	EASEL 600 West Cummings Park Woburn, MA 01801 (617) 938-8440	Supports EIS screen design and information presentation
EIS-EPiC	EPiC Software 25 Burlington Mall Road, Suite 300 Burlington, MA 01803 (617) 270-0610	A full-capability EIS product
FOCUS/EIS	Information Builders 1250 Broadway New York, NY 10001 (212) 736-4433	The Lightship product serves as a front end to the FOCUS database

TABLE 12.5   Selected Commercial EIS Software Providers (*Continued*)

PRODUCT	VENDOR	DESCRIPTION
Express/EIS	Information Resources 200 Fifth Avenue Waltham, MA 02254 (617) 890-4433	An EIS front end to the Express DSS
EISTool Kit	MicroStrategy One Commerce Center Wilmington, DE 19811 (800) 927-1868	Supports EIS screen design and information presentation
Executive Decisions	Contact local IBM sales representative	A full-capability EIS product
Pilot Decision Support Suite	Cognizant Corporation One Canal Park Cambridge, MA (617) 374-9400	Complete, extensible decision support environment built on open standards. This is an extension of command center
RediMaster	American Information Systems P.O. Box 367 Wellsboro, PA 16901 (717) 724-1588	Supports EIS screen design and information presentation
Resolve	Metapraxis 900 3rd Avenue, 36th Floor New York, NY 10022 (212) 935-4322	A full-capability EIS product

Adapted from Watson, H.J., B.A. Hesse, C. Copperwaite, and V. Devos, "EIS software: A selection process and the western mining experience," *The Journal of Information Technology Management*, 3(1), 1992, pp. 19–28.

commercial EIS product, introduced in 1984 by Pilot Executive Software. It was also the first programming environment to exploit the power of microcomputer–mainframe co-processing. In addition, *Command Center* was the first to include hypertext linking of text that mimicked human thought processes to facilitate use of the system. Today, *Command Center* has evolved into *Pilot Decision Support Suite,*™ a programming environment for EIS that includes editors, debuggers, screen formatters, data acquisition bridges, and OLAP capabilities to deliver a product consistent with open standards.

Comshare's *Commander EIS* is currently the most popular EIS software. The EIS applications are designed for the non-computer-oriented executive who has neither the time nor the inclination to become more familiar with computers. All EIS functions can be performed using a mouse or touchscreen. *Executive Edge* is a tool that makes data capture and analysis easier. It is an open development environment that allows the designer to exploit the organization's existing infrastructure rather than provide a separately built one. In addition, it utilizes artificial intelligence technology to improve the quality of information presented to the executive and to reduce system maintenance. Often EIS are developed using fourth-generation languages (4GLs) coupled with front end interfaces built with natural language systems. These are easy to use but limit the detailed analysis and the data consolidation generally found in an EIS. For example, *RediMaster*, a product from American Information System, can be used to build interfaces to databases, graphics tools or modeling tools such as Lotus 1-2-3. Similarly, *EIS Toolkit,* from Ferox Microsystems, Inc., provides tools for building limited, financial oriented EIS.

EIS proprietary packages are outgrowths of 4GL. These languages, such as *SAS, IFPS, EXPRESS, and EMPIRE,* are designed to enable executives and their staffs to develop a personalized EIS to run on a personal computer or a mainframe. An important advantage of 4GLs is the facility to generate customized reports or graphs to summarize key statistics and highlight trends. Most 4GLs are less successful than the proprietary pages because they tend to be weaker in the data analysis and consolidation even though they are stronger in data management tools.

SAS is a 4GL that has made significant progress as an EIS. *SAS/EIS* is a development environment that includes objects for building an EIS. SAS uses object-oriented programming and concepts to create predefined objects for use. These predefined objects can be used by non-computer oriented users to develop customized screens and functionality in an EIS. A screen illustrating the available objects is shown in Figure 12.5. In addition, the object-oriented programming concepts also allow more experienced users to create additional, customized objects and to build more powerful, yet flexible and user-friendly, systems. The inherent analytical strength of the SAS language allows users to build models with powerful statistical tests behind the drill-down menu. Its recent data warehousing facility has made data browsing and data management easier for the executive.

As with any kind of computer-based system, there is always room for improvement and ways to refine the system. Not only is there a need to update the technology, but there is a need to focus the manner in which executives plan and use the system. Crockett (1992) suggests that for improvement in strategic decisions the key is to link stakeholders' expectations to performance measures. Oftentimes, executives fail to identify all possible stakeholders or their expectations in their decision process. The expectations and critical success factors should be

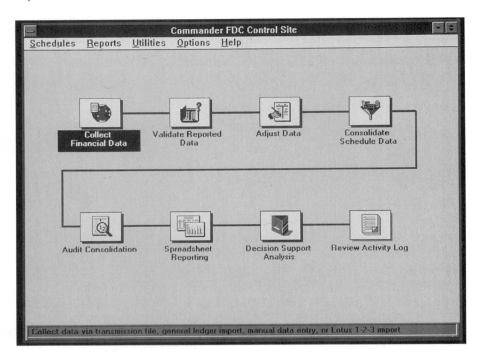

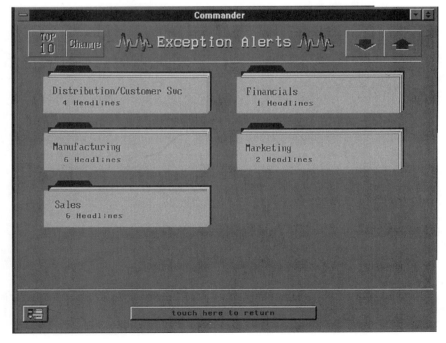

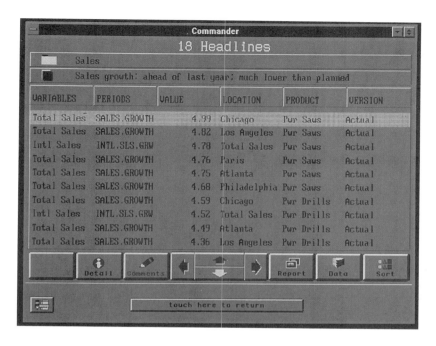

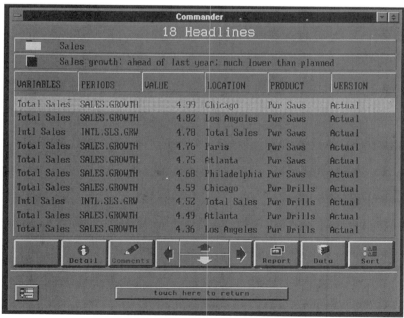

Figure 12.4 **A,** Control site. **B,** Desktop folders contain alerts of the most important exceptions within a multidimensional database. Automatic surveillance of large databases helps ensure managers they're not missing something important. **C,** Briefly book screen with choice of items for dynamic reporting. **D,** Exception reporting for managers.

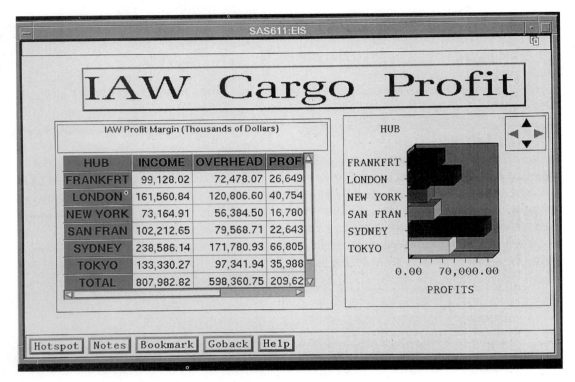

Figure 12.5   EIS from SAS.

identified, and then performance measures that monitor them should be documented. By clearly understanding the strategic goals of the company and expectations of stakeholders, designers can create EIS that should provide better support.

DISCUSSION

Executive information systems provide decision support technology to high-level
managers. In many ways, they resemble the decision support systems addressed
elsewhere in the book. Among the most significant difference, however, is that
the EIS generally provide a number of prefabricated, standard analyses selected
particularly for a decision maker. In addition, since EIS are designed to support
high-level managers, their needs for implementation and monitoring are different.
Finally, since EIS tend to support strategic decisions, the kinds of analyses provided must be different.

QUESTIONS

1. Discuss how the design components of a EIS are different from those of a DSS.

2. Why have many senior executives not become hands-on users of EIS? What implications does this have for documentation of an EIS?

3. Describe the factors that would influence the design of a transnational executive information system. Include how cultural factors that are either unique to a country and/or strongly influence the decision making process, as well as the specifications of design that would be affected. Is this effect more or less than you would expect with a DSS?

4. Critique the concept of using a standardized methodology to design executive information systems.

5. Select a particular corporation or industry and outline the trends and/or events one might monitor in an EIS.

6. Justify, in a convincing manner, the adoption of an EIS to a top-level executive of a corporation.

7. One of the prerequisites to successful EIS implementation discussed in the chapter is technological maturity of the organization or executives. Discuss how you might address this need if such maturity does not exist in the organization.

8. Discuss why using prototypes for eliciting users' needs is so important in EIS design.

9. What does it mean for a user-interface to be intuitive?

10. Describe how a content-sensitive help menu differs from a context-sensitive help menu.

◆ O N   T H E   W E B ◆

On the Web for this chapter provides additional information about executive information systems. Links can provide access to demonstration packages, general overview information, applications, software providers, tutorials, and more. Additional discussion questions and new applications will also be added as they become available.

- *Links to overview information about executives and their decision making styles and needs.* These links provide access to bibliographies and overview papers about group decision making, both with and without EIS tools.
- *Links to products.* Several EIS providers have pages that allow users to demonstrate their products. Others provide testimonials and/or reviews.

- *Links provide access to EIS examples in business, government, and research.* Some links provide access to papers on the Web describing EIS applications and their uses. Others provide descriptions of the process for developing the application.
- *Links provide summaries of applications in particular industries.* Examples of how specific business problems have been solved using EIS are identified and reviewed.

You can access material for this chapter from the general WWW Page for the book, or directly from the following URL.
http://www.umsl.edu/~sauter/DSS/eis.html

SUGGESTED READINGS

Bergerson, F., *et al.,* "Top managers evaluate the attributes of EIS" *DSS '91 Transactions,* Manhattan Beach, CA: College on Information Systems of the Institute for Management Sciences, 1991.

Burkan, W.C., "Making EIS work," in Gray, P., (ed.), *Decision Support and Executive Information Systems,* Englewood Cliffs, NJ: Prentice-Hall, 1994, p. 331.

Burkan, W.C., *Executive Information Systems,* New York: Van Nostrand Reinhold, 1991.

Chapnic, P., "Editor's buffer," *Database, Programming and Design,* 2(4), April 1989, pp. 7-8.

Coffee, P., K.D. Moser, and J. Frentzen, "Software tools support decision making," *PC Week,* 7(25), June 25, 1990, pp. 119-121.

Crockett, F., "Revitalizing Executive Information Systems," *Sloan Management Review,* 38 Summer 1992, pp. 17-29.

Darrow, B., "EIS put data at users' fingertips," *Inforworld* 12(33), August 13, 1990, p. 13.

DeLong, D.W. and J.F. Rockhart, "Identifying the attributes of successful executive information system implementation," in Fedorowicz, J. (ed.), *DSS '86 Transactions*, Washington, D.C.: College on Information Systems of the Institute for Management Sciences, 1986.

Eliot, L. , "High ROI on modern EIS," *Decision Line,* May 1994, pp. 7-8.

Ferranti, M., "Pilot aims windows-based EIS at non-programmers," *PC Week,* 7(36), September 10, 1990, pp. 39, 50.

Gray, P. (ed.), *Decision Support and Executive Information Systems,* Englewood Cliffs, NJ: Prentice-Hall, 1994.

Houdeshel, G. and H.J. Watson, "The management information and decision support (MIDS) system at Lockheed-Georgia," in Sprague, R.H., Jr., and H.J. Watson (eds.), *Decision Support Systems: Putting Theory into Practice, Third*

Edition, Englewood Cliffs, NJ: Prentice-Hall, 1993, pp. 235-252.

Korzenlowski, P., "C/S opens data access tool door to fresh competitors," *Software Magazine,* February 1994, pp. 71-77.

Oland, D., "The impact of a powerful new process at Moosehead," *CMA Magazine,* February 1994, p. 6.

Rockart, J.F., "Chief Executives Define their Own Data Needs," *Harvard Business Review*, March-April 1979, pp. 81-93.

Rockart, J.F. and D. DeLong, *Executive Support Systems,* Homewood, IL: Dow Jones-Irwin, 1988.

Scheier, R.L., "Information Resources unveils tool set that combines best of EIS with DSS," *PC Week,* 7(46), November 19, 1990, p. 11.

Sprague, R.H., Jr., and B.C. McNurlin, *Information Systems Management in Practice, Third Edition,* Englewood Cliffs, NJ: Prentice-Hall, Inc. 1993.

Volonino, L. and S. Robinson, "EIS Experiences at Marine Midland Bank, NA" *Journal of Information Technology Management* 2(2), 1991, pp. 33-38.

Volonino, L. and H. Watson, "The Strategic Business Objectives Method for Guiding Executive Information Systems Development," *Journal of Management Information Systems,* 7(3), Winter 1990-91, pp. 27-39.

Watson, H.J., "EIS user interface design guidelines," *Information Systems Management*, Summer 1995, p.   .

Watson, H.J., B.A. Hesse, C. Copperwaite, and V. Devos, "EIS software: A selection process and the western mining experience," *The Journal of Information Technology Management,* 3(1), 1992, pp. 19-28.

Watson, H.J., "Avoiding hidden EIS pitfalls," in Sprague, R.H., Jr., and H.J. Watson (eds.), *Decision Support Systems: Putting Theory into Prac-*

tice, Third Edition, Englewood Cliffs, NJ: Prentice-Hall, 1993, pp. 276-283.

Watson, H.J., R.K. Rainer, and C. Koh, "Executive information systems: A framework for development and a survey of current practices," in Sprague, R.H., Jr., and H.J. Watson (eds.), *Decision Support Systems: Putting Theory into Prac-*

tice, Third Edition, Englewood Cliffs, NJ: Prentice-Hall, 1993, pp. 253-275.

Watson, H.J., *et al., Executive Information Systems*, New York: John Wiley and Sons, 1992.

Watson, H.J. and M.N. Frolick, "Determining information requirements for an EIS," *MIS Quarterly*, September 1993, pp. 255-269.

Photo Credits

◆ ◆ ◆

CHAPTER 1   Figures 1.1, 1.2, and 1.3: Developed by the Fund for the City of New York with the Vera Institute of Justice. Page 14: Graphics courtesy of Erik Riedel with assistance from Bernd Bruegge and Ted Russell, Carnegie Mellon University.

CHAPTER 3   Figure 3.3: ©1996 Reuters, Ltd., All rights reserved. Figures 3.4, 3.5, and 3.6: Courtesy of Visual Components. Figure 3.11: Courtesy of MicroStrategy, Inc.

CHAPTER 4   Figure 4.2: Screen provided by Reality Online Inc. Figure 4.3: Courtesy of CACI. Figures 4.4 and 4.5: Courtesy of Arlington Software Corporation.

CHAPTER 5   Figures 5.24 and 5.25: Used with the permission of Aaron Marcus and Associates, Inc., Emeryville, California (http://www.AMandA.com) and Copyright ©1993 by Aaron Marcus and Associates, Inc. Page 173 (bottom left): Courtesy of General Reality Co. Page 173 (bottom right): Kermani/Gamma Liaison. Page 173 (top): Courtesy of Microsoft. Page 173 (center): Frank Pryor/Courtesy of Apple Computers, Inc. Figure 5.26: Interaction Development Corp.

CHAPTER 6   Figure 6.1: Courtesy of Lois & Paul Partners. Figure 6.3: Courtesy of ON Technology Corp. Figure 6.6: Banyan Systems, Inc.

CHAPTER 12   Figures 12.1 and 12.2: Courtesy of Information Builders. Figure 12.3: Courtesy of Pilot Software, Inc. Figure 12.4: Courtesy of Comshare, Inc. Figure 12.5: Courtesy SAS/Graph Software.

Index

◆ ◆ ◆